FENWAY LIVES
THE TEAM BEHIND THE TEAM

Also by Bill Nowlin:

Mr. Red Sox: The Johnny Pesky Story
Ted Williams: The Pursuit of Perfection (co-authored with Jim Prime)
Ted Williams: A Splendid Life (co-authored with Jim Prime & Roland Lazenby)
Fenway Saved (co-authored with Mike Ross & Jim Prime)
Tales from the Red Sox Dugout (co-authored with Jim Prime)
More Tales from the Red Sox Dugout: Yarns from the Sox (co-authored with Jim Prime)
Ted Williams: A Tribute (co-authored with Jim Prime)

Edited works:
The Kid: Ted Williams in San Diego
The Fenway Project (co-edited with Cecilia Tan)
The Russian Tragedy
The Guillotine at Work

FENWAY LIVES
THE TEAM BEHIND THE TEAM

The People Who Work in and Around Boston's Fenway Park

BILL NOWLIN

Photography by Andrea Raynor, Emmet Nowlin and Bill Nowlin

Rounder Books
Cambridge, Massachusetts
www.rounderbooks.com

To my sisters Joyce Arnason and Lisa Doran,
and to all the hard-working folks at Fenway Park,
past and present

Copyright © 2004 by Bill Nowlin

Published by Rounder Books

an imprint of:
Rounder Records
1 Camp Street
Cambridge, MA 02140

ISBN: 1-57940-090-6

Design by Sarah Lainie Smith
Front cover photos of Fenway Park employees by Andrea Raynor
Back cover photo by Bill Nowlin

Nowlin, Bill 1945-
Fenway Lives: The Team Behind the Team
1. Fenway Park (Boston, Mass.)–History 2. Boston Red Sox (Baseball Team)

First Edition
2004093572
796.357'092

ISBN 1-57940-090-6

Printed in Canada

9 8 7 6 5 4 3 2 1

Table of Contents

INTRODUCTION

The Boston Red Sox baseball club has a long and frustrating history. Their penchant for reaching the heights of glory before snatching defeat from the jaws of victory endears these perennial underdogs to fans around the world. Each year miles of copy – measured in column inches – are published about the Sox. Torrents of words stream out over TV and radiowaves. At home, in the workplace, on the streetcorner, and now in internet chat groups, everyone's got an opinion on this team, the players, the manager, the GM, even their ballpark – venerable Fenway Park (est. 1912.)

This book isn't about Nomar or Pedro or any of the other well-known names in the news, it's about the people who work in and around Fenway Park, the team behind the team. This is the supporting cast, the people behind the scenes who make it all work. Sure, the games could be played with just the eighteen players on the field – well, twenty, since Boston is an American League city where the designated hitter still prevails. But no one would see or hear the games without the people who make it possible.

Fenway Park currently seats over 2½ million fans every year. Millions more put their Sox on via radio or TV. Most home games are sold out, or close to it. That puts 34,000 people per game in the old, narrow seats. For a few hours on game day, the population of Fenway Park equals that of a small city, with all the hallmarks of a community, the shared language, the common experience, the sense of belonging, of togetherness.

These days, players come and go. Current contracts tend more to be of the "rent-a-player" annual deal than the long-term type. Yaz played 23 straight years for the same team. Ted Williams played for the Red Sox in four decades, from 1939 to 1960. That would be almost unheard-of today.

While the players all too often seem transient, one thing that has been remarkable about the Red Sox organization is the longevity of many of its staffers. During the 1941 season when Ted Williams hit .406, Helen Robinson began working as a switchboard operator and was still there into the first years of the 21st century. Jerry Shea, an usher who worked out in right around sections 1 and 2, into the 21st century, too, could still remember seeing Babe Ruth play. It's not hard to find people with twenty or more years of service, still plugging away at far-from-glamorous jobs, just for the joy of being at Fenway.

The Red Sox have about 150 full-time employees, including some scattered in Florida and the Dominican Republic. As Opening Day approaches they take on more help, and during the course of the actual season will employ 700-plus. Some are full-time seasonal employees; some are day-of-game help. Some are retirees, keeping active. Some even hold other jobs, as successful stockbrokers or businesspeople, who just want to keep a hand in. When you add in all the people who work for the concessionaires, primarily Aramark, there are between 1200 and 1500 people working at the park during the season, serving those 2½ million fans and the millions more who follow the game through the media. Many workers return year after year.

When I co-authored the book FENWAY SAVED with Mike Ross and Jim Prime, we told the story of Fenway Park itself. Our brief there was to describe the park – the oldest in baseball – but one the John Harrington administration planned to replace with a more economically suitable modern stadium. We kept our focus on the park – its physical structure, its history, how players felt about The Wall, the lack of foul territory, the odd angles and corners – the park as a venue for baseball.

During this process I discovered that in addition to the physical structure that was the park, there were also the people of the park. Characters like Sherm Feller, the veteran public address announcer. One day, maybe ten years ago, I was waiting for him before a game. At his invitation, I was going to join him in the booth. He showed up with not many minutes to spare. Acting like he owned the place, he pulled his Cadillac into a Tow Zone right in front of the press entrance. Feller casually arced his car keys through the air to a Boston policeman on the street, confident that the officer would look after the car for him, giving a new twist to the term "public servant." Feller himself was a true character who (among other things) wandered off during the course of that game, leaving me in charge of the balls and strikes for a full half-inning.

In the course of talking with people about Fenway Park, I kept running across any number of fascinating stories. Christian Elias told me about working inside the manual scoreboard where the scores are still posted by hand. Dennis Keohane told me about his first day as a vendor in the stands, getting all sticky with Coke. There were many such stories, but they didn't fit FENWAY SAVED. Yet, I realized, there wouldn't be any ballgames at Fenway Park if these people, often unheralded and well behind the scenes, didn't perform their duties. Before we finished working on FENWAY SAVED, I resolved to tell the story of the people who work in and around the park.

Some work inside, some outside, some in official capacity and some as independent entrepreneurs seeking to reap rewards from the gathering crowd. Approaching the park along Yawkey Way, you feel like you're in a street carnival. Vendors hawk their wares. "Peanuts! cashews! pistachios!" "Get your Nomar sunglasses! Manny sunglasses!" You run a gauntlet of sausage carts side by side with guys selling baseball caps. George Higgins called it a "Bostonian souk" and it does indeed have a bazaar quality to it. There have been efforts by the Red Sox to roust the vendors, but people love the atmosphere and the attempts to clear the streets (in the name of "public safety") have come across as clumsy and over-reaching. The vendors have organized and the PR battle looked like Goliath coming down on David; even though some of the sausage vendors in particular seem to rake in big bucks, reportedly into six figures in some cases. In late 2002, the new owners of the Red Sox found a way to secure much of this income for the team and at the same time offer a little more walking-around room for ticketholders by closing off Yawkey Way before each game. Although in the process, the feeling on the street became more structured and less free-wheeling, a significant degree of the old flavor survives.

In early 1999, the Red Sox discovered the virtue of building on the festival atmosphere. They hired the Hot Tamale Brass Band to play on the street before Opening Day, Kids' Opening Day and on a few other occasions, a regular gig that, as of this writing, has lasted six years. They brought in Tony Lupo, one of the last hurdy gurdy men in America to work the street with his capuchin monkey Coco. They had Billy Bedard the stilt walker, and others to entertain.

Opening Day, always exciting enough, has became even more so. The new owners have added Eric Royer, the one-man band, and introduced a number of new features inside the park, like Autograph Alley where a former Bosox player signs for one and all. Many of the new changes at the ballpark, like the Green Monster seats, have been huge hits with Sox fans.

Around the Fenway neighborhood, merchants draw on the crowds to make their living. Arthur D'Angelo used to sell newspapers with his brother to ballpark fans for 2 cents a pop and is now a wealthy man with a thriving business. His company, Twins Enterprises, has become the largest manufacturer of baseball caps in the world. Jimmy Rooney of the Baseball Tavern on Boylston Street serves small crowds during the off-season, but it's wall to wall after a game, packed with ushers, vendors and baseball fans. Yet proximity itself seems no guarantee of success. There was a bowling alley underneath Fenway Park, right under the ticket office – but many people didn't even know it was there and passed it by.

A full complement of television cameramen, producers, directors and editors, broadcasters and the like brings the games to TV. The radio team also has its own technicians and "statistician." Without the rights money these stations pay to the Red Sox each year, the team could never compete.

Likewise, without the cleaning crew, which begins work right after the game and will be finishing up at 6 AM following a night game, the park would never be ready for the next day. One of the crew comments that the millionaire players would never be able to draw the crowds they do were the park left filthy for the fans. Without someone to sell the tickets, to offer food and drink, without security or the cleaning crew, you can't hold a game. The hundreds of people who work in the park are as essential to a successful game as are the players themselves.

These workers are rarely heralded – usually aren't even noticed. For many, they blend into the background. This book will try to give recognition to those who work to stage the ballgames. Based on interviews and conversations with over 200 workers, I will try to tell the stories of the people who work in and around Fenway Park.

Sometimes these are family stories – three generations who have worked at the park, or seven members of the same family who all worked there. Some are stories of longevity – people who have worked for decades at the same job. Some are stories of kids just starting out, making a little money while they're in school. A surprising number of these people stay on. They get hooked in some way. There really is a sort of family atmosphere about the place. Any number of cousins and nephews of someone who knew someone who used to work there dot the landscape. The more you probe, the more you learn of these familial connections. Even those without kinship ties often express a feeling of belonging to the community, to a greater whole if you will. It's a powerful force, a local legacy. It remains to be seen how new ownership and increasing rationalization of job expectations affect these patterns of the past.

Workers will always come and go, as is true with any dynamic organization. Some of those interviewed no longer work at the ballpark. Others have shifted responsibilties. It would be impossible to preserve a snapshot in time as though there would be no changes. Nonetheless, the basic tasks still have to be fulfilled and the folks you will meet here are the folks who handled these tasks at the time of their interviews.

Most jobs involve little glamour. It's not like everyone gets to meet the players and hang with them after the games – though in earlier days an usher like Mike Pucillo might throw a party at his home and most of the players would show up. Michele Julian, the director of human resources who oversees hiring for the front office, stresses that the jobs are like any other jobs. You have to be qualified. You have to be good, and you have to do your work. The Red Sox are going to hire the applicant with the best resume, not the one who comes to the interview wearing a Red Sox cap. A little enthusiasm can't hurt, but it's surprising the number of Sox employees who don't bother to watch the games taking place on the other side of the wall from where they work, or who even turn out to be

Yankees or Orioles fans! Many don't follow the team's play at all, but nonetheless take great pride in their work and haven't missed a day in years. Their community is that of their fellow workers and their sense of pride comes from a job well done.

The positive feelings most of these workers express may well reflect the fact that for most of them the work they do is elective – in many cases, supplementary work – a second job. In many instances, the job is one they undertake not out of necessity but for extra income and even for some of the social pleasures that work can offer. Associating themselves with a well-loved baseball team conveys status, too, no small factor for many.

Work can ennoble and foster dignity. Work can also be back-breaking sheer drudgery. Work is hated by many. They seek to escape it the moment the minute hand reaches the top of the final hour. One reason so many people continue their work in and around Boston's baseball park is that the rewards here more than compensate for that which tedium and obligation might otherwise make oppressive. These are people fortunate enough to find some sense of contentment in the responsibilities they assume.

They're not heroes, not by any means, though the dedication, feeling and care many of them bring to their work is admirable. As individuals, the work they do may not make the headlines, but it is work that must be done. That so many do their job, and do it so well, is in many ways a tribute to the capacity in each of us to reach for something satisfying in our life, and to derive a measure of satisfaction out of what it is we do.

As I accumulated the stories of scores of Fenway Park people, my long-time friend Henry Horenstein told me that the Library of Congress was looking, as part of its Bicentennial celebration, to collect and preserve stories of "local legacies" from around the United States, and that each Member of Congress and each United States Senator had been asked to sponsor projects in their Congressional district. I contacted Representative Michael Capuano of Massachusetts, whose district embraced Fenway Park (and also my residence) and he immediately agreed to sponsor the research. This was not financial sponsorship, but a recognition that the work I was undertaking seemed to have value and fit in the Local Legacies initiative of the Library of Congress.

Knowing that Congressman Capuano had sponsored the project, the Boston Red Sox were very cooperative and provided access to a dozen or so important people within the administration who might otherwise have been hesitant to talk as freely about their own personal work history with the team. Only one person I contacted refused to talk – a street vendor known as The Sausage King. To be precise, he didn't refuse; he wanted to be paid. I declined. By and large, though, no one seemed shy and I found that almost everyone enjoyed the opportunity to talk about the work they did, and many have expressed ongoing curiosity about how the research was going. It was the reaction of people who I'd interviewed, telling me, "You ought to make a book of the interviews" that finally prompted me to try and close the circle that Mike Ross had first suggested – to try and capture much of what people had told me in book form.

FENWAY LIVES is the result.

Bill Nowlin
April 2004

~

Interviewing for this book began in 1999, so some of the interviews reflect or refer to people in positions they no longer occupy - such as former General Manager Dan Duquette, for example. In other instances, the number of years of their emply will seem off. Debbie Matson, for instance, was among those interviewed in 1999 and stated that she had been with the ballclub for 13 years. As of April 2004, when final editing for this book was done, that thirteen has now become eighteen years.

It is inevitable in any evolving, dynamic organization that personnel will change. With the sale of the Red Sox in early 2002, there has probably been more change than there otherwise would have been, but no immediate and wholesale purge ever occurred. Nonetheless, new - and in many cases younger - leadership has taken the organization in new directions. A quite large percentage of the people interviewed right at the start of the project still work at Fenway Park.

Sometimes it is possible to date a given interview by references made within the transcribed words. I chose not to present the actual date of each interview, though, simply because the dates never seemed as important as the functions and responsibilities of the given position. The people who work at Fenway Park have counterparts at other stadia. Though Boston and Fenway both have their own unique circumstances and traditions, one will find similar jobs at other ballparks around the country and, indeed, in other lands as well.

~

Thanks for assistance on this work go to, among others:

Peter Bartis, Library of Congress
Dick Bresciani, Boston Red Sox
Congressman Michael Capuano
John Caron, Boston Red Sox
Phil Castinetti
Patrick Cavanagh
Sue Costello
Lib Dooley
Ronald J. Fitzgerald
Scott Fitzgerald
Sue Halpern
Henry Horenstein
Arthur Kaufman
Jack Lyons
Kerri Walsh Moore

Tim & Joannah O'Connor
Johnny Pesky
Jim Prime
Captain Bob Rigby
Mike Rutstein
Paul Sajovec, Johnson Consulting
Peter Seligman, Library of Congress
Kevin Shea, Boston Red Sox
Louisa Kasdon-Elias Sidel
Mark Sternman, Greater Boston Chamber of Commerce
Adele Travisano
Jim Wahlberg
Debbi Wrobleski
David Wunsch

Extra thanks to Jim Parry, Ken Melanson, and Tim Samway.

1

GETTING IN ON THE GROUND FLOOR

Edward P. Kenney, Assistant General Manager
Edward F. Kenney, former director of the
   Red Sox farm system
Casey Erven, Ground Crew Manager
Mike Ferrara, Ground Crew

Tom Barnard, Ground Crew
Paul Gordon, First Base Ball Boy
John Giuliotti, former ground crew
Al Forester, Stadium Operations Staff
Dave Mellor, Director of Grounds

Joe Mooney and
Dominican grounds-
keeper, Santo Domingo
PHOTO BY BILL NOWLIN

"Get in on the ground level" – good advice for someone wanting to break into any field of endeavor. With the Red Sox, many who work for the club literally started at ground level...on the ground crew.   A mere point of entry for some, a life-long career for others.

One of the most powerful memories people have of Fenway is the lushness of the grass. The unexpected greenness of it on a sunny day as you enter from the street and pass through a darkened concourse under the stands. The care and maintenance of the natural turf is a delicate job, requiring far more effort than most people would expect. It's a science and an art, a never-ending chore but the result admired by thousands of fans.

Joe Mooney, long-time head groundkeeper at Fenway Park was nothing if not passionate about his grass. Any number of celebrities have wandered onto the field and been ordered off, by a shout and a curse from Joe.

Mooney has been with the Red Sox since 1970, when Ted Williams helped him get the job. Ted was manager of the Washington Senators at the time and Joe had been there for 10 years. Asked to explain why he keeps working at Fenway after all these years, Mr. Mooney replied, "If I didn't like what I did, I'd get out tomorrow morning. As long as I'm healthy, I'll stay. Coming to the ballpark everyday is good. It keeps me younger."

Joe Mooney spent the better part of a lifetime on the ground crew, but there are those who started out there and advanced to other jobs. Employees such as Jim Healey, who walked in the door and got a job on the grounds crew, then worked his way up to team vice president.

One of the more impressive Sox family lineages is the Kenney family. Edward P. Kenney was Assistant General Manager. His father, Edward F., was Vice President for Player Development, and his grandfather Tom began the family Fenway dynasty on the ground crew.

EDWARD P. KENNEY
Assistant General Manager

My father was with the club about 46 years, from the early 40s until he retired in 1989 or 1990 as Vice President for Player Development. He's Edward F. Kenney. I'm Edward P. Kenney. A lot of times I'm referred to as Junior. My grandfather was Tom Kenney. He was the first one who worked at the ballpark, for Mr. Yawkey, during the late 30s and early 40s. He was more or less a personal assistant for Mr. Yawkey, and did some driving for Eddie Collins, too. I don't know if there was an exact title. He was just around the ballpark.

Eddie Collins was the general manager when my father played in the minor league system for the Boston Red Sox. He was an infielder they tried to convert into a pitcher and he hurt his arm. Eddie Collins talked him into coming into the ticket office to help out. Then he talked him into running tryout camps around the country. That evolved into front office work.

Edward P. Kenney's mother Anna and his father Edward F. met at Fenway Park. Anna worked in the minor league office from 1946 to 1948, when they married.

EDWARD F. KENNEY
former director of the Red Sox farm system

My father was on the ground crew at Fenway in the 20s. I was at Fenway when I was 13 years of age, in 1934. He had been working there for several years by then. Joe Cronin was the manager. He let me work out with the team, batting practice and all. Hughie Duffy was a great man there and I used to work out with him. He had tryouts in the morning, before the regular players came in. He had young players from high school and college come in.

Duffy signed me to a Red Sox contract. I played the infield in college. He thought I had a good arm. He watched me hit but I guess he didn't think too much of it so he said I ought to try pitching. Then I went in the service for four years. When I did come out after the war, I went to spring training with the minor league club and, well, I had a sore arm.

Eddie Collins was the general manager. He said to me, "Do you know how many young players make the major leagues? The percentage is very low." They were winning the pennant at the time, 1946, so they gave me a job in the ticket office. I fit in pretty good. He said to me, "If you do all right, it may lead into something." It did, because I was there for 45 years.

I worked in the ticket office for one or two years; then Joe Cronin had me going all over. We ran baseball schools throughout the country. Texas, Louisiana, all over. Tryout camps, schools. We'd be on a certain field at a certain time and anybody of a certain age range could show up for a tryout. I was on the road most of the time that first year.

When I came back, Johnny Murphy was appointed farm director and he said, "Would you like to work for me?" I worked in the minor league office in 1947. I think they called me, at that time, executive secretary. A fancy title. My wife Anna was in the ticket office and then she was secretary to the farm director George Toporcer; we met by being around the office. I moved up in the office and eventually became the farm director, responsible for all the minor league development. Then they made me Vice President of Player Development for the whole operation. I retired at the end of 1991.

My son Ed started in '78. He worked for a few years in the minor leagues, down at Bristol and New Britain. Then Haywood Sullivan said, "We'd like to have you working in Boston." He came into the minor league system. We had five children, but he's the only one who works for the Red Sox. I'm proud of him, really.

It was great working for Mr. Yawkey, and then Mrs. Yawkey. In fact, Mrs. Yawkey asked me if I wanted to be a trustee of her Foundation. I still am a trustee of the Yawkey Foundation.

Ed Kenney, Assistant General Manager, picks up the story with regard to his own career:

I grew up around the ballpark with some other young kids in the same age group, like Marc Sullivan. I went to work in 1978 for Joe Buzas, who owned the Red Sox Double A team in Bristol, Connecticut. I had just graduated from Boston College and Joe talked me into working for his club in the minors. I did that for a couple of years and then was named General Manager of the Bristol Red Sox. We moved the team to New Britain in 1983, and I worked there. After the '83 season, Haywood Sullivan offered me a chance to come up to Boston and work as assistant in the minor league scouting office. I became assistant farm director and then Minor League Director. I was Director of Minor League Operations, and then was promoted to Assistant General Manager.

I work now with player movement and trades, the whole baseball operation, signing players and contract work during the off-season. It's a lot of work with our scouts, trying to look for trades, improving our ball club, and evaluating our own talent. The weeks before the July 31 trading deadline are very busy.

I'd hoped to play ball when I was a kid, when I was younger and in high school, but I realized that I'd better find another way to make a living.

My own sons, they're turning 11 and 9 this summer. Hopefully, if they work here, they can work out on the playing field and make the type of money that they make out there. They're growing up around baseball. They have a great love for it already. I can bring my kids on a Saturday and they can go running around by themselves and I don't have to really worry about them.

I guess you could say it's in my blood.

Note: In September 2000, Edward P. Kenney resigned the Red Sox to become Special Assistant to the V.P. of Baseball Operations of the Baltimore Orioles. He may have seen the writing on the wall, knowing the team was to be sold and hoping to advance in another system – but what a shock, for a third generation Red Sox employee to move to another team.

CASEY ERVEN
Ground Crew Manager

After the season is over, the grounds crew prepares for the winter. This may involve re-sodding areas of the field. After the 1998 season, the outfield was re-done. After the 1999 campaign, all the infield grass was stripped off, both inside and outside the baselines. (There for the taking, part of my own backyard now sports Fenway infield grass.) New sod is laid down and, as winter approaches, a white felt covering is placed over the grass to protect it from the harsh weather. Mooney developed this approach some years ago. The felt, supplied by the Harry Miller Company in Boston, allows the field to breathe, but also keeps it warmer than it otherwise would be when covered by snow and ice.

Casey Erven was the Ground Crew Manager for many years, and currently head groundskeeper for the Pawtucket Red Sox. He joined the crew as a 15 year old in 1981. His mother Carol had begun in the ticket office just the year before, and Casey just showed up one snowy day looking for his own entrée.

I had actually applied before, spoken to Joe [Mooney] and filled out an application. He'd said, "Hold on. We'll see what happens. We'll call you back." The following Spring, he had never called back, but with the snowstorm around Opening Day I thought I'd go in and see if he needed anybody.

We had school off and I went in first thing in the morning. He hired me, and I've pretty much been working there ever since. They provided the shovel.

I worked all through high school and college, during my breaks and my vacations. Joe kept me on for summer work. I didn't really enjoy too much what I took up in college and I decided I wanted to stay in baseball somehow, so I just stuck with it. It just kind of rolled into what I'm doing now.

During the summer, we have a crew of about 25 to 35 guys. We do everything, from cutting the grass, to fertilizing, to watering, to cleaning up the warning track. If stuff needs to be touched up with paint, if pads need to be redone, we'll do that. We set up the screens. We break them down. If deliveries have got to be made, we end up doing that. The souvenir give-aways or something – if there's a truckload that comes up to the gate, we'll help with that. Informally, we're like the receiving department, too. We'll do pretty much anything that needs to be done.

By the time I get in about 7, Joe's usually been there about a half an hour. Joe takes all the heat off me, the heat from upstairs. He's a good buffer. He's definitely still very hands-on. Whenever he sees fit, he's still out there taking care of the infield, or watering. I'll still see him jump on the lawnmower.

We try to get everybody to know how to do everything. There's a huge turnover every year, probably about 70%. We have a big turnover in the spring when you need bodies around to pull the canvas, the tarp that we use when it's rain-ing. We pretty much take everybody, weed them out as we see fit, and bring back the guys we like. Most of the time, they're young kids in school, or just guys that don't have very much ambition. You're always going to have those types in every manual labor job.

On a regular non-game day, we'll get out of there around 3 o'clock or 4 o'clock. It's tough being in the sun all day in the heat of the sum-mer. These guys put in 70, 80 hours a week during a home stay, so we try to get everything done fast in the morning and get them out of there in the afternoon. In the off-season, that's when we do all the work. When [the team's] not there. When they're home, you can't really do anything other than the routine game day stuff, because you've got to have everything ready for the game that night. You're just maintaining when they're home. When they go on the road is when we do all the re-sodding.

If it's calling for rain, we'll get rid of a lot of the full-time guys that have been there all day. A lot of guys, frankly, don't want to stay for the game. If they want the overtime, they're more than welcome to stay but a lot of them are like, "Get me out of here."

We've got a lot of people who have regular jobs, and can come in for a nighttime game. We've got a couple of guys that work at Fidelity. One that works for the state. Essentially, it's like a season ticket for them. They come in and help take the screens off and watch the game, maybe do the foul line. If it does rain, they help us put the canvas out. Those are the guys that we depend on at night.

Casey Erven
PHOTO BY: BILL NOWLIN

About 18 to 20 people pull the tarp. If there's any chance of rain, we'll keep twenty guys on. We don't aim for any time in particular when it rains – just to get it out as fast as possible. I haven't any idea what it weighs. How long it takes us varies on how hard it's raining, on how many guys you've got pulling, if you've got good guys pulling it that know what they're doing or if you've got guys who have never pulled it before. People fall sometimes.

I'm there until the game's over. Rain delays and extra innings I hate. They kill me. I shut the lights off at night...well, I tell the electrician to shut them off. We shut them down in stages. We kind of try to let the crowd thin out, then turn the lights off and say, "OK, the show's over." Once they all get out and they're completely cleared, then we go quick. If you leave the lights on, they'll hang around all night long. I lock everything up and – boom – I'm out of there.

The baselines are latex field marking paint, made by California Paint. That's what the base-line is, from the dirt part until you get to the warning track. Then it turns into a 2 x 4 with a strip of rubber put on it. It gets painted every three or four days, to neaten it up. Maybe around 1 or 2 o'clock, I put down the foul lines. We just use a pressurized tank to spray on the paint – you pump it up and it's got a little noz-zle on it in the middle that fires out a perfect four-inch wide strip. You put a string down to follow, and just walk the line.

We replace home plate about once a year, unless someone comes in and steals it. Once every couple of years, somebody gets in and clips one.

Before the game, we'll just throw a clean set of bases in there. Occasionally, if the game's on Fox, they have their own set of bases that have microphones in them. So if you ever saw us going out and changing them in the middle of the game, it's most likely Fox or ESPN and the batteries have gone dead. If it's really raining during a game, if the bases get all muddied up, we'll try to put three new bases out there partway through. Ninety percent of the time, though, before the game, we just put three bases in and that's it. They're heavy, heavy rubber. They have an indefinite life – ten years, twelve years.

After the fourth and after the seventh, we do the drag. We smooth out the surface of the infield dirt. We used to do it after the fifth, but a few years ago, one of the managers asked us if we could do it a couple of times. Four guys go out and pull those big heavy screens, wide enough to make one pass each way. Then one guy comes out and is raking around first base, where the first baseman stands, and he just kind of pulls the pile [of pebbles and dirt] off to the side after these guys lift up their drag.

The drain system has about 60 drains. There's a whole grid system of PVC that runs off the field. The whole field is pitched towards each individual drain. We well them up with dirt and put some grass plugs on them. The grass plugs grow right into this 4 or 6 inch PVC. I know by memory where those plugs are. After a week or so of not pulling them up, they blend right in and you could easily lose them. Now and then, you lose one. Occasionally, we'll try to spray them very lightly with vegetable dye so it stands out against the natural color of the grass. We only bring them up when we're expecting heavy rain. On the track, there's another drain system that follows the side of the track pretty much, foul line to foul line.

They had an old kind of pipe – Orangeburg, I guess it's called, where it's kind of tar wrapped in paper and stuff. Mooney put that in, when

he came here in 1970 or 71. When he first came to the ballpark, there wasn't any drain system here whatsoever. He found the low spots and proceeded to start a drain system and did it in two or three years, a little bit here and a little bit there. He eventually got the whole thing where it drains pretty good. It's the same system that Mooney laid out almost thirty years ago, with a few more added.

We have an old impact sprinkler system, 35 or 40 years old, with the big plug-in sprinklers that shoot about 100 feet. We have guys go around with hoses getting the edges, getting the spots the sprinkler missed. You can do a more uniform job with a hose than you can with a sprinkler. It's just a brass plug with a rubber coating to hide them; we'll just glue a piece of Astroturf on the top and that blends right in. The whole thing is flush. We've never had a complaint from a player.

We re-seed throughout the year where needed, like the wear spots where the three outfielders stand. Occasionally, you get a disease or you get a fungus in there. A lot of times we can bring it back with chemicals, herbicide or fertilizer, and cut back on the water, but if that gets a little ahead of you, I'll go in and throw some seed.

Usually in the off season, we'll slice seed the whole field. The slice seeder, it's got maybe ten to twelve vertical blades that cut the soil about two inches deep. There's a bucket on top, a hopper that holds all the seed and there's some chutes that go down and they drop seed into the slices. We slice seed the field usually in two directions, crisscross it.

The pattern that you see in the outfield grass is just the rollers of the lawnmower. The pattern depends on how you cut the grass, if you cut it all one way or if you cut it crisscross. There's no special magic to it. All you've got to do is know how to drive that lawnmower straight and the rollers in front of the blade just push the blades of grass one way and then when you come back the other way, it lays down light. It's just different shades because the grass is laying one way or the other.

We do like the pattern. The more you go over it, the more the pattern stands out. You could go over it the same way five or six times and eventually the other direction will disappear. Or you can crisscross it, the way the kid put the star in the outfield for the All-Star Game. Ted's number 9 on the field was done with the same dye that we use for the drain caps, but the star was done with the lawn mower. He came in at night, marked it out with strings and then just followed the pattern. Then once he did it, he could see what he was doing and he just kept going over it for three or four nights until it really got emblazoned into the grass.

Different managers have different requests. Some of them are very particular with how they want the field and others couldn't care less.

A lot of players like things done certain ways but you'd have 25 to 30 different guys asking you to do different things. Occasionally, some guy asks if you can keep it loose where they're at, or maybe roll it a little extra for them. Usually they're infielders. We can do a little quick stuff. Maybe a pitcher now and then has a preference on how they like the mound.

You can only do so much. You've still got to stay within the guidelines of the American League rules. When push comes to shove, we're the ones that have to take the heat from the American League, not the players.

The American League does send people in every couple of years. They come in and check the distances between all four bases. They check the Red Sox bullpen and the visitors' bullpen for the pitch of the mound and the distance between the plate and the mound, and the height of the mound. Make sure it's ten inches. That's just to keep everything fair. It's a good policy.

Some teams do [doctor the field.] Some guys do, some guys don't. A few guys do ask for certain conditions and usually it's the height of the grass. I've never had anybody want the baselines pitched any particular way. I think that's a practice at a lot of places but Joe tries to keep it by the book. What you think is going to help you might come back and haunt you. Like The Wall. It gives but it also takes away, and the same thing is true with any extra things that you do to the field. You might keep the grass longer to slow down a ball so it gives your guys a chance to get to it, but there might be a guy on their team that's very, very fast and now the ball's slowed down. He bunts and he gets away with a lot more bunts than he would have. It works both ways. It hurts you and it helps you.

If I choose to, I can pretty much see the whole game. Most of the time, I'm just kind of walking around the stadium and making sure everything's going all right. Hopefully, come game time, if we did everything the way we're supposed to, our job's pretty much done. The only thing we'll usually have to do during a game is something like go fix a seat. The seats break a lot. They're old, ancient. If we can't fix it, we'll just move the people somewhere else.

If it's going to rain, I'll be right down in Canvas Alley the whole time, talking to the umpires. Between innings, I'll run out to the first base umpire and let him know the forecast. I'm usually there from the start of the game through the first inning and then I kind of disappear and just go through my business unless it's going to rain and then I'm down there the whole game. I like to let the guys just enjoy the game and not have me staring over their backs, not babysitting them. They've seen me all day! They just want to sit and watch the game, too.

It definitely has its highs and lows, but I've been doing it a long time and I guess I like it.

Mooney's fantastic. We get along tremendous. He's definitely one of the fairest guys I've ever met in my life. If you do the work and you do what you're supposed to do and you're honest with him and you don't try to horseshit him, you're not going to find a guy that's more loyal to you. He's like anybody else. He's still a boss in a manual labor position, so his temper flares now and then but he's great to work for. I hope he sticks around for a while. I learned it all from him.

Who is the guy who walks along on top of the Wall to collect the balls hit there in batting practice?

It's one of our guys. I used to do it but now my wife won't let me. There's a walkway that's about a foot below the top of the Wall, and you're safe up there. The walkway's a piece of heavy planking a foot wide that goes along the whole length of the Wall. It's kind of a catch basin for all the balls that come off the net.

It's a fishing net, just one big net. The whole thing. We take it down in the offseason to keep it from freezing up.

The felt we put on the field over the winter does a great job. It gives you extra growing time in the winter. It keeps the grass from going dormant and in the springtime, it helps jump the grass right back about three or four weeks before anybody's lawn. It depends on the weather, but we usually take it off around the first of March.

A lot of people say they'd like to put in on their yard, but of course we're out there eight or nine hours a day every day maintaining it. Watering. It's got a lot of chemicals in it. The stuff doesn't just stay green – magic turf. It's a lot of hands-on maintenance that keeps it that

Mike Ferrara
PHOTO BY BILL NOWLIN

way. Anybody that puts the time in and the care we put in could have a lawn that looked like that, too. I have an apartment — so my lawn is pavement.

[*Not only does Casey's mother still work in the ticket office, but Casey met his wife Joanne at Fenway, too. And Sox team photographer Jack Maley's son was the natural choice to make their wedding pictures.*]

We've got a couple of brothers on the ground crew. A lot of sets of brothers come through. It seems that a lot of the people who work here stay and bring their whole families in. Most of the people really love working here. You kind of have to be a baseball fan, because you don't make a lot of money. Either you like the game or you don't, and if you do, it kind of runs in the family.

Casey is now head groundskeeper at McCoy Stadium for the Pawtucket Red Sox.

TIM SAMWAY ON JIM GATELY

Jim Gately used to like to be the one to line the batter's box just before each game. Tim Samway, a long-time Sox fan very active in the Bosox Club, once told me a story about Jim, one which says a lot about the Red Sox as well. This is Tim's story:

Jim Gately worked at Fenway Park for over 50 or 60 years. He came to the ballpark right after the war and he got a job in maintenance. Jimmy was an usher on the work gang but then he got so much seniority they promoted him upstairs. One of the things he did before the games – at 7 o'clock, when the games started at 7:30 – he would go down and he would line the batter's box. I said to him, "Jimmy, have you ever had a photo of you doing that?" "No, no, no." He had done the job for so many years that when he got the job with the jacket and tie, upstairs in the press box, he refused to give up this one.

He used to run down and he would do that and then he would go back upstairs and wash up. Come seven o'clock one night, I'm down behind the third base dugout and I've got my big lens on and I'm taking photos of Jim out there putting down the lines. I'm noticing this contraption that he has. I focused on one end of the big contraption, it literally has some Johnson & Johnson athletic tape, the white tape, around the corner.

I got the photos back and I was showing it to him. Jim was – I'm saying this nicely, but he was just a simple worker – he's saying, "Oh Geez, thanks a lot. That's really great." I said to him, pointing at the tape, "What's this?" And he said, "Oh, the thing cracked. We just took it to the trainer and I put some tape on it."

I'm thinking to myself, now here's the game of baseball. There is such precision. And he's out there lining the batter's box and he's got trainer's tape wrapped around this thing. I said to him, "Jesus, Jim. You've been doing this since 1940?" He said, "Yeah." I said, "And that thing broke? How many do you use a year?" He says, "Ahhh, one." I said, "What do you do then, make a new one?" He said, "No, that's the same one I've been using since 1946. It broke and I put the tape on it."

I said, "Jimmy, you cannot be telling me the truth. Since 1946, you've used that one thing?" And he said, "Yeah, Jesus, don't tell anybody it's broke! They'd get really pissed off."

All these years, he had ONE since 1946. That is so Red Sox!

But here's this guy, religiously goes out and puts this thing down and takes like ten minutes, very precise about it. And of course, the first batter comes out there and scratches the lines out anyhow.

MIKE FERRARA
Ground Crew

Casey mentions climbing the Wall to collect the baseballs that gather in the net. Mike Ferrara's been the one doing that the last few years. Fenway Park is noted for the ladder affixed to the Green Monster. It's the only in-play ladder in baseball. Once in a while, a ball will hit the ladder and ricochet unpredictably off into the field, and the ground rule is that the ball stays in play. After batting practice, Mike will make his way out to "the Yaz door" – the doorway which opens up onto left field from under the stands, and climb that ladder to retrieve the b. p. balls.

I've been up on the Wall every day for four years. The ladder is under the stands. I bring it over and put it up, to meet up with the ladder on the wall, then I'll climb up with the bags and collect the balls from the net.

The most I ever got was the night of the home run contest before the All-Star Game. I got 150 then. Many games there's around 50.

People call out at me. They want me to throw them a ball. When I don't, they throw stuff at me. Coke bottles, softballs.

With the installation of the new Green Monster Seats on top of The Wall prior to the 2003 season, this long-standing tradition has come to an end. And the net is no more.

TOM BARNARD
Ground Crew

Picking up on another point which Casey mentioned, laying down the foul lines, Tom Barnard describes that process further, as well as his own little ritual he developed during the drag.

Tom Barnard
PHOTO BY BILL NOWLIN

I happen to own my own garden center and I work for the state as a horticultural inspector. I inspect nurseries and garden centers for insects and disease damage. Somebody at the state knew somebody who used to work over at Fenway and it fit into their schedule. So one day I walked out onto the field and met Joe Mooney. I told him my situation and he hired me on the spot. It was great. I remember, when I got it, coming out the back there and going "YEE-HAH!" A little excited!

I was a Red Sox fan growing up in Brockton, and I spent many nights with my grandfather listening to the game on the radio while we played Scrabble. That's how I became a Red Sox fan. It was mostly my grandfather. Later on, I used to take him into the games. He had a weird tradition, I'll tell you. He had an old-fashioned bicycle horn and every time the Red Sox did well, he honked this horn. Everybody around the stadium got to know when my grandfather Joe was there. We used to sit right in section 21, right behind home plate.

I enjoy the heck out of it. Last year we took a couple of days and used a level and some pins and string to make sure that the pitcher's mound was built properly. That took a few days. Casey can spend a whole day leveling the mound and the plate and down in the bullpen.

We put in the actual foul lines. Nobody really realizes that those are made out of wood, with pieces of rubber on top of them and then they're pounded into the ground. We take them out at the end of the season and then it takes us one whole day to put them back in.

Before the game, we all have our assigned jobs here. I like to take the broom and sweep the foul lines. I started here about five years ago putting the foul lines down with the carpenters – so I kind of treat those lines as my babies, you know. Paul [Gordon] asked me before every game, "How do the lines feel? Does it look like it's going to be a win or a loss?" He got the feeling as the ball boy. "Feeling pretty positive tonight" – and then we'd win that night. One night, I'd say, "I don't know, Paul. I'm not getting good vibes tonight." We'd play like that back and forth.

I'm involved with the drag, the raking of the field between the fourth and fifth and then in between the seventh and eighth. I have a cousin, Peter Monsini, on the crew with me and every drag, we go out and we're the first ones on the field with the screens there and when we're coming around second base – nobody's picked up on it yet – we sort of give our hats a little tip, honoring all the past players that have been on the field. Our grandfather was a really big baseball fan, so every time we go around second base there, we'll say "A salute to Ted Williams" or "Salute to our grandfather." It's just our own funny little salute.

The screens aren't that heavy, probably around ten pounds. They're attached to two pieces of rope and we hold the end of the rope and we go around. I steer it so it keeps away from the edge of the infield. I'm the outside guy, the one who actually controls how close it is to the infield. I actually got to rake around first base the other day. It's all interesting stuff that happens there. As we're running out, I step on the first base foul line. That's my little thing. I try to step on it as we come back in, too. You notice Nomar. Nomar always skips it. He hops right over it.

I've taken down the flag after the game. Richie Dean 's usually the one who goes out and takes down the flag. They said, "Hey, Tom. Want to help Richie with the flag?" It's a big flag. You've got to make sure it doesn't get caught up in the Wall there. It comes down and you fold it up and put it down back near the grounds crew room.

I haven't missed a game. I enjoy it. After the Red Sox season, I go on and I work for the New England Patriots grounds crew. At Fenway, you have the turf management but you also have the dirt conditions there. It's a little bit different work over in Foxborough, completely turf. There's a lot of painting of the field and putting up goal posts. It's a completely different ballgame, no pun intended.

PAUL GORDON
First Base Ball Boy

Paul Gordon, as Tom indicates, took over not that long ago as one of the two ball boys. A ground crew member, he works during the games from a very short and pretty beat-up old metal stool he sits on just inside the right field foul line. After new ownership assumed the reins, the ground crew's ball boys were replaced by ball girls. No reflection on Paul, but the ball girls seem to be better fielders than some of their predecessors drawn from the ground crew.

I'm the first base ball boy. I was playing Yawkey League baseball with one of my buddies last year and he worked on the crew for Joe. I called Joe up the day before Opening Day at Fenway and said, "I'm just wondering if I can come in and work for you tomorrow." I said, "Any time." He said, "Show up at 9." I just took it from there.

I'm an intern for a large Boston-based financial services firm. This is my third summer interning. Eventually I want to get into the finance or the investment side of things, fixed income or equity research or into venture capital.

I grew up in Boston. I was one of the most loyal Red Sox followers you'll ever find. My first day on the job here, I looked up and there was Jim Rice over me – my favorite baseball player ever. He just seemed so untouchable and now he was five feet away from me. To have that feeling and then, an hour later, to sit and watch the Red Sox take a full batting practice...

[As the ball boy on the foul line] if you average it out over a week, you usually get two or three balls a game. You get as few as zero and as many as seven or eight a game. There's one game I remember, I got five in the first two innings, and then none the rest of the game. It's not predictable. The only thing that's predictable is when Pedro pitches, they're usually not going to hit a ball down the line. They either swing and miss at everything or they guess right and put it into play. There's no in-between. It's pretty amazing.

There are more righty hitters, I guess, but we always joke on the ground crew that Anthony [third base line ball boy] makes way more errors than any of us. He gets so many more balls over there. We don't keep fielding percentages. I know that I've made two errors and misplayed one so I guess you could say that I made three errors all year. That's all. That's with about two hundred chances. .985? Maybe I can get a Gold Glove.

I joke that I was the ball boy for the All-Star Game. I was on the field for three and a half innings. We split that up. The previous week I had made this catch, jumping into Canvas Alley to get a Lou Merloni liner. Saved a couple of my buddies from getting hit in the head. Supposedly it made Sportscenter and everything.

There's no infield practice, nothing like that. You've got to prove yourself on the first ball.

If there's a pop fly over there, you're supposed to pick your stool up and jump into Canvas Alley. You've got to jump over the top. The first time it happened to me, I jumped over. It was during an afternoon game, late in the game, so the sun was setting over Valentin. I lost sight of the ball. I had no clue where it was, so I hopped over the fence. It came down and hit me on the shoulder. I didn't see it at all. It just plunked me from behind. There were three players over there.

If you get a ball, absolutely throw it to the fans. It's good PR. Obviously, you're going to give it to the little guys and girls out there, who are dressed up in Sox colors with the Red Sox hat and Garciaparra T shirt.

A lot of the guys don't want to do ball boy, because they get too nervous out on the field. Usually on the weekend games when I show up there early, I clean up around the tracks. Clean out the bullpens. Rake down the bullpens to make them look nice. When you're a kid and you went out in the bleachers, you'd always look down and watch the pitchers pitch. It was always raked so perfectly. Everything looked so perfect out there. I try to get it to look like that before every game. Fill in the divots where pitchers were throwing from and where their feet were landing. Just make it look all nice.

I don't come in every single day. I just come in when the games are played. Like I told Joe, it's the internship that will get me my job, and Fenway is my work for recreation.

They have one person out in the Red Sox bullpen getting the beachballs that go out on the field. That's your only responsibility – run out, pick it up, pop it and take it back. That is the only thing you do. John Wasdin said last year's game record was around fifteen. Usually, you're not counting. You're just trying to catch your breath after running out there.

Paul Gordon
PHOTO BY ANDREA RAYNOR

After the game, I take care of the visitors' bullpen, pull the tarp out from the corner, place it over the top, throw the concrete blocks on every corner. I usually look underneath where the pitchers sit out there in the bullpens for any balls that are still left over from batting practice. I usually throw those up to the fans afterwards.

The players leave all kinds of gum and food out there. Usually, you take care of that the next morning. Sometimes you come across some interesting stuff, like stat sheets and scouting reports from the other team on the Red Sox.

We'll put out the tarp if it starts to rain. We don't time it. We just want to get it over with. When the rain's pumping down on you and you're pulling it and you've got the infield dirt under your fingers...you're pulling it and it's ripping at your skin and it's raw and cold out, you just want to pull it and get that darn thing out there, and then seek some shelter in the over-flooded dugouts.

That Yankees game! It was the top of the ninth. It was 6-0 Red Sox. It wasn't even close. I think they had a runner on and one out. Jim Corsi was pitching and then all of a sudden, the skies just opened up and it started pouring. So we fumbled out there, we sprinted out there, laid the tarp on finally, then sat in the Sox dugout for about 35 minutes. I was actually sitting next to Nomar and Jim Rice, listening to them talk! Then they called us out to pull it off because it had cleared. Finally we had got the whole thing pulled off, all the water drained out perfectly, had it folded up and ready to be put back onto the metal roller – and the skies opened up again! We had to lay it right back out again. And wait another 35 minutes until we could pull it off. It was rough.

Sometimes after the game, we'll hit the bar scene up on Boylston. That's where all the players go after a good win. They go to the sports-type bars by Hynes. Pedro's a great guy. Making, what, $13 million a year but he talks to every one of us. He's always happy, always bouncing around. When the media's not around, and the fans aren't around, he's just so hilarious out on the field while they're taking batting practice, or just around the clubhouse. But game days? You don't go near him. He's so focused.

Right before the game, we break down batting practice and roll the cage out to center field under the stands. You come in and take the three screens from in front of the dugout. There are three of them side by side. They plug in, they have metal rods that go into the ground. Two legs that come out and each of those legs goes into a hole. Believe it or not, it's actually a round peg into a square hole. After we take the three screens in from in front of the dugout, we have these other plugs that we put on top of them so no players get their cleats stuck in them.

Then we have the screen in front of the pitcher's mound. One in front of first and one in front of second. We've got a mat on the one right outside of second base that they stand on.

Better than them standing on the field and tearing it up.

The bases have the metal part that comes out of the base and it just goes into a little square hole that's sunk into the ground. They actually have a big scooper to scrape the dirt out, so that second base isn't raised at all, so nobody comes in and jams their feet. We pull the dirt out of the hole so the base sits level.

I have not done the drag yet. It almost is a prestige thing.

JOHN GIULIOTTI
Ground Crew

John Giuliotti used to work on the ground crew, and one of his duties from 1982 to 1987 was to work inside the Wall, operating the manual scoreboard.

I worked on the ground crew all through high school and all through college. My father is Joe Giuliotti, and he was a BOSTON HERALD sportswriter. He started as a copyboy and then 48 years later he retired as a sports columnist. When I turned 16, I needed some summer work and my father put me in contact with Joe [Mooney.]

My older brother Ed was already working there at the time. Same thing, grounds crew. I grew up in East Boston, so I never had a lawn of my own. The first lawn I ever cut in my life was probably the most famous lawn in Boston. I was amazed how often you had to cut it. There were times during the summer that we would cut the outfield twice in one day. We would fertilize and fungicide. Joe Mooney, that was his baby, so he would take care of that.

When I first started cutting the outfield grass – it was my job for a couple of seasons – I used to see what the other ballparks would have on TV and I used to take some pride in the lines that we would cut. I remember I would put the news on when I got home, not so much for the replays of the game, but to see how my outfield grass looked.

I was just a young kid and I was fascinated by the scoreboard. I remember my first time walking through the Wall and I was just amazed that it just looked like the corner of someone's cellar, dark and dusty. Nothing like the outside looks.

My first couple of times out there, the people who were training me said make sure you keep the radio running. Well, what's that for? "You'll find out." They ended up telling me that there's rats that run around out there. The first time I was out there and the radio was broken, sure enough, I looked down the far end of the scoreboard during the game and a couple of heads poked out of some drain pipes and were looking at me. So from that point on, the left fielder probably got a dose of my terrible voice because [my partner and me] were singing the rest of the game!

Sometimes we'd tune in and listen to the game. Other times we'd just listen to music. Every now and again, before we'd head into the scoreboard, we'd call a local radio station and say, "Can you play a song for the guys in the scoreboard?" We'd listen to that station and they would maybe later on play a song like "I'm Trapped" by Bruce Springsteen.

We had to be there at 7:30 in the morning. We would work all afternoon in the hot sun, taking care of the field, whatever – raking, watering, cutting. If you're doing a ten or fourteen game homestand, it really weighs on you. You'd come in at 7:30 in the morning and you'd leave at 11 o'clock at night only to be back there the next morning, so you kind of get all baseballed out.

Once the door shuts, once the game starts, you're pretty well trapped in there. They had a little porta thing in there, but that wasn't used very often, except in a rare emergency. The left fielder would come over once in a while, between pitching changes, chat or listen to the music. Some of the guys are cool. My first year was Yastrzemski's last year and Yaz would come over to the Wall and talk to us. Bo Jackson came over a couple of times to say hello. They would come over and just chew the fat. Hang out.

I have my name written in there. I worked the night that Clemens struck out his 20 and we carved our names in there. That was one of the games that we were listening to the radio – but not the ballgame. We generally didn't pay attention to every pitch, you know, because of other things going on. You'd read the paper, chat…but that night by the fifth or sixth inning, every time he's striking someone out, the crowd is really starting to go ape. We weren't really sure what was going on until the final out. I came out to take all the out of town name plates off the front of the scoreboard and the message board read that Roger Clemens has just set a major league record. While he was setting the record, we weren't really aware he was setting it!

My first year there was an Old Timer's Game. It might have been one of the last times Ted actually had a uniform on and played in left field. I was working the scoreboard at the time and I had the opportunity to peer out through the scoreboard and see Number 9 play left field. I savored that.

We almost felt like we were a part of the team because we were there just as much as the Red Sox were. You'd develop speaking relationships with some of the guys. I remember during off days they would have optional workouts and we would go out there and maybe shag balls out in the outfield and do some things like that.

The rain delays were kind of fun. Pulling the tarp out; it was kind of a rush. Sometimes people would lose their footing and fall. It was really a tight knit group of guys. There was someone – it might have been in S.I. [SPORTS ILLUSTRATED] – they timed the grounds crews. We were one of the fastest in the league, so we would take pride in that. Joe would make sure that we would get that thing out there as quickly as possible. It was tough love with him. He was very, very demanding – but he was great for kids who were in high school or college. He taught me one thing – you always had to be on time. You were there at 7:30. If you were there at 7:31, you were late and got sent home, no matter what. No ifs, ands or buts about it. It was just a great learning experience.

During the '86 series, I was a freshman. I came home for the Series and worked as the third base ball boy. I wasn't really too popular at the time – but next thing you know, a couple of foul balls, and I was on national TV retrieving some ground balls. I came back to North Adams and it was, "Wow. You were the guy on TV at the World Series." Everyone kind of knew me after that.

There are a lot of family connections at Fenway. The Kenneys, of course, but also Carol Erven and her son Casey, who married another Red Sox employee. Tom Barnard and his cousin Peter Monsini. The Giuliottis. There are several others, in other departments and particularly within Aramark, the concessionaire. We will meet some of them in later chapters.

AL FORESTER
Stadium Operations Staff

Al Forester, listed as Stadium Operations Staff, is sort of a jack of all trades around the park. When they need someone to drive Ted Williams in on the electric cart, Al's the one they call for. When they need someone to watch a gate, Al's the man.

April 10, 1957. That's when I started. I was in the florist business in Woburn, with my four brothers. We had five greenhouses plus two flower shops in West Medford and down in Winthrop. Everybody retired, sold the business.

When I started, I did a little bit of everything. I started on the ground crew. Connie Sullivan from Dorchester was the head back then. There was another guy after him, and then I was in charge for a couple of years. Then Joe Mooney came in. I used to drive for Mr.

Al Forester
PHOTO BY BILL NOWLIN

Yawkey and Mrs. Yawkey, too. I've done a little bit of everything.

I come in every day and I work 7 to 3 on the off days. I just stay at Gate D, watch everything that's going on, all the deliveries. [Today] I had twelve trucks out here that were unloading. Everything from beer to paper cups to hot dogs to Coca Cola. All these different things that they deliver – not just for the Red Sox, but for Aramark, for the skyview seats, the 600 Club.

Every day I work the gate here, when the team is away. Now, when the team is at home, if it's a night game, I come in at 3 in the afternoon and work until midnight or 1 o'clock in the morning. I have to find what time the visiting team bus is coming from the hotel. I take care of the bus down at Gate B. Once the bus backs in, I close the gate. Nobody gets no autographs. They don't allow that.

The same at night. The visiting bus leaves at least an hour after the game is over. Once all the ballplayers get in the bus, when the traveling secretary gets there and he says we're ready to leave, all I do is open the gate and let them leave, close the gate and that's it.

The nights that the Red Sox and the visiting team are both leaving, then I may have four buses down there. Most of the time, they'll go off together. Anybody hanging around, we don't allow it.

I have stayed here overnight. I was working until 3 o'clock in the morning so I stayed overnight in the first aid room. After the last playoff game, I had to wait until all the Yankees left, with their buses. So I just stayed over, rather than go home. Why go home? It wasn't the first time.

The main question I get asked here is can I go out and look at the field.

A lot of people don't have time for the tour. They've got to go catch a plane or a train, and they say, "Can we just go look at the field?" I say, "OK. One minute. You go up to the top of the ramp." They want to see the Green Monster. They come from all over the world. Australia. The Netherlands. Sweden. Denmark. They come from everywhere, and all they want to see is the Green Monster.

After the season, there are no more tours but I still have my own one minute tour.

The biggest event was 1999. I drove Ted in during the All-Star Game. All the ballplayers come around us, while Ted and I were sitting on the cart, so I introduced each one of the ballplayers. Started off with Mark McGwire, Sammy Sosa, Tony Gwynn, Ken Griffey, Jr. and then Cal Ripken. The producer said, "We're running late" so I had to kind of cut it short.

I saw Nomar to my left and I said, "Nomar!" Ted said, "Where's Nomar?" "Nomar, come back here and shake hands with Ted." So he shook hands with Ted. Then I looked over my shoulder and there's Joe Torre. I can't forget him. I said, "Ted, here's Joe Torre from the Yankees." So he come around and shook hands. That's when he got out of the cart to throw the first pitch.

I used to drive the relief pitchers in from the bullpen, in that baseball cap cart. They walk in now to limber up their legs.

I also set up the microphone for the National Anthem, yes. Every game.

Usually, in the seventh inning I start heading down to Gate B to get ready for the bus. I usually sit outside. They have a little monitor on the side of the truck. One of the TV trucks. I sit right down there and watch the game right there.

Sometimes I'm upstairs the whole night. We have sixteen cameras there and I watch the monitors. If there's a fight or somebody gets hurt, I can just put on whatever monitor I want to and pick them up. It's good to pick it up on the camera because now you've got it on tape. You can never tell when somebody might get drunk and start swinging at our guys or the cops. Now you've got it on tape if you have to go to court.

I watch every game. Even if they're away. I leave here at 3 o'clock. By the time I take a shower, it's 4 o'clock. I get home 4:30, 5 o'clock. I'll have something to eat. The games around here, like Baltimore or the Yankees, that's easy. If they're playing out in Anaheim, which starts at 10:30 or so, I'll just take a nap. Set the alarm for 10 o'clock and wake up and watch the game. Oh yeah. I love baseball. If you love baseball, you just want to watch it all.

I'll keep doing this until I die.

DAVE MELLOR
Director of Grounds

Before the 2001 season, a new groundskeeper assumed responsibility for Fenway's grounds. David Mellor's grandfather Big Bill Mellor was a major leaguer, his career shortened by a knee injury. Big Bill played for John McGraw's Baltimore Orioles in 1902 – the same Baltimore team which metamorphosed into the New York Yankees. Given the family history, David could well have been raised a Yankees fan.

Dave Mellor
PHOTO BY BILL NOWLIN

Mellor began work in early January, assuming responsibility for the hallowed turf of Fenway Park. Long-time legendary groundskeeper Joe Mooney, 71, was ready to cut back on his schedule.

David Mellor's lifetime dream was to make the major leagues as a ballplayer, but life offered other challenges to him. His father, Bill Junior, died of a heart attack when David was just three years old. Bill Junior was a staunch Red Sox fan, his son says. "He had a passion for baseball. He and my brother were season ticket holders at Fenway Park; they actually had the two seats right next to the dugout when they lived in Andover back in the late 50s, early 60s. They were avid fans."

After his father died, young David, too, was raised as a Sox fan by his mom. "My mother knew the passion for the Red Sox that was in my father's side of the family and she just continued that passion with my two older brothers and myself. I was born and grew up in Ohio, near Dayton, so I certainly went to Cincinnati Reds games. We never missed a Game of the Week on TV. I watched the 1975 World Series. I went to two of the games there and I was certainly one of the few kids wearing Red Sox things and carrying a Red Sox banner. My brothers and I had every-

thing we could think of that was Red Sox. I was 12. They won one and lost one."

David wanted to follow in his grandfather's footsteps and he was apparently quite good on the mound. "I pitched. I pitched all the way up through Little League and Legion and had planned on playing in college, but right after I graduated from high school, I was walking into a McDonald's restaurant and a car came off the street and hit me. I had people talking to me but my coach said if I do well at the tournament, I'd have more offers. So just hold off, and I did but then I got hit by a car." It was his knee that was damaged, the same knee that did in Big Bill Mellor.

"Everybody aspired to be Luis Tiant or Carlton Fisk or Carl Yastrzemski. Before I got hit by the car, my dream would have been to become a Red Sox player." Between this and a later accident – again, to the very same knee – David has had 18 knee operations. It goes without saying that his pitching dreams were over. Another calling offered itself. "My brothers advised me to find a career I loved where I would look forward to going to work every day." He'd done a lot of lawn work as a kid, and began to realize that – after all – someone had to take care of major league baseball fields. A secondary dream began to formulate itself. David applied himself to the study of landscape horticulture, agronomy and – ultimately – the specialty of sportsturf management. He landed an internship with the

Photo taken March 27, 2000 of the materials they were using to put in the new foul lines. Rubber strip hammered onto top of 2 x 4. String line stretched to show foul line.

PHOTO BY BILL NOWLIN

Milwaukee Brewers in 1985 and after graduating from Ohio State began to work for the Brewers full-time. David Mellor had made it to the major leagues after all.

He spent 16 years working his way up in Milwaukee, and had a number of interesting experiences. There was the "hundred year rainstorm" in Milwaukee in 1997, which saw much of the city – and County Stadium – under water. One game had to be canceled but a postponement the next day was avoided after David arranged for the Channel 12 helicopter to hover over the field for six hours at a height of 12 feet, blow-drying the field! Another time play was halted by the appearance of a skunk on the field in mid-inning. A cautious ground crew gently urged the skunk to leave and everyone breathed a fresh sign of relief. A nearly unbelievable insect invasion presented another quandary as hundreds of hungry gulls settled in and made it clear they planned to stick around. This crisis was solved in a humane manner by bringing in six trained "soft mouth" bird dogs which scooted around the field between innings and over the course of a couple of weeks discouraged the birds enough to bring about their search for more fruitful pastures.

When David came to Boston, he moved from the newest park in the major leagues – the brand-new Miller Park, which he saw from inception to completion – to the oldest, Fenway Park. David left Miller Park before the first game was played in the new facility, but he was going to the home field of his beloved Red Sox. Milwaukee used to be an American League city, of course, before the Brewers switched to the National League. Was it a special treat when the Red Sox came on a road trip to County Stadium? "Oh, absolutely! It was a real treat. Our ground crew sat in the left field corner, so I'd be either there or in my office. I'd be a quiet rooter at that point – but everybody knew I was a Sox fan."

It was at County Stadium where Mellor suffered another bizarre car accident, again to his right knee. "I was on the field and this lady came driving her car right onto the field. She drove through a delivery gate behind the bleachers. It was just kind of a freak thing. She was a mental patient off her medicine. It could have been a lot worse." Where can you go to be safe from getting hit by a car? Apparently not the ballfield at County Stadium.

County Stadium, though, is where David Mellor developed his skill and artistry with mowing patterns. To some extent, Paul McCartney was responsible. In 1993, Paul played a concert at the stadium and it rained throughout. The stage had been set up in the outfield and a couple of thousand sheets of plywood were laid down to protect the grass. Felt carpeting was laid as well, but when everything was broken down there was serious damage to the field. Safety and playability were, as now, David's priorities – but once those problems were addressed, he turned to aesthetics. He and his crew mowed a pattern into the outfield grass to try to disguise the damage that had been done. Tricks such as sprinkling fresh green grass clippings into the worst areas helped, but Mellor wasn't satisfied. To attract attention away from the outfield, he and his crew mowed a pattern into the infield grass. The patterns were so engaging that all comment was on the artistry – everyone wanted to know how they could replicate them on their own lawns.

How are those patterns created? Mellor tells all in his book, PICTURE PERFECT, released by Sleeping Bear Press. The answer is deceptively simple – the use of a roller following behind the cutting blades on a mower. Mellor points out that in Victorian times, the wealthier often used hand-powered push mowers to create stripes and patterns in their lawns. As gasoline-powered mowers became more popular in 1902, this became an easier craft. It's the roller, not the mower, though, which causes the blades of grass to bend in the direction they are pushed by the mower. Simple stripes are created by rolling the grass one way, then rolling an immediately adjacent strip in the other direction. "Stripes or shapes that look light when viewed from one direction will look dark from the other direction," writes Mellor – who then proceeds to give detailed instructions on creating patterns.

Mellor is proud that for the last ten years of his stay in Milwaukee he successfully avoided the need for any herbicide. "Quality seed makes a difference. You get what you pay for. Buy seed that's cheap, you end up getting weed seeds and things like that. Different times of year, we use different products. If you have a thick, healthy, lush grass there's not really room for a weed to get established."

With the care for Fenway's field passing from the capable Mooney to the artistic and capable Mellor, Boston baseball fans can feel the hallowed grounds are in good hands.

Fenway facts abound:

- The mound is composed of a full five tons of clay

- The sod used at Fenway comes from Kingston Turf in Rhode Island. The Yankees buy sod from the same company.

- Over the winter, a felt covering is placed over the field which acts as a sort of thermal blanket and protects the field

- One of the most effective forms of snow removal at Fenway is to pile snow high against the Green Monster. The heat the Wall absorbs from the sun more quickly melts the snow.

- The tarp weighs approximately 2800 pounds. The size of it is 175 feet by 175 feet. The material is a 10-ounce per square yard vinyl laminated polyester.

- Fenway's warning track is comprised of 130 tons of crushed brick.

- In 2001, even Brian Daubach's younger brother Brad worked on the ground crew. "Just did what everybody else did, really. The grass and the grounds. Some of his patterns. It's a neat place. Sometimes it's hard work but it's definitely rewarding."

2

TICKETS & FACILITIES

John Smith, Fenway Painters
Thomas Queenan, Director of Facilities
    Maintenance
John Caron, Property Maintenance Manager
Glen McGlinchey, Facilities Management Staff
Donnie Gardiner, Carpenter
Butch McDougal, Maintenance Supervisor for
    Aramark

Jane Alden, Bunting Provider
Carol Erven, Ticket Office
Joe Helyar, Director of Ticket Operations
George Rivetz, Ticket Seller
Larry Corea, Ticket Seller
"Jimmy", Ticket Vendor
"Danny, Ticket Vendor

On a sunny day in early April, the Fenway grounds are immaculate. After the long gray winter, the field can seem startlingly green and alive. Since December or January, tickets have been on sale, the lifeblood of the team. There certainly is plenty of revenue from other sources – broadcast rights and Major League Baseball licensing shares among them – but a team that doesn't put bodies in the seats doesn't attract as much for their broadcasting rights (nor do they earn as much in concessions.) The Red Sox are one of the most popular teams in baseball, with a remarkably loyal fan base. Season ticket renewals are typically in excess of 95%. Tickets are available in person, by phone, over the Internet and by mail. Most tickets are sold well before the day of the game.

Before the gates can open, though, a full off-season of repairs and preparation has taken place. Not only has the ground crew toiled to prepare the field itself, they have worked with others to repoint brickwork, recondition and improve the stadium itself and repair damaged seats.

Visit the park a day or two after the last game of the season and you will see Aramark employees with water jets pressure-cleaning the concession stands. Visit again two or three weeks before Opening Day and you'll find them scrubbing down each stand with detergent. This is also when Jane Alden drapes the bunting, usually the day before the long-awaited home opener. John Smith of Fenway Painters gives the Green Monster a fresh coat almost every year and paints throughout the park upon request.

The park was built in 1912, renovated fully in 1934 and undergone a number of very significant changes and upgrades over the years, including dramatic changes in 2002 and 2003. It's costly to keep up an older stadium – estimates are it takes an annual budget of a million dollars or more to maintain the park.

JOHN SMITH
Fenway Painters

We paint everything at Fenway Park. Inside and outside.

My father, Ken Smith, founded the company in 1937. He gave it the name because we used to live in the Fenway.

We began 26 years ago when we got a call from one of the vice presidents, who was looking to get the seats painted. They were changing colors and looking for another painting contractor. They just picked the name out of the Yellow Pages because they saw the name Fenway Painters. What the heck, give 'em a call!

I was involved right from the beginning, the first day there. We started doing the seats and painted all of them, they're sprayed. We spray the box numbers, too, refresh the numbers. We paint the stairs.

We've done the Wall about twenty times now. It is done when needed, usually every other year, or when they want to brighten it up. It takes about 38 gallons to do the Wall itself. Two people do it in a day. We hire an aerial lift and we spray it. Sometimes we do the Wall along with the pads and some other stuff. The scoreboard is done every year.

You wouldn't be able to find any of the colors we use in a store. They're all custom mixes that we put our own names on: Fenway maroon, special green, fence green, scoreboard green. The yellow is a safety yellow, an OSHA color. You could buy safety yellow. The gray on the light towers is another standard color. But the green, it's fence green, not "Monster Green" or "Field Green." We order it as "fence green."

We paint everything – the light towers, the bullpen, the girders. It's constant maintenance. It's an older ballpark. I think they do a very good job in trying to keep up with it.

THOMAS QUEENAN
Director of Facilities Management

I started here in 1982. I was working for the Radisson Hotel chain in food and beverage services. In April of '82, they were going to open up 21 private suites on the right field roof. They needed someone to come in on a seasonal basis and get involved in the food and beverage servicing of those first 21 suites and I was offered the job.

That winter, they built the 23 suites on the left field roof, and the job just grew from there. Those opened in April of '83. We also purchased a barroom known as King's Row, which was in a corner of the ballpark but had a public street entrance to it. We made that into a function facility called the Player's Club. We tied it in to group sales, packaged it in order to be able to offer various groups a place to come in, eat, drink, hold their affair a couple of hours prior to the game and then go up and watch the ballgame.

In the winter of '88-'89, the decision was made to do something with all of that lovely area behind home plate, which is now the 406 Club. That was a huge project, and once that had been completed, I was named Director of Facilities.

The ballpark in Fort Myers does not come under me. We have the ballpark here and the other properties here, which would be the Ipswich Street garage and the Brookline/Maitland Street parking lot across the street. We own that parking garage on Ipswich Street that butts up to the back side of the parking lot. Before that, it was the Hospital Laundry Association, a functioning laundry. That building has quite a bit of history to it. There have been several different businesses in that building, including an aircraft factory, an automotive parts factory. Where the triangular surface lot is now, that used to be the Dawson Brewery building. Dawson Gold Crown Ale. *[After the 2002 season, the old parking garage was converted into the right field/bleachers concourse and to receiving/storage/office areas for Aramark.]*

Where the bowling alley is now, that whole building was an automotive distributorship. Vehicles were serviced on the different floors of the building. There were freight two elevators in that building. There was one opposite the Cask and Flagon on Lansdowne Street, and there was one where the main executive office entrance is now, next to the ticket office.

There is a supplemental first aid room by the visiting clubhouse. It was used as a film processing center. Most people aren't familiar with all the support areas around the building.

I'm a fan. Born and raised in Winthrop. I used to come over here all the time on the Blue Line. I remember paying fifty cents to get in the ballpark, and by the fifth inning I was in the box seats. I came with my family and by myself as well. I used to love coming over here when there were doubleheaders on Sunday. That was a big attraction. Used to bring a lunch and spend the day.

John [Caron] works for me. John's the manager of property maintenance. As the director of facilities, I'm a little bit more involved in planning, in devising maintenance systems, getting involved in construction and renovation. It's the same job as any building manager would have in any privately owned office building.

It's difficult when you're dealing with a park that was built over 85 years ago. The maintenance budget is probably among the highest in baseball. Still, I think you'll find that most colleges and several high schools have better clubhouse facilities than we do here. It's just the nature of the beast. You're in the original footprint, with essentially the same capacity.

John Caron
PHOTO BY ANDREA RAYNOR

JOHN CARON
Property Maintenance Manager

The keys to Fenway Park

PHOTO BY BILL NOWLIN

I've got keys to pretty much everywhere in the park. I know a lot of the history – not everything – but I know all the nooks and crannies.

I'm the property maintenance manager for Fenway Park. I oversee the park itself, year-round and on a day-to-day basis, getting the place open every day. Cleaning companies, electricians, plumbers. Air conditioning. Heating. Everything from the pictures on the walls to the carpet on the floors. The roofs. The offices, locker rooms, all that stuff.

Aramark handles the cleaning of the outside seating, the bleachers, the concourse downstairs and the reserved grandstand and the box seats. My cleaners – contracted through the Red Sox – clean the rooftop box seats, the private suites, the offices, the 600 Club, the press level. The press box is done in-house. The 600 Club is done by a separate company. The suites and the roof are done by another company. The offices are done by yet another company. Why do we have so many different companies? I ask that often. They're different for different reasons. What those are, I don't know – but it works out well. It was that way when I arrived.

'86 was my first season. I started in marketing – group sales, advertising. I sold advertising with Johnny Pesky for a couple of seasons. Marketing was very small. Bob Montgomery, Johnny Pesky, myself. Larry Cancro was there then. He started in '85. Jeff Goldenberg was there, then. He's still here, in advertising now.

It's busy every day. Weekends and nights in the off-season, we get to go home. But we have functions all year. Everything from anniversary parties and weddings to bar mitzvahs to birthday parties. During the off-season for me, though, it's like forty hours a week. During the season, it's like 90, 100.

On a weekday game, I would get in like 10 A.M., I guess, because I would be here until about 11:30 or something. The cleaners, they get in like 5 or 6 in the morning, but my staff – the actual Red Sox staff – would get in like 7:30. They bring the trash down. They fix seats. They start their day with whatever there is. I have an assistant, Glen, and he comes in and opens the doors, gets things started.

Most days are regular and you have your regular stuff. Things breaking down, you coordinate so that the contractor – whether it's elevators, escalators, ice machines, air conditioning, heat, plumbing, electrical, whatever, they'll come in the next morning. We do have our own carpenter. We have an outside plumbing vendor, but they come in as needed. We don't have them here all the time. We don't even have them on for a game. We have a union electrician on during the game.

I stay like an hour after the game, in case someone's stuck in an elevator, or the Red Sox locker room loses their hot water or whatever the problem may be.

GLEN MCGLINCHEY
Facilities Management Staff

I grew up in Somerville. I live up past Teele Square. I was a Red Sox fan from an early age. I started here in May of '86. A friend of mine had worked here, they needed help, and he just brought me on. After the summer ended, my job ended but the ticket office had gotten so busy that they called me back. I worked during the playoff in facilities and then I worked in the ticket office all that winter, and went back on to facilities in March and pretty much stayed ever since.

When the crew comes in, first of all we have to clean everything, do some repairs. We kind of let the suites go after the season. We shut them down and we turn the water off. When contractors come in, I work with them. We bring on

ten people for seasonal work starting around the third week of March.

The ground crew takes care of everything downstairs and we take care of everything from the third level up. We take care of the offices, too. They paint some of the offices, while people are away for spring training.

Glen McGlinchey
PHOTO BY ANDREA RAYNOR

I show up at 7:30. The crew is supposed to be here before 8. I get them going, which is a big task for the day. After a week, you pretty much get into a routine. Then I usually walk around the building, the suites, the club, through the offices and check for anything that broke. Usually, someone will leave a voice mail for John or myself: "During the game, this thing broke and we couldn't fix it. Take a look at it in the morning." Things break a lot, usually a thing every day. Seats happen a lot. Holes in the roof. That happens a lot. The roof over the suite level, it's not in great condition up there. I'm in seven days a week if they're home. We stay until an hour after the game ends. About 11. This year, we're going to start to rotate. There's three of us now. John Caron and Donnie Gardiner and myself.

During games, most of the time, it's quiet. You could watch the games if you want, but unless it's a big game or if Martinez is pitching or something, I don't really watch the game. The first year, '86, I think I watched probably 60 games here. I was watching almost every game. Then it kind of dwindled to maybe 20 and then it dwindled down further. I'd rather do other stuff. I bring stuff from home, a book, stay in the office. It'll be on TV in the background. They'll call us if they have a problem.

I have an 8 year old son now. He comes in to some of the games. He just loves it.

DONNIE GARDINER
Carpenter

Electrician and plumbing are subbed out, as the carpentry was – to me. I was independent, with my own company They brought me in-house, because I can do more than just carpentry. I was working here like eight or nine months out of the year anyways. I was a one-person operation. Ninety percent of what I did could be done by one person.

Donnie Gardiner
PHOTO BY BILL NOWLIN

I worked for the Red Sox as a contractor about ten years. Walsh Brothers was finishing up the 600 Club and they were looking for somebody just to hit some of the punch list items. Word of mouth through their guys got back to me. "Are you interested?" "Yeah, I'll take a run in and see what they got." It just escalated from there.

Now I'm just a member of the facilities staff. Carpentry, cabinetry, remodeling. It could be anything. I just re-did the counters up in the fifth floor bathrooms. Whatever needs to be done.

I have to be here for all the games. We get here at 7 in the morning and if there's a game, we stay through 'til 11 or 12 o'clock, in case things go bad. One of the gates last year got ripped off during a Yankees game, a gate by one of the turnstiles. I had to put that back on again. They were hanging on it and broke the hinges. It's a sight call whether you fix it right then and there or if you have to call in one of the other trades. The biggest thing here is keeping the place safe.

I really don't get to watch much of the game myself. All I do for the most part is just walk around from right field to left field and back. I try to stay in the middle, so I can get anywhere

pretty quick. And I know the little short cuts. I'm basically on call and I keep my eyes open.

Height was against me being a ballplayer. I'm a realist. I was excited, though, when I got the call to come in and do some work at Fenway Park! I was a fan, but it wasn't something that I lived for. Now that I work here, to me it's blasé. I love it when the team does good, because everybody's in a better mood and I'm a team player, but my life is the building. The players have their jobs and I have mine.

There's a saying that goes: we're the team behind the team. We're the ones that no one sees. Personally, I don't want to be seen. I just want to be behind the scenes. If it's not working right, it's going to come down on my boss. It's going to come down on us.

The place is old. It's time for a new one. New place or old place, I have a job. This place has a history and it's a tremendously interesting place. I've been here a long time but there are guys who've been here decades longer than I have. It's neat. It's still a learning experience.

I can do what Butch [McDougal] does, but if it's a building issue, I'll usually be taking care of it. We own the building. Aramark uses the space. If it's an equipment issue, it's usually Butch who takes care of it for Aramark. He's their employee.

BUTCH MCDOUGAL
Maintenance Supervisor for Aramark

Butch McDougal is the maintenance supervisor for Aramark, the concessionaire which handles all of the sales of food and beverage and souvenir items throughout the park. When it comes to repairs and maintenance, the Red Sox and Aramark have a remarkably collaborative relationship. Butch McDougal married into a family which represents one of Fenway's local legacies.

I got the job through my wife Patricia, since my father-in-law [Vince Orlando] worked over there. We started working around the same time, but she's been over there since she was born.

I've been working here since 1978. I maintain all the equipment, everything that we have whether it be plumbing, electrical, ice machines, refrigeration. With Coca Cola, as part of their contract, they take care of the Coke equipment. We call in somebody for any of the refrigeration now, if it's major stuff. They just decided to have somebody come in because it ties me up too long when we have problems, especially if it's during a game, but I know how to do it. I've done it for years.

I just went in as temporary help working in the office where my wife does – in the vending station. The people that they had really didn't do much of anything maintaining stuff so I used to just fix things. I got to be very friendly with Rico [Picardi] who used to be very good friends with my father-in-law and my wife. I stayed on through the winter months and we did a lot of projects. I laid out all the stands and the countertops. I did all the designing of the countertops, where the drop-ins go, the frank units, even to the vending poles that they use now, to carry the cotton candy and the popcorn. The covers that we use to protect the registers. All those things there I designed. I never patented anything. It just made my job easier if people didn't ruin registers.

We'll put the walls and stuff up. I'll get the units made that have to be made. If it's gas or major electrical or gas plumbing, I have guys that I call.

We work 8:30 to 5:00 on a regular day when there's no games. On a game day, a night game, we'll get there about 9:30, 10 o'clock and I'll usually stay a couple of hours after the game. If the stands all come out right, and everything balances, and there's no problem like stuck shutters or somebody left something on, then we're out of there. If there's any problems, I'll stay and fix them, especially if it's refrigeration. If it's reading 60 degrees, we can't leave it 'til morning.

You know when they pull down those shutters on the stands at the end of the game, sometimes they're in such a rush to get out of there

that they'll jam 'em. Those shutters have been there longer than me.

Anything that's within the stands – from the doorway in to the stands – is mine. Anything on the main gates coming in, that's Red Sox, but I've fixed those, too. They'll call me if they need some help or if they don't have anybody right then. They borrow my stuff; I borrow their stuff. Joe Mooney's more than willing to give me a hand with anything. The same way, if he's having trouble with his lawnmower, I'll go out and fix it for him. There's nothing like "that's not my job." They just brought in union electricians recently, and I thought I'd have trouble with them, but they're great. We don't step on their toes and I give them whatever work that's major, and they have no problem giving me help.

I was not even into sports as a kid. I never had been to Fenway Park before I met my wife. That's probably why I get so much stuff done, because I don't go out and watch the games that often.

We got modernized this year! We got a forklift truck! I never had a fork truck. Once in a while if I had really, really heavy equipment, I'd go across to the Twins and the guy over there would help me. I used to get ten bucks out of petty cash or we'd give him some shirts. Something like that. Twins [Enterprises] have been very nice to us. Years ago, we unloaded every 40 foot trailer from the street. We didn't even have those couple of little Cushmans we drive around.

Butch McDougal
PHOTO BY BILL NOWLIN

We've got names for all the rooms. We've got Coffee Room, which is the chowder room, which is now the kitchen. That's where we used to prepare all the coffee for the stands. That's the one that's just down by the ramp heading towards Joe Mooney's room. We used to have 5 or 6 big 50-gallon stainless steel drums that we used to brew the coffee in. With a big net. We've got the Linen Room, which is now basically storage for souvenirs and stuff. That's where they used to keep the linens when it was Harry M. Stevens. Our barrel room, which is for the empty barrels. That's the big room out by Gate B, the big metal thing out there. Under the ramp across from where the nachos stand is now, that's our little truck room where we keep all of those little yellow hand trucks. When it was Stevens, we had 22 big ones and 24 small ones. Every year we'd paint them and take the wheels off and de-grease them and then re-grease them. That was a job every year. You can't stand up in there! You have to keep your head down while you push the trucks all the way to the back. It's got a little slanted door. We keep all the pallets in there now.

One big advantage of a new park – if they ever get it – would be that you'd be able to do the concessions the right way, Right now, when we try to put anything new in, it's really a pain. Like exhausts. Out in the bleachers, we tried to do those portable fryers for the French fries, but there's really no place to vent. You can't vent it outside because there's nothing to attach to and you have to go up beyond the 600 Club. All those vents are grandfathered in, basically. They suck the smoke out from the stands and they blow it back into the stadium! With a new park, you'll be able to get more ventilation.

It's a challenge every day there, what you can put into one little tiny spot. You know those two Papa Gino stands there for the pizza? Those used to be souvenir stands. They gave me like a week after the team went out of town to rip out the souvenirs, put up the wall, put in the plumbing and get a couple of their ovens in there.

For Kowloon, they have a plug, a big 3-phase 200 amp plug. They have to unplug it, because we move the cart out of the way at the end of the night. We push it over by the beer thing. The other one [the sausage stand across from the Kowloon stand] the wiring actually comes all the way out from the left field vault, all the way out to the panel that's right by the sausage cart across the way. From there, it's the big heavy duty cords that go into their own little power panels in each unit. They're all self-contained; they have their own hand sink where they've got hot water. They've got refrigeration. They've got their grill, the lights, ice tub. They've got everything in there.

During the games, I walk around. I have my radio. I check the stands and make sure that people are in their places. I've done all the concessions, too. Posting sheets at the end of the night…all that stuff. You don't get away with just doing one thing in that place.

There are things we thought we'd never sell. They said that Richie's Slush wouldn't go. Rich Roper's the one who said he wanted to try lemonade. He's the Vice President. We went for years not trying too many new things. Rico's statement to Jackie Lyons was, "The lines would be too long." It's true. It's amazing. We put those lemonades in and they can't keep up. We started off with a couple of makeshift carts and then we ordered two. Now we've got four. The kids' arms go broke squeezing lemons but the line doesn't stop. Same thing with the ice cream. We had very little soft serve in there before, maybe 2 or 4 machines. The lines were so long. Now we've got 14 machines, and the lines are still long!

I've got my son, who's 35 [Wally McDougal, former batboy] and my daughter, who's 11. Ever since my daughter's been born, she's been there. Some times she hates it over there because she'd rather be home. But that's like anything else. So wouldn't I!

JANE ALDEN
Bunting Provider

Fenway Park, the facility, is decked out in its finest the day before the first ticket-bearing patrons of the season arrive. Jane Alden provides the bunting for the park. Not the bunting that's done during a game, but the flag bunting that hangs from the stadium during special occasions such as Opening Day.

I hang the red, white and blue bunting – which is always cloth bunting. I only use bunting that has stars. That's sort of traditional for the park. I've seen by looking at the TV at other ballgames at other parks they seem to use just red, white and blue, which is not good enough for Fenway. Fenway deserves the best.

The first thing we do is hang a piece of bunting on the Commissioner's box down on the field. Then we continue on around the lower level, and then we go upstairs and we put bunting around the luxury boxes.

It seems like it's always going to rain, or snow, and it's some days that it's so cold that you think your fingers are going to freeze right off. This is my 25th year of doing it, this year. In 25 years, I laughed to the fellow who helps me, "Do you recall how many times we've done this park when the sun has actually been out?" My father, Edgar Freeman Alden, he decorated the park for I don't know how many years.

The bunting gets weathered, so you have to replace pieces from time to time. I can almost predict where the pieces are going to get stolen. It doesn't matter whether it's upstairs in the boxes or downstairs on the field. You lose several every year.

The bunting itself has changed over the years. It used to be beautiful, heavy, what they called bulldog bunting. It hung very nicely because the weight itself would help it hang well. About the last five years or so, they came out with some nylon bunting and that was just about all you could get, so I had to go with that. Now they've gone back to a heavier cloth bunting, but it will never be the same as the other. You're at the mercy of the supplier. There are not a lot of companies in the country that produce this stuff.

Evenings I'd be taking stuff down after they'd finished playing. There'd be no one in this ballpark and I'd be the only female there. I'm 5 foot 1, small, blond, blue eyes, you know, and I move rather quickly. I'd be racing around there getting this stuff down and I'd be the only person in this park.

David Batchelder helps me now. He comes down from Narragansett, Rhode Island. For about 22 of those years, he's been doing it along with me.

When we first started I really have no idea what Dad did, so I just used to try to find some way to use the metal brackets that are attached to the padding on the wall, that go over the concrete. They're spaced very poorly but I used to try to tie them on. I wanted them all to be even. I would either wire or tie them on. I guess you learn after a few years. Now we staple them on from the rear. There's a white header that goes along the top of the bunting and you always try to hide it by stapling on to that.

Jane Alden
PHOTO BY BILL NOWLIN

Over the years, technology has advanced and you hopefully advance with it. You can use those cable ties. If you see someone who has been arrested and they have their hands behind their back, they put those white plastic ties. They are called cable ties. You can snug them up real tight. And then I always tape them.

It's a little hard to explain but it used to come in one long flat sheet and then you had to tie them up – you'd fan them up, that is, you'd make the pleats yourself, with your hands. Then you'd have to tie the two halves together – you'd do that to two of them – and they made one full fan. Well, about seven years ago, they finally got smart and came out with a piece that had this white header with grommet holes right along the top of the piece and it was already one full fan for you. It was all pleated, which certainly made things easier.

I certainly am not doing anything great for the Red Sox. But they make me comfortable here, and I think that says a lot for an organization that – let's face it, the bottom line is profit – but that they can do that and still make outside people servicing them feel accepted, I think that's pretty good.

I don't stay for games, though. I try to get in and get out. The noise drives me mad. Now they have loudspeakers right in your face. I come home and I watch it on TV. I have a mute button and I can push that.

TICKETS, TICKETING, SCALPING

Many teams must resort to endless promotions to sell entries to their games; they can hardly seem to give away tickets. Since the 1967 Impossible Dream season, tickets to Fenway Park have become hot items.

In the first chapter, we met Casey Erven, who headed the grounds crew. His mother Carol is a phys ed teacher in the Woburn public schools, but has worked a full 25 years in the ticket office.

Carol Erven
PHOTO BY BILL NOWLIN

CAROL ERVEN
Ticket Office

I love the ballpark! I really enjoy the ballpark. In 1978, I got season tickets. I still have them, section 14, box 110. That was the year of the Bucky Dent playoff game. I split them with another person initially. I don't need them now, but I keep them just in case – when I'm not working there, and there's a new park – I will have a location. You just don't want to give them up.

I started the year before Casey. I started in 1980 and he started in 1981.

Since he was five or six, we used to go to games. In our home, we always had the radio on with the game on. It was just a constant. My mother and father would watch the games.

The year I started, I worked in the ticket office. I answered the phone, took reservations and processed them. We did it by hand then. It was the old system. Right around the change when Joe [Helyar] came in and Arthur [Moscato] left, they went to the computer. We used to pre-print every ticket. They had the

vault where you had to store all the tickets. They would put them out daily. Whichever game ran out, they'd just keep replenishing it. It was what we would call a "hard ticket."

After one year I started to work at my reservation window – Window One – which is a hotbed, believe me! Actually, I had a whole three page series in the *Globe* – when I was accused of being a conduit for the scalpers. My name in the paper and everything. Someone passed tickets down through the office and they came down to me, through my window, and we just passed them out.

If someone was a scalper and wants to drop off two tickets for someone – they try to control it somewhat. We make them go through the office. But even on a regular night, if someone comes and says, "I want to drop off two tickets," we're so busy you just take the name, put them in an envelope and hand them out to the person who comes. It's really hard to eliminate and that's why it's such a ridiculous thing – that I was called a conduit for a scalper. It was not good. And then the heat was on Arthur, and he got let go the year after the World Series. For a while, they didn't allow any dropoffs.

John Basmasian is my partner. He and I run the window. When we've VERY busy, they bring down everyone else to help. It was awful the last night of the season. When the reservations go through the ticket office over the phone and when they're more than the two of us can handle, that's when we get help – like four or five or six people, whatever is necessary. When Pedro pitches, they use that 24-hour touch-tone thing and it's just almost nonstop.

We do have a late window and we're there for about seven innings and when they close the service window down at Gate D, we hand out the baseball players' tickets and the military tickets. They show their military ID and get in for five dollars. Subject to availability, of course. Ours is the last window to close. A regular game, we close about the seventh inning.

Sometimes, during the week when I have school, I go right home, but every game in the summer, I go up and watch. If I've given my own tickets away to someone else, I'll find an empty seat, or sometimes the ushers know where there's a seat available. I listen to most of the away games. I love baseball. I don't follow any other sport. Not like this, no.

Once in a while, we'll have a problem. People can get frustrated if their tickets are not there. My feeling is always: Don't worry, there's no problem if it can be taken care of. If someone has the wrong day in their envelope, or the tickets are not there, we send them to Customer Service. They follow up on it. As far as obnoxious fans, no. 99% of the people are very happy to get their tickets.

I'm more than willing – if we have tickets available – to upgrade. Because of the nature of the window, we get a lot of cancellations, and people love cancellations. Let's say someone in the organization, whether it be a Dan Duquette or a John Buckley or anybody makes a reservation and the people are going to come in and pay. If they don't show by the second inning, we sell them. Anything that's left over, we sell. Extra standing room, bleacher seats, anything. We can do as much as four or five thousand dollars at the window, just in a short period of time, getting rid of everything.

The Red Sox have always been good to me. I've been a good worker, though, believe me. I've always been there. I've given up many a weekend because I've had to work. I've put the Red Sox first. Always.

We handle everybody important's tickets. All of Buckley's, Duquette's and Harrington's, and you definitely don't want to make a mistake. Sometimes two people will come in with the same name. Any mistakes reflect on Window One. If you've ever seen it during the playoffs, it's just like a den of lions waiting for a piece of meat when a ticket comes up. They'll hover around Window One even in the second inning, waiting for something to come down.

You must be proud of the job Casey's done here.

I certainly am! He's worked hard, and no one gave him anything, believe me. He had to work very hard. It's funny. I remember, the first or second time he came home from work, Casey said, "Ma. He called us all cocksuckers!" Joe

was strict with him, which was good. His father and I didn't live together. I was married a long time ago, but when we separated, it was kind of good for Joe to give him some direction. He certainly gave him discipline.

You couldn't be late for work there, you know. Not even five minutes. And my son...I'll never forget the time I didn't bother to wake him up. He was literally five minutes late, and Joe sent him home. This was when he was just a teenager, about 16 or 17. Sent him right home. Couldn't believe it.

I think all the little people are the ants of the organization. The people that work for Aramark, the people that do the field, all your ticket takers and ushers – and the ticket office people – work very hard. They really do.

Upstairs, they do, too, but in a different way. The marketing people always start a rung or two up on the ladder. There's a little bit of social distance in the organization. Definitely.

In general, the ticket office and other parts of the park, I can see the effort to be a lot more customer friendly. It really has changed, a great deal. And the security, they're not just a bunch of brutes. I think maybe they learned, too, that you just can't handle people the way they used to.

It's been an interesting experience. It's been fun.

JOE HELYAR
Director of Ticket Operations

I grew up in Plainfield, New Jersey. But I went to Boston University. I've always been an Oriole fan. When I came to BU, I used to always come over here and ask if there was a part-time job. Never a job. But that's back when they only had about twenty employees. They didn't hire a lot of people. You didn't have phone rooms. Tickets were sold on the day of the game. There wasn't a lot of work outside of [former concessionare] Harry M. Stevens.

The one year I didn't come, which was my senior year, a friend came and got a job, which really got me upset. He got married at the end of the year. When he left, Dan [Marcotte] called and asked if I wanted to come to work here in the ticket office. Like a gofer. So I started in '68. I worked two years as part-time full-time, so to speak – you worked from January til the end of the season and then you'd take two months off. You're an hourly employee. My last year, '70, I was a full-time employee. I got into the game just by being known – which is how most people really get into this game. I've said to so many people, "Just get your foot in the door. Just get hired somewhere." Then you have much better leverage because people know who you are. Back then you didn't have all the sports adminstration programs like you have now, so you had to be sort of lucky. Or know somebody. Almost everybody who works here knows somebody. There's very few people who have been hired without some sort of an "in" here. They may say there wasn't any, but you'll find a connection somewhere when you go back.

That's how I got into it. A little bit of luck, being in the right place in the right time and being known. Once I went full-time, I was Arthur Moscato's assistant. I think Arthur started in '48. He left in '88, forty years doing basically the same job. I don't have any aspirations to go any higher. Plus, I'm getting ready to retire.

1970 was my first full-time year here, but it was my last as well. Then I went to the minors. I always liked minor league baseball. So I worked in Pawtucket for two years. There were three full-time people. Bristol for two years. I owned a ballclub in West Haven for two years. The West Haven Yankees. It was a Yankee farm club. I took a year off – I went to Australia with a girl. Sold the club and went to Australia. That's back in my younger days.

I was an assistant at the Braves for like ten years. When Arthur retired, they called me. I liked living in Boston. But it was still sort of comfortable in Atlanta. It was a tossup whether I'd come or not.

I think there's about 5900 season ticket accounts. You've got to multiply that by the number of seats they have. Some accounts have ten seats. Some have two. That gives you your full season equivalent. We have about 8300 full season seats that are sold. Some clubs – California only used to sell full season plans and they had like 14 or 15,000. In our case, we'd sell partial plans and we might have 17,000 seats sold as full season equivalent.

Once we get the prices, we get everything ready, do the renew, get your season tickets out, your renewals. Then you have a big rush when you first put tickets up for sale, usually the second week in January. It goes about a week, very heavily. Before, it was line up, and that was it. Now we have various forms of ordering, with faxes and everything else, you can call on the phone…all those orders have to be handled somehow. With the internet, they're doing their own work, so it's not as bad as the IVR. That takes some of the load off. IVR is Integrated Voice Response, where you're actually calling in and being recorded, but there's still work to be done, to transcribe the names.

Then, it's sort of steady until about the middle of March when you're into your spring training schedule. Then your casual fans start thinking baseball. You're still in the middle of hockey, still in the middle of basketball, but they start thinking baseball. Now you've got a rush right through to the first couple of days that you play. Then it settles down into rote. It's the same stuff over and over and over again until the end of the year.

There are people with bleacher season tickets. It was probably in the early 80s they started to put the backs on the seats out there and started selling season tickets. Before it was those wooden benches.

They used to open the park after the seventh inning and you could just walk in. I'd come over from college and just walk in for the last couple of innings. "Put a dollar in the Jimmy Fund box" and they'd just let you in. Those days are long gone. It was a sport then. Now it's a business.

When I was first here, you'd call Globe Tickets and say, "This is what I want. These are my areas for season tickets. Print all of this." They'd come in boxes. You'd count them, you'd put them in the drawers. Hand-pull the season tickets. I used to be pretty good at that. Then of course it got a little better where you could tell somebody, "Here. We want this seat collated this way. We want this one collated this way…" We're only talking maybe 1500 accounts back then. It wasn't like it is now.

You'd sit down and look at the schedule and you'd say, "OK, these games will sell and these games…" and you'd order from Globe, with enough time to bring in what seats you need piecemeal, so you're not doing the whole park. We also sold general admission, so you didn't have to print the whole park. You knew on a Wednesday afternoon against some club that finished last in the league, you're probably going to sell general admission, so you didn't need to print all those other seats you weren't going to sell. If you got into a bind, you always had a couple of emergency sets, no date on them, which had the locations printed for those areas – a complete set. Game A was good for that day's game. Then you'd say to Globe, "Print me another set."

Today, if our computers go down, we're screwed. If we can't get on, we don't know what's really sold because you can buy from many different areas now. We've been very lucky. Never had a crash. It's caused us undue grief. It's been stressful, where it's been four hours, but you know you're going to get back up. Meanwhile, you've got a lobbyful of people. Now, we don't run our own system; it's through Next Ticketing. We rely on them.

Ignatius Giglio is the oldest season ticket holder. 1935, if I'm not mistaken. You see patterns. There are a lot of dates after the '67 season. A lot of dates starting in '88 and '89.

How many season ticket holders don't renew? When you get to a good area, and you're in the infield, you don't give your seats up. You either have to have died or go through a divorce or economic ruin. You're going to keep those seats because you know if you give those seats up, you're never going to get them back. A lot of people buy small plans when we're good, to be able to be in the hunt for a playoff date, but when we start to lose, and lose continually for two or three years, they drop out.

You get some corporations coming in here and they expect to sit in the baselines. It's such a small park.

I think Larry's talked about seat licenses but I don't believe we're going to do it. Larry [Cancro] can give you a much better idea. We've never actively sold season tickets here. We don't have a sales force that tries to sell them. We're such a small park and we have such a limited inventory. We have enough people beating on doors that we don't need a big sales force for season tickets.

We're selling so much here we don't really analyze that carefully how many we sell via phone sales, the Internet, and so forth. It only really goes up and down 100,000 maybe between a good year and a bad year. You look at your season ticket number, and basically you might say 65% sold by the IVR, phones, mail and 35% at the window. It may be 60/40. Say the season tickets account for half of your sales. Now you're looking at just the other half. If you take your Internet figure and add it to your TTT, you're talking about 430,000 so it's about the same as the window but then you throw your groups in – some of them are mail, some of them are phone. The group sales, a lot of it's repeat business. Probably the window is maybe 40% and the other categories when you're not actually walking up here is the other 60%.

Day of game walkup is not what it used to be. Most of the stuff is sold. You have maybe a thousand tickets to sell, your obstructed views, all your standing room. Plus, you have all your dumped stuff, which can be another thousand tickets all told with just odds and ends, singles, leftover stuff. Even on a sold-out game, say the Yankees, you might still sell 1500 tickets on the day of the game.

Do a lot of people claim to have lost their tickets?

On Yankee games, it happens a lot. It's amazing how many people lose their tickets for Yankee games. The guys use them to get in and just go stand in the back.

I don't go in to watch the games. I work in the office here until sometime in the seventh inning. You oversee sales. You have to balance the game out, do the game statement Richie [Beaton] does the game statement but I'm here doing the money end of things. The stile count is done by one of us in the office. Someone will go out and take the stile count, match it up against what the sales are to get you the no-show figure. Once that's done, most of us want to be out of here before the crowd breaks, because we're back here the next morning.

Kids when they come say, "Wow! You can go to the games!" After twenty years, you don't care about going to the games. You want to go home. It's a job. It's not that I don't have any love for the game. I love the game. But I want to watch a game from start to finish. I'll maybe watch an inning, but I'm not going to stick around just to see whether we won or lost. I used to watch away games on television, until they made all the away games on cable. I'd rather go down to Pawtucket. I'd rather go to New Britain. I'd rather go watch live athletes play as opposed to sitting down at home and watching television.

Group sales do not reserve seats. They sell right out of open stock, but what they do is they have a good clientele base that they will call and say, "What games you want to go to? We'll block you in." Then before we go on sale, they'll block those tickets out. They're repeat customers. If you call late, no, you can't buy forty seats all in one bloc. You have to buy early here. We have a real problem with some Dominicans; they probably think we're screwing them and we're not. They come up to the window and they've got their hundred dollar bill and they point to the dugout and go, "There. There. There." And our guys are going, "There. There. There." And they think that we're putting them in right field

Old ticket windows – and old prices!
PHOTO BY BILL NOWLIN

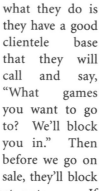

because we don't like them. Sorry. That's all we have. You have to buy early.

The stories people tell us – why they HAVE to have tickets for this or that game – go in one ear and out the other. Well, there are some. Everybody "has" to be at the so-called event.

The Red Sox do have their club seats. We have stuff that we will hold for the players, too. If Ted Kennedy wanted to come for a Yankees game, they'd get him in somehow. There might be some shifting around of club seats here and there. Somebody who's on the lower end [of the Red Sox club seats] would probably wind up in the grandstand seats. We don't per se handle the club seats. We're given a list and told, "These are the people who are going in them." But then Richie and I have our own seats, too, that we hold and take care of people. Sometimes Larry will call down and he needs some really good seats for somebody. We'll take care of those people. Every club does that. It's not a lot of seats. They're seats that the players get, behind home plate in the grandstand. Not in a lower box seat. There's only so many of those that are left to work with. I have a couple. Richie has a couple. We take care of the other clubs, take care of leftover stock that we need to take care of. There's not a lot of those.

The players [for the visiting team] have to get their list in about an hour and a half...just before we open the gates. On a Sunday, sometimes it's after we open. But you have an idea. You can ask the traveling secretary. You can look at the previous list and know last time they were here, they didn't buy much. They got in last night. They haven't had time to go out and give away their tickets, to Krissy and Bambi who don't seem to know who their last name is. The home team uses roughly about the same. Yankee game, it's about the same. If you get Kansas City in here, Kansas City hardly uses anything. The players have some friends. They know some people, but they may give away 160, 180 tickets. We might give away 200, 220, that type of thing.

It used to be that they would send out passes to most of the Catholic priests and area baseball coaches, but we've cut way back on the passes. There are some going to former employees. I get an American League pass as the Director. If I were a Vice President, I'd probably get a Major League pass. I don't think I've ever used my pass. I always buy my tickets if I go anywhere. I just feel that they're in business, just like we are. That's me, personally. Other people don't look at it that way.

We never had much of a problem with true forgeries. We saw some this year in the ALCS, because of color copiers, but we caught them.

Richie Beaton basically runs the place. When I leave, he probably will be the ticket manager. He was considered when I first came, but he was like 22 or 23 years old at the time. Richie is a very dedicated employee.

Amy McCarthy does all the phones, and she basically is the babysitter. There are a lot of high school kids that work here that we don't pay real…we're almost now to where minimum wage is more than what we pay. It hasn't changed in twelve years. We put in for an increase, but I don't know if we'll get it. The quality of help that you get has gone downhill drastically. You're not getting people who can spell or type or know how to handle situations. They don't stay that long, so it's a continual training process. She becomes like a little mother to all these people. She does all the customer service stuff.

Joe Helyar left the Sox employ after the end of the 2002 season. Richie Beaton did become Director of Ticket Operations.

GEORGE RIVETZ
Ticket Seller

These days most of the tickets for the year are sold before the first game is played. In earlier times, day-of-game sales used to provide the bulk of those sold and many of them were sold at windows at the various gates around the park.

I'm a ticket seller. What else? 1966.

We started with about thirty ticket sellers. We're down to about four. There used to be six of us at the bleachers, two to a booth. Now most of it is done in the main ticket office.

George Rivetz
PHOTO BY ANDREA RAYNOR

I've lived here all my life. A Yankee fan. I still am. Nothing to be ashamed of. When I was a little boy, seven years old, I got Babe Ruth's autograph. Lou Gehrig's autograph. They were nice. They treated us all right. So I became a Yankee fan. They were going into the park. Same place they go in now. They signed a piece of paper. I still have it.

They used to have a knothole gang. Five cents a whole summer. Braves and the Red Sox. We had a pass, a nickel for the whole summer. We'd sit out in right field, but I didn't care.

They don't have Ladies Day anymore.

I report to work at 5:15 and the gates open at 5:30. We stay there until roughly quarter of eight. Then they close down those windows and keep Window One open.

I started at the bleachers, for one year. Then I worked the service gate for twenty-odd years and then over here to Gate A.

I always work window 8 now. We're there when they raise the grates until about 45 minutes into the game. Second inning, something like that.

They give us whatever tickets are available. Mostly grandstand, and right field. Behind the plate.

It all depends on who the team is. A lot of people don't want to see Kansas City or Detroit. Montreal. The better teams, we get nothing. On an average night, we each get 50 to 75 tickets. We used to get in the hundreds. Right now, we've been getting 25, 50 tickets. That's it. If we run out quick, either they'll give us more or they'll give us standing room.

We don't take any credit cards. Just cash. Sure, they get irritated sometimes. I can't believe people walk around without any money in their pocket.

Sometimes people will give me an extra ticket. I'll give it away to somebody. We're not allowed to re-sell the tickets.

Scalpers, sure. I tell the police about them. Everybody knows who they are. I hope they're cracking down more. They're still working there. If it's not here, they'll go to the Garden, they'll go to Foxboro. It's a living.

I like the benefits. I like meeting the people. I like to be able to get in free. I can even take my family in if I want to. Free. If they want to scrounge around for a seat, OK. They go in for nothing. That's the benefit. They give us opportunities to buy playoff tickets, World Series tickets, All-Star tickets, everything.

On the weekends, I go in to watch the game. On the week nights, no. I've got another part-time job and I have to be up early in the morning.

It gets quiet. We can go as much as an hour without selling a ticket. Most people have tickets now. Very little gate crowd this year. Very little. It's all in advance. Internet. Everything is on the Internet.

We're not full-time people. If it's sold out, we don't come in. When Atlanta was in, we didn't work that Friday or Saturday. Yankees. We don't work the Yankees games.

We get paid by the game. We don't get as much as the ushers. It don't make any difference if we work one, two, three hours, you get the same pay. I don't know if the Red Sox want me to tell you. It's over forty. Closer to fifty. When I started, it was seven dollars.

Sure, I was working the window when the playoff tickets went on sale back in '86, '88 and then. When you get a lot of people, that's good. I like a lot of crowd. More people, more excitement. I don't like to just sit around and do nothing. Then people are choosy and ask you all kinds of questions.

No one ever caused any trouble. They've got too many police on. The only time I was almost robbed was when they had a concert at Fenway Park years ago. They caused a lot of problems – shaking the bars and trying to grab the tickets and the money and everything. But not with the Red Sox. We have a phone in there. We're locked in – they can't get in – but we can get out. It gets hot in there all the time. Maybe when they build a new stadium, they'll have some ventilation.

What about the ticket takers? Do you know one or two of them?

No, I don't know them. We don't bother with them. Different department. They're in the union. We don't have anything to do with them. Ushers, takers. That's a different department.

No one sells down at Gate B anymore. That was years ago. They used to have exchange windows. They used to have windows where you go from the bleachers to the grandstand. No more, though.

There's only four of us. One guy's been there almost 55 or 60 years. He's Johnny Pesky's brother-in-law, as a matter of fact. Larry Corea. He started as a bat boy. He was a ticket seller in the 40s. His wife and Pesky's wife are sisters. They're all gone. All retired, died, left, whatever reason. There's only four.

After new ownership assumed the reins, there was a concerted effort, spearheaded by architect Janet Marie Smith, to make the park more open and accessible from all sides, which resulted in the opening of the ticket windows at Gates B and C once more, and the old ticket booths at Gate A were closed as points of sale.

LARRY COREA
Ticket Seller

Johnny Pesky on Larry Corea: "He was my clubhouse boy. He was there as a kid before I ever got there. We had four of them, two were on the visitor's side and two were on the Red Sox side. What they did, they all worked together. Larry and Frankie Kelly were on our side. He used to call me a Johnny Come Lately. He's a hell of a kid."

I'm just a part-time ticket seller, just like George Rivetz. I work in one of the booths at Gate A. I'm in Window 6.

As a kid, I was hanging around there in the clubhouse. This goes back to about 1940.

When I first started, it was all day games and they started at 3 o'clock. They didn't go much over two hours. They didn't have that many people there for a traffic jam but it always broke around rush hour. I'd get in there maybe at about 10 o'clock, way before the players got there. We'd take stuff out of the laundry and put it in their lockers. Sweatshirts and stuff like that. Hang up their shirt for them.

I worked in the clubhouse up until 1952. My uncle was the equipment manager. We used to hang around there and watch the games from the little edge of the dugout. His name was Johnny Orlando. His brother Vince Orlando took over after he left. Johnny Orlando's sister – and Vince Orlando's, naturally – was my mother. I have a brother Frankie. Frank Corea. He worked there, too, in the publicity department, years ago. He worked for Ed Doherty. [Astute readers will thus notice that Butch McDougal is therefore also related by marriage to Johnny Pesky.]

I wasn't paid. We were just helping out then. My pay as the visiting batboy was two practice balls a game. They were worth about a half a buck apiece. I started work in 1942.

After being the Red Sox batboy in '43, I went in the service, in the Navy out in the Pacific. I got back in '46 and worked there until '52.

Years ago, they used to travel with equipment trunks, six trays to a trunk. The days they were leaving town, after the game was over, we'd have their road uniform in there and then we'd put in the stuff they wanted to take on the road. We had an extra trunk with the extra uniforms. We had a bat bag and a bat trunk. You didn't have all the things they have today, like helmets.

They didn't get a clean uniform every day. If one wasn't that dirty, you'd just let it go another game or two. It was that hot flannel. They'd kind of refresh themselves with spurts of ammonia when it got really hot. Now they have their own laundry.

I got paid a salary, yeah. It wasn't much. Two or three dollars a game. Tips was a big thing. We had something we used to call the scandal sheet. I had the concession there. If a guy took a Coke, I'd mark "10 cents P" (for pop) and then at the end of the homestand, you'd total up all the Cokes and cigarettes and chewing tobacco – they had a lot of chewing tobacco – you add the total and if they owed you four or five dollars, the good tippers would give you maybe seven or eight or ten dollars. Ted Williams tipped at the end of the year.

We took care of the umpires, too. Actually, they were in the same clubhouse area, kind of upstairs. Years ago, the two clubhouses were together. The umpires had their own little room – they still do – and their own shower. You had the two clubhouse guys for each clubhouse and then you had the bat boy who also helped around the clubhouse. Sometimes they'd run out of baseballs and we'd have to rub them up. The umpires started with, I think it was four or five dozen. If they needed more, we'd have a few on hand. They weren't rubbed up, and we'd rub them up with the special mud they had from Maryland or somewhere like that.

After the game, we picked up the towels and hung up the uniforms. Throw them in the lockers. After the game wasn't too bad. We'd be out an hour after the game. We cleaned the clubhouse, swept the floor and washed it. Grab this big broom and wet a towel and just go up and down. It was a hardwood floor way back then.

Some day games we'd hang around after and work out with Mr. Yawkey. You'd pitch to him and he'd hit them. We'd all get our turn to hit. He was great. He liked to play pepper. We had fun doing that. He was a great guy. He used to change in the manager's room. He had his own uniform. He enjoyed getting out there. If he wasn't hitting, he'd feed the pitcher the balls to throw in to the batter. It wasn't what it is now, but we had a batting cage. We didn't have any protection as far as the pitcher goes, though. You had to be alert.

Larry Corea
PHOTO BY ANDREA RAYNOR

I quit the clubhouse in '52. Joe Cronin got me the job. After I quit the clubhouse, I was standing up watching the game and he come out of the office and says, "Well, why don't you go down and sell tickets?" From then on, I was a part-time ticket seller.

I'm retired from the government, Veteran's Administration. I spent thirty years with the V.A. In the meantime, I was working part-time, day of the game, at Fenway. Then most of them became night games, so I could work that much more. Selling tickets.

I still enjoy going over there. We watch batting practice. We only work a few hours. Eight o'clock maybe, we close up. After we close up, I go in now and then to watch the game, but most of the time, I'll listen to it on the radio going home and then watch it on TV. Then I beat the crowd. I watch most of the away games.

The tickets used to be printed. They used to play 77 home games. They'd have 77 drawers, one for each game, that would hold, say, thirty thousand tickets. They had one window for advance tickets. As I recall, they would just sell advance tickets for the homestand [not months in advance.] To buy other tickets, you'd go to the advance ticket window. There were usually ample tickets for every game.

Years ago, they had general admission, unreserved grandstand. Your upper boxes used to be grandstand. They'd chain off about five rows and they would be reserved grandstand, and back of that would just be general admission.

We start with a bank. We start with a hundred dollars of one dollar bills and a hundred dollars of five dollar bills. They give us tickets to sell. It varies by the demand. If we sell out, we call the office and they just send more down, if they're available. Even the standing room tickets now come out of the computer.

Do you ever have much trouble with customers? They give you a hard time about anything?

There's always something turns up. If it's threatening rain or something they always ask you, "Is it going to stop?" My answer to them is, "Eventually it will." You know, wise guy.

Re-selling a ticket is illegal in Massachusetts. A large notice advising patrons of this law is posted in the window of the ticket office, facing the street. The law makes no distinction as to the price a ticket might be re-sold at – even the casual fan stuck with a spare $60.00 ticket offering it to someone for $20.00 is deemed breaking the law. It's not hard to find people selling tickers, though, right on the sidewalk in front. The police are dealing with thousands upon thousands of people all arriving at the same place more or less at the same time and they may have greater priorities, particularly given a recent court case which seemed to permit individuals selling their own personal tickets. For the 2003 season, the Red Sox even launched a system by which season ticket holders could post and sell tickets they themselves were unable to use.

The current system is what it is and it's been this way for decades. It permits – really, it encourages – the growth of a group of enterprising men who will risk arrest to buy and sell tickets for a profit – the "scalpers." Regular fans notice the same people working the same locations every game. Joe Helyar is a smart, perceptive man; he knows who these "ticket vendors" are, by name, even as he instructs his staff in ways to discourage them. It's not a secret that tickets can be had and, in fact, a good case can be made that these scalpers provide a service. They'll try to buy cheap and sell high, like any business. Inevitably, some will gouge. Some will misrepresent the game as being sold out, when it is not. Many will sell tickets at face value, though. Having bought them for less – maybe just minutes earlier – they can still profit adequately.

It's a risky business. The Boston Police are charged with enforcing the law and do have plainclothes officers who will make arrests if they catch someone re-selling a ticket. The trick, of course, is not to get caught.

"JIMMY"
Ticket Vendor

On June 18, 1999, my son and I saw a scalper in handcuffs, being led away from the bridge, where he had been busted. Just a few games later, though, on June 30, there he was again with the usual crew, down by the corner of Kenmore Square, chatting at some length to a couple of uniformed policemen.

Some days later, I approached another scalper working another side of the park. He agreed to talk with me by phone anonymously and gave me a number. Call him and you may get his voice mail; a simple reverse lookup provided me with a real name – not an unlisted number – but for these purposes he'll be known as "Jimmy" at his request.

Interestingly, Boston seems to have bred some very talented ticket sellers. The degree to which there is organization and the degree to which it's an individualistic effort remains unclear, probably because it's a little of each.

The interview:

It's illegal but it's not immoral. We provide a service. I get a lot of dumps from ticket brokers and stuff like that. I take them to the street. I give them a cut back. It's on consignment with a lot of people.

Some people just give me tickets. I want to give them something for it. I tell them flat out I'm going to sell it.

I've done tickets all my life. I know tickets inside and out. Sporting events, concerts, World Series, Final Fours. I travel a lot. I've been doing it about fifteen years. I always liked selling tickets. There's a few dollars involved.

When the tickets go on sale in December, do you buy up some big games?

No, no. Unless you know they're going to have a huge, huge year. You can just get them.

When the Yankees came in in May, the ticket wasn't that big, because it was too early in the season. A lot of people invest, but I just buy them as I need them.

I buy from a lot of ticket services. They can't sell them back to the Red Sox, so they sell them to a street vendor. Basically, that's all ticket people are is street vendors. It's not that lucrative as a business as everyone thinks it is. There's a lot of pitfalls, a lot of aggravations, lot of headaches.

The law in Massachusetts since 1969 says you can't re-sell a ticket on the street for anything. You can't sell them for five cents. You can't do it blatantly, wide open. You're not going to rub people's faces in it. That's why a lot of guys that do it regularly stay in Kenmore Square, and they do it away from the ballpark.

Selling tickets is a full time job for you?

Yeah, basically, but no one makes all 81 home games. And you do a lot of nights drinking or something like that, you're not going to make a Thursday 1:05 start against Detroit. I'd say 99 percent of the guys that sell are good guys. They're not out there to rob anybody. I mean, they might charge ten dollars over that, fifteen dollars, but it's for a seat you can't get. Like that seat I sold you last night? You can't get that ticket if you go to the window and buy that in January. You can't get that ticket. Box 28. The guys who have that season ticket has had that probably since 1965.

I go in maybe ten or fifteen times a year. I love baseball. I dig Fenway, right? I'm like a real Fenway nut. I've scalped, I've sold tickets all over the world. I've worked Wimbledon, I've been all over the place. There's nothing like Fenway Park. I mean, the seats are so close. Granted, they have obstructed views and granted, the building's how many years old? People complain that you can't get good seats, that the seats are bad. Well, if you've got to get good seats, go to a guy in the street! Exchange

Arrest of scalper by plain clothes policeman
PHOTO BY BILL NOWLIN

your seats, give a guy twenty buckets a ticket and your tickets and you get a pair of good seats!

If the game's at seven, I get there maybe about four. I'll work until about the first or second inning, when people stop coming. Sometimes you get stuck with some, but most of the times, you know how to get rid of them. You know, discount them late. Last night, I sold everything. They only give you like ten or fifteen of them. So if you get there early, you can sell ten or fifteen of them any night.

Have you ever been arrested yourself?

Yeah, four or five times. You go to court and pay a fine. This shit, where they say the police turn their heads to this stuff, that's bullshit. People get arrested left and right for this shit. You can bail yourself out. It's like a fifteen dollar bill. They can give you a fine up to five hundred dollars. I've been fined $500 a lot, for resale of tickets. The law in this state says you can't resell without a license, on the street, and you can't get a license to resell tickets on the street. So it's impossible. That's life.

Is there any possibility of doing time?

They say they can get you for repeat offender, if you've got a lot of offenses. It's your livelihood. It's like arresting guys for selling peanuts.

They don't turn their heads! That's a fallacy. They're out there. They do their job. They pinch people left and right for this. That's just the fucking assholes on the radio that think that. And the fucking shitbags that write in the newspapers. The Will McDonoughs, the Eddie Andelmans, the Dale Arnolds. It's easy to say. That's cemented in their stupid heads!

It's a victimless crime. The only time there'd be a victim would be if you sold them a fake ticket.

You're not going to get rich doing this. On an average ticket, you might get five or ten dollars. You're not going to get rich doing this stuff. You make fifty dollars a night, and then you go out drinking with it.

Most of the guys aren't out there robbing people. Everybody thinks, they're all stealing robbing, lying, you know. There's some that do.

There's some lawyers that will charge you three thousand for a case, and you can go down the street and get that case for six hundred. They're doctors who will tell you, "Oh, you need a hernia operation, and that's four thousand" and the other guy will tell you, "I can do like a laser thing" and that'll cost you three hundred.

I don't lie to the people. I don't want to look at myself and go through life thinking that I'm a rotten liar. A lot of these guys do that, but that's just the way I do things.

Do you call yourself a scalper? What do you call yourself?

Ticket vendor. That's all we are. Half of the time, you just sell them for the price on the ticket. I get them on consignment. I'm supposed to give the guy fifty percent.

The word "scalper" has a bad connotation. You don't have to buy them. The bottom line is: don't you live in a free society, in a free country? The United States. Are we living in Moscow, Leningrad, or Massachusetts? If I want to go see the All-Star Game and I'm a baseball fanatic, and I've got the money, I'll pay the three thousand dollars. That's my money. If I want to take hundred dollar bills and rip them up and throw them in the sewer, I should be able to do that. See what I'm saying?

Arizona, it's legal. Idaho, it's legal. It's not really legal in any other state. California, it's not legal to sell tickets on the premises. The agencies are supposed to have a certain markup. A lot of these guys are just scalpers with a phone and an office. That's how that shit works. You're supposed to only charge ten percent over. But if these guys get their paws on a first row Springsteen ticket, they're not going to sell the ticket for ten percent over and make three dollars on the ticket. They're going to sell the ticket for $550, $750, something like that – whatever the market bears. That's where they do break the so-called quote/unquote law, keeping the price structure. I don't know. It's basically all semantics.

"DANNY"
Ticket Seller

Just call me "Danny," who has been trying to sell tickets, who has been dodging police for however many years. It's the absolute, God's honest truth. I've never had a green light from any policeman down there. Even friends of mine. If they caught me, they arrested me. I know a lot of people don't believe that, but it's the truth.

They call me the Mayor of Kenmore Square. I've been doing this 35 years. I'm in my late 40s now. I was at Boston College, a kid trying to get into a game, and I used to ask the priests for tickets. I don't know how old I was, maybe ten or eleven. I was getting them free and I'd go in the game. One day, I got a ticket – I think they were playing Army – and there were people everywhere looking for tickets, so I went and sold it. Then I kept going back and getting more for free, and re selling them. Then I just started buying them and re-selling them.

Then the Bruins, with Bobby Orr – which was the biggest thing ever. That was the biggest era ever, for tickets. It just took off from there.

I grew up in Brighton. I think I was about eight when I went to my first Red Sox game. I remember my father taking me to Ted Williams' last game.

Around '67 I first started selling tickets at Fenway. The year they made it to the World Series. I was a big fan. It was just a part of going to the game. I wasn't really thinking about it in those days, like, "Hey, I'm a scalper." I was just always hustling around.

The Sox never drew before Yaz. Then it kind of leveled off a little. Then '75 brought it back a little, and '78. Then the early 80s, it was dying out again. And then Roger Clemens came. Since Clemens has been there, even when they're bad, there's still a high level of interest. When Clemens would pitch, you'd have an extra five thousand people at the game.

Right now it's my main source of income, yeah. It has been for a long time, maybe fifteen or twenty years.

I sell at a lot of other events in Boston. A lot of the scalpers, they travel now. The Patriots, you can't go down there anymore. You get arrested down there now. You used to be able to work there all the time. Everywhere in Boston, they've cracked down pretty much. It's unbelievable. I work on music shows, too. If you needed opera, even, I could get you opera tickets.

There are 38 states where it's not illegal to re-sell tickets. In Arizona, for instance, you can sell for as much as you want to, anywhere you want to. In New Hampshire, it's legal, too, and New Jersey...most places now.

I think it's illegal here because there's a lot of jealousy here. There's a lot of hypocrisy, because everybody's scalping. The politicians are scalping. The business community's scalping. Everyone's scalping. The ticket agencies are scalping. They're not supposed be selling for more than three dollars over face value, but they're selling for three hundred, four thousand, whatever they want, and nobody's doing anything. People are re-selling tickets at the office, up the State House, people are re-selling tickets in exchange for favors – like if a company owns season tickets and they're giving them out to people in exchange for other stuff...you know what I mean? Everybody, everywhere's scalping. The only people that are getting nailed are the people that are re-selling tickets on the street.

I remember in '86, all the major league baseball players were out there scalping tickets. George Scott pulled up to me. He was trying to sell me tickets. Don Sutton was calling a friend of mine, at 3 o'clock in the morning. Willie Stargell. They all wanted crazy money, too. They wanted big money. They wanted more money than I was getting.

You'll see somebody getting arrested for scalping on BC property while all these underage people are getting drunk and smashing bottles and anything. It's crazy. The only explanation I can come up with is that people are jealous. They don't want to see someone else make it. You know how Boston is, New England. They kind of begrudge anyone who makes it. It should be like, "Hey, good luck for him. Good for him. This guy's doing good." It's the other way round around here. I've lived here all my life. I've noticed that. It's just there's too much back-biting. They hate to see anybody do well.

I've got all kinds of sources. Ticket brokers that unload them. People on the street. No, not from the Red Sox.

The biggest thing now is NASCAR. The Boston scalpers, they follow NASCAR all around the country. I don't know why, but you always find a lot of Boston scalpers all around the country. They're just better at it. I guess if you can work here, you can work anywhere. A lot of those regulars are leaving Boston because the laws are so strict now, so they go elsewhere now. Like one guy moved to Arizona. He said, "I don't need this headache all the time, worry about getting arrested." He moved to Arizona and it's completely legal. Isn't it unbelievable?

To tell you the truth, though, the stricter the laws, the better it is for me. It doesn't have any effect on the price, but there's less competition. I'm better at it. Like if you asked a cop, "You know that guy, right? How come he doesn't get caught? Do you leave him alone?" They'll say, "No. He's just very good at it." They have to catch you. Most of the cops know me. I get caught once or twice a year, it's a cost of doing business. They're giving out crazy fines now. That's why some people have left. They're trying to charge people with third and subsequent offense. They're making it really, really difficult. There's so much at stake when somebody gets arrested now. It used to be – years ago – you'd get pinched, you'd go in, they give you a fine, you pay the fine, you go back out. The more you got arrested, the higher the fine. If you got grabbed, you'd get a hundred dollars. If I got grabbed, it'd be a thousand because of all my prior arrests. So it's getting harder and harder and harder.

If you went over there this weekend for the playoffs with the Yankees, you didn't even see anyone over there in Kenmore Square selling. They had fifteen detectives out there and it's not worth the risk.

You can't really blame the police. Their job is to enforce the law, but they're also getting pressured by the public. Certain people are going to the games and they're seeing certain people out there all the time selling tickets. A guy may come down and he wants a ticket. He wants to pay twenty and the going rate is forty, and he gets mad so he goes over and says, "Hey. This guy's over here selling tickets." He tells someone at Fenway Park. Fenway Park says to the cops, "Hey, we're paying you detail here. What're you doing?" It all comes down to money and jealousy. The legality has nothing to do with the price. The only thing that affects the price is supply and demand.

There are some days I end up losing. Absolutely. It's all speculation. It's constant speculation. It's speculation on the buyer's end and it's speculation on the seller's end.

People always say, "You just wait to the end, when the game starts, and you get them cheaper." A lot of times that doesn't work. The seller is speculating earlier, too: "Maybe I oughta get rid of these." You never know. Nobody knows. I've been doing it all my life and I can't predict it from minute to minute, nobody can.

I bought two tickets for my kids for the All-Star Game, and paid $1500 myself, $750 each, right? I wanted them to sit in certain seats. My oldest boy, he's a high school baseball player. He said it was the greatest day of his life. How do you put a price tag on that?

Everybody's competing with each other down there. And they all grew up in the same neighborhood, so they all know each other all their lives, too. It's crazy. They're all like South Boston, Dorchester, all city neighborhoods, you know. People do have to get along out there to get along, because if they didn't, nobody'd make any money, but underneath, deep down, there's unbelievable resentments of one another out there. It's funny, because everybody grew up together. And they hate each other. Everybody sticks together, but you work together because you have to. Some guys have partners but nobody has other guys that work for them.

I enjoy it, sometimes. It's very, very hard work. If I had to do it over again, I wouldn't do it. I'd go to school. I'm a high school dropout. I would have done something else. I'm getting by, though, with my kids. It's been a struggle.

The other scalpers, some of them are not nice people. It's a tough business, let's put it that way. It's a tough crowd, you don't need a resume to do it! You know what I mean? You might get people right out of jail. They've got nothing else to do so they go down there. It's a tough racket. My kids will never do it. I know that. I tell them all the time, I do it so you won't have to do it.

My regular people who buy and sell to me, they know that they're getting the best deal they're going to get. If they're paying over [face value], they still know they're getting a good deal in terms of paying over. And whatever I give them for their ticket is fair market. They know I'm making money, but I'm making a fair profit, and I'm giving them a fair shake on their ticket. A lot of people just hand me their tickets and tell me "Do the best you can" – they have faith that what I'm giving them back was fair. I'll give them the money the next day or the next time I see them.

People call all the time on the phone. Or they just see me on the street, or whatever. Some people don't even know my name. That's the funny thing. They'll just come up and say, "Here. Here's a couple. I'll catch up with you later." I'll see them later and say "Here you go" or I might even give the tickets back [if I can't sell them.] I've been down the park so long that people will walk by everybody else and go over to me because they trust me. Whereas most of those guys down there, they'll tell them it's a box seat and it'll be out in the bleachers.

I could never compete any more, at my age, with these kids on the street running around and trying to beat me to the customer. I depend on regular people coming by and looking for me. I could never just go out there...they're all competing with each other for the same customers. Running to get ahead of the other guy. It's so cut-throat. Now with the cellphones, there's some business that comes that way even in the last hour or so. They'll call and say, "I'm coming down. Hold me two."

Do they turn each other in? Oh, yeah. All the time. Oh, yeah. If somebody from the suburbs comes down and starts trying to scalp tick-

ets, he'd be locked up within fifteen minutes. The college kids come down sometimes. They're in cuffs like within seconds.

It's been going on since the beginning of time, right? They were scalping the gladiator games, weren't they?

Scanning ticket barcodes, May 2004
PHOTO BY EMMET NOWLIN

I think the Jacobs brothers were scalpers originally. Not the two that own it, but the original Jacobs, in Chicago, they scalped tickets and sold souvenirs. They use to scalp...remember the movie *Eight Men Out*? The guy who fixed it, Rothstein. He was a scalper originally.

A lot of the guys went over to Europe for the World Cup. They said that was like having twelve Super Bowls go on at the same time. One guy made more money than he would have made here in five years. The Olympics doesn't compare to the World Cup. The English scalpers and the Europeans were cleaning up. Even the Boston scalpers who went over there and didn't know what they were doing when they went over there made gigantic money. The English scalpers are the best.

The cops usually have two or three guys outside, but it's a gigantic park, and there's also public drinking and stuff. They're looking at that. The cops do the best they can. I mean, how far away from the stadium are they supposed to go? If they go one direction, then they're missing a whole different direction. How many cops are you going to hire, how much manpower and how much money is going to be spent, and how much court time? They have to enforce it, but it's difficult. You've got to be careful. Don't put it in their face. Even if you know the guy, he can't let you just break the law in front of him.

It's a victimless crime. It's so ridiculous when you think about it. I know one guy that went to Japan for the Winter Olympics. It's completely legal there. Japan! Nothing's legal there, but scalping they had no problem with it.

There's been some sad stories, too. I remember when they had the World Cup here. There a guy from Argentina that came up with his wife and kid and he had an extra ticket down at Foxboro for one of the games. He was just trying to sell it for face value – $75. An undercover Foxboro cop arrested him, in front of his wife and kid, for selling the ticket for $50. The guy couldn't even speak English. They made him sit there – they had a specially made holding tank – in front of his kid. Missed the game.

If a concert goes on sale in the Fleet Center, the first guy [in line] will get a loge seat. The next guy will get like a floor seat. The third guy will get a balcony. Where did all the seats so quick? You don't see that with the Red Sox. I think every team in every sport does it, and every band, every concert, there's some shenanigans going on, but I would say the Red Sox are probably the fairest I know. I don't know of anything going on myself.

I don't know of anyone who has done jail time who has just scalped tickets. But I know that there's guys that have stopped because of fear of it.

Joe McDermott,
Vice President,
Stadium Operations.
Joe McDermott
maintained a consecutive game streak for over 28 years, before having to miss a game on April 16, 2004 due to prostate cancer. When Joe topped Lou Gehrig's 2,130 games, it was a real milestone. Sadly, Joe's streak ended at 2,247 consecutive games. Any organization would be exceptionally fortunate to have such a dedicated and loyal employee.
PHOTO BY EMMET NOWLIN

Fenway facts abound:

You never know what's going to happen at Fenway Park. When it rains exceptionally hard in a short period of time, Charles River water backs up in storm drains and causes flooding of the dugouts. When it rains really, really, really hard, Joe Mooney explained to the new incoming head groundskeeper David Mellor, the first base camera pit will flood and an occasional fish will flop out on the field. Skeptical, but fresh to Fenway, Mellor respectfully did not question the veteran Mooney.

The Saturday before Opening Day 2001, three inches of rain fell on the field. Mellor surveyed the field early Sunday morning, and found eight bass (each 6 to 8 inches long) on the field between the first base camera pit and second base. "I thought I was on Candid Camera," Mellor said. In constructing the "dugout seats" prior to the 2002 season, a jammed valve was found in the camera pit and the problem has been fixed. Probably.

3

BEFORE THE GAME

Sam Santiago, Parking Lot Manager
Dylan Thompson, Parking Lot Flagger
Michael Thompson, Manager, VIP Parking
Nick Jacobs, Peanut Vendor
Jim Parry, Sunglasses Vendor
Dave Littlefield, "The Sausage Guy"
Jim Dioguardi, Sausage Vendor
Ken Melanson, Baseball Card Vendor

Keith Durham, Baseball Cap Vendor
Mike Rutstein, Editor and Publisher,
    BOSTON BASEBALL
Ryan Goldney, BOSTON BASEBALL Hawker
Hai Ho Nguyen, BOSTON BASEBALL Runner
Tony Lupo, Hurdy Gurdy Man
Mickey Bones, Bandleader,
    Hot Tamale Brass Band

You've got your ticket now, ready to hit the game. Parking lots around Fenway fill up quick; frequent visitors develop strategies for finding spaces. The Red Sox encourage people to take the T, it certainly is cheaper and can be a lot less hassle.

Sam Santiago collects fees from cars arriving at the Lansdowne Street Garage, right across from the back of the Wall on Lansdowne Street, a/k/a Ted Williams Way. Before working at MASCO, the parking lot company, Sam used to work nearby at Northeastern University doing shipping and receiving.

Ken Melanson
setting up shop
PHOTO BY BILL NOWLIN

SAM SANTIAGO
Parking Lot Manager

Sam Santiago
PHOTO BY BILL NOWLIN

I work for MASCO. At least four years in this garage or the other one that belongs to the Red Sox [down on Ipswich Street.] Usually, we have six to eight employees here.

Baseballs coming over the Wall are hard to get, there's a bunch of people waiting for them. I got a bunch of them during practice ball [batting practice]. Two years in a row, I had Valentin's home run.

We have a sign, if the ball breaks a window, we're not responsible. I just hope you got insurance. People have a choice to park inside or outside. Some of them will be like, "I want to park outside". We tell them to read the sign. Some say, "Ah, I'll park inside."

[The sign reads: Please note: Management assumes no liability for damage or injury resulting from baseballs that may be hit out of the ballpark."]

It's fifteen dollars. We open two hours before a ballgame, at 5. It's heaviest twenty minutes before the game.

I work 6 PM until 3 AM – because of the night clubs. During a ballgame, we don't get many incidents. It's the night club people. Thursday nights, it's 18 and up. They can't drink in the clubs, so they come drinking before they go in.

One night when I was working at the Red Sox garage, I seen Tom Gordon. Flash. I've seen Nomar. I've seen a couple of ballplayers.

Dylan Thompson
PHOTO BY BILL NOWLIN

DYLAN THOMPSON
Parking Lot Flagger

Around Fenway, outside the various parking facilities, there are seven or eight flaggers who try to wave drivers into their lots.

I'm a flagger for VIP. I've done this for about two years now. I stand here [on Brookline Avenue] and wave the flag and try to get cars to come in. We get here about an hour before the game. We knock off whenever we're full.

I live in Burlington. I'm in middle school, eighth grade. I'm the owner's grandson and the manager's son. Being a flagger, it's about the only thing I can do. I can't be a valet because I can't drive yet.

MICHAEL THOMPSON
Manager, VIP Parking

Dylan's father Michael Thompson is the manager of VIP Parking.

I'm the supervisor at VIP. That covers the lot here, the one across the street, another lot behind the Il Giardino Cafe and another one down Brookline Ave., little lots tucked in here and there. Overall, we have about 300 slots. It's privately owned.

We only have two or three flaggers. Dylan's trying to earn some money to get into BC. He's 14 now. He wants to drive the cars, but he's got a couple of years to go. The flags are just orange plastic and we stick a stick on it. Just a regular flag.

For a 7 o'clock game, they start coming in about two hours before. I come in a couple of hours before that just to get everything straightened out and ready to go.

Normally, we're $20. Non-baseball, it's $9 a day. Sometimes people don't have enough money. We just take their license and they run down to the ATM or whatever.

An hour after the game's over, usually everybody's out. If not, we tow them. No overnight parking.

Once the game starts, all we do is move cars around into different spots. People keep coming out throughout the game. I don't really understand it myself. Two innings go by, it's a nice day, and here they come. Somebody wants out. So you move them out and you put the other car back in. It's a pretty dopey job.

We have a TV in the store [Short Stop] but in the garage we listen to the radio if we can. My wife usually kind of keeps her ear to that because I'm trying to get everybody unblocked. She works at the Short Stop. It's a little convenience store. She's in there every single day. It's the whole family. Her, my father-in-law, my kids. Grandfather down through us, and the grandkids. All of us. My father-in-law owns the store and the parking garage. The parking business they've had for 25 years or so. The store we've only had for five or so.

NICK JACOBS
Peanut Vendor

Once you've parked your car, you might want to get a snack or a meal before heading into the park itself. There are plenty of spots to choose from. The newer Boston Beer Works always has a line out front, and so does the venerable Cask & Flagon.

One of the more unique features of Fenway is the action outside the park. Often imitated, never duplicated, there's tradition here. And controversy. Tradition is perhaps best exemplified by Nick Jacobs, whose grandfather began selling peanuts the first day Fenway Park opened in 1912. Nick's father took up the work, and Nick continues the tradition today. The Red Sox have from time to time tried to ban the vendors. They take business away from the concessions inside the park – lost revenue of a million dollars or more each year.

Joe Castiglione: "It's a privilege to have [Fenway Park] be my "office," to have the opportunity to be there every day. I get a kick out of knowing the vendors, the groundskeepers, the ushers, the people who make their livelihood at the ballpark. I never tired of seeing the fans who get there three or four hours before the game starts, patiently waiting for autographs. I always look for that one old peanut vendor who's been here forever, and the sausage guy right across the street. They're all part of the lure of Fenway – the feeling of a real city neighborhood spilling over into the park itself." (Our House, p. 184)

Michael Thompson
PHOTO BY BILL NOWLIN

The "old peanut vendor" was George Jacobs, Nick's father, who seemed to never miss a game.

My grandfather, Peter Davis, was already into the business before they built Fenway Park, the Red Sox were the Red Stockings and they played at another park off of Huntington Ave. [Huntington Avenue Grounds.] One of my uncles used to peddle his wares down at Braves Field. He had a horse and carriage type thing.

[Now the vendors have an arrangement with the City where those who have established themselves over the years are more or less "grandfathered" into an understanding that they may continue to sell on the streets under certain regulations. However, in late 2002, the Red Sox received temporary game day permission to close off Yawkey Way outside the park – in effect expanding the footprint of the park, not unlike the way restaurants are allowed to place tables and chairs on the sidewalk outside their premises. In the process, the vendors who had benefited for many years by setting up on Fenway's doorstep are now shunted further away from the park – and the potential profit that proximity conveys.]

You're basically locked in. Nobody else can go in there now and sell their wares, just people that have longevity. It's a vendor's license. You need an occupancy permit from the property owners to sell outside a building, unless you're moving constantly. You gotta reapply every year. Back when my father was doing it, the licenses weren't as strict as they are now. There's a lot of red tape to deal with now, with liability insurance and so forth. You never know, a car could come down the street and hit the cart and that could hit somebody, too.

Nick Jacobs
PHOTO BY ANDREA RAYNOR

I used to go down there [with my father George] when I was real young. My mother had a spot there too, years ago.

I really don't know how the family first got involved with the business. I guess a lot of Greeks were involved with selling on the street, with pushcarts way back then.

The cart I have now is about 4 or 5 years old, but I still have the original cart my father had. Now, my grandfather's cart, I used parts off that to build the cart that I use now. It might not look it, but a friend – a carpenter – helped me. A lot of planning went into that, everything was hand-crafted and fabricated. There's not a company out there that makes peanut carts.

I have a company in Cambridge that I buy supplies off. I buy a couple of hundred pounds at a whack and they roast them for me. I pick them up the day of the game and they're fresh roasted every day. I hardly ever have any left over.

[In recent years, Nick has sported peanut earrings. I asked about that.]

We come out with the earrings about 3, 4 years ago. We were goofing around one day. It was a Yankees game. One of the Yankees fans gave me the idea of wearing these peanuts on my ears. People love that stuff. They think it's cute. Anything for a laugh. It's part of the shtick, you know.

Do you wear them when you're not at Fenway Park?

Oh, of course...I've got a diamond studded one [jokes] – no, I'm only kidding.

We've had cashews about 5, 6 years now. We have cashews, pistachios, crackerjacks, and a new line we're trying out this year. They're hot and spicy in the shell; Cajun style, it's going very well. I do all right. Enough to make a living, to pay the bills.

The old fashioned stuff, the traditional stuff sells the best. A lot of people don't like salted peanuts. We do have the salted in the shell, too. A lot of people just like the regular peanuts with no salt; it's more health conscious.

In hot weather, our business goes down. The best time is early spring and the fall. Parts of the summer are nice, too. It's kind of a tossup between night games and day games as to which are better.

I live in Whitman, on the South Shore. I drive the cart to Fenway in the van. In the old days, when my father was alive, we had a little storage place in the North End, off of Endicott Street and we used to wheel the cart over, all the way down Boylston Street. We'd wheel that wagon a couple of miles, and some of it was uphill too. Whether it was rain, hot, cold, we'd get up early in the morning – my father was like that.

[For a 7 o'clock game] I usually leave around noontime and go pick up my supplies for the day and then I'm down the ballpark by 1 or 1:30 and I'm out there selling by 4 o'clock or so, and I stay 'til about the third inning. Most of the business is for about an hour before. I don't usually wait around for the out crowds, because no one really buys peanuts on the way out. Sometimes a sausage or a pretzel, but not peanuts.

My father had a knack of selling the peanuts. He used to throw them and you'd have to catch them. Things were different back then. People would get a kick out of it. If that bag hit you in the head today, you'd probably sue him! When I was there working with him, I was kind of embarrassed a couple of times because people would get teed off and they'd throw the peanuts back and ask for their money back. You never know who you're dealing with out there.

We say things like, "Hey, come on down! Get your peanuts for the ballgame! Bigger, better, fresher, cheaper! The best of Boston! Come on down! The baby cries, the daddy buys!" We just make up stuff as we come along.

I don't really know any of the kids who sell inside the park. Well, maybe one kid. I'm good friends with Robbie. He actually throws them inside. [The reference is to Rob "Nuts" Barry.]

I just fell through the cracks and the loopholes of the law. That's why I'm still there. And I'm glad to be there! It's part of the nostalgic values of the City of Boston. Thank God the City of Boston stepped in and gave me a hand with this. And the City Councillors, and definitely the newspapers – the people at the GLOBE and the HERALD, Dan Shaughnessy, Bob Ryan...I owe those guys a lot of thank yous, I'll never forget what they did for me.

I want to be careful what I say [about the conflict between the Red Sox and the street vendors.] The Red Sox have been very cooperative. They understand the situation. They gotta remember the nostalgic values of some of the things around that ballpark, that they should not eliminate. There's a few vendors that have been there a long time. Like myself. This is my bread and butter. This is how I make my living. It's not like I drive a Mercedes Benz or anything like that. I'm just a regular working guy.

I've spent my whole life down there in the streets around Fenway Park. I've put a lot of time in down there and it was time I could have went to school and did something with my life. Sometimes I wish I did. My father was there for so many years. People know me down there. The fans know what I am, know what I represent and they knew my father and grandfather.

What I represent down there is like a time capsule.

I love going in there on a day game and the nice weather and the people around me. I might even bring a bag of peanuts! It's nice, you know. It really is.

JIM PARRY
Sunglasses Vendor

Jim Parry was a disc jockey on Boston's most popular station, WBCN, during its most freeform alternative days. In a later stint, Jim did a number of folk radio shows in New Hampshire and Concord, Massachusetts. Radio is not a stable business, though, and for many years now, Jim's distinctive voice has been heard outside Fenway selling sunglasses.

It was around 1984 that I first started selling sunglasses. After WBCN I went back to graduate school, anthropology and archaeology. Harvard and Brandeis. I kept getting poison ivy, which is what you get in New England archaeology.

A friend of mine, Phil Krampf, was financing his way through graduate school at BU selling sunglasses at the park. I worked for him for a couple of years, and then went out on my own. Phil's actually still there. He mostly sells caps now. I never really sold anything else. I didn't want to conflict with the Twins, who was right across the street. I like selling sunglasses more than hats. It may sound sort of strange, but there is more scope for creativity.

Jim Parry
PHOTO BY BILL NOWLIN

I just sell at Fenway Park, Foxboro gets too cold. The Boston Common gets too expensive.

It's a city license for the Storage and Sale of Merchandise on a Public Way, specifically for the Fenway area. Back in the early or mid-80s they started trying to enforce no vending there. It was in court and back and forth for four or five years and they finally decided to legalize and regulate it. So they started issuing licenses in, I think it was 1990. There haven't been any new people since then.

The longest, of course, is Nicky's family. [Nick Jacobs]

Everybody else pretty much started in the mid-80s, or before.

I sell more during day games, it's dependent on the weather more than anything else. Sunny days in late May, June and July when it's 80 and there's not a cloud in the sky are the best and then it starts slackening off. It starts getting dark a bit earlier, but it hangs on through August. The last week of September is usually pretty bitter. You have to be out there with your thermies on, and your insulated boots and caps and mittens.

The Yankee series are really big sellers for everybody.

It varies [whether I sell more before a game or afterwards.] For a long time it was about half and half. Now it depends on the game. Sometimes 60/40, sometimes 70/30, sometimes still 50/50.

When did you start selling sunglasses after dark?

In '96, there was a late game on Saturday. It was going to end at 7 or 8, and I was pushing it, "Come on, come on, come on! Get done before it gets dark. Come on. Come on." It was a long game, and it got dark, and I was still there and so I figured, well, what the hell? It's ending. I don't want to leave, because people are coming out. I just kept selling and discovered that people buy after dark. Which is possibly the most counter-intuitive thing I've ever encountered.

People say things like "Where is the sun?" People think they're being really original and witty, giving you shit. There are about a half a dozen lines and you just get them over and over and over. Sometimes you just ignore them and sometimes you have to come up with a line. It's like, "Where's the sun?" and you point and say, "Ninety three million miles that way" which isn't a particularly original line, either, but it stops them. They're just being wise-asses.

Ever turn any of those into sales?

Usually if people are giving you a line like that, it's just to hassle you. People will say, "Do you have Stevie Wonder glasses?" or Ray Charles glasses, and they're not going to buy, even if you say yes.

Is there any celebrity than you DON'T have?

(extended laughter)

I mean on the spur of the moment, you have everybody, right?

Well, I've got a lot, yeah. I've always done that and then a couple of years ago, the guy who publishes BOSTON BASEBALL came by and said, "Oh! That's the kind Wade Boggs wears." So I adopted that into the rap. People started buying them because of that. It's sort of the celebrity thing.

I look at PEOPLE magazine and the HERALD – which has better sunglass pictures than the GLOBE – and find one that my supplier has that is a copy of that.

So you do identify particular people with particular sunglasses? I kind of figured that you half made up these names.

Oh, no. Pedro Martinez, I have one actually. There was a picture in the HERALD, but he seems to be wearing clip-ons for prescription lenses. I have never seen him wearing regular glasses. I don't know if he wears contacts when he is on the field, or what.

Did you ever have a player or a player's relative come by?

Oh yeah. Mrs. Vaughn – Mo's mom – and she didn't like it because she thought the one that was the "Mo Vaughn", was ugly. She didn't like the style. But that was the kind he was wearing. He later changed to a better looking style. She was really nice. She came by a lot.

Derek Jeter is the biggie. I figure at some point I will find something that he wears, assuming that he wears them. Some people don't. Sammy Sosa doesn't seem to wear glasses. I've had people looking and nobody came up with anything. I've got something similar to Mark McGwire's, but nothing that's Sammy Sosa. Some people get a little ticked that there's a McGwire and not a Sosa. The problem is that nobody has ever seen him wearing glasses.

The Nomar one is also a David Duval one, which gets all the golfers.

Everything is five dollars. I figure that this is not a high-end crowd. Nobody is going to buy the hundred dollar Oakleys or Serengetis from someone on the street. But at five bucks, people are going to buy them.

It's getting tighter. Expenses are rising, so I've got to find something else. The sausage people are the ones who really rake in the bucks.

This year we can be there two and a half hours before the game, because they started closing the street. For a 7 o'clock game, I'll leave Cambridge about 4 or 4:15. I drive over, loaded up. I have a two-seater, so it gets completely filled. I have a folding table, a large package shelf, a two wheeler, two to three boxes of sunglasses and umbrellas.

Umbrellas are awful because the boxes disintegrate in the wet. And they always un-pop. You know how you push them in and the handle clicks in? When they get bumped, the handle clicks out. They only sell if it's really raining, so you have to keep lugging these damn things. You have to have them, but they're a drag.

What's the most umbrellas that you ever sold in a game?

I sold maybe a hundred or so, all that were available at that time. This was years ago. The timing has to be right, the surprise storm comes in, so they haven't brought an umbrella. There was one in the last home stand, a real gully drencher. [May 19, 1999] I sold about twenty in that. They're five dollars also. It's a very simple price structure. It keeps the rap simpler.

It's interesting. I do the hawking and you can see people looking and sort of veering toward the stand. You try and figure out what it is that pulls them in. You have to tailor the spiel to who's passing by, and sometimes you hit it and sometimes you don't.

I'll bring somewhere between sixty and ninety dozen pairs of sunglasses to a game. I won't sell anywhere near that many, but that's backstop. You get about thirty dozen in a carton.

What do you do during the game – when most people are inside?

Sit there and yell occasionally whenever people pass by. There's usually a significant amount of business during the game, you've got people using the Square and you get BU students going by. I get kind of antsy sitting and reading. People are passing by and I kind of feel, "Ah. Business is possibly being lost" so I tend to keep going during the game. It's much slower, obvi-

ously, but there's still something going on. You might sell ten or twenty during the game. A lot more during a day game than a night game.

What if you have to go to the bathroom?

You can go to McDonald's or into the park. We know most of the gatekeepers. They know that we're just going in and coming out. I give a discount to people that work in the park, and to people that work in the street.

People hang out much longer after day games than night games. A lot of them are kids and autograph seekers waiting for players to come out. Friday nights are good, you get a lot of the club people. They're preparing to hang out in all the bars: the ones on Lansdowne Street, Who's On First...they keep coming by. That is a significant amount of business that you don't get other days. During day games, you get a lot of tourists and BU students.

We have to be out of there an hour after the game. It picks up from about the 8th inning on, as people start coming out. Sometimes the seventh inning, if the score is really lopsided. If it's just been a long game, then they're usually not that interested in buying. They just want to get out of there.

It doesn't really seem to be that much of a variable, whether the Red Sox win or not. It's mostly the weather – that's the predominant thing – and if the teams they're playing are hot.

The first five or ten minutes after the game ends, everybody just wants to get out of there. Then it slows down as people are picking up souvenirs, eating, hanging out – they're more likely to start buying things. So it's maybe forty minutes after the game, sometimes up to an hour or so. Sometimes it's just fifteen minutes if they're grumpy and just want to go home.

I'm pretty sure there are a few light-fingered people who come by. Sometimes they're just really inept. I mean, I've had people who are so obvious about it that you just go down the street and confront them. But it's not a major problem. Most people, even the drunks, are there for a good time. After years of doing this, you know pretty well how to handle people. By and large people are happy. They're coming to the park, they're having a good time. Some of it is because it is a family thing, so they are more restrained.

I came out of the whole sort of Sixties hippy thing and this is kind of the antithesis of that, so this was sort of culture shock for the first couple of years.

A lot of people get thrown out of the park. Between 5 and 20 at an average game, and I'm right there where they get thrown out. They come by [feigns drunken speech], "Can you believe it? We were thrown out for saying, 'Yankees suck!'" They were probably doing something else, but that's what they say.

You get like feeding frenzies. On a really sunny Saturday, it'll be hands reaching with money from every direction and there's just no way that I can make change. It varies a lot between evening and day games. I've had a couple of really awful days when I've sold a few dozen. Some days I'll sell more than a hundred.

I bring a radio to the games and every time you're trying to listen to what's going on, someone shows up to buy glasses. About half the vendors bring a radio. You do want to know, since some of the vendors will roll away. The Twins people will go back into their warehouse and only come out in the sixth inning. Some of the people are there because they're really sports fans. Some of the people are there to make the buck. It's kind of a range. I guess I'm probably in the middle of that.

There are some really rabid autograph collectors, who make a living buying and selling memorabilia and autographs, they are really good about finding where players are staying, they'll hang out in the hotels and get their signatures. Last year I was next to Kenny, the baseball card guy. They would come by and compare what they'd gotten and they would sell him stuff. Some of it was business but I got the impression that it was kind of like the people who have life birding lists. It's sort of a personal trophy.

You get balls coming out during the games. On Yawkey Way, it's always foul balls, of course. All of a sudden, you'll hear this "THONK!!" and hordes go screaming up and down the street. You'll get like half a dozen people chasing it. They go under cars, down the alleyway. Year

before last, there was a new van with a plastic moon roof. The ball came out and "WHONK" – right in the middle of the moon roof. Nick the peanut guy put a note on the car telling the people what happened. Someone got the ball.

The first one I got – well, maybe the third one I got – was a Jose Canseco foul. You know the sloped roof, glass-fronted thing on the Twins where WEEI broadcasts? It hit one of those panels. There's this "FROSH-KUH!" and tinkling of glass. It hit and bounced out, so I ran over and grabbed that.

Do you have a good relationship with Twins?

They're kind of ambivalent. They haven't been pleased with the lineup of carts blocking their entrance – even though we're on the other side. It was always the same thing, though. Until this year, it was handicap cars blocking. At this point, everybody is sort of modus vivendi-ing along.

I used to like sitting in the bleachers. You get these guys and they have had the same seats ever since they were kids. They sit there talking about the new aluminum storm windows they're putting in. You come and socialize with someone you only see at Fenway – and then you yell at Dwight Evans or whoever. You rag him for a while and then you go back to talking about storm windows.

Busty Hart, the stripper, who was sort of the Morgana the Kissing Bandit for Boston, would come by occasionally after doing her thing, which was another one of those wonderful 80s Red Sox traditions.

[Jim is a real observer of street life around the park.]

I was watching the bottle bill amendments last year and someone was inveighing about the bill and the people who pick bottles. I really disagreed with that, because those people are very industrious. There are three or four regulars who come around and pick up the cans and bottles and take them and redeem them. This is someone who is working, with a measure of self-respect, and it's a hard job. Some of them just go around and around the park. I run into one of them once near Harvard Stadium. I didn't know he had quite that wide-ranging an orbit. You kind of have to say, "OK. This is someone who has found a niche that is ecologically responsible. It is not panhandling. It's someone who is working hard, and they deserve some respect for that."

Some of the people were caught up in the de-institutionalization of the 1980s, and have no place to go. You get a lot of different kinds of regulars. Last year there was Karaoke Man, who would sing "Dock of the Bay" and this very melismatic version of the "Star Spangled Banner" and "Take Me Out to the Ball Game." A lot of people figure out their own little hustles.

There are the guys who play percussion on upturned plastic buckets.

They showed up a couple of times this year. There's a blues singer that's come by a couple of times that I like. I'm not sure how well he does, but it's kind of pleasant having him down the street.

I really like Fenway. It sort of reminds me of the Roman Coliseum, which has seen every kind of thing coming by and happening to it and is still there two thousand years later. Now you get Yanni at the Coliseum. I'm not sure that's necessarily a concert that I would go to, but two thousand years later, the place is still in use.

Fenway is one of the fairly early reinforced concrete structures in the country. You think, "Is this still going to be here in two thousand years?" Clearly not, and that's kind of a shame. This is something that has a lot of history attached to it and there has to be something that you can use it for.

There's a lot of symbiotic structure that's evolved around it, that people support themselves with, that provides the sort of support structure for the park, that the Sox, I think, don't really recognize. It is in a lot of ways a functioning sub-segment of the culture.

It's interesting because it is ephemeral – four or six hours there and then it's gone. Then it reassembles. I read the accounts of the people who show up at the Esplanade a week early to get front row seats for July 4th, or the people who did the Star Wars thing. People set up temporary communities for the companionship and order

and organization, and for entertainment and mutual reinforcement.

There are really not that many places for people to assemble and interact. Too much of modern city planning has been for business or for shopping, and hasn't been oriented toward people having some place they can actually assemble and do something. I don't think the Sox realize that. Those are the kinds of things that I think are very valuable about the park and about baseball in general.

Keith Durham, the hat guy, got married on Saturday for the second time. He did the in-crowd and then about 2 o'clock he was bustling down the street with his table under his arms. "Is this the day, Keith?" "Yeah, getting married, getting married." He got married at 4 o'clock. We were taking bets as to whether or not he would show up for the out-crowd. With his bride.

[Jim works with a Coleman lantern to illuminate his stand during night games. It's part of his rig, which does all fold up nicely and neatly onto his two wheeler afterwards.]

DAVE LITTLEFIELD
"The Sausage Guy"

I'm the Sausage Guy. That's my M.O. I'm wearing the T-shirt today. It's not just a shirt; it's my life.

The Phantom Gourmet had me on TV when they did a show about late night foods back in February. After that, we hammered out a sponsorship agreement. They're going to give me mentions on the show and so forth, they hooked me up on their web site and created a "sausage link" to my web site. It's the sausageguy.com [www.sausageguy.com]

I'm the sausage guy for the nightclubs as well. I've been on Lansdowne Street for the last six years. 1999 was the first year I'd actually done the Red Sox games. In the past, I tried to

Dave Littlefield
PHOTO BY BILL NOWLIN

do business for the games, but there's 8 guys there and it seemed as though the guys who wanted sausages would walk on the opposite side of the street. They still tend to do that, but I yell and they come over.

I rent the space from the Lansdowne Street Garage, from MASCO. It took me three years to put that little location together. I have a decent sized lease there and I paid to build it out to the specifications that you see now.* I'm on private property. That's how I'm exempt from the forced move of the other vendors. One of the vendors actually tried to offer triple my rent to take my spot. Being a good guy, my landlord stuck by me.

[*sits on top of a concrete block platform, with side railings built in and wooden posts on both front corners. Maybe 6 feet square.]

I became The Sausage Guy because nobody knew my name. They're like, "Hey! Sausage Guy! What's up?" Week after week after week. So eventually I just ran with it.

They're pork. You've got to cook them well. The chicken is notoriously hazardous because if it's not handled correctly you could be in trouble.

The Board of Health come by all the time [to inspect the food.] I've already been inspected three times this year. The vendors have been doing what they've been doing for so many years, the guys are professionals. I have people begging me for like X sausage on the grill, but it's not cooked and I have an argument with them. They're going, "Come on." I'm like, "No, If I feed you that, you'll wake up dead tomorrow and you'll be mad at me."

My stand is built to meet city and state codes for Board of Health requirements. Running hot water, running cold water as well as a catch basin for the disposal water. I clean everything down constantly. The Sterno is for the hot water heater. We keep it going constantly. We steam-clean the sidewalks once a month. I want a good relationship with the city.

[Up top in the stand, there is a compartment, with some extra ketchup and mustard, napkins and a water bottle for Dave. He keeps a boom box on a shelf behind him.]

I've had instances where I've sent cabs to get mustard. They think you're crazy. You run up to them. "Look, I need some mustard." Some of the poor guys can hardly speak English, and I'm holding up the bottle pointing to it. Actually, they're pretty good sports about it. It's a bad situation to be in, though. I've been out here when the clubs have just let out and I'm running low on mustard. They get angry when you don't have mustard. "What do you mean, you got no mustard?"

There are kids who stand out here looking for balls that come over the Wall. I don't see them coming sometimes. The angles are unbelievable. If a ball hits behind me, it's like a pinball. I'm ducking. Just recently a ball broke the cart during batting practice. The ball hit right off my radio, it smashed my thermostat control right off. I looked down and everything was burning. I didn't know what it was and I looked down at my knobs and everything was gone.

I sell just one item, and try to be the best at it. Sweet Italian sausages, cooked to perfection. That's the goal.

I get them from Cara Donna. That's over in South Bay. [Cara Donna Provision Co. – Dave picks them up once a day.]

When do you sell better, day game or night game?

You know, it doesn't really depend on the day. It depends on who they're playing. Obviously, the Yankees games are very busy for everybody and it's always a good time to be out there. Monday night's a little bit quieter. The weekends tend to be pretty consistent but not very busy. It's hard to say. It's a bizarre business. I always tell my guys, "Prepare for the best, and prepare yourself mentally for the worst." It depends on whether they win or lose, but on the way in is usually better than on the way out.

On a game with a 7 o'clock start, people will be leaving around 10:00, 10:30 and then the nightclub people come in. I'll be there until 2:30 in the morning. I have a long day, my friend. I started at 8 and I'll go to bed at 4 AM.

Any other problems, people running off without paying?

Sure, sure. When it's busy, you might set a couple up on the shelf and somebody might reach through and grab one and run. You can't chase them. You sort of laugh about it. We got a guy one time, he ran like hell. He ran like he just stole a million dollars. I thought he was going to kill himself running. It was hysterical. I'm like, wow! That guy was really hungry!

The confrontations with people that are drunk, though, that's the discouraging end of it. That happens more so, the night club side. I always tell my guy, it's up to myself and him to set the tone for the night.

The cart was custom made for me. Just under five thousand. My grill's actually electric, and then we have working sinks underneath. A pop-up top for storage and that's about it. I plug into the garage. I store it in the garage sometimes.

With leftover sausages, we just throw them away. I try to run out every event I'm at. I don't mind running out. It's fresh and that's what I like about it.

What do I have for dinner? Sometimes I run up to the Cask 'N Flagon and get a grilled chicken sandwich. Sometimes I pack a lunch. I don't eat the sausages as much as I say I do. It's like anything. A bartender doesn't drink that much, because he's pouring them all the time and he's tired of it. I'm the same way, I guess.

The good part of it: I enjoy it. I'm out there with the public and I open myself to, well, anything. I sort of enjoy the excitement of that.

I'm trying something a little different than somebody just out on the street. I market the place as more of a retail shop. I have a sponsorship with BCN, which is just phenomenal. I put up an ad for them [painted on the side panel of the cart} and they give me on-air ads. They mention me fairly often. They say, "Go see The Sausage Guy. The BCN Sausage Guy." They try to tie me in to whatever they may be doing on the street. The idea was just to make it a little more fun. It's worked out great. It's been fun for the public, it's been fun for me. They've been fantastic over there at BCN; they've just been great.

JIM DIOGUARDI
Sausage Vendor

Jim has the most modest stand on the street, advertising Italian sausage, kielbasa and all beef hot dog. His white truck which he drives over for pickup afterwards has on it these individual letters: JIM GEMS CHE-CHI [he once sold jewelry] and he sports a SAVE FENWAY PARK bumper sticker on the back.

I started about 27 years ago back in East Boston. This friend of mine had a variety store. Fruits and vegetables. I was real young then, my early 20s, so now I'm 50 and I'm still at it. It's my livelihood. I've been here at Fenway Park about 25 years.

I used to do a jewelry [business], back in the 60s, and I'd call it JIM GEMS AND CHE-CHI'S CHARMS. Che-Chi's comes from my son's middle name, Joseph Chechi Dioguardi. I sold handmade jewelry, all kinds of stuff. Then I got into slush, I was doing slush and jewelry at the same time. Prior to that, I did newspapers and I used to go down to the Wonderland track and sell the track books. I used to mark the ones I thought were going to be winners so that I'd get more money from the bettors. They'd be giving me money for the books plus the tips, as well.

I buy mainly sausages from a business back in East Boston that started close to sixty years ago, DiLuigi's Sausage. Everybody knew each other back then. We all helped each other out in businesses.

I don't talk about how many sausages I sell, I talk in pounds. It could be anywhere from fifty to two hundred pounds. You never know. Weekend nights are the best. Saturday might not be too bad. Sunday afternoons might even be the best. Because of the families, you know.

I try to keep everything frozen, or fresh. Otherwise, I don't sell. I don't feel right if everything's not fresh. I seldom bring pre-cooked.

I'm the only barbeque guy here. I'm like the Burger King of sausage. I use briquettes. I've got my own sauce. I play around with different sauces at different times.

I've been at Boston College for almost twenty years now. Years ago I went to the Common – the Cambridge Common, the Boston Common. I was at Northeastern for a short while; I was at Boston State College for a short while. I was at Boston University. I was at Harvard for a year. I'm just at BC now. Only on the weekends. I did days up there for close to ten years; I had a day spot up there.

I had my problems. I took a jump about thirty, thirty five feet over there [up by the ticket windows] because of a problem I had with people attempting to rob. They'd try to grab cash, that and the stand. That was years ago. I was a lot younger then and I didn't give a fuck one way or another. The way I looked at it, if I had to go down for the count, at least it was for a good cause: my living. That's the way I looked at it.

Ken Melanson
PHOTO BY BILL NOWLIN

KEN MELANSON
Baseball Card Vendor

1986 was the year that the Red Sox were pennant winners and went to the World Series. That was a benchmark year because the Sox were doing so well that crowds flocked to the ballpark. A large number of vendors started selling their wares and foods and so forth around the ballpark. There were probably a half a dozen card dealers. That's kind of how I got into it. I pretty much exclusively sell baseball cards.

I'm a human resources manager for a services organization. Training, employee relations, benefits, that sort of thing. We operate mental health clinics or social clubhouses for mentally ill adults.

I'm at Fenway Park 81 times a year.

Around 1979, I read an ad in THE SPORTING NEWS, of all places, and somebody was selling a complete set of 1979 baseball cards. That was something I had never had as a kid – a complete set of cards. So I sent away for it. Then there were some card shows in Massachusetts in the early 1980s that I went to. By '84 I started setting up in card shows, selling off my duplicates.

I wouldn't give up my day job. Sure, I make a dollar or two, but the people who can really make a living without doing anything else are the sausage vendors, people eat every single day. My thing has too many variables. I'm at the mercy of the weather, the team that's in town. I view this more as something I'm interested in.

The Yankees are coming next week. That will be very good. But when Toronto comes, or Minnesota, or Kansas City, the crowds aren't here. I'm at the mercy of the numbers of people that come.

I'm unique in the way I set up. Well, probably the sunglass guys are the same way. I load the stuff in my car and bring it to work. Then after work, I drive to the ballpark and scrounge around for a parking spot. I built a platform on wheels, so I'm able to put the folding tables and showcases and boxes and so forth on this platform, and then I just wheel it to the ballpark.

For each series I bring a different selection of cards. When the Yankees are in town, I try to have some Yankee cards. Jeter is the most popular Yankee, but Bernie Williams or Martinez or O'Neill or Cone or so forth. Then when Toronto comes, I'll put out some Blue Jay guys. Admittedly, there's not too many Blue Jay stars to choose from, but for those people who ask for players that are playing against the Red Sox, I try to have a little variety.

For the most part, people are just looking for cards – particularly Red Sox team sets – as souvenirs. I have some customers who've been there all fourteen years, but most of the business is the casual kid or adult who is looking for a card of a favorite player or a team set, as a souvenir of the game.

I am usually there after the game, too. Obviously, the better business is prior to. It's not so much the shorter period of time after the game as the daylight. You can sell more cards in daylight than in darkness. It varies a little bit on the afternoon games.

What do I during the games? Watch paint dry! I mean, there's nothing to do! You can't go in and watch the game. It's literally just standing around and talking to the other vendors. Nick has determined that peanuts don't sell to the out crowd. Cards do, adequately anyway. I don't bring a radio, but if another vendor has one, I'll at least find out what inning it is, or what the score is.

After the game, and if I know that, say, Garciaparra just hit two grand slams, I'm calling his name out as much as possible. People are very funny. The same cards that I had of Garciaparra prior to the game, I've got after the game but people are prone to buy them because he's in their minds.

In the heyday of baseball cards, in the late 80s and early 90s, theft was a significant problem. Having two people handle things cuts that down. The way I set up, the single cards are in showcases under glass, but the packs of cards are out in the open, for people to touch and feel and pick up. Theft is clearly the number one problem.

Rain, that's my worst enemy. Almost all the other vendors can set up in the rain, but I can't. I can't sell cards in the rain.

KEITH DURHAM
Baseball Cap Vendor

I'm a wrestling coach and a public school teacher in special needs, in Boston.

The summer of '77 I sold hot dogs outside the park. It was just total bedlam over there. I can't say how many vendors were there. It was just as crazy as can be. It was the year before that great team the Sox had in '78. They were in it until the second to last day of the season. It was kind of a fun year.

I didn't do it for nine years. I was a legislative aide for City Council President Joe Tierney. I taught at the Department of Youth Services in Roslindale as well as the Hayden Goodwill Inn School in Dorchester. I was still coaching

wrestling at the time and some football as well. Then I went on to start my own silkscreening business in West Roxbury. It's funny. I just wasn't able to do it. I just didn't have the best managerial skills, handling money and everything.

I went back in '86. This guy from Venus Sportswear in Ipswich said to me, "Why don't you take some hats with you?" I said, "All right, I'll take 100 Red Sox caps." It was the day before the Yankees came in. I went over there with 72 hats. I sold them all! I couldn't believe it. I went over to West Roxbury, picked up the other 28 and sold the other 28 after the game.

I've been there in the Fenway area ever since.

I was substitute teaching at the time. After my last class, I drove up to Ipswich, got another hundred caps, came back and that was it. I paid two dollars a hat – this was back in 1986. I sold them for four dollars a hat, two for seven. It was fantastic. One weekend – it was when the Tigers came in – I sold a gross of hats each day. I bought a gross of hats on Saturday afternoon from the Twins [Twins Enterprises] and by Sunday morning, I had to buy another gross. It was just incredible. It has never been like that since. Financially, it was a special year – and it was as close as you can get to winning a World Championship. One strike away!

Keith Durham
PHOTO BY BILL NOWLIN

I've been a fan since 1964. I'm one of those Dan Shaughnessy types that went to the game with my father and grandfather. I fell in love with the Sox and I've gone to Fenway ever since. I grew up in Arlington. My family's from Charlestown and I live in South Boston now. It's special being a Red Sox fan.

I have sold T shirts a little bit. I sold sunglasses, but sold even less. Through my years, it's probably been 97 or 98 percent hats. After the Red Sox season, I'd gone over to the old Garden and sold after the game. I used to go down to Foxboro. During the World Series, I was in town selling them because it was just a hot item. I'm really just a Fenway guy now.

75% of my inventory throughout the year is just Red Sox hats, and of that 75%, probably 50% or better is the Red Sox blue hat.

I just love talking to people from other cities. The only ones who are unapproachable are the New Yorkers. The Mets fans are absolutely the worst. Yankees fans, they're obnoxious but they buy hats.

The Angels were always bad. The Angels, the Twins, the Royals – those are the teams which do worst. It's funny. Probably the best selling hat I've had over the last couple of years has been the Cardinals. Obviously when you get a new expansion team, that's pretty good, like when the Rockies and the Marlins came in. Nobody ever asks for Marlins, now – occasionally the Rockies. Diamondbacks, they're kind of popular. Tampa Bay, not so much.

These days I get the hats from two or three wholesalers. I deal with the Twins for years. I will buy Twins hats from other people as well. Sometimes it's just quicker than from the Twins.

I think just about all of us who buy hats, at some point have dealt with the Twins. Over the years, probably somewhere between fifty to eighty percent of our business has gone to the Twins either directly or indirectly.

They're not too interested in really cutting us a great deal because they've got their own stands on the street. Actually, the two guys that run the stands now are great guys. Pat and Brian [Smith], they're brothers. I don't know their last name. Their father, Jerry, is an usher in the park. They're just great kids. The people that are vendors, by and large, they're really nice people.

I would say it's pretty close to fifty/fifty with maybe the edge going to the out crowd. Definitely if the Red Sox win, and especially on a Sunday afternoon. This past Sunday when they lost after having that 5 to nothing lead, between the heat and blowing that lead, people were just so lethargic coming out. They were walking with their heads down. I can relate to that. When the Red Sox win, I'm the first one to put on Ted Sarandis or Johnson & Mustard after the game is over. When they lose, I listen to a classical station. I want nothing to do with it once they lose. I don't know – maybe it's a form of denial.

Day games are great because you've got the kids. Whenever the kids are there, you sell much more.

I've got some regulars that are just characters. This guy Dickie [Boynton] comes out from West Boylston. Dickie's 68 years old. He really is one of those people that lives for the Red Sox. I remember one time, "Christ's sake, Keith! Christ's sake! Christ's sake! Christ's sake, Keith, you won't guess what happened!" I said, "What happened?" "My car just caught on fire." I says, "Where?" He said, "Some place in Newton. I jumped the T. I just barely got here in time for the game." Dickie let his car burn, but he didn't want to miss the first pitch.

There's a guy, Herbie Keough from Dedham. Herbie's got a cane and he's got cerebral palsy. Herbie lives for sports. He comes down all the time for the games. He used to go to the Dedham High games. He knew Peter Gammons when Gammons was a high school baseball reporter.

Charlie Arkamando used to be a vendor over at the ballpark. He used to be good friends with Charlie Moss. Charlie would sell all sorts of trinkets and baseball caps and jewelry and things. In April of '97 he figured he'd go down and spend the winter in Fort Myers and catch the Sox in Spring training. He came out of the bar in Fort Myers and got wiped out by a truck.

Then there's this other guy Robbie. Robbie was a poor homeless type of guy. I think he lives with his family up in New Bedford now. He'd hang around the park all the time and if one of us had an errand to run, Robbie'd be around. There's a lot of those – I call them the characters of the park. There's this lady, Carole [Williams]. She lives in Belmont. She's in a wheelchair. She comes to quite a few games and she'll always come by and say hello.

When the Sox have lost a game or if they're in a bad losing streak, that's when people are most miserable. Or Friday night. The Friday night crowds are awful. They drive you crazy.

Usually it's something derogatory about the Sox or something derogatory about whatever you're selling. If the Sox are losing, they'll get down on you a little bit. Usually they'll come around the fourth inning – that means they got thrown out of the park for being unruly. Then they start giving you a bad time. That's when you can't have a thin skin. They'll come by and say, "How much are your hats?" You say, "Ten dollars" and they'll say, "I'll give you two dollars for it." "Sorry, sir, they're ten dollars." "I'll give you two." You just have to walk away.

When I got married for the second time, this past May 22, I worked the game before I got married. I worked the before crowd but I didn't work the after crowd. I got married around 5:30. I worked 'til about 1:30, rushed down to Southie, showered and shaved, and met up with my parents who were staying down the South Shore. I changed there and got married. What I would have loved to have done, I would have loved to get married here in Southie, rushed back and got the out crowd and then done the reception. We could have been the newlyweds, in our wedding clothes. It would have been a good gimmick.

The Tiger series back in '86 was the best one ever. I probably sold over 500 hats. My price is ten bucks these days.

Occasionally, I do go into a game. Lots of times friends will come by and if they've got an extra ticket, you'll go in and catch a couple of innings. One of the other vendors will watch the stand for you. There's something about being at Fenway. There isn't a time that I walk in there that I don't get excited.

There is a home run roar that you can tell. If you don't have a radio, you can run down into Who's On First and see it on three or four screens, and then you can run right back up. It takes about a minute.

What's interesting is the people. They'll come up to your stand from all over the country. Whether it's Wrigley or Fenway, they've kind of hit their baseball Mecca. That's their whole raison d'etre, their reason for being. To hit Fenway, to hit Wrigley. Once they've done it, it's almost like they've fulfilled their baseball dreams. A lot of the baseball tours end at Fenway Park.

Some of the people, they're shut-ins but they live for the Sox. I think baseball is more likely to embrace the shut-in. That's one of the reasons that FDR never stopped baseball during World War II, because he knew it was just too important to the morale of the country as well as people that were physically challenged. This was just a big part of their life. That's what made FDR so special. He saw life through the eyes of someone who was physically challenged and was much more sympathetic.

I always give out a couple of hats. I've got to give out at least two a game. Otherwise, I don't feel good.

MIKE RUTSTEIN
Publisher & Editor, BOSTON BASEBALL

Others work the streets before the games. A team of BOSTON BASEBALL hawkers and runners work the crowds, selling copies of the unauthorized fan magazine outside the park. Boston city police are present to maintain order and "meter maids" penalize those who ignore the parking laws. Travel agencies hire people to distribute flyers advertising travel packages to New York, Toronto or Baltimore for Sox away series. Scientologists hand out invitations to Dianetics workshops. Others advertise exotic dancers. For one stretch each summer, Boston firefighters park a fire truck alongside the park on Brookline Avenue and collect contributions to fight Muscular Dystrophy, urging passersby to throw money (or an extra ticket) into the fireman's boot they use as a collection box.

BOSTON BASEBALL describes itself as "the best selling publication on the Boston Red Sox." Despite going to glossy paper throughout with the May 2000 issue and raising its price to $2.00 an issue, the paper has remained a candid and critical voice, a contrast to the Red Sox in-house scorebook magazine which by its nature is a traditional ballclub publication. Mike Rutstein, publisher *and editor of BOSTON BASEBALL, would probably have liked nothing more than to devote his prodigious energies to working for the Red Sox, but conflict with the team seems to have soured that possibility.*

I'm a third generation Red Sox fan. My dad's father and mother were big Red Sox fans. She had Alzheimer's and couldn't even remember my dad's name or my name. To make a connection with her, my dad would run down the lineup of the 1946 Red Sox. He would say, "Johnny...." and she would say "Pesky." It was one of the only things they could still talk about when her memory was completely gone. It's a sad story but it shows you the depths of involvement with the Red Sox in our family.

My father's father, who I never met because he died when my dad was a teenager, used to take my dad into games at Fenway. He apparently was a smoothie. I wouldn't call him a bootlegger, but he did sell liquor during Prohibition. He didn't make as much money as the Kennedys but through his liquor sales, he was on good terms with several people in the Red Sox front office. He used to be able to get in for nothing. He took my dad into the clubhouse after they lost a game in the '46 Series to St. Louis. The liquor salesmen were going in and coming out. My dad said it probably would have been better not having been there. Everyone was very surly.

My parents took me to a game when I was about six. I remember the CITGO sign made a huge impression on me. If you got bored with the game, you could just watch the lights go in and out...that was before they renovated it. It had some missing bars, some missing neon but I thought that and the scoreboard were fascinating.

Then we moved out to California and as I grew up, I was loyal to the Boston teams. I was a Yaz guy and if we visited relatives in Massachusetts, I'd get a new Red Sox hat. My aunt had wonderful season tickets for many years, four rows up from the Red Sox dugout. She used to take me whenever I was in town.

We moved back to Sudbury and my folks still live there.

A friend of the family had given me the 1967 IMPOSSIBLE DREAM album which I played religiously all through my childhood, even before I really understood all of it. It's great. Even now, even though I haven't listened to it in fifteen years, I know the whole thing by heart – forty minutes! It's wonderful. I strongly recommend it. It's beyond corny now, in this day and age, but me and my friends used to act it out. They would be describing a catch and we would act it out in my room – you know, LEAP across the room and land on the bed with your glove stretched all the way out.

I'm the biggest fan. My father and I still go to games together. We went to Fantasy Camp a couple of years ago.

I did not have a journalism background at all, but I was the editor of my high school newspaper. I wrote basically everything that was in it. I went to Penn, an English major there. But I was excited to get back to Boston. I always liked to score, but the program that the Red Sox sold back then – it was $1.75; it later went up to $2.00 – there were only three editions in a year. All through April and May, you were buying the same magazine. Two dollars was a lot of money then, and the scorecard was terrible. It's on that glossy paper, so you have to use a pen. You can't make any mistakes because you're using a pen. And because they're trying to fit the beer ads on the bottom of the page, the boxes in which to score are very, very small.

It dawned on me that if someone came out with a magazine that had a good scorecard and maybe some good minor league information and information about visiting teams, that would be something that people would buy.

I sent my resume to the Red Sox when I got out of grad school, you know, just kind of on a lark. They never even got back to me. I decided, maybe if I did something like this and showed the Red Sox how they're missing the boat, I could get their attention and we could do something together. This is 1990. I was 25.

My dad loaned me money and I bought the computer and some desktop publishing software.

I started fooling around and then by Opening Day, there I was. It was a twelve page newsletter. It was called BASEBALL UNDERGROUND then. I have a copy of it in my office. It says "Rookie Newsletter Steps Up To Plate."

Believe it or not, I've seen them for sale at card shows. Five or six years ago, I saw one in a bin for ten dollars. I laughed. Then I thought about buying it because I don't have that many first editions!

The first issue we printed up 2400 of them and just handed them out. With the second issue, we started charging a dollar. The whole business was started for less than ten thousand.

I think we had ten issues the first year. Every issue sold more. That was really encouraging. I think we only sold a total of about 16,000 magazines that first year, but we had definitely gotten to where people were interested in the publication and were looking for it.

Over the first two years, I would occasionally send them copies of the magazine, and...nothing. Just completely stonewalled. The first meeting I had with them really was kind of negative.

By the summer of '92, we were selling a couple of thousand a game. The magazine had grown from 16,000 the first year to something like 40,000 the second year. The third year, it tripled. We were on the pace to sell 120,000, 130,000 magazines. At that point, we were beginning to be felt in sales of the Red Sox official product. So, the Red Sox said, well, this is an annoyance. At that point, I would have been so flattered to have been invited into the Red Sox organization – if they had said "we want to work together" or "maybe we can give you some credentials in exchange for a share of whatever you're taking in outside the ballpark". But what the Red Sox chose to do, being the Red Sox, was that they went to their buddies at City Hall and they said, "Look, get rid of this kid." You know, "Scare him off."

One day in the summer of '92, Richie Iannella – who was then the code enforcement director for the City of Boston, and later a City Councilor (in fact, planning his run for City Council at the time, which kinds of figures into the story) – shows up at the ball-park, plainclothes, walking around, telling my hawkers that their magazines are going to be confiscated, they're going to have criminal records, and that they should clear out while the clearing is good.

I hadn't just gone out and started selling the newsletter. I had gone to the Boston Police and said, "This is what I'm going to do" and they said, "OK by us." I had gone down to Ashburton Street and said, "This is what I'm going to do. Do I need a license?" and they said, "No, because you're selling a periodical publication on public streets." I said, "Great. That's all I needed to hear."

So Richie Iannella came down and told us all these things. I called my mother, who happens to be a lawyer, luckily for me. She said, "Stay the course, this guy obviously has no idea what the relevant laws are. He's just blowing smoke and trying to scare you. Publish your next issue, and keep going out there."

[The city of Boston filed a criminal complaint in Housing Court for vending on public property without a license, but Kevin Cullen of the BOSTON GLOBE heard of the issue and wrote a story, "Sox Look to City to Settle Score" which in turn prompted coverage in other publications and on local radio. Iannella quickly dropped the case and the issue went away.]

Then in 1993, they dropped the price of their program to a buck. We get more great media attention. The price of something in the ballpark had gone down! When had that ever happened? That may have been a singular moment in the entire history of the Red Sox franchise, possibly in the history of all of major league baseball – that something inside the ballpark went down. Not a nickel, not a quarter, but fifty percent! So we declared victory.

For the next couple of years, we had to compete with them at the same price point. Which was great, because I think that that finally

Mike Rutstein
PHOTO BY BILL NOWLIN

showed the Red Sox that the price wasn't important, that their product really was not very good. They began to try and make it better, with fold-out posters and stuff like that. They copied a couple of our innovations. We had begun putting stat inserts into the magazine, with up to date statistics. They started doing that, too. We continued to sell more and more magazines all the time.

The maximum crew we like to put out there is about fourteen guys. Twelve guys selling, and two guys running. The runners just bring magazines out so the guys never need to leave their spots. They get paid depending on how many magazines they sell that night, so they have incentive to make sure that the magazines get out there in a timely fashion. Everybody at BOSTON BASEBALL is on commission. They make thirteen cents out of the dollar.

We are the best selling publication on the Red Sox, by a wide margin. The Red Sox don't want to draw attention to the fact that – probably alone among all major league teams – they're being outsold at their own ballpark. My guess is that we have anywhere from 60% to 2/3 of the market.

We've made an effort to address their advertisers saying, "Why are you paying twice as much for half the circulation?" They want to be associated with the Red Sox and enjoy the kind of perks that the Red Sox can give them, that we just can't match.

Every other team in major league baseball is at three or four or five dollars. In the American League East, I don't believe there's any team that's under five dollars now. If the Red Sox would be at five bucks and instead they're at two bucks, everyone who buys a program – even theirs – has saved three bucks. We have saved Red Sox fans millions of dollars. Even if they've never bought our magazine, we're still saving them millions of dollars.

The truck drops off the magazines at VIP Parking, the whole month's worth. Sometimes the printer's not able to print up everything that we need. We'll need 40,000 magazines but they might not be able to bind all the magazines by the time the first game rolls around.

For a night game, I'll show up as early as noon or as late as 4:30 depending on who's in town, what day of the week it is and how much work there is to do. I'm there a minimum of three or four hours. An average day might be more like five hours. I've got to drive into town, go to Sir Speedy which does all the insert printing for us and pick up the inserts, take them to the ballpark and get all the guys organized. Usually it's 85 degrees, we buy a bunch of Powerades, and then sit there drinking Powerades, chatting and listening to the radio and getting the stuff ready. You can do ten boxes an hour, but that's only 1200 programs. For the beginning of the Yankees series, when we think we might sell 10,000 magazines that weekend, that's a lot of hours to stuff. Me and Hai and Lemon all going at top speed might stuff 25 or 30 boxes an hour and that's still only 3600 magazines. The goal is to get as many of them done on the first day of the homestand and then Saturday we can then just show up around 10 o'clock and stuff for an hour, and then go out at 11.

If it's a 7 o'clock game, the guys are usually out there selling until 7:15 and then they come in. Some guys like to stay out a little longer to try and pick up a couple of extra bucks with the late arriving crowd. Everybody's in by 7:30 or 7:45, and with any luck all the programs and all the money is accounted for by 8 o'clock. I'll hit the road and listen to Joe and Jerry on the way home.

There have been overtures from the Red Sox. I think there was an interest on their part to find out who I was, what my plans were, where I was going with BOSTON BASEBALL and if there was any possibility that we could work together. We had many chats in a non-specific way. When the chats started to get specific, that's when talks started to break down. It's difficult to figure out, at the end of the day, how serious they really were or whether they were just seeing maybe this was a problem that could be easily dealt with.

In 1991, if they had offered me a job in their public relations department, that would have excited me a great deal. Now it's 1999 and that's not what I'm looking for.

There are people that are concerned about working with us because they're concerned that they're going to get a black mark against their name with the Red Sox. I know of people who have been given a hard time, but the Red Sox are very selective about who they give a hard time to. Some people are above that. Rico [Petrocelli] is one example – he really doesn't care – and Jerry [Remy] is another.

Jerry works for NESN and NESN is partially owned by the Red Sox. It all depends on how beholden Jerry feels to the Red Sox, and how picayune they're willing to get. How petty would you have to be, to say, "Jerry, we don't want you giving interviews to BOSTON BASEBALL any more." They could do that, and in certain senses they have done it but they tend not to pick on the Jerry Remys.

Over ten years, I probably have missed only a dozen games. I read a great quote the other day. It said, "Find a job that you love and you'll never have to work a day in your life again."

RYAN GOLDNEY
BOSTON BASEBALL *Hawker*

Everybody down at Fenway calls me Nomar. Even my family and friends, 'cause they say I look just like him.

We're hawkers. We don't get paid on the hour. If you just stand there and don't put any effort or time into it, you're not going to make any money. I started from the bottom and worked my way up and now I'm the best seller in the company. I sold close to 8000 magazines last homestand.

Certain gates are better than other gates. When you're a rookie, you're not going to come right in and get gates that veterans have who have been there longer. I proved to Mike the first year that I can sell. He'll put you where he thinks you'll do best, but if you're a good seller, you can sell anywhere.

When I first started, Gate A was the best gate and the bridge wasn't. The bridge record

was 536 magazines. No one really did more than that. I went up there against the Atlanta Braves and I did 811 magazines. Everybody was just in shock and in awe: "Oh, my God!" Ever since then, the bridge has been like the best gate to sell magazines.

I was 19 when I started, three years ago. I wish I'd started earlier.

Say we have a 7 o'clock game, we go out at 5 and I get there at 4:30. I get my apron, my magazines ready. You know the Short Stop store on Brookline Avenue? That little garage there, VIP, is where we work out of. Everybody gets there about half an hour early and just talks baseball. Everything's ready there, all the magazines. It's a nice little get-up we got in there. It's fun.

A lot of people show up only on the weekends. That's OK, but if you show up in the middle of the week, Monday through Friday, that says to the boss that you're dedicated, you're dependable and he's going to give you good gates. It's usually the guys in the middle of the week that are out there making money and selling magazines for the company.

I stay out until 8 o'clock for a 7 o'clock game. You have a lot of late people who come. The flow of crowd comes to at least 7:30. Then I stay out there for another half hour.

A lot of people give me free tickets. They'll say, "I'll give you a free ticket for a program." Most of the time I'll say, "Why not?" I'll tell my boss. It's only a dollar. I'll put up the dollar and he'll say, "Fine."

People don't really give me a hard time. There's one guy, though, that I can't stand. He says, "Why are you saying it's cheaper outside? They don't sell it inside!" I say, "That's right. They don't. We sell it out here for one dollar. It's two dollars inside and you gotta pay for a pencil. You get a free pencil from us, a scorecard, a program. It's only a dollar."

Ryan Goldney
PHOTO BY EMMET NOWLIN

Gate B, down in right field, is the best gate for people to talk baseball. That's one of my favorite gates. I love going down there. You get tourists, you get people from out of town. You sit down there and sell them the magazines. I'm the only hawker, so they've got to buy off me. We talk baseball after I'm done selling.

We have two runners. One we call Lemon, his hair's yellow – and the other's name is Hai. Hai is Vietnamese. These are the two best runners. These two guys are always on point. If I run out, they're there to give me more magazines. They're always on the run. They have two-wheelers, both of them, and they run around the ballpark all day, seeing if we need more magazines.

Hai Ho Nguyen
PHOTO BY EMMET NOWLIN

HAI HO NGUYEN
BOSTON BASEBALL
Runner

I was 12 years old and I started collecting baseball cards and getting autographs.

My family comes from Vietnam. I was born in '78. We were boat people.

My father was a general in the military. If he had stayed in Vietnam, he would have either gotten killed or he would have been in prison, so he took the shot of escaping from Vietnam.

We landed in The Philippines and lived there for two years. It was really hectic, a resettlement camp. My parents said, "Anywhere." Boston was just a random selection.

The first time I ever heard of baseball was here. We saw it on television. My parents didn't like me coming out here on the streets late at night and coming home at 1 o'clock from getting Frank Thomas or Ken Griffey Jr's autograph.

It was easier to get the Red Sox players back then. You could see through the gate and stick your hand through. Now it's heavy plastic.

There are some players that are super nice, about ten percent of them. The rest are assholes. Frank Thomas is a really good guy. Ken Griffey Jr. is an asshole. Griffey grew up rich, because Griffey Sr. was a baseball player and had lots of money. Frank Thomas grew up in the 'hood. He knows how the kids are, wanting autographs. Frank Thomas gives the benefit of the doubt and don't care because what's the name to him? It takes him five minutes to write his name for a lot of kids. Even if people sell them, still. Five minutes out of your day.

I started off working for BOSTON BASEBALL about four or five years ago, by meeting Lemon. He's the other best runner of this company. I met him doing the autograph thing. We were chasing players every single day, every single night. That's how we become friends. Lemon had this friend from Southie. He found out how to work for BOSTON BASEBALL.

I have people out there that offer me more than Mike's been paying me, but I still like Mike and I still like BOSTON BASEBALL enough that I prefer to be here. People have been offering me either selling sausages over there or selling baseball cards and souvenirs inside the Twins. I could be a scalper. I know all the scalpers over there. I know the head scalper.

I like running. It's fast paced. You can see everybody and you can say "Hi" to people. I get a penny a book after they sell the first batch. On average, we usually go home with about twenty dollars for two hours, which is good. You can make an extra twenty bucks before the game, stuffing [inserts into the magazines.]

By the fourth inning, we don't get much sales. I come back here then. I neaten up the place. I help the guys count out the money. Oh, my God! I have never seen money in my life before I see these companies. Mike needs to buy a rake, a gold rake or something to rake all this money in. These guys come home with thousands of dollars.

It really is amazing how all these guys work. Some of these guys can't think. They're kind of slow, and when they come back they're a little tired. I still think runners should be more tired than sellers because all they do is just scream and stand in one place. Runners have been running around with whole boxes for two hours, so I would think we would be more tired, but we have the brains, I guess. Sometimes I go down to the game, but I've been down only three or four times this year.

I like to follow the Red Sox on TV when they're out of town. Most of the time when I finish working here, like on a seven game series, I'm really tired.

I was selling last night for the vendors. I started doing that this year, selling souvenirs after the game. Last night I worked for Patrick Smith. This year the Red Sox have been so hot that he can't keep up with the supplies.

The top of the seventh inning I go over there and get dressed up. Actually I'm kind of like a model, advertising baseball caps, T-shirts of Nomar, things like that. In the eighth inning, I start selling. Whatever I sell, I just give to the Twins at the end and I get a commission. Ten dollars is the least you can get, and then it goes up from there.

Twins is a multi-million dollar company. Actually, Arthur D'Angelo, the owner of the company, came over and asked me to work for him. I was running around the park and Arthur D'Angelo walked over and asked, "Can you work for me?" I was shocked. A man who has a billion dollars like that, I couldn't believe that he actually walked over and talked to me. He is a very modest guy. I told him that after I worked for Mike through the end of the regular season, yes, I would do it. I wouldn't screw Mike over for any money in the whole world.

I'm trying to write a movie type of story, about the dark sides of our lives. Stories that only the runners and people would actually know, like when Lemon got robbed. Some black guys put a shotgun to his head, for thirty six dollars.

Ryan, he sold 7000 magazines – three times! Never been done before. This guy is a selling maniac. I think he has this drive to be the best. But I think most of all, he just wanted the money. It's very competitive. The more competitive you are in this company, the better gates you get. If you're at a good gate, you make the best money.

TONY LUPO
Hurdy Gurdy Man

The Red Sox decided to join in the festivities in 1999, and on certain occasions such as Opening Day and the two Kids Opening Days, they have entertainers to liven the atmosphere and add to the "Friendly Fenway" experience. What was already a carnival-like atmosphere became much more so with the addition of clowns, jugglers, musicians and even a hurdy gurdy man.

The Hot Tamale Brass Band kicked off the 1999 season playing outside Gate A on Opening Day and for the first night game of the year. Joining the band were a number of street performers, such as a man on stilts, a juggler and Tony Lupo the monkeygrinder, whose his pet monkey did tricks with a baseball while wearing a Red Sox helmet.

I was there Opening Day and Children's Opening Day. I also did Fan's Day a couple of times.

The Red Sox hired me. I think this was the first time they've actually had anything like that, entertainment at the park for Opening Day. I've been a part of the entertainment scene in Boston for twenty years now, so I think they just thought it would be appropriate to have me as part of the event. Billy Bedard was there; he was the stilt walker. Spunky the Clown was there. Joe Howard. Curly the Clown.

I've been doing this for twenty years. This is full time for me. I go everywhere – I do festivals, fairs, private engagements, corporate events

Tony Lupo
PHOTO BY BILL NOWLIN

Mickey Bones
PHOTO BY BILL NOWLIN

in Boston. I do everything. You name it, I do it.

The monkey is a Capucin. The traditional organ grinder monkey. Her name is Coco. She's my oldest monkey. She's 18, so I've had her almost since the beginning.

She plays the shell game, plays catch, shoots a basketball, plays the piano, the maracas, a tambourine, the guitar, the cymbals. She wore a Red Sox cap at Fenway Park, but I just got her a Patriots helmet and she's catching a football now. I try to keep to the sports that pertain to Boston, to New England.

I've been on David Letterman, Saturday Night Live, the Today show.

I'm the only hurdy gurdy man in my family, the only one in New England, in fact. As a young child, I can remember going to the North End of Boston and to what's now called Downtown Crossing and seeing them. Very few people continue the tradition. I think there's only six of us in the country now.

I think finally, after twenty years I can say that I've achieved my goal. What I've tried to do is to take the image of the organ grinder, which at one point in history became very shady, and revert it back to its original lustre, which was to be an entertainer. They originally brought the monkeys over, had them do shows in order to provoke people to pass a coin to the monkey, but over the years so many different guys got in it – unskilled – and just had the monkeys trained to take coins. It kind of destroyed the vision.

At some point in the show, I'll often demonstrate how the old-fashioned monkeys were trained to take a coin, place it in the cup or pocket and tip their hat. She's trained in the same skills, in the same traditional way, because of the historical value of it. Coco, of course, has been updated a little. I have her take the coin, put it in her pocket or her cup, tip her hat, slap

me five, give me a high five and then give me a kiss. I kind of enhanced it a little bit.

The Red Sox don't really need people like me outside the door. The team itself and the park are enough of a draw. I commend the Red Sox for doing something like this. It just enhances the flavor of the park.

I'll tell you, there's very few things that I consider pinnacle points of my career and being at Fenway Park for Opening Day is among the most precious moments that I've had.

MICKEY BONES
Bandleader, Hot Tamale Brass Band

We did Opening Day and then the first night game. I was opening up for G. Love over at the Paradise and I talked to this guy backstage. He remembered me like from three or more years ago. I guess I was probably smoking a joint with him backstage or something like that and he remembered me. This guy named Tim McKenna. He called me several times setting it up for me to talk with Marcita.

They paid us $800 a day. It's certainly not the most we've ever been paid, but it's very high visibility, lots of press – especially for the playoffs. We were on TV all over the place! If it was free, I would have done it!

We showed up for Saturday's 4 o'clock game – we started at 2:30 – no sound check – pretty much the minute they opened the gates, that's when we'd start.

We played the same stuff we always do. We play some songs where we could interject – we have a lot of songs that we sing in unison – New Orleans brass band style – so we'll pick a little phrase like "Red Sox are gonna win! Red Sox are gonna win!" Something like that, with some chanting and yelling that we like to call singing.

I love playing on the street, eye to eye with people. That's the best. For some reason, on stage, there's this barrier that comes up. To me, that's my favorite, being in the crowd.

I liked playing at Fenway Park. That's one of those gigs that'll go with me to my grave. I'd love to do it next year. We had people dancing out there and everything. The second and third day we went out on the field for twenty minutes; we just followed Wally around wherever he went. We just followed him; we even made up a little Wally song for him.

I saw Wally naked! No, I'm just kidding. I asked Marianne [Comeau] who Wally really was and she said it's top secret. We were asking her if it was a woman, was she wearing any clothes underneath....I didn't get any information. We talked about getting our picture with him, and it was, "No." They were afraid we'd use it for pro-motional purposes – which we would, of course!

They were very nice about it. I'd say that "Friendly Fenway" is the way to go. I have no idea if they're as friendly to everybody. Usually – you know the corporate world – somebody that's in charge of putting on a private party, I'd

say 60% of the time they're total assholes. But the Red Sox people were very nice.

It was a great experience. It was beautiful. Everyone was being nice. Nothing was thrown at us. No loud, scary language. For people all pumped up, it was pretty comfortable.

The pizza guy across the street, though, kept trying to bribe us with free pizza if we'd move down the street. "You're killing my business!" he said. We would have loved to move for some free pizzas, but it was just so crowded and we wanted to be right where they told us to be.

Chris [Poteet] was out there selling T-shirts. He got busted by the Boston Police. They didn't take him in. They just took all his stuff. He was going around saying, "Yeah! Friendly Fenway! Right!"

Fenway family:

Nick Jacobs' family has been selling peanuts at Fenway for 3 generations: "The cart I have now is about 4 or 5 years old, but I still have the original cart my father had. Now, my grandfather's cart, I used parts off that to build the cart that I use now."

George Jacobs, Nick Jacobs' father
PHOTO COURTESY OF NICK JACOBS

Peter Davis, Nick Jacobs' grandfather
PHOTO COURTESY OF NICK JACOBS

George, the peanut man
PHOTO COURTESY OF NICK JACOBS

4 RED SOX ADMINISTRATION: MAKING IT ALL POSSIBLE

Dick Bresciani, Vice President of Public Affairs

Larry Cancro, Vice President, Sales and Marketing

Michele Julian, Director of Human Resources and Office Administration

Kent Qualls, Director of Player Development

Marci Blacker, Baseball Administration Coordinator

Tom Moore, Assistant Scouting Director

Billy Broadbent, Video/Advance Scouting Coordinator

Al Green, Customer Service

Paul Lazarovitch, Fenway Park Tour Guide

Marianne Comeau, Community Relations Intern

Sam Zoob, Human Resources Intern

Ron Burton, Community Relations Manager

Debbie Matson, Director of Publications

Jack Maley, Team Photographer

Rick Dunfey, Publisher, Red Sox Yearbook

Kevin Shea, Director of Communications and Baseball Information

Kate Gordon, Communications Credentials Coordinator

Glenn Wilburn, Baseball Information Coordinator

Guy Spina, Press Steward

Mary Rodrigues, Manager of Staff Dining Room

Like any business, the Red Sox have developed an organizational structure to achieve their goals. This requires hiring good people of varied business capabilities to run the club, as well as finding talented ballplayers, manager, coaches and staff. For decades, Tom Yawkey ran the club more as a sportsman than a businessman and surrounded himself with a management team he enjoyed — congeniality and even conviviality were highly valued traits. Since his passing, and increasingly following the death of Jean Yawkey, more professional management has been hired, and management has evolved more in line with contemporary business practice. Today a businesslike corps of dedicated professionals looks after the team's development.

There are veterans in top management. Ed Kenney, as noted, was a third generation Red Sox employee. Dick Bresciani, the Vice President for Public Affairs, has been a valued leader since 1972. Larry Cancro has been with the Red Sox since 1985 and has played as important a role as anyone in shaping the new direction and image of the Red Sox. The real transformation of the Red Sox as a modern organization has largely been on John Harrington's watch, and fans have found a much more consistently competitive club on the field since Harrington assumed primacy, supplanting the squabbling among executives which had characterized some of the years after Tom Yawkey's death. Respected throughout major league baseball, as witness his appointment to the more important committees in MLB, Harrington's decision to bring Dan Duquette in as General Manager was probably his greatest contribution to Red Sox success on the field of play in recent years, even though Duquette was never a popular figure.

Clearly, the hiring of upper management is done at the highest of levels. The Red Sox have grown as an organization over the years and the front office staff is much larger than it was even ten years ago. The club has a professional in charge of human resources, Michele Julian. Though she has been with the team for only a short time, the very creation of a position of this responsibility exemplifies both the growth and the rationalization of today's occupational structure. It's her job to populate the offices with the best employees for the job. This means hiring based on resumes and not on who you know.

The scouting department is charged with finding and signing up the best players, and then getting the most out of these players. The minor league office works to develop players within the system. Major league scouting is much more international in scope and increasingly takes full advantage of computer and video technology. Kent Qualls, Tom Moore, and Billy Broadbent each offer perspectives on these realms.

For over sixty years, the first voice of the Red Sox was that of Helen Robinson, with the team as switchboard operator since 1941. "Red Sox" she answered, taking each call personally and routing them to the proper recipient, no doubt covering at times (as any good receptionist must) for those looking to avoid certain calls. It's been suggested in jest that she was the one who really called the shots, with John Harrington and others yielding to her. There may be an element of truth in this, on some matters of office management.

Befitting this discreet elder stateswoman, Helen Robinson is one of a very few persons contacted for this project who declined to be interviewed.

I wanted to interview Wally, the Red Sox mascot, but Wally does not give interviews, either.

Also dealing directly with the public is Al Green, who runs the customer service booth located under the grandstand behind home plate.

Interacting with the public on a regular basis are the guides who give tours of Fenway Park and various interns. Paul Lazarovitch has conducted tours for several years now. Marianne Comeau and Sam Zoob both worked at Fenway as interns.

Ron Burton is the Community Relations Manager for the Boston Red Sox. His charge is to interact with the public and to foster good relations throughout communities across New England.

The Red Sox also proffer a number of publications for the public, from monthly editions of the official scorebook magazine to the annual Red Sox yearbook and the Media Guide. Debbie Matson and Dick Bresciani are both involved with publications.

Dealing directly with the media is something else, of course. Kevin Shea, Kate Gordon and Glenn Wilburn each offer comments on the work they do in support of those who Ted Williams dubbed the "knights of the keyboard" and their broadcast counterparts.

Sustenance is provided to both media & Red Sox staff: Guy Spina, the press steward and Mary Rodrigues, the manager of the staff dining room, each discuss their work.

DICK BRESCIANI
Vice President of Public Affairs

I grew up in central Massachusetts, the little town of Hopedale. I grew up watching the Red Sox and the Braves both. My dream was to play baseball, but once I got into college, reality set in. I decided to get into sports some other way so I became involved in a lot of things, sports editor of the college paper, broadcasting games on the college station. When I graduated I was offered a job in the athletic department.

I was there for eleven years. I did a lot of work with the baseball team and one of my duties was to travel with the team in the spring. My contract with U. Mass gave me the three summer months free. For seven summers, I was head of PR for the Cape Cod League. That helped me meet a lot of people and work in a great atmosphere of amateur baseball. Eventually I decided I was going into professional baseball. I contacted a lot of teams and got a lot of rejections, including the Red Sox. I knew Bill Crowley, the PR director and he just told me, "Keep in touch."

Come May of '72, Bill called and told me, "My assistant is being interviewed by the Milwaukee Brewers. If Arthur [Keefe] goes to Milwaukee, could you be here Saturday?" I said, "I'm there."

Arthur got the job with the Brewers and, ironically, we had a Memorial Day weekend series with Milwaukee. When they left town, he went with Milwaukee and I went with the Red Sox. I worked with Bill until he retired after the '81 season.

When I came here in '72, there was Bill and [secretary] Mary Jane Ryan and myself. No marketing, no broadcasting, no community relations, no promotions – none of that. The feeling was that if you won games, you drew a million and that was what the teams needed to be successful.

By the end of the 70's, other sports grew in stature and popularity. Baseball had to start addressing this situation. They had to get radio/TV contracts to bring in money. That's how these other areas started to develop here at the Red Sox.

A few years ago, we became the Public Affairs Department. A separate Baseball Information Department was set up to deal with the team and the General Manager. They also handle credentials and the press box area. We handle publications and pictures, archives and history, the Red Sox Hall of Fame. Community Relations and Customer Relations moved to our department. We started the Red Sox alumni group. We do all the publicity and media work for Marketing.

In the off-season you work normal hours, but once you begin playing games, everything revolves around the team. When the team's away, you're still kind of 9 to 5 – but once the team comes home, I come in between 9:30 and 10, but I'm here to the end of the game.

During the game, I float. I usually go up in the press box and talk to the media. I know the people on the opposing teams and I spend a few minutes with them. A lot of times I'm in with John Harrington, or in our executive box – kind of our headquarters during a game. Or I might be in the office. I float between those three or four areas. I want to be accessible during the game.

We started the Red Sox alumni group a few years ago. We have about 55 people primarily in New England, former Red Sox players, managers and coaches. Joe Morgan, Dick Radatz, Jim Lonborg, Walter Hriniak, Richie Gedman, Jerry Remy, John Kennedy, Walter Dropo, Dom DiMaggio, Johnny Pesky – a good group of guys. They've helped us a lot. We're fortunate that it's easy for them to help us with some of these community projects.

Larry got "Friendly Fenway" going in the marketing department, and we all kind of embraced that. It's caught on.

Debbie Matson is in charge of publications and photography. There's a variety of internal things that she works on. The magazine and the media guide are the two prime publications. The yearbook has been done outside, but we still assist them. There are six editions of the magazine, and she's in charge of subscriptions and sales.

Ron Burton's job has expanded tremendously in the last few years. The misconception was out there that the Red Sox help the Jimmy Fund and that was it. We're helping all kinds of people. He's constantly meeting with neighborhood groups. We get loads of letters and calls, so his intern has to go through and help him with weeding out. With an intern helping, he has time to work on the rookie league, the hospitals and all our major programs. He's also been instrumental in helping us with the new ballpark project.

Lou Gorman has been invaluable as a consultant. Lou is the overall coordinator of our Red Sox Hall of Fame that we started in '95. Lou's involved in making sure the money's going to the right charity, organizing the people who sell the tickets to bring in the money. Lou is a big name and a very personable guy. He'll assist us with groups and companies; he does a lot of appearances for us.

Helen Robinson...and the kinds of calls that come in sometimes...some of them are very nice. Some of them are very difficult, especially if the team isn't doing well. If there's a problem, they're all yelling at her. She does a great job. She knows everybody in baseball and she knows what to do with the calls. When there's a game, she's here for an hour after. She doesn't close the switchboard until the visiting team leaves. She's so dedicated. At one point, we had her taking a little time off, but she keeps saying, "What else am I going to do?" We can't keep her away! And she really knows what she's doing. She's seen it all. When she first came here, there were probably eight people in the front office, and the old plug-in switchboards. She's seen the whole growth. She knows people all over baseball, owners and everyone. When they come to town, they all come say hello to her or send her flowers. She's a real legend in the game.

What I enjoy most, is when the team is successful. That's what we're all here for. This team has been competitive for over thirty years. A lot of teams, in their hearts they know they have no

chance. Whereas here, in our off-season meetings, we always talk about, "We're going to win it. We're going to be competitive. We're aiming for the top." Every year, we're aiming for the World Series. That gives you a rebirth every year. That keeps you excited. That's the great thing about this organization.

When you're an extremely popular franchise in a highly competitive media market, you have a lot of people who want access. You can't accommodate everybody. We help many people, but it's not 100%, and sometimes people get upset. It's like autographs. A guy signs maybe three hundred autographs and then he finally has to leave to get ready for the game, and five hundred people are mad that he didn't sign for them. You can't please everybody.

I really felt fortunate that I was able to be associated with Mr. and Mrs. Yawkey. Luckily, I had four years with Tom before he passed away. It was such a terrific thing to come into this organization and see how he treated everybody, no matter who they were. He was just down to earth, no matter what job you had in the organization. He'd go down to the clubhouse, but he wasn't talking strategies, he'd be talking about families and what they did in the off-season, things like that. He liked to know them personally. He wasn't down there to interfere. He was in there as a friend to those guys. He saw them as part of his family.

In 2003, Dick Bresciani became Vice President/Publications and Archives.

LARRY CANCRO
Vice President Sales & Marketing

Larry Cancro grew up as both a Red Sox and a Yankees fan.

I grew up in New York, Westchester County. My two favorite teams were the Yankees and the Red Sox, because they both had tradition and old, classic ballparks. Neither one of them was ever good at the same time, the years I grew up. In '67 the Yankees were horrible. In '75 the

Yankees were horrible. In '76 the Red Sox weren't so good. It was '78, when I was already a professional in baseball, that they finally had a good year at the same time.

I loved sports growing up. Baseball by far was my favorite, and still is. I wanted to be a ballplayer, but I wasn't a very good athlete. I wanted to be marketing a baseball team before that job existed in baseball.

I used to check the boxscores. I always checked the attendance. I wondered why it wasn't more, why yesterday was higher than the day before. In a way, I was preparing for this job my whole life, but it wasn't a job that existed in my youth or even in my college days. When I went to the placement office, they'd say, "That isn't really a job." I'd say, "Well, that's what I want to do." Oddly enough, I ended up doing it.

Larry Cancro
PHOTO BY ANDREA RAYNOR

I started in Boston University, applying for jobs in baseball and sports and got nowhere. When I went to graduate school, I found out St. John's in New York had an athletic administration program. I asked if there was any way to combine my degree with that discipline and was told, "No, ours is strictly undergraduate, but I have an internship if you want to go interview." So I did and ended up getting a job with the Jersey Indians, a double A team for Oakland. We had Rickey Henderson on the team. John Kennedy, our former utility shortstop, was the manager. That's where I got my start.

That year I got a job with the Atlanta Braves. I was there for six years. One of the things I did there was start the first sports catalog merchandise program. Apparel and caps, souvenirs, the whole bit. It went very, very well and I gained some notoriety and then the Red Sox came to me – after years of me applying –

and asked if I would be interested in heading their marketing department.

I began as Director of Marketing. For the most part, other than a title change and a few additional responsibilities, it's been more or less the same job the whole time I've been here.

The department was really in its infancy. The Red Sox were more resistant to these ideas than most teams. I had been with a team that had struggled and tried a lot of things so I had a different perspective. In fact, I think a lot of people were kind of horrified by me at first. I'm not a wild promoter. I'm not a Bill Veeck, but I realize you have to do more than nothing.

I think we're good at what we do. If you look at the attendance numbers, since '86 we've never drawn below two million people. I'm real proud of that. Prior to my arrival, we only drew two million on three occasions. I think that the strategies we use now keep us on solid ground.

I have the biggest department here. Twenty-two full time people and the whole organization's 60 or 65.

We do all our advertising in-house. We do our creative in-house. We write our ads. We don't produce them, obviously, but we do the concepts in-house. We sell all the advertisements in the ballpark and in the scorebook. We create the ads, the brochures. Everything in-house.

The Coke bottles [mounted on the Green Monster] worked out well. It brought in a lot of money and it prevented us from having to go up even more on ticket prices. That's why we do the advertising, to ease the burden on the fans a little. The Coke bottles really don't look any different than the Schenley ad and the Buck Printing and White Fuel and all the other things that have been right outside the park that DIDN'T help. This one does.

Jeff Goldenberg is director of advertising and sponsorships. Somebody might come in and sponsor Wally Bean Bag Day like Fenway Franks did, or Coke, one of the things they sponsor is the calendars, or the mall tour that we do in January. He oversees the sponsorship deals. Then you've got Marcita Thompson. She oversees the actual promotions, the special events, the on-field stuff. They handle Wally.

Me and John Harrington had the most input in creating Wally. John said, "I want somebody that everybody is going to be happy to see. I want a two-year-old to love him. I want an adult to love him." So we came up with Wally, the basic concept was mine and I worked on it with Rick Dunfey. Rick put some polish on the story, actually, he came up with the name Wally. Up until then, we just were saying "The Green Monster."

It took a long time to get our organization to embrace the concept, even some of the fans were critical. Hey, listen. A four-year-old is at the ballpark and losing interest. A visit with Wally puts him right back into place, and he's fine. When we go to a special event, Wally goes. We don't have to find a player to represent the club. To be honest with you, kids recognize Wally faster than they recognize the players.

He's a vehicle to teach kids the history and traditions of the Red Sox. He's not counter to the history and traditions. He teaches it.

All he's doing is teaching kids about the Red Sox. He's not a San Diego chicken and that's not what we'll ever do with him. He's at the gates, he works the concourse and the suite level at every game since he started. We've been putting him into the stands where he can be seen.

I was the architect of Friendly Fenway. Believe it or not, I had the idea years ago. This was always a team that was marketed on the ballpark experience. When I was at the Braves, it was, "Come see Dale Murphy. Come see Bob Horner. Come see Phil Niekro." Here it's always been, "Come to Fenway Park." Part of this ballpark experience has been that there are stars involved through the years, but it's always been sold as an experience and not a "starring so-and-so."

The truth of the matter is any given day a star can disappear, but you still want to sell your next game. So, with that in mind, I jumped right into the idea of selling the experience and I wanted to have a name for it. I read VEECK AS IN WRECK for the umpteenth time and – I think it was his father – said, "From now on, any time we say 'Wrigley Field' we're going to mention the word 'beautiful' first, so it's always going to be 'beautiful Wrigley Field.'" And if you notice, people still say "Beautiful Wrigley Field."

I thought to myself we're trying to get the concept of friendly and that Fenway was welcoming. "Friendly Fenway" has alliteration, so I thought let's go with that. Then I wrote a whole position paper about how this notion, this phrase, should affect the behavior of everybody in the organization and how we should live up to it. If people love the experience, the results on the field are going to have less impact than it otherwise would.

A few years ago, when my daughter was maybe eight, she was at the ballpark with me, and she's sitting in the front row. It's pre-game, before the gates open. She's got her feet up on the wall enjoying the summer day, talking to two people she doesn't know. I walked up to her and I said, "Well, don't you look comfortable! Sitting here making new friends and enjoying yourself." And she looks at me, as children do, and she said, "Dad! That's why they call it Friendly Fenway!" I said, "Oh, that's why!" Of course, "they" was me.

[Larry oversees food & concessions, as well as fan research.]

There's over 2½ million hot dogs sold per year, also sausages and chicken and hamburgers

The changes we made – bringing in Legal Sea, Bob the Chef, Kowloon...our dollar volumes went up, our share went up, and the fan approval ratings went up dramatically. All we did was ask, "What would you like to eat? What don't you like?"

Aramark was so different from Stevens. One time, some of the guys who worked at Stevens went to the head person and asked him to add slush. He said, "We can't have slush. The lines would be too long."

Now, who ever heard of not selling something because the lines are going to be too long? That was the mentality we dealt with, but when Aramark came in our approval ratings went way up. I had fans come up and say, "Thank you for adding cotton candy. The little one couldn't take more than three innings. Now when he gets antsy, I buy him a cotton candy, that holds him until the seventh, and then he's anxious to see the end of the game."

As of 2003, in another of the changes implemented by new ownership, Larry was made Senior Vice President/Fenway Affairs. The September 2003 concerts by Bruce Springsteen capped the summer season; Larry Cancro organized the event.

MICHELE JULIAN
Director of Human Resources and Office Administration

I am involved in the hiring of all full time employees on the business side of the house. This includes Broadcast, Technology, Stadium Operations, Marketing, Sales, Accounting, Public Affairs and Facilities. To a lesser extent I am involved in seasonal hiring for the same groups. I have some involvement in seasonal hiring for the baseball side of the house. I do not get involved in hiring players, scouts, coaches, trainers. For the most part the baseball side takes care of itself. Good thing too, otherwise all I'd ever do would be to hire people.

I have been in human resources for 20+ years. The majority of companies I worked for were high tech or financial services. I did not have a background in sports. I started here in January 1998.

People call because it's quote/unquote a glamour industry. We get calls that say, "I'll do anything!" People don't understand that the Red Sox, like any other business, is staffed by trained professionals. You're limited to positions related to your experience and education. For example, my Marketing people all have either experience or a degree in Marketing.

People also forget that working with the Red Sox is a pretty good guarantee that you'll never get to watch a game. You'll be working!

Full-time employees, we're up to around 155 people, worldwide. During the high season, we have probably 700 seasonal employees. They work from two to ten months. That's only Red Sox employees. That does not count Aramark and Gourmet and Boston Police and all those folks. It takes considerably more than 700 people to put a game on.

The ushers are unionized. I think ticket takers are the same union. Some of my grounds crew people are union. We have a very friendly relationship with our union. Joe McDermott is the one to speak to about that. He handles the negotiations.

The biggest problem is not turnover, the biggest issue is just the whole idea of an incredible seasonal business. The last week of March, all bets are off and things just kind of get wild.

We play to the end of September and most of the students go back to school Labor Day-ish. So we have three weeks, maybe four weeks, of being short-staffed. That becomes one of the headaches. You don't even have to make the playoffs.

During the off-season we get a limited number of applications, probably only slightly more than your average company would. The instant the newspaper writes about baseball, the volume goes through the ceiling. As people start buying tickets and the season starts, that number just becomes phenomenal. If I count telephone and mail, there could be fifty a day – and that's just what's coming in to me. People will often send resumes to everybody in the Media Guide. We'll get 10 or 12 resumes from the same person.

The business is like any other. I tell people, "Think Fleet Bank. You're done." The business side is the same. How you treat people is the same. It doesn't – shouldn't – vary from company to company.

Baseball has its industry meetings and the h.r. group gets together once a year. We have sort of a mini-conference. One of the things that I've noticed is that teams like the Red Sox, the Yankees, the Mets – the older teams that have not moved around – are thought of completely different in their cities than teams which have been bought and sold, or changed cities. What you find is that if you work for one of the newer teams, it's just like working anywhere else. People go, "OK, cool." If I tell people I work for the Red Sox, it's like, "O-kay!! Now we want to talk to you!"

People ask all sorts of things. For people in this area, it is seen as something magical or mystical. I often tell people I'm in human resources and avoid the company name, because people always want to know if they can get discount tickets. Often it's not in your best interest to tell people where you work. As soon as people find out, you immediately have gone back to work.

KENT QUALLS
Director of Player Development

I got into this line of work originally with the Montreal Expos. I was at the University of Kentucky, majoring in business administration, but at the same time I was an athletic trainer with baseball, football, basketball – pretty much all the sports. My first year in baseball was as an athletic trainer during the summer in Bradenton, Florida. Once I completed my education, the Expos offered me a full-time position in the front office. An entry-level type job, administrative assistant in player development. The minor league director was Dan Duquette. I was with Montreal from '87 through 1994.

I'm a certified athletic trainer, but I also have a degree in business administration. I don't practice as a trainer any more, but actually I got back into that the first year I was with the Red Sox in '95, the strike year. There weren't many openings and it was a way to stay in the game. It actually worked out well, because after one year, they put me back in the front office, in Pawtucket.

I'm based at Fenway Park, but I travel quite a bit. I oversee all minor league operations. We have seven teams, the Pawtucket Red Sox, our double A team is the Trenton Thunder in Trenton, New Jersey. We have a team at Fort Myers, the Red Sox. We have the Greenjackets in Augusta, Georgia. We have the Sarasota Red Sox and the Lowell Spinners, and a team in the Dominican summer league.

We own Sarasota, Fort Myers and the Dominican team. The other teams, we have what's called a PDC – player development contract. It's a standard contract between major league teams and minor league affiliates. It used to be that every city used the nickname of their major league teams. In recent years, they've gone away from that for marketing reasons, although in Pawtucket's case, they remain the Red Sox. Lowell could have been the Lowell Red Sox, but they chose to be the Lowell Spinners.

All the coaches and staff work for the Red Sox [at the minor league teams.] So we're providing the talent and they're providing the venue. The PDC is supervised by Major League Baseball. We pay a good chunk of the freight. The basic division of expenses is the coaches and the players payroll, insurance and all that is from us. There's a sharing of the cost of equipment. We pay for meal money. The minor league team pays for travel, which in Triple A can be quite expensive because they fly. Flights and buses and hotels, the minor league team pays for. They do bus in Triple A. There are some cities that it just makes more sense to bus.

I work closely with Dan [Duquette] and the scouting department. We have a terrific computer program. On a daily basis during the season, we get game reports from each of our teams. We can sort it different ways to get the information that we need. We also have medical reports and scouting reports, all computerized and automated.

Spring training, I'm down at Fort Myers for seven or eight weeks. Once minor league camp starts, we have a staff meeting every morning, myself and all the coaches and our field coordinator, Dave Jauss. It's kind of a planning session for the day. I normally work in the office in the morning. We're still finishing contracts and things like that, so I try to get a lot of the administrative duties out of the way and then watch the games in the afternoon.

Towards the end of spring training, we have to make personnel decisions – who we're going to release, who's going to what club, and so on. That's in conjunction with Dan Duquette and several other persons, but ultimately, I'm the point person. The higher the level, the more input there is from the major league people.

Our affiliates are great to work with. They understand that the best players leave to move to a higher level, though I've heard that people get upset when you move their best player. But that is what the business is all about. In Pawtucket, they announce it – so-and-so was just promoted to the Boston Red Sox – and the fans give them a round of applause.

The major league team leaves before the minor league camp's over. We stay there wrapping things up and putting our teams together before they break camp. Our job at spring training is to make sure the teams are ready to start the season.

We handle the travel arrangements for all the minor league players. It's a big chore. We have thirty coaches, one hundred and fifty players and you don't know, up until that last week or so, who is going where. In January, we have to get all those players to spring training. We handle all the visas, too.

I normally come back to Fenway right away and spend a few weeks here. Fortunately for me, we have several local teams. At least half the month, maybe a little more, I'll be out on the road. The other times, I'll be here at Fenway.

There's constant voice mail going on. We get reports from the managers, from the trainers. I'm in pretty much daily conversation with all of our managers, not so much with the coaches. Dealing with injuries, doctors and trainers and medical people is part of my job. We get medical reports and voice mail reports from them every day. With my background as an athletic trainer, I think I have a better understanding when we discuss injuries.

Just like the major league teams, players go on the DL, off the DL, certain players move up and down. So we have the same number of roster moves in the minor leagues, and we're overseeing seven teams rather than one. People go from single A to double A and back again. It's a constant reaction: the major league team needs this player from triple A and we're reacting to replace that player. It's a trickle down effect.

There's also movement due to a player deserving promotion to that next level.

The rosters are close in size. Triple A and double A are 23. All the other teams – class A and below – are 25. We start with five teams,

our top four plus a team in Fort Myers. Then once we get into the draft, we get more players. Lowell begins – and basically a new season begins in Fort Myers – and then our Dominican team starts. We've got five teams in April and May, and by mid-June, all seven teams are playing.

From the middle of September to the end of October, we have our winter instructional league in Fort Myers, a six-week program devoted to some of our best young prospects. Also, we participate in a couple of fall leagues. In Arizona it's a co-op type team, six of our top prospects, normally from double A and triple A. In California it's the California Fall League, which is more like A and double A players. We also play winter ball in Mexico, Venezuela and the Dominican Republic.

There's not a lot of time for vacation. Christmas, that two weeks is the slowest time. Other than that, it's very busy. In the fall, we typically renew our staff contracts, so any coaches or trainers that we're rehiring, it's done in fall or winter. Up until late January, we're signing minor league free agents.

I don't know if we rely on the draft less than other teams, but I think we recognize that if you rely only on the draft, it's not enough. The draft has expanded a little, but it's for players from the United States, Guam, Puerto Rico and Canada. Players from the Dominican, Korea, Japan and so forth don't go through the draft. Ray Poitevint oversees the Asian part, and Levy Ochoa oversees the Latin American part. I'm also very involved in our Latin program. Actually, before the job I have now, one of my main responsibilities was starting up that Latin program from the scouting and development side. We've come a long way in three or four years.

I'm on the phone a lot trying to find players and agents. They all have agents, all the way down to single A. The frustrating thing is they change agents so frequently. There's not a whole lot of loyalty out there. The number of agents has grown a lot over the last twelve or thirteen years. There's a lot of agent wannabes, too, that'll take any player.

I'm at the top of the spectrum on the minor league thing, but it's not a one-man show. It's a group effort.

MARCI BLACKER
Baseball Administration Coordinator

I'm from Sudbury. Babe Ruth used to live about a mile from where my parents live. I went to U. Mass., a sport management major.

I started as the administrative assistant in the scouting department, in July of '95. I was only seasonal, so I left in October, after the play-offs. I came back in February, and did a lot of scouting and minor league administrative assistant work. Typing up contracts, putting information in the computer. A lot of the scouts send in hand-written reports.

That fall a job came open, the coordinator of Florida operations. I applied and got it. I moved to Fort Myers for 2½ years and ran the spring training facility.

My main function was preparing everything for spring training, overseeing the ticket office, the souvenirs, grounds, maintenance, day of game operations – everything. After spring training, we had our Gulf Coast team there, so I did administrative stuff for them. It was slower, but there was a lot of player movement.

They promoted me back here in April 1999. As the baseball administration coordinator, I'm Kent Qualls' assistant. My main duties are health insurance, worker's comp, immigration issues and I am responsible for the Dominican team.

When I was the scouting administrative assistant, I did a lot of preparation for the draft, putting stuff in the computer, getting things ready and organized for Wayne [Britton.] I know what goes on during the draft so I'll help out if they need anything. They do the draft from Fenway, by telephone.

Every year we tell the Commissioner's Office how many visas we would like. They'll go through Immigration and allot each team a certain amount. Immigration's usually done by the end of spring training, give or take a few people that we might bring in.

I'm still involved with health insurance. The major league health insurance goes through the Players Association. Once the players get to the major leagues, I'll give them all the information to fill out and they can send it in, but that's as far as I go in regards to the major leagues.

Worker's comp takes up a lot of time, unfortunately a lot of injuries [throughout the minor league system, with a few hundred players.] I deal with the major league players, too. It's a little different, than say, if I was to get workmen's comp, because they have guaranteed salaries. We just pay for their medical and treatment.

I live close so even after a night game I can sleep in a little and still get here around 10. The minor league game reports come in every morning, and as a courtesy to all the scouts and minor league coaches, I give an update on the voice mail. "Pawtucket beat Norwich, 3-2...."

There is a box next to the press box where baseball operations people can sit. Ed Kenney [Assistant General Manager] will come in there sometimes, and some of the scouting people. Some people watch in their office. The executives can watch in their suite. Every now and then my friends are at the game, so I'll go downstairs and watch with them. Not 'til May, when it's warmer.

Tom Moore
PHOTO BY BILL NOWLIN

TOM MOORE
Assistant Scouting Director

I didn't play ball in college, but in high school I did. I was talented enough in evaluating players at that time to realize that I was not going to pursue my playing further in college. I always had a passion for the game. I was an intern, starting in '95, and then I was hired full time in '96. In Springfield College I double majored in sports management and business. Our senior year, we had an internship and I was fortunate to come to the Red Sox minor league and scouting department.

About halfway through, after I had become a seasonal employee, I was moved down to the major league video position. The position that Billy Broadbent holds now. I did that for two years.

I grew up a Red Sox fan in Berkshire County, about two hours west of here. Ever since high school, I had been contacting general managers and teams. I got a lot of positive responses. I met with probably half a dozen of them. It really was remarkable – and it's even more remarkable now that I know what kind of schedule they have.

For '95 and '96 I traveled with the team as the video coordinator. In '97 I moved back into the minor league and scouting office and saw the operations a little closer. I would say it was kind of training for what I'm doing now.

It was kind of a catchall in minor league and scouting, with some major league responsibilities. I had some responsibilities in the office but the majority of it was video. I had a hand in developing our minor league and scouting computer program.

Our minor league managers fill out game reports that track certain information and the progress of our players on the scouting side. Our scouts track their reports on the computer of both free agent players and pro players during the summer.

It was the brainchild that Dan had brought here from Montreal. He wanted to get everything computerized. There's a lot of administrative work involved with preparing for the draft – organizing the reports, making sure that he sees what he needs to see while he travels.

In '96 I was given the title Baseball Operations Assistant. If there was a project that the minor league department needed to get taken care of, I'd move over there, or if there's a project in scouting that had to get taken care of, I would take on that. If there was extra work to be done in any department, it would just kind of fall my way.

Wayne Britton is the person I work most closely with, but I also perform kind of the same job for Ray Poitevint in the international scouting department. I also have a hand in advance scouting.

I'm the person in the scouting department who spends the most time at Fenway. Sort of an anchor here. We've gotten to the point where I would say that we're 100% computerized. We're also starting to take charge on the video aspect of it. Video scouting is becoming a big part of our program.

The Major League Scouting Bureau does video of high school and college players for the purposes of the draft. They'll send videotapes or CDs in for viewing. Most of the players who go in the first several rounds of the draft, every major league team will have received materials from Major League Baseball. Definitely in the first round, every player's been seen by a few scouts, the scouting director, cross-checkers, even the GM sometimes, if not in person, on video.

I think the basis for scouting will always be with the eye evaluation, but as technology improves we want to take advantage of the tools out there. That's going to improve your evaluation process, but the success of a scouting department comes down to your area scouts and your people out in the field that have their actual eye on the players. That way, you can pick up things like work habits, character.

Dan Duquette, Dave Dombrowski, and all that line of GMs that have come from an analytical background, are really an inspiration to everybody else. You don't have to be a star in the game to excel in the front office. Being around top-notch baseball people, you can't help but learn their ways. It's a process of osmosis.

I remember when I was showing video to a big league coach and maybe a player. You're saying to yourself, "I'm sitting down here with Joe Kerrigan, who's one of the best pitching coaches in the game, listening to him evaluate what this guy's doing wrong, what he's doing right, how to pitch to this hitter." You're learning hands-on from some of the best baseball people.

If you rely solely on the draft, then you're going to live or die by the draft. If there's a good crop of players, then you're going to be fine, but if not, then you're going to be in trouble. Even if there's a really good crop, you're just getting one every 30 picks. So is every other team. In today's game, you definitely have to have other avenues to acquire players. That's one thing I've learned from being here. The more creative you can be, the more players you can bring into the system, and that's what the game's about, acquiring players.

We have three Koreans that are pretty close to major league and two others at the entry level. The same thing in the Dominican, with Pedro and Ramon Martinez, anybody that's a pitcher has got to be thinking about the Red Sox. It's kind of a domino effect. Once you have a stronghold in a certain area and those players are successful on your team, they get worldwide recognition and kids from that country just want to be like their heroes.

Everybody likes to see variety and flavor on the team.

Frank Malzone and Eddie Haas are major league scouts for us. We have about five major league scouts. They pretty much do the same thing, if Dan needs them to see a player here or there, but Eddie's done a little more than that. [This is why he had the additional title of Special Assignment scout.] Lee Thomas and Jerry Stephenson are also a couple of our major league scouts.

Our scouts work regionally. We have Eddie in the midwest. Lee's region is the central US. Jerry's out on the west coast, Frank does the east coast. We have a group of about fifteen area scouts that cover territories in the US, and then we have two cross-checkers for the purpose of free agent scouting that just kind of bounce through the country, cross-checking all the top players. Wayne will do that, too.

I work out of Fenway Park maybe 75% of the time, other than spring training. I go down to spring training for the duration.

One of the big responsibilities I have is servicing our scouts, both domestically and internationally, to make sure that they're operating on full power. If they need certain things, I'll make sure that they are operating with what they need.

It could be anything from administrative to technical to whatever. It could be personal, too. If their wife is pregnant and needs some insurance information...if they need anything from the office, whether it's in the scouting realm or not, I can either guide them to what they need or get it for them myself.

I like to stay late, it's a good time to get stuff done because it's quiet. You can see what's going on in the baseball world at the same time, with games finishing up. I do a lot of work during the game. If it's really a busy time, I'll bring work with me and do it as I'm watching the game.

We have closets of old video, but we're getting to the point where all of our video from here on out will probably be recorded on the computer. The beauty of having it on the computer, Dan will be able to sit at home and say, "Gee, I wonder if we have video on this guy" and he can just look it up.

BILLY BROADBENT
Video/Advance Scouting Coordinator

I've been major league video coordinator since '97. We record everybody's performance on tape and then you're responsible for getting charts and graphs – statistical information – on the opposition and on our guys for the coaches.

We tape both home and opposing players. We don't have secret cameras or anything like that. We have a satellite dish and we'll record off of their regular broadcast feeds.

We have a large archive housed here at the park. We rotate it every couple of years, because obviously the stuff from '96 and '97 is not going to be as applicable as the stuff from '98 and '99.

A picture is worth a thousand words. You could have all the statistics in the world on a guy, and then you see him and you say, "Wow! How did that guy do that?"

Joe Kerrigan uses tapes every day. There might be film on this particular guy that would help Joe see how his pitchers are going to approach him.

99 percent of the players look at tape, some are adamant about looking at everything, and some just want to look at stuff when their mechanics – whether it's at the plate or on the mound – aren't exactly where they want them to be. Sometimes Jim Rice [hitting coach] will come up and take a look at it. Then he'd say to them, "Look, this is what you might be doing wrong. You might give this a try to correct it."

These are professionals trying to perfect their skills. They use it from the aspect of where their hands might be when they're at the plate, or is their body opening up too quick when they're on the mound – something that might be throwing their performance off. It's used to help their performance, but also to prevent them from getting hurt. If a guy's not throwing correctly he could end up hurting himself.

For a night game, I'll get in between 9 and 10 in the morning, and I'll acquire all the information that we need on the opposition. I'll have tape work to do, breaking down things for different guys.

There's a lot of statistical information than I have to keep track of, as far as pitchers performances. That's broken down in terms of the number of fast balls, curve balls, changeups, the percentage of strikes with them in certain counts. As you can imagine, that keeps you pretty busy.

Bill Moloney charts all the speeds. He charts every pitch the entire game, whether it was a ball or a strike. He was a former pitcher, so his ability to recognize pitches is great. He throws left-handed b.p. for us also.

All that information's broken down statistically on what's working and what's not working. If you've got a guy that's struggling, you've got to figure why.

For the first game of a series, there's tons of information and reports to acquire, to make sure they have all the accurate information, make sure that they have the spray charts on certain individuals. That's coordinated through the scouting department; they do a lot of that work beforehand.

The second game of the series, there's just the night before to look at, but there's a bit of lag time, too, and by the second game of a three day series, you're starting to get ready for the next team that's coming in. That'll take a couple of days to do, because we might have to get film on a new guy.

If we had to go to Major League Baseball to request film, that would take so much time. Normally, you can find something on just about everybody. You like to have the most recent, but if you can only get something a couple of months old, then that's going to have to do. At least it will give you some idea.

For instance, that shortstop that got called up by the Yankees. What you do is, look up the games that he played in – you can find that on America Online – it will have his batting logs and you'll say, OK, he played 9/2, 9/3 and 9/5. So you ask the scouting department, "Do you have Yankee games on these days?" You might be able to find six at bats or so and then the pitching coach and the manager can watch that and come up with a game plan on how they're going to approach him.

A digital system is in the works, but we're not fully up on that right now. We're killing some man hours rewinding tapes by hand, but the system's better than it was five years or ten years ago. There's no way to make a copy in anything other than real time. It is time-consuming, but it goes fairly smoothly.

Three VCRs are going during the game all the time. One records the game in its entirety. One records all the opposition – whether it's pitching performance or at bat. And one records all of our pitching or at bats.

In the off-season, I break down the statistical information on the people we're going to be playing next season. What they did against the rest of the league, what they did against the Red Sox. That type of stuff.

There's still nothing more final than the numbers that come out in the STATS, Inc. books. Say we don't play the Yankees until June. I have all the information in what they did in '99 versus the Red Sox and what they did in '99 versus the rest of the league. What I'll have to have plugged in is what they've done in 2000 from April 1 until whenever we play them. That would be the day to day stuff.

I was just a kid and the ballpark was close to my house in Pawtucket. You could see the lights of the stadium from my mom's house. It's very much like the Johnny Pesky story. It's probably one of the reasons he's taken a shining to me like he has.

In 1980, I lived in Pawtucket, Rhode Island and I applied for a job to sell popcorn or peanuts, and they asked me if I wanted to be batboy. I guess somebody was looking after me and knew how much I liked baseball. I was very, very fortunate. I did get to sell some popcorn, when they had college games while the team was on the road and they needed our help in different areas.

I was the Pawtucket batboy in '80 and '81. I worked different jobs around the ballpark in '82 and '83, and then in '84 I worked in the clubhouse again. I did everything, whether it was selling tickets or working on the ground crew. I was full time during the season. I was only 15 when I started at batboy. I got a little older, and they said, "OK, you can work in the clubhouse now." It's a big responsibility and long hours. By that time, I was in college. I was responsible for both clubhouses. I guess you would call it the clubhouse-slash-equipment manager. I did that from 1984 to 1992.

I saw just about everyone you can imagine pass through. I've seen all kinds of things. My brother and I were batboys for the longest game in baseball history. Had the game been on a Wednesday night, they would have probably sent me home. It was a Saturday night; that was why I stayed the whole game. My mother came down and threatened us about going home, and I'd be like, "Who'd take care of things? Just a little bit longer. Just a little bit longer." Next thing you know, they called it at 4 in the morning.

Starting in September, 1990, we used to come and help out up here. They were in the playoffs and the kids had to go back to school, so they needed extra hands during the day. The people in Pawtucket were kind enough to let us come up here and work. Joe Cochran and Jack Rogers and Steve August got me approved by the front office to work on the visitors side and I worked there from '92 to '96. Then in '97, they promoted me to major league video coordinator.

It seems like a lot of the stuff is repetitive, but every time the guy plays another game, the information has to be updated. Everybody that plays for the Red Sox, if they've played for the team for the whole year, they might have a couple of tapes. I'll make copies and I send them to them. As a matter of fact, Pedro has a tape that we recorded when he was with Montreal. A really good game that he had thrown. We hold onto that tape because he did a lot of things with his mechanics correctly there, and the pitching coach Joe Kerrigan will occasionally refer to that tape. So you have to be able to access things in the tape library because somebody might want to see something. Say, for instance, John Valentin. The last two playoffs against the Indians, he's been very hot. Say in April, he struggles like he usually does. He might ask you, "Get me my at-bats in the last two playoffs against the Indians. I want to see what I was doing there and compare to what I'm doing now." That's up to Jim Rice and Jimy Williams and John Valentin to figure, though. My job is to have the stuff so they can see what they were doing right.

AL GREEN
Customer Service

Al Green worked for Harvard, doing mechanical engineering and quality control for 27 years. Harvard was generous and let him get to Sox games, where he worked first as usher and then as head of customer service.

I've worked for the Red Sox for 27 years. I've never missed a game and I'm never late.

I started in 1974 as an usher. I used to work at Star Market at Porter Square in Cambridge. There was a white guy there who

Al Green
Beginning on Opening Day, 1974, Al Green has worked 2,402 consecutive games (as of June 1, 2004, when this book went to press.) He has also worked 31 post-season games, without missing one. He's closing in on Cal Ripken's 2,632. It takes twice as long to get there as a park employee, since the team only plays half their games at home.
PHOTO BY BILL NOWLIN

used to pack the groceries. He was an old guy, so I told him I would help him. Then he said to me, "You know, I work for the Red Sox. If you come over, I'll let you in the ballpark." I said, "OK."

I would go over and go to the game. Then I said to him I'd like to be one of those ushers, too. He said OK, go and put in your name.

But they gave me a hard time, every year they told me, "Come back." "Come back...come back...come back." I didn't know any different. I was the only black at the time there, and every time they would tell me to come back, so I would go home and come back the next year. I didn't know that you could come back the next *day*.

One day this white guy said to Andy Anderson, the supervisor of the ushers, "Hey, you're making this guy come here a long time. It's time to give the guy the job." The guy said, "So what do you want me to do? Where do you want me to put him?" The guy said, "Give him a job. I got a card here for him." It's a union, so you've got to get a card. So they give me the job as an usher.

I was the first black usher. I had problems with the other ushers, sure. People were putting pressure on. When I first went in, those guys said, "I don't want to work with him." Cold shoulder, very cold. They wanted to put on a girl there and the other ushers didn't even want a girl to work. I took the girl with me. The father said to me, "You know, you're the only person that ever treated my daughter right." They gave her a real hard time. She left and never came back.

They'd send me everywhere the other guys didn't want to go. I never complained. One day, the supervisor said to me, "You know, everywhere I send you, you never complain." I said, "Why should I complain?" One time, they sent me to work with a school group in the stands. Another usher didn't want to do it. I went and got the kids all quieted down. The teacher come to me and said, "How did you manage to get all these kids quieted down?" I said, "I used psychology on them." What I did was, the big kids in front, I told them that they was the boss.

When the other kids come down, they run them out and got them quieted down that way.

The teacher said he would recommend me as to how I calmed these kids down. I say, well I know how to deal with people.

Then one day they sent me to work at home plate, up at the top in the back. I never complained, I went there and worked. When the game was over, the guy said, "I want you down on the field." I said, "Why? The guys who work down in the boxes, they go on the field. The guys in the back don't go on the field."

I know what the story was. I played the game. I was no stupid idiot. They wanted me on the field so that people could see that they had a black guy there. So I did it.

Then, the guy came to me and said, "The vice president wants you to work in the information booth." I said, "Why do you want me? I don't know anything." He said, "Well, they want you." I said, "OK, I'll go."

I would walk around the place and check all the sections and everything. Learn about the place. Then Dick Bresciani would bring these leaflets to me and I would read them.

People would pass and show one another — hey, look, they got a black guy there. They never said that to me, but I could tell that, the reaction of them. They would touch one another to get them to see me. I plainly saw that.

I think they were trying to see if I would steal from the Lost and Found. I had better character than that. I never touched nothing. When I first went there, it really was the Lost and Found. When somebody has something, they still come here. If anything's lost, I take it in and then they take it upstairs. People lose everything. Wallets, pocketbooks, earrings, watches, credit cards, briefcases. Somebody lost their teeth once. They dropped out and they couldn't find them.

I was a baseball fan back when I started. I came here from Barbados when I was 24, in 1951. I played cricket. I used to be a bowler. Here you'd call it a pitcher. Cricket and baseball are similar, only in cricket, when you bowl you hit the ball on the ground. In cricket, you could stay there and play the ball for a whole day. You don't have to run. In baseball, if you hit the ball inside the crease – I mean inside the lines – you've got to run.

I knew about baseball in Barbados. I read about Jackie Robinson and Mickey Mantle and those guys.

When I came to America, I came right to Boston. I had an uncle here. Then I met this guy who used to tell me about baseball. I decided to like baseball. It looked a bit like cricket to me. I went to a lot of games at Fenway Park in the 50s before I ever worked there. One time I saw Ted Williams passing by and I got him to autograph a ball for me. I said to him, "Well, I never knew you in your glory days, because I was in the islands." He said, "Oh, I go down there fishing, man." That's what he told me.

I never played baseball. Only softball. I hit and I pitched, too. I played mostly first base. I've seen a lot of great guys. I saw Frank Robinson make a mammoth hit. One of the players I liked best was Carl. Yaz. Yaz was a man, he'd play hurt. He hustled. Another guy that played hurt was Reggie Smith. They didn't cry baby and stuff like that. Another guy that I really loved – I couldn't believe this man was hurting so much and would play like that – was Mickey Mantle. I saw him take a catch off the center field wall, I couldn't believe it.

Pesky man [Johnny Pesky], he always say, "Hey, us old guys have to stick together." He's a good guy. Johnny Pesky's a very nice person.

I was a Red Sox fan, but I liked the Yankees, too. When I was a little guy, I had an uncle in Canada, his sister-in-law was in America so I went to Brooklyn. I had on a Yankee cap. I didn't know the difference and people gave me hell. "You better take that cap off in Brooklyn." I didn't know the story. I just thought it all was America.

One time I left to go to Florida, in the Sixties. When I got to Palm Beach, we had to catch a bus for Miami. I sat beside a white lady. I looked back and I saw all these black guys standing up in the back, I didn't know there was a reason. Coming back north, I sat beside this other white lady and she said to me, "You know, they don't let blacks sit beside white people." I

said, "What are you talking about?" Another time I was in Washington and a woman said to me, "You can't eat here." I said, "Why can't I eat here?" She said, "Where are you from?" I said, "The Caribbean." So she said, "OK, you're different. You are all right." That's what she said to me!

I get there about two hours before the game. I stay until about forty minutes after. I've got to see if there's any lost and found, turn them in.

People ask me questions all the time. More than a hundred a game. More than that. Are you kidding? I get a million questions. Firstly, they want to know how to get places. How to get to Maine, New Hampshire, the Cape. They want schedules. They want tickets for the Yankees games. They want to know about different clubs in Boston, night clubs. Nothing to do with the Red Sox. Because they see information, they think you should know everything. A woman came in and said she lost her husband. I said, "How did you lose your husband?" She said, "Well, he dropped me off and I don't know where he went." I said, "Well, you should take a ticket and give him a ticket."

Some people come there with a little kid. Instead of looking out for the kid, or giving the kid a ticket, they let the kid go, say "Go and get some autographs." Then they don't watch and the kid gets confused. It's the mother that's more confused than the kid. "Oh, I can't find my kid." But the kid is all right. Someone will find the kid and bring them right there. We never lost a kid there.

You get a million questions. More at rainout time. "I'm from out of town. How could I get my money back?" I said, "Look. All you got to do is go to the Red Sox office and you get your money back or you get tickets for another game." Forty minutes later, the same question, the same guy.

A guy came once with a $9000.00 check to present for the Jimmy Fund. He lost the check! So this guy said to me, "You know, I had a check for the Jimmy Fund, but I lost the check." Well, somebody else found the check. I said, "I got the check!" He was so happy.

One night Jim Rice's father came here and he went to go up to the stands and the ushers kicked him out. He came up to me and said, "Where do the player's families go?" I said, "Who are you?" He said, "I'm Jim Rice's father. The guys kicked me out up there." I ran right up the ramp and I said to the guys, "Listen, do you know who this guy is? This is Jim Rice's father. You were in a hurry to kick him out." He said, "Oh, I'm sorry. Excuse me. I'm sorry. I didn't know." I said, "Well, apologize to him right now." So he apologized and put him in a seat. Other guys, like the Spanish guys who don't know English, they come to me. I speak just a little. I talk to them. I understand. Other people don't have that patience.

The Red Sox are trying harder now to accommodate. When I first went there, if I was a black person from America, I wouldn't work there. In the Caribbean there's a lot of white people [who interact normally]. My mother used to work with some white people and they used to call her "Ma" and I used to call their mother "Ma." I never knew the difference. But when I came here I saw things that happened, but I still had things in me that I didn't care what color you are, you're the same. If I had been raised here, it might have been different. I can see how people got hurt. That's what makes me different.

Paul Lazarovitch
PHOTO BY BILL NOWLIN

PAUL LAZAROVITCH
Fenway Park Tour Guide

I was born and raised in Hyde Park. In the summer, my cousins and I tried to make as many of the day games as we could. You'd get in to the right field grandstand for 75 cents. We'd eventually end up behind first base or home plate, because the games weren't sellouts.

It was the time of Dick Stuart. Frank Malzone. Eddie Bressoud. Bob Tillman behind the plate. Wilbur Wood was pitching for us at the time. It was nice to see a local guy out there.

Growing up in the city, if you lived in Hyde Park there were two sports: baseball and politics. I remember during the Mantle/Maris home run craze, seeing how many home runs we could hit in our playground on the corner. We were all shooting for 61 that year.

I don't remember Ted Williams, though. He quit after 1960 and it was another year before I was really cognizant of the Red Sox. That's one part of the tours that I love – when people talk about Ted Williams. I get to hear the stories. Everyone has their own story.

I started in '96. I teach at Wentworth during the day. I just called and said I'd like to give tours, I remember how much it meant to me going to Fenway, and I still feel magical about it. They told me to come up, interviewed me and told me, "You've got the job."

For training, everyone would go with someone who would be a little senior. I tend to have all the kids follow me around this year. I'm the old man now, I'm 46. They're mostly all college kids. Last year, though, we had a gentleman who was older than I am giving tours.

The first year, I only taught one course, so I was there every day. This year I'm there less, because I've got two young daughters and my wife works. I work two scheduled days a week and then some other times if they need me. In the beginning of the season, I think I worked every day until my summer classes started in May and then they brought in the college kids to do tours. I think we had eleven kids this year. Sports information or sports management majors from U Mass. A couple of kids from Harvard.

I was thrilled the first time I was in the clubhouse, but I was disappointed it was so small. I expected to see something a bit more glamorous. Realizing it was Fenway Park, I shouldn't have anticipated that. I've thrown the ball a couple of times in the batting cages under center field. I've been inside the scoreboard – in fact, my name is in there. I tell people that some greats are in there – Piersall, myself...

If you walk down right field and look up, there's some bumper sticker. I think it might say WEEI or something. On the tour one day, before we headed down to right field, a guy says, "You're going to see a bumper sticker, and I put that up there!" He was just so proud that he had something at Fenway. That's his permanent reminder.

It's an hourly wage. Nothing I will buy a second house on the Cape with. Sometimes I wait for weeks to pick up the paycheck. I just like being there.

We were issued Red Sox IDs to get into the games. It's a great benefit. Also, we get tickets for seats subject to availability. They've really treated us nice. My kids are loaded with Red Sox hats. Wally the Green Monster bean bags. Pennants. My daughters are 7 and 9. My girls are good for four innings and then it's a lot of trips to pizza and so forth.

I'm an associate professor. I teach communications. I do see a connection. I bring my classes over for tours and also I bring in guest speakers. In fact, I'm teaching an oral communication course this semester and I want to bring them over so we can see how they present information about the Red Sox. As a guide, you have to use your oral communication skills some times, when individuals ask questions that may not be appropriate. You've got to keep the crowd moving along.

We do get offered tips sometimes. It's usually a camp group or something. I used to say, "No. Just give it to the college kids." But I had one priest who was adamant. He was from New York, and he knew his baseball. He told some great Dodger stories. He handed me a ten dollar bill, and I said, "Father, I can't. You give it right back to the kids." But he wouldn't. He really knew his baseball. I should have paid him for what I learned from him.

There's something magical about being on the field. To me, the biggest thrill is when I see people when they open that gate. All kidding aside, it's like FIELD OF DREAMS. I see their faces light up. I've seen people say everything

from, "Oh, my God!" to "I can't believe I'm here." They'll kiss the ground, take home pieces of grass. I like to see people in that spirit. That's the way I feel when I'm there.

I always get asked if anyone's ever hit a home run over right field, up over the numbers. The question I get asked the most is, "Do you get to meet all the players?" You don't. You see them come in in the afternoon. They have no idea who I am.

This may sound corny, but people are usually there to see the shrine. On the last day of this season, there was a couple there and that's what he said, "I'm here at the shrine. Here at the shrine." A couple of times, old retired ballplayers – not from the Red Sox – were there and one guy said, "I remember playing here back in 19 such and such a year." His eyes lit up when he got out in the left field area.

Everyone pretty much stays together. They only wander a bit because they're taking their 100th picture, it seems. I'd do the same thing. I still do. I bring my camera and I've got videos essentially of nothing – walking through the hallways, the empty 600 Club, the media area. Just the love of being at Fenway.

Yes, I get to eat in the staff dining room. That was a big thrill. It was almost surrealistic the first time I ate there, the Red Sox game was going on literally five feet behind me – and I'm watching the game on television. Dan Duquette walks in. It was a Fellini moment. I was watching on television and then all of a sudden, oh my God, Duquette's there. It was a big thrill.

I always do this one routine. I say, very seriously, "Well, you know this is major league baseball and we have certain ground rules. First, please stay together on the tour. Second, don't go on the grass. The most important one, if there are any Yankee fans here, back of the line, please." Or I'll get to the fourth level and say, "OK, Yankee fans. The tour ends here." It's fun. People get into it. But when the Yankees are in town and the fans are here, they rub it in. I hear every Bucky Dent joke. It's a great rivalry.

One guy was sort of shaky and a little nervous and excited. I didn't know what to expect. I brought him around to the Green Monster and at that moment he said, "Okay!" He had a back-pack and he whipped out a glove and a ball. All he was doing was having his picture taken catching a ball off the Green Monster. I didn't know what was going to come out of that backpack.

If you ask me why do I do it, what did Sir Edmund Hillary say? Because it's there. And I love it. It's just exciting. I'll always be twelve years old as long as there's a Fenway Park.

MARIANNE COMEAU
Community Relations Intern

I am Community Relations Intern for the Boston Red Sox. In the late 80s and early 90s, I was doing week-end news and sports for a radio station up in Lowell, WCAP. I couldn't get full-time work in radio so I decided to go to U. Mass. in Amherst and get my degree in Sport Management.

After I graduate, I definitely want to stay in sports, in marketing or special events planning or community relations. I'll apply with the Red Sox, but I don't know if that's where I'll end up.

I started working as an intern at Fenway this July. I was working in Marketing before, as a tour guide. Then I went over to Community Relations as an intern. When it's all done, I'll have earned 12 credits.

I put in a full forty-hour week. When there are games, it's forty-plus. I work until December. Then I'll go back to school in January.

When I first applied to the Red Sox, I was just looking for a summer job. I started as a tour guide and for a couple of years I just did tours. Then I moved up to gate promotions and then up to escorting Wally.

They really didn't have a lot of training. Someone from the Red Sox took me around and told me the things they wanted me to cover. Preparing for questions from the fans is something you have to learn on your own, though. They probably spent about an hour, and then they gave us a script. I knew most of the information from being a fan from seven years old on.

I was raised as a Red Sox fan. My mother took me to my first game in 1967. She became a fan from her father. The whole family's into sports.

I never really had any problems with anyone. The groups were much smaller then than they have now. I liked meeting the public, you got to meet people from all over the world.

I did gate promotions too, giveaways during the game. We gave away Wally the Bean Bag Buddy, helmets, books, calendars. I passed them out myself but I also oversaw to make sure everything was going OK.

You have to make sure all the materials are down there and you've got to make sure the people stay at the gates, too. Mostly people have volunteered to come in and do this, from ROTC units or something. Afterwards, they get to see the game free. I'll give out the Bickford's restaurant coupons. Those are by location. They're chosen and then I have to go and find the seats. Then there's one family per game that I choose on my own. The Family of the Game. I choose them early so we have a chance to take their picture. I have a Polaroid and I take the photo myself. I try to pick a family with cute kids.

Recently, I've escorted Wally around. We walk around the park, but I've gone outside to parades and things.

I've gone to Sox Talks. It's sponsored by the Red Sox and Boston Parks and Recreation. We take players to different places within Boston and they talk to the kids.

Now, I'm organizing different functions like the Pedro Martinez benefit for [paralyzed Dominican jockey] Rudy Baez. I made sure everything was in order and when people went to have their pictures taken with Pedro, I organized the people and sent them through the line.

The other day I was organizing letters from charities. If a church is going to have a fund-raiser, they write a letter to us. They just ask the Red Sox to help in any way they can. They might ask for a player to come and visit, but they usually get autographed pictures, a team ball, something they can auction off. We get two or three hundred of those a week. The Red Sox are very good about it.

SAM ZOOB
Human Resources Intern

I worked as a human resource intern from May into September. The head of the department, Michele Julian, and her assistant Adis Benitez make up the entire Human Resources department. I have been interested in getting into sports management and had just graduated college. I called around to the local sports teams to see if there were any summer internships, and I just lucked out timing-wise, I guess, and they called me for an interview. They ended up placing me on the front door and gave me work at the All-Star Game.

When you start out at the bottom, you do menial work, but I got to do a lot of exciting stuff for the All-Star Game. I got to put together data bases for the volunteers we used for picking up people at the airport, welcoming committees, dinners, orientations, bus scheduling. We received a couple of thousand applications for volunteers.

As for my daily routine, I come in at 9 and unlock the offices. I have a key, yes. People higher up have their own keys, but as far as a door open to the public, no one could come in until I got there. I'd take care of any work that Michele or Adis sent down – phone calls or things they wanted me to take care of, and then just read and take care of questions, or take the occasional phone call.

Helen Robinson, she's tough. She's 89 years old. She likes things the way they used to be. She's very ensconced in her daily routine. She likes things her way, and no one's going to tell her differently. She likes to make it seem that she's being crucified, and that her life is tougher than it is but she's a nice lady. She's there all the time. I asked her if she slept over and she said only once. She won't open up the office, take any phone calls or do any work before nine – but she's there, having breakfast in one of the cafeterias. She'd leave at five if they're out of town, but on game days, she's there until the end of the game.

I'd say you'd get anywhere between five and ten people a day that just wander in and ask questions, and you'd have probably ten to fifteen people with actually scheduled meetings. Some days, you'd get a total of five people all day long. When the team was at home, you'd get more people.

A lot of people neglect to read the doors and see that the ticket office was actually next door. I had people coming in to buy tickets, three or four a day. You'd have people wondering about employment. I'd hand out applications. You had your not mentally well people come in now and then. I've had people who lost keys to their apartments thinking that the Red Sox had them. Lost and found is upstairs, so we had people come up for that. We had solicitors. I had one guy come all the time with personally addressed packages for every single member of the Red Sox with Dianetics packages and poems and what not. You smile and you take it and you say, "Thank you very much" and you put it in the trash when they leave.

A lot of people came in asking about tours, which ran out of Gate D, two gates down. After 2 o'clock, we stop offering the tours and I would get people saying they're from California, from Nova Scotia, from Spain, saying we're only here for this day – and you have to turn them away. They just want to take a peek in. I tell them you could go down to Gate D and see if someone will let you in. I left it to the guys at Gate D.

When school started up again you have a lot of college students rushing frats come in and do silly stuff on the field. We had one guy from the Toronto Maple Leafs hockey team who wanted to dress up like a bear and dance on the Green Monster. That was one of the stranger requests.

I did some projects for one of the head secretaries upstairs. We give out clergy passes and I had to organize that for her because she has about 500 or 600 clergy requests. Not all of them are legit. And people move and change parishes, so I had to see if people are still

Sam Zoob
PHOTO BY BILL NOWLIN

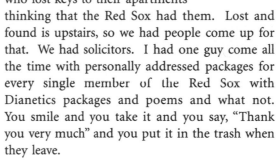

around. They get a year-round clergy pass. It's in their name and a guest, standing room, or if they can find an open seat. There are also discounts for military.

I could see as many games as I wanted. I probably saw 15 or 20. I worked until 5 and then I'd get some dinner in the staff dining room and go into the game for a bit, but since I lived a little far away, I'd leave around the fifth or sixth inning. I saw most of the Pedro games. That was enjoyable. I watch all the games on TV, though, for sure.

Ron Burton
PHOTO BY BILL NOWLIN

RON BURTON
Community Relations Manager

I started in community relations in 1993. I heard about the job through my brother Steve, who's a sports broadcaster. Ron Burton [Boston Patriots football player] is my father. I went through several interviews and ended up getting the job.

I was in real estate before this. I was pre-law at Northwestern. It had nothing to do with real estate and it had nothing to do with what I'm doing now. The program at Northwestern is excellent. We used to go into the court systems and do all these wonderful things. I wanted to go into criminal law, but seeing what these guys actually do and what they go through, I said, "This is not for me."

I deal with all the functions and liaison for the club as far as community concerns. We serve all the functions, the events, the player appearances. I'm in charge of all charitable donations and things of that nature. We also work with the community, not only in the Fenway and in Boston but in Massachusetts and New England. That is our fan base and we take care of various groups as best we can.

When I first joined the Red Sox, I did some work related to minorities issues. Major League Baseball wanted to take a look at that. For over forty years, we've had great athletes in the sport and yet how come we don't have any minority managers? Latino. Black. General managers. Where are the coaches on the field?

And then you look at the front office and say the same thing. So, that was part of a study that we were doing. It wasn't so much a committee as a group that out-sources to each team and says, "Let's look at this". It was both a Red Sox thing and a Major League Baseball thing.

We have been doing things in the Dominican community even before Pedro. We've had our Latino Youth Recognition Day. The population, the demographics are changing. Even as a business decision, it's wise to make sure we are marketing to these larger demographics that are emerging today. Especially with Latinos, where the sport is so big for them, for them not to be filling the park all the time, we have to be figuring out what's wrong.

The issue is not really that we've alienated people per se, but the fact that we have 20,000 season ticket holders, and there's 34,000 seats. There's really only 14,000 seats for public sale. It's time to open up some of our lower box seats. It doesn't look so good if all the minorities are out in deep right field. People pass their season tickets down from generation to generation and nobody gives them up. Which is fine, but it doesn't look right.

Obviously, the baseball season is just incredibly hectic for us. Most of the players don't live in the area and so during the off-season there are fewer player-related activities. When we do have the season, we make sure that the players are involved. The season is when everything really starts to kick in for us.

There were a lot more Asian faces in the park when Jin Ho Cho pitched. It is amazing, but you'll find that it's not the same as it is in the African-American community. It's a little bit different. You'll find that when a Jewish player plays, you'll have a lot of Jewish people in the stands. The fact of the matter is, there's a different connection. With the Dominicans, it's a patriotic and linguistic connection.

The Yawkeys philosophy was – as really it should be – you did good and you didn't say anything. But the corporate climate has changed a little bit. They say, "Well, you've only helped the Jimmy Fund." Well, that's not exactly true. There are a LOT of people that we've helped. It's just that we've never said anything before. Sometimes you've got to put the word out a little bit.

We help over a thousand charities. We can't help everyone at the same level, of course. We offer tickets to some, autographed items to others, some sponsorships. Different levels depending on the relationship with us.

We get 200 requests a day from all over the world, we can't honor them all but anybody from New England who calls generally will get something. They come in by mail, by phone, and e-mail now.

We will often have people come in and show them around the park. For instance, we get a great many requests from the Make A Wish Foundation to meet players or to have a tour. We had a bunch of kids come down to spring training. That's their last wish.

Often we have people come before the game for check presentations or to have a photo taken with a player. We have many other programs now, not just the Jimmy Fund. I'd say we do something at around 70 percent of the games.

Some of the stranger requests we've had are the death requests. Having their ashes buried on the field. We had one kid who wanted to be driven around the park as part of the funeral procession. We have requests for people to be buried with certain Red Sox memorabilia. We have a lot of peoples' ashes scattered at Fenway. Some people will just do it during a game, even, but we do have people that will call up and we allow them to do it. It's unbelievable the mystique this place has and the feeling that it gives to people.

There are so many facets to what we do. The youth leagues. We have to make sure we have the right coaches for kids. That is vitally important to the Red Sox organization. We want to make sure we have parental involvement. That can be a big problem. To make sure that our programs run right, we have to have the right people.

As far as I'm concerned, you can hit off a T as long as you're having fun. Let the kids learn to love the game first, whether the bases are 20 feet up the baseline or whether they're 100 feet up the baseline. It doesn't make a difference. Just have them run around, hit, catch the ball, have fun. Even if you just play pickle all day. The main thing is to like the sport first. Then you'll get into it.

The thing that I love about the position is that I have a chance to help a lot of people. That's the essence of the job, the ability to reach out from an organizational viewpoint, and help people. To get paid to do that, it's unbelievable.

In 2004, Ron serves as Manager of Community Athletic Programs.

DEBBIE MATSON
Director of Publications

I've been with the Red Sox 13 years. I was the managing editor for a small publisher in Boston who published the Red Sox Yearbook and through that job I got to know Dick Bresciani, my present boss. I would come to Fenway periodically to run ideas by him and get his input for the yearbook. On a few occasions I expressed my desire to work for the Red Sox if any openings should occur. 1986 was my lucky year.

I was hired to help out during the pennant drive. There were no full-time openings at the time, but I was willing to stay on for however long they could use my services. In November, I was hired permanently as the publications manager, overseeing the publications and photo files, a position I've held ever since.

I coordinate the Red Sox publications. We produce six issues of the official Red Sox Magazine. We started with three issues a season, increased to four, then about four or five years ago we decided to try six editions, one per month during the baseball season. We produce an extra edition for the Division Series. Major League Baseball produces the LCS and the World

Series magazine, and we contribute material for our local section.

We employ three photographers. Jack Maley and Dennis Brearley shoot the games. We hired Cindy Loo to photograph community and special events. Jeff Goldenberg is in charge of advertising sales and is assisted by Jeff Doyle. We employ an outside graphic designer for the design work.

We have a core of writers that we use. Oftentimes writers are interested in submitting stories. We always look at what new writers have to offer. We have a group of writers whose styles are just right for our magazines. It's a mix of regular and occasional guest writers.

We have a base of subscribers. We've been focusing on our subscription base more than ever now, especially with the Internet. Mary Jane Ryan mails out copies of each edition to our alumni ballplayers. I don't know how many copies we sell in the ballpark. Aramark, our concessionaire, handles in-park sales.

The yearbook is distributed more widely that the magazine. It's also produced by an outside publisher, Dunfey Publishing. They handle the editorial for the yearbook. I assist them with any specific photo needs they may have.

The Red Sox Media Guide is out in early March. We produce a post-season media guide when it's necessary. Each year we try to incorporate new material, and each year, the guide gets larger. We promote it on television, and on the Internet where we can reach people beyond New England.

The pocket schedule and ticket brochure are produced by our marketing department. They might ask me to assist with photo selection and proofreading on these projects.

I'm here at 8:45 in the morning, and I stay until 6:00 or 6:15 p.m. for a 7:00 game. By that time my work for the day is done, however, I'll often bring work home with me, cataloging, editing, etc.

_____

As of 2004, Debbie has been with the Red Sox for 18 years. Dennis Brearley has since passed away and a number of other photographers now work with Jack Maley. Mary Jane Ryan has retired.

JACK MALEY
Team Photographer

I'm the Red Sox team photographer. Myself and Dennis Brearley. I work just about every other game. The photos are used in the scorebooks, the yearbook, the calendar and whatever advertising they want to use it for. I've been doing this since 1975.

I was a photographer for the state, for the MDC. I started with them in 1949. I photographed everything you could think of. I worked at Deer Island when they built the initial sewer treatment plant down there. All the deep rock tunnels that carried the water from Quabbin down, I worked on those.

Photography started out as a hobby with me. A couple of my friends were going in with their dad to a hobby show at the old Mechanics Hall. I was the boy from the country going in to the big city. They had all kinds of hobbies, and there was a little darkroom that a fellow had built and he was taking pictures with a couple of floodlights and a roll film camera. Then he'd bring us in, under the safelight and we'd see him develop the film.

It just kind of turned me on. It was like magic seeing the image come off the paper. I was about 12 years old. That was during the Depression years. My folks didn't have any extra money, but my mother let me buy a 39 cent plastic camera down at the drugstore. Every week I'd buy a ten cent roll of film. The developer used to come in tubes, like test tubes.

I made an enlarger out of an old cookie can. Of course, it had no ventilation system and I used to practically cook the negatives. They looked like waffles when I got through. Talk about starting out at the bottom.

In high school, I had a friend who had a Kodak Bantam camera which was really sophisticated – it had a two way lens. I used to really drool when this kid let me borrow it to take pictures for the yearbook.

My mother had this old Kodak folding camera. I think it took 116 film, which they don't even make any more. She let me use that and getting a bigger negative I was able to start making contact prints. When I started working in high school, I was able to buy a better camera.

When I was 19 I went in the Army. When I got out three years later, I went to the University of Massachusetts three nights a week. Kodachrome had been invented but they were just starting to work on color negatives. It was about the same time I started working for the MDC.

One of my friends, Jerry Buckley, was the Red Sox team photographer. In 1975 he asked me if I would give him a hand, because things picked up when they were getting closer to the World Series. I worked with him for a number of years. He did the Celtics, the Bruins, the Patriots and the Red Sox. Then, when the seasons started to overlap, he gave up everything but the Red Sox. At some point, he and I started alternating just like Dennis and I do now.

Before they put the sky boxes up, they used to have cages that hung off the face of the balcony up there. They were called photo cages. They used to have one on the home plate side of first, one at first base, and on the third base side of the infield. Frank O'Brien and I covered the World Series from those cages. We had to come down through the roof box seats and climb down a ladder to get into those cages. They were very sturdily built, so there was never any fear of falling off. Once they built the luxury boxes, that was the end of that. Those were great, though, because you could cover second base, home plate, third and nobody'd be in your way.

The press photographers used to be right out on the field during the game. It's a wonder some of them didn't get killed. Man, you didn't have time to blink and the ball would be there! I generally sit on a little folding camp stool, up against the wall where the gate comes out onto the field, right next to the dugout.

I usually show up at the park around 4 or 4:15. I'll go upstairs into the p. r. office where Dick Bresciani and Debbie Matson are. I find out any pre-game activities that I have. Generally, they'll have an Anthem singer and a color guard from some ship that's in the harbor or some high school or military group or what-

ever. If they're going to do an article in the next scorebook on a certain player, they'll tell us. We'll try to get him in the field and at the plate. I roam around wherever I need to go. It all depends on what they're looking for.

Jack Maley
PHOTO BY BILL NOWLIN

We shoot the whole game, whatever happens. Not too much during batting practice because we have so many shots from Spring training. We go to Florida with the team and we shoot a lot of stuff down there. We do the portraits of the players down in Spring training. Then as they make trades and so forth, we'll bring them into the family room, just down the hall from the players' clubhouse. We have a background screen and a set of studio lights. Any new trades, we'll have the player notified and at the quickest opportunity, we'll just bring him in for maybe 2 or 3 minutes. We'll shoot him in Ektachrome and black and white.

If you're a fan and you wanted a picture of Nomar or someone, p.r. have 8 x 10 head shots that they send out made up from the black and whites that we shoot.

The photographs all belong to the team. During a normal game I probably shoot about 6 rolls of film. If something special's going on – a ceremony or some big shot's there to throw out the first ball – we might do an extra roll. It varies. As the season goes along, we probably tend to shoot less; how many shots can you get of a guy at home plate?

We both use Nikon equipment. I usually have two cameras minimum and I usually have one or two in the car because if you don't have some backup, you can feel kind of stupid. If both of them conked out at the same time, it's only a matter of a couple seconds to get some new equipment and carry on.

I have about five lenses. Dennis has a couple of longer lenses. Primarily for the game action, I use a 400 Nikon 3.5. Dennis has a 400

2.8 and a 600 5.6. It's the 400 2.8 that's the heavy one. There's so much glass in it.

We used to try to shoot Ektachrome at night, but with the black players you don't get any detail under the hats at night. It goes completely black and you couldn't tell one guy from another. So we gave up and only shoot chromes during the day now. We use color negative film at night, Kodak 1000 or 1600. The normal exposure for me at night is 1/500th at f3.5. Wide open. Especially where there's some action, if you don't shoot at 1/500th you get an awful lot of blurring. That's why I shoot wide open. The 1000 film holds together pretty good when you enlarge it. If you're not forced to use high speed, you can get away with the 400.

Ordinarily, the exposures at night are always the same so you're never going to go wrong that way. At 7 o'clock I'd be shooting at whatever the meter called for and then when it gets dark, I just go 1/500th at 3.5 and leave it at that. The lighting in the park is always the same. Of course, the light falls off pretty fast after you go past second base.

The processing is done by Campus Camera over in Kenmore Square. We turn the film in and they pick it up the following morning, so actually Dennis and I very seldom see what we're shooting.

If a player's having a tough time or if he's in a slump, or if he's a pitcher on a losing streak, you just steer clear of him. Don't aggravate him, like the writers do! If a guy's having a tough time, just give him plenty of room.

In the Red Sox camera pit, on the outfield side of the dugout, there's usually about five photographers. Sometimes I'll go down there with Bill Belknap or Jimmy Davis – from the HERALD and the GLOBE. Of course, there's always somebody from the Associated Press. I like that spot up in Jimy Williams' seats, because from the camera pit, it seems every time there's a play at second base, the first base umpire blocks the shot.

A lot of people ask me what some of my favorite shots are. That World Series in '75, that was quite an event. Then when Carl Yastrzemski got his 3000th hit and his 400th home run, when

he went out and waved to the crowd. All the games were good.

RICK DUNFEY
Publisher, Red Sox Yearbook

I started the Dunfey Publishing Company in late 1985. We're a custom publisher of magazines. The first magazine we published was called THE SOX FAN NEWS, later renamed DIEHARD. I launched that in 1986 – an infamous year – and ran the magazine up until the summer of 1998, at which time I sold it to Coman Publishing.

I started by publishing what was really a tabloid SPORTING NEWS style publication about the Red Sox, and then they asked me to take a bid on their yearbook. It's a completely different kind of publishing. THE SOX FAN NEWS or DIEHARD was really a news and information style publication, whereas the Yearbook is really much more of a picture book.

The first issue [of SOX FAN NEWS] was a spring training issue in 1986. It had a picture of Luis Tiant on the cover. I went to the Red Sox fantasy camp that year, the Sox Exchange. Luis was there and we got him adorned in one of our t-shirts. It said THE SOX FAN NEWS on it. He's my all-time Red Sox favorite, along with Fred Lynn. He was the cover boy; It was mainly a spring training oriented issue, a preview of the Red Sox and their competition.

I worked 10 years for the International Thomson Organization, one of the largest media companies in the world. A huge Canadian firm, they own newspapers, magazines, data bases. At the time I left they were a $4 billion company, they're much bigger now. I worked in a college textbook division and was a sales rep, an editor and a manager. Then in 1980 or '81, I started their venture into electronic publishing, which was a euphemism for personal computer software. This was three years before the IBM PC was introduced. The Apple II had just come out. We were one of the original software programs on the Macintosh. Mainly boring stuff – statistics, databases and forecasting tools.

I grew up a Reds fan. I was born and raised in Ohio, and moved here when I was 10, then moved back to Ohio when I was 15. I became a Red Sox fan when I was here. Radically.

In 1975, up until the Reds landed in Boston, I was undecided. I had gone to 51 games in 1975. I worked in Kenmore Square as a waiter. It was the first disco in Boston, called Mirage. I worked the lunch and dinner shift there and in between, I'd caught a zillion games.

My best friend in Boston was Sharon Williams. Her father is William D. Williams, the principal owner of the Reds. Sharon knew all the ballplayers and coaches and introduced me to Rose, Bench, Morgan, Foster. When she introduced me to Sparky Anderson, though, all I said to him was, "Sparky, I have two words to say: Carl Yastrzemski!" At that moment, I knew who I was going to root for, I absolutely changed allegiances.

When Fisk hit his home run in 1975, I was jumping up and down with Johnny Most, hugging and kissing him.

I went to all seven games. I was lucky enough to hook up with an outfit called Sportscom. They had a service in the press boxes where they would take the writers hard copy as they were finishing it on their typewriters and put it on an early version of the fax machine. They put the paper into this weird looking machine and the piece would be bounced back to their desks in Chicago and LA. I got hired as a runner for Jim Murray and Peter Gammons and a whole slew of famous writers. They would put their hand up as they finished a sheet and I would take it to the fax machine. I got to see every game from the press box in both stadiums.

DIEHARD was never an official publication, but the Red Sox liked it. We were fairly journalistic about our approach. We had plenty of criticism in it, but the purpose was not to take potshots at the team, the criticism was more directed at the play on the field and front office moves, rather than ownership, which was a big dartboard at the time. They generally liked it. Right from the beginning, we were sold inside the park by H. M. Stevens.

We weren't insiders. We weren't a mouthpiece for the team. Nobody ever tried to get us to say anything or recant anything. But we weren't like a talk radio show, either. I started publishing the thing because I loved baseball. It wasn't because I was a great Red Sox fan. We never kowtowed to anybody. We called it as it was, but we never wanted to get the vitriolic stuff going.

They asked about a half a dozen companies to bid on the yearbook. I got a call from Dick Bresciani asking me to meet him up in the press box. I didn't know what he was going to say, and I was surprised when I got it.

In 1991, I sold my company to Times Mirror magazines, which owns THE SPORTING NEWS. I worked for them through 1994. While I was there, we were the official publisher for Major League Baseball for four years. We did all the All-Star Games and World Series games. I reacquired the company in 1995.

For years, we came out on Opening Day. We don't any more. One of the strike years, we ended up coming out late and we noticed it really didn't affect much. Usually we'd have a spike in sales on Opening Day, and then nothing until the kids got out of school and families started coming. So now, we come out in mid-May.

Rick Dunfey with his son, watching the Sox in Santo Domingo
PHOTO BY BILL NOWLIN

The Red Sox have final decision on anything we do, but I'll generate most of the ideas. I'll talk them over with Debbie and Dick, and Larry as well.

We sell pretty equally distributed among the park, newsstands, direct response via TV and radio and our own direct mail campaigns, then through souvenir stores like Twins.

Sales are pretty steady from year to year. There was a big dip after the first strike in 1991, not just us; across the country. When we started in '87, ESPN was just getting up and running. There weren't the mega scoreboards. There weren't the nightly Baseball Tonight shows.

Newspapers didn't have four-color capability. There weren't all the talk radio shows, the Internet and everything else. The yearbook, up until around 1990, had a real niche. It was the only place you could get four-color photographs of your local heroes. You couldn't see them on TV. You couldn't see them in the newspaper. Now we're competing with all those other media forms. Sales were very, very healthy up until 1991. You would think they would follow how well the team is doing, but not really – unless the team is in it in September. If they're in it in September, everybody wins.

I published THE LEGEND OF WALLY THE GREEN MONSTER. I wrote the book. I named Wally. My wife did the illustrations. We basically created the whole legend. The Red Sox had a couple of ideas – he lived in the Wall – that's about as far as they took it. Larry [Cancro] called me the first week of March and told me, "We need a book by Kids' Opening Day in five weeks." In five weeks, we wrote the story and got it illustrated. We got 20,000 copies up to Fenway. When you only have a couple of weeks, the pressure's on, but we enjoyed it. That was hard work. It's like giving birth. You forget about it later.

Kevin Shea
PHOTO BY BILL NOWLIN

KEVIN SHEA
Director of Communications and Baseball Information

I began working for the Red Sox as a group sales representative and marketing assistant for Larry Cancro, which was a great opportunity because that's one of the best places to see the whole operation. You have dealings with the ticket office, with accounting, with the baseball side of the operation. I worked for Larry for about 2½ years.

I went to Holy Cross. I was a psychology major and I just applied out of the blue. I got a call and came in and met with Larry. It was a great conversation, we kind of hit it off. I got a call at about 10 o'clock at night – "If you're interested in the job, come in tomorrow."

Our challenge always was to make sure our fans understood what we were doing. We were one of the first teams to develop a web site. That's been one of our best vehicles for communicating with our fans. It's not being filtered through another medium. It's direct to your fans. And fans love it. Our numbers rival the BOSTON HERALD's on a daily basis, as far as people going on our web site.

From marketing I went over to PR and was Publicity Manager for a while. We developed another department called Corporate Communications. Community relations and customer relations were under that department. I headed that department up. That was around the beginning of the Clemens situation and some of those negative things. Out of response to that, we created the Communications and Baseball Information Department, which responds to negative publicity. We're on the baseball side. I report directly to Dan. We deal with the players, all the sports media, local and national. We deal with all the baseball matters.

No matter what position you have in this organization, everything is geared towards winning on the field. What goes on in between those lines is the most important thing that we do here.

For three years I went on every trip, the whole season. They've taken me off the road a little bit, because they want me close to home, with Dan [Duquette] and John [Harrington]. Glenn [Wilburn] does most of the traveling. If Dan goes on the road, I'll go with him, and I'll also give Glenn a trip off here and there. It was an amazing experience, but it was very difficult to have any sort of life. I'd still be doing it, though, if they wanted me to. Whatever it takes.

It varies, depending on what time I get out of here at night, but if I get in here at 10 o'clock, I'll spend the morning – depending on how quiet it is – doing phone work. Then, as the department's getting ready for the game itself, I'll make sure everything's on schedule.

Once the players are in the clubhouse, I'm usually down there on the field, working with the media. Once the game starts, I'm up in the press box, and I work with the media up there. Postgame, I'm in the clubhouse. I go down right after the game is over and meet with Jimy [Williams]. Then we let the print media in to talk to him. Then the electronic media comes into the clubhouse. I kind of orchestrate that changing of the guard as the print media come out and the electronic media go in. The print media always goes into Jimy's office first; it's just the routine, just tradition. It seems to work.

Jimy gives the overall picture of the whole game, and then, if the GLOBE has three writers there, one guy will be doing the game story, one might be doing a story on the starting pitcher – maybe Pedro – the other guy might be doing the star of the game. So, they'll get quotes from Jimi on all three, then they'll go in the clubhouse and one guy will talk to Pedro, one may talk to a couple of key players in the game, and the third guy will talk to the star of the game. It's kind of like a symphony!

Everyone gets what they need and then they head upstairs. The clubhouse is the players' office, their home away from home. If you have something to do in the clubhouse, get your work done and then move along. There's no need to hang around.

The clubhouse is open up until 45 minutes before the game, and then again after the game. That is a LOT of access. There really isn't a heck of a lot of time for the players to have private time.

The media has a lot of access to the players before the game and after the game. After the game, they can be in and out of there within 45 minutes. The regulars get their work done and then get going. That's what I watch out for, too. You don't want anyone down there just hanging around.

Tony Massarotti's a perfect example of someone who handles himself very professionally. Here's here to get his work done. Because of that, the players respect him. They know that Tony handles himself professionally and they

respect him for that. He benefits from that. His paper benefits from that.

I wait for the last one to go and then I'm usually last out of the building, either myself or Joe Cochran from the clubhouse. Sometimes, after the game is the best time to get work done. The phone's not ringing. Sometimes I take advantage of the quiet. It's a long day, but I wouldn't trade it for anything in the world.

Off-season, it's different. You put in almost as many hours. The main writers will call me at home – which I don't mind as long as they don't call too late. It's not a 9 to 5 job. It's a full-time job.

Dan has a foreign-born players program, throughout the minor league system, that addresses not only language hurdles, but things as simple as food. Ordering from a menu. Things you wouldn't even think of. A player's coming from Japan to the United States. Just grab your glove and go out and play? It's far more complicated than that! This person's coming from another culture. You can't take that for granted. The players are people first, players second.

I remember a few years ago, a player was at a hotel down at spring training and wanted to cook rice in their room. The hotel had a rule against it, so we had to find a place where he could cook in his room. He didn't want to eat out, order off a menu. This person was losing weight. Things like that, Dan doesn't take for granted. Sometimes I'll ask one of the Korean media or the Japanese media to translate for the group of media down there. The media appreciates that, and the player appreciates that.

There's a support mechanism in place for the whole organization, not just our foreign-born players. Players are human beings. For a ballplayer going to spring training and playing for an entire season, that's an incredible stress on a family. We have a system in place that if a player needs help, that is available.

Every spring training, Pedro says to me, "Kevin, whatever you ask me to do, if you're asking me, I know it's important for me to do it. I know it's important for me, I know it's important for the organization, and I'll be happy to do it." That's the way he is. He's amazing to work with. Nomar's the same way. They're very accommodating and helpful. They understand the business. They understand what's important for them to do. That's why people love this team. It's a hard-working group of players who just want to win out there.

I check out the fan chat groups, online. We get a lot of e-mail. A lot of fan feedback. It amazes me that people take the time to write very thoughtful comments, on the team and the organization. They care. Our fans are our lifeblood. They're the reason we're all here. They're the reason I have a job. Dan and John and John [Buckley] – they know that our fans are important. They never, never take that for granted. People say, "Oh, the Red Sox are going to sell tickets. They'll always pack that place." It's never taken for granted here. It really isn't. The loyalty's appreciated, and it's never taken for granted.

Prior to the 2004 season, Kevin left the Red Sox to explore other opportunities and was replaced by Glenn Geffner.

Kate Gordon
PHOTO BY BILL NOWLIN

KATE GORDON
Communications Credentials Coordinator

When I was in high school, in Pittsfield in western Mass, we had minor league baseball for years and years and years. We had the Red Sox back in the '60s, but it was the Pittsfield Mets single A New York-Penn League affiliate. They're still there now.

It was all my mother's side, my grandfather and my grandmother. My mom has three sisters and the four of them are sports fanatics. My dad doesn't know anything about sports.

Since I was born, I've loved baseball and that was the first job that I wanted to do. A single A team, there are probably fifteen employees total so you do everything from working the concession stand to cater parties to pull the tarp. You do just about everything. I was just summer help, I don't think they even gave us a title. You did anything you could. It was a pretty small group of people; the owner's mother is the receptionist. She does the ticket sales. You get a little flavor of all the different aspects of how a team works.

Did I pull for the major league Mets? Oh, God, no! It was just a team in Pittsfield as far as I was concerned. My family is Red Sox only.

I did that for a couple of summers. Then I was deciding between Williams College and Tufts. I came to Tufts because I wasn't going to be able to get the Red Sox games on TV or radio out there in Williamstown. That's why I came to college in Boston.

Then the owner of the team – you know everyone there because it's so small – he is on the board of directors of the Hall of Fame – he suggested to me, "Would you ever think of working for the Red Sox?" He said, "I know a couple of people. Maybe you could do an internship or something." I just about died. I couldn't believe it, but I followed up that fall and I got a position. Larry Cancro was my boss the first two years I interned. I did some group sales work, marketing, that sort of thing.

They were interested in hiring me full-time so since the spring of '96, right out of college, I've been here. I was just in the right place at the right time.

I handle all media access to Fenway and our Spring training site. A lot of times when people want to do interviews, I'll do the preliminary screening on what they're looking to do. Get them to send videotapes, and see what kind of show it is if it's radio or TV, or see what kind of publication it is if we haven't worked with them before. Years ago there was one corps of writers that covered your team. Now, with all the international players, it's not unusual to be talking to someone from Korea or Japan or the Dominican or whatever. You really have to be attuned to who's in your organization, on the minor league level, too. A lot of time media people will call from other countries and want to know about the minor league players. It's interesting. Even in four years, I've seen that evolve.

I get by pretty good with my Spanish. In Florida we get a lot of Spanish-speaking media. I speak Spanish to them and it's been a huge help. Most of them have decent enough English, but there's some – especially at Spring training – their English is really limited so they feel welcome when somebody's able to – even thought I'm not completely fluent – speak to them and tell them what's happening.

Our players appreciate it too. Certainly some speak English better than others. The toughest thing is players from Korea or Japan. Just about nobody that works in American baseball speaks Korean.

In terms of credentials, there are some people who get season credentials and others who come in for a single visit. It's a hard thing to quantify since it's existed for so long. There are a lot of people out there – the Baseball Writers Association members – who have lifetime passes.

There are probably twenty people from the HERALD and the GLOBE. They have their main beat writers and then a couple of guys every night – or girls – and then they have five or six photographers on a regular basis, so we've had to create a system which is fairly strict. Otherwise, everyone and his brother would be having a season pass. It's basically for those people who are here at least a couple of days a week. We have five traveling beat papers. The HERALD, the GLOBE, WORCESTER TELEGRAM, PROVIDENCE JOURNAL and the HARTFORD COURANT. They're represented at every game throughout the year, home and away.

Then we've got maybe ten to twelve home-only beat papers, which are like your MIDDLESEX NEWSes – I guess they're METRO WEST NEWS now, NASHUA TELEGRAPH, LOWELL SUN, things like that. They don't travel. We've got a good group here at Fenway but on the road it's just five or six guys.

The traveling beat papers apply through the American League for an American League pass so they don't have to contact each park individually.

We credential our own regular broadcasters. I think they go through Jim Healey for a regular American League pass. The other broadcasters who are coming into our park all have American League passes, so we usually don't have to worry about them on a game-to-game basis unless there's a fill-in.

When you've got fifty or more colleges in the area, too, it's difficult. You get a call, "I've got this big project due tomorrow. Can I come down and interview some players?" They just don't really grasp how many people are making the same request and the fact they can't really just do it today. It's difficult. People need to be able to gain experience, but a lot of the time – especially with the college reporters – I'll urge them to try to get more experience at the college and minor league level.

We have the Media Credentials window at Gate D. We have Ray Cormier down there. Ray checks in with me on a daily basis and if there's anything out of the ordinary that somebody's doing, he gets a list. It's a daily thing. He can phone up if there's anything that comes up. Sometimes it takes a while to find me because I'm all over the ballpark, but he gets me.

Kevin [Shea] and I pretty much work side by side. A lot of people will contact me first, having dealt with me on a daily basis. Especially for Pedro and Nomar, who are asked to do a million and one things – Kevin will usually take the reins on that and decide whether or not it makes sense for the player to do it.

Pre-game, just beat writers are allowed in the clubhouse. Some radio people, too, but no cameras or TV. Usually a couple of us are down on the field during batting practice to assist with media interview requests, to disperse information, any transactions that have happened that day or anything that's going on. Any pre-game ceremony, like when Babe Ruth's daughter was here, we'll kind of clue all the media in before the game. On the weekends, the sports crews are different people and they're not always over here, but Monday through Friday we usually get a decent crowd doing their stand-ups for the 5 o'clock and the 6 o'clock news.

I come in for the night games at around 10:30 AM and usually leave around midnight, maybe an hour or two after the game. We have interns that help us with post-game notes. There are different things that we post on the web site in terms of post-game information and if there's any things that need tying up, you'll be up in the press box for half an hour to forty five minutes after the game, finishing the media notes and getting the box score out.

I'm sure a lot of the newspapers go through STATS, Inc. or whatever to get the box scores electronically, but all the guys who write their stories after the game are all looking at the hard copy box score that we pass out in the press box. I doubt the newspapers are retyping that; they must get it off the wire or something.

We don't really monitor the chat groups. There are just so many of them out there. If something comes to our attention, something offensive somewhere, someone using our name, certainly we'd take care of that, but we realize there are a lot of fan sites out there – most of them, they're just fans!

During the off-season it's a little less intense, but there's a schedule that you need to follow. There is certain information that needs to be released from time to time – ticket information, the schedule, signings of players, shaping the roster. This year, some post-season awards, which was nice. It's certainly not the hours it is during the season, but you stay pretty busy.

Kate left the Red Sox soon after, replaced by Kerri Walsh. Tom Moore was pleased; he and Kerri married a couple of years later. In 2004, Meghan McClure fills the position. Kerri Moore became Assistant to the Executive Vice President/Public Affairs, Dr. Charles Steinberg.

GLENN WILBURN
Baseball Information Coordinator

I was a college student at Northeastern and I took Joe Castiglione's class in 1990. Joe loved the fact that I knew something about baseball. It was my favorite sport as a kid. I knew Red Sox history even though I wasn't a Red Sox fan. I just knew from watching TV. It was a one semester class. It really helped me a lot.

Joe kept track of students who he thought took the course seriously. I happened to be in New York doing some co-op work about 7 or 8 months after the class was over. He called me out of the blue. He said that his current statistician in the broadcast booth was graduating and wanted to know if I would be interested in being his new stat guy. When he offered me the opportunity to work at Fenway Park for 81 home games, I couldn't pass it up even though at the time I was a Yankees fan. I'm from New York originally. Whenever Joe tries to rip on me about being a Yankees fan, he admits that he was, too.

For the whole season of 1991 and most of the season of 1992, I was the stat guy for Joe and Bob Starr. I was paid, I think it was, twenty-five bucks a game.

It's called "statistician" but it's more of an assistant position, you already have all the stats done by Red Sox PR people. Basically, I would just update averages as the game went along, and ERA. Give Joe or Bob the advertising drop-ins that they had to read on air. I put those together. I did some historical research, as the game went along. If Jody Reed tied some record or he was approaching some record set by, oh, Rico Petrocelli, I'd look in the encyclopedia or media guides and highlight that so they could have that information in front of them.

I kept the out-of-town scores. We had a huge sheet and I would look up on the sports ticker and update the scores every half inning. We had a ticker back then in the press box. Now it's a computer screen.

Basically, I'm assistant PR person here. I travel with the club extensively. Every game at Fenway, I do the pre-game notes. They're printed up and available in the press room.

Generally, Kevin Shea and Kate Gordon work out of the home office and I'm the contact on the road. I set up interviews between the players and the media. I try to provide the media with statistics, records and research, what have you. At Fenway Park, Kate or myself do the PA system [in the press box.]

We also do a game summary, on the web site. www.redsox.com. It's our department, with the aid of New England Sports Department. Kate does most of the work on the web site. I do the post-game story and the Manager's out-look page, and I'll post the pre-game notes. During the game, an intern enters the play-by-play.

[This stopped when MLB took over all the websites for each major league team, creating a more uniform (and less individualistic) look and feel. The original Sox site had a number of nice touches, such as old P.A. announcer Sherm Feller's voice welcoming fans to the site.]

My whole premise was to use Joe's course as part of building towards a TV career, until Joe thought enough of me to ask me to come along with him. That was when I really got to know what goes on behind the scenes of a major league baseball club, and that intrigued me more than what I was doing in TV. NESN is right down the hall from us. I've got the best of both worlds. I'm pretty happy right now.

GUY SPINA
Press Steward

The press steward is basically an usher for the press box. The media's usher, rather than the fans'. The visiting press, as well as the local press, if they need any encyclopedias, any record books, any media guides on various teams. Any publications made available to the media are maintained by the local ballclub. We have several secure cabinets where we maintain all these materials.

Ralph [Rodolfo] Cid brought me into the ballpark. We both started in 1975. He started, I believe, at the beginning of the season. I was kidding him, "Boy, what a job that would be. Fantastic. That's not a job; that's fun." It turned out that 1975 was when the Red Sox made a drive to the World Series, and they needed to supplement their personnel because they were getting tremendous crowds. They asked, "Anybody know anybody who was interested?", and Ralph mentioned my name. They said,

"Bring him in for an interview" one thing led to another and here was my first day at Fenway Park. Right in the middle of the season, 1975. It was a good year to start.

Guy Spina
PHOTO BY BILL NOWLIN

We have one media guide for every team in the major leagues. We have the encyclopedias, baseball record books, baseball guides. We have some biographies, histories of the Red Sox.

The local print media have their own seats. It's not the person, it's the publication who has the seat. Whoever's working that night for, say, the HARTFORD COURANT or the PROVIDENCE JOURNAL or the WORCESTER TELEGRAM – goes to that seat. We also maintain seats for the visiting press. The radio and TV media have sort of general admission seating in the press box. I'm also the steward for them. It's a throwback to the old term of being press steward, when press was everybody except the one radio broadcaster. We maintain that title, but in essence I'm the media and communications steward.

My primary functions are all taken care of by the end of the first inning. At that point, there's really nothing for me to do except to be [available] if they need something. As a part of my function I maintain a small beverage bar – non-alcoholic because of Major League Baseball rules. In the old days, it was very alcoholic. Nowadays, it's just soft drinks and such. A few snacks or something like that. That's also a throwback to the old tradition of what the press box is.

I'm in the lineage of Tommy McCarthy. He was up there in the old press box when it used to be in the middle of the roof seating. It was a flat area, maybe two rows of seats and nothing else. It was in line with the roof seats. That was the press box. Since then, they've renovated the roof and they've put that 600 Club in. Directly above the 600 Club is what is now called the press box. It is extremely high. For the casual observer to come up there and watch a ballgame, you get kind of a distorted view. You can over-react to a simple pop-up and think it's going to be leaving the ballpark. Everything is below you. It's very rare that a fly ball will come as high as we are.

We maintain three different TV receivers. That's for exclusive coverage of the game. They can see an instant reply.

I'm usually there about 2½ to three hours before the game. The Red Sox publicity office has staff downloading all this information, from first thing in the morning. They collate it and get it all together, make sure they have complete sets, then they start printing it. I'll bring it upstairs and do the local distributions.

It's between half an hour and forty-five minutes after the game by the time I shut every-thing down and make sure everything is secure. I wait for the media to start flowing back because they leave a lot of expensive equipment around and we don't want the press box to be completely empty with that equipment out there. So I wait until there's an influx of post-game interviewers, when they're coming back. I'm gone before they leave, though. The press box is theirs. They can be there as late as they want.

Chaz Scoggins is the primary official scorer. There are a couple of backups because nobody's expected to be there every game. He is a reporter so he also has to work his regular job.

I've never had any difficul-ty. I find that the media are a great bunch of people. I've never met one that I didn't like. You don't always agree with what they write, but we have the best coverage here in Boston. The best.

Mary Rodrigues
PHOTO BY ANDREA RAYNOR

I suppose I've been a Red Sox fan since I was a kid. I probably was a Braves fan first because that was my father's allegiance.

I started as an usher in uniform down on the field. This is an usher's position and I just matriculated to it.

I started in 1975 and the Red Sox went to the World Series. My son, when he was 14 years old, started at Fenway Park as a vendor, in 1986. And the Red Sox went to the World Series. So we looked at each other...uh..."does your mother want to come to work?" Every time we start a new member of the family in here, the Red Sox go to the World Series.

MARY RODRIGUES
Manager of Staff Dining Room

I manage the staff and press dining room. Staff people eat on one side of the dining room and press on the other. Staff people eat earlier. They have to finish before the game. The press, I think, are a little more flexible.

We serve between 200 and 250. The food for the suites come from the third floor kitchen. I am located on the fifth floor. There's a few different kitchen areas. There's also the Players Club, down on the ground floor, and they have their own kitchen.

I'm a special ed teacher. Actually, the sched-ule works very well because I have summers off. It gets a little hectic in the spring and fall, but I manage. It's usually Opening Day that's a real problem and I reserve a personal day for that.

I started as a fill-in waitress about fourteen years ago. They gave me a chance to work there, and I kind of worked my way up. I started in the same dining facility.

My boss, Brian Aitchison, and I will sit down and go over menus. We have a head chef as well, who is also included in on that. Brian manages the 406 Club, the suites. He works alongside Patricia Flanagan, the Red Sox Director of Foods.

We offer two or three entrees as well as a full salad bar, with cold cuts and two or three different salads to pick from, hot soup and assorted desserts.

We only serve breakfast for the 1 o'clock games on Sunday. It's a combination brunch and breakfast, a wide variety of fresh fruits and bagels, really a very nice breakfast. We also serve lunch, on Saturdays, and for 4:00 games, and for any day games. Most of the games, Monday through Friday, are dinners.

During the summer, I'm usually there by 1 o'clock. I usually stay – because I also manage and serve Mr. Duquette's box. He usually eats in the dining room [GM Duquette] with regular staff people, but he does have a variety of guests coming into his box. I usually bring them appetizers or hot dogs.

I'm there usually to the eighth inning, but I'm quick enough to get out of there and beat the traffic. When I leave, the radio definitely goes on. WEEI is permanently set on my radio. I hear all the talk shows, too. I think when you work there you really become very devoted. It's exciting.

During the off-season, I definitely look forward to spring. It keeps me very busy, but I love going to work there every day. It's nice to be able to say that. I don't get home until 11

o'clock and then, if I'm teaching, I'm up usually by 5. I'm a runner, so I have to do my running. Then shower, and then off and in school by 7. It's a long day. I don't find it exhausting, though. My adrenalin is pumping by the time I'm in Fenway. And I kind of carry it over into the schools, too. The kids love to hear stories about Fenway Park. It's a nice connection. I think it's sincere, too, because they see how excited I get when I talk about it.

I have eight girls working for me and they're very reliable and friendly. I hear that Fenway Park is the best park to receive your meal at, whether it be breakfast or dinner – for the press. I really enjoy it there. I don't even think of it as a job. Every year, I hope that my work lasts deep into October.

Bob Levin, Stadium Operations and gatekeeper at Gate D for the past 15 years.
PHOTO BY EMMET NOWLIN

5

GETTING SET

Warren Curtin, Ticket Taker
John DeRosa, Usher
Rodolfo Cid, Usher
Larry Nowell, Head Usher
Tom Gilmartin, Usher
Cynthia Russell, Usher
Jerry Smith, Usher Supervisor
Mike Pucillo, former usher

Gene Brundage, Usher
Tom Castiglione, Emergency Medical Technician
Richard Giglio, Organist
Ray Totaro, Organist
Ed Brickley, Public Address Announcer
Kevin Friend, Sound Engineer
Katryna Nields, National Anthem Singer
Jim McSherry, National Anthem Singer

WARREN CURTIN
Ticket Taker

I go way back. My first baseball game I ever went to was the 1948 World Series. Braves Field. In 1967, I went to about 55 games. I saw all those World Series games. I first went to work here in 1968. The pay at the time was kind of low and I was working at the Post Office, I'm a letter carrier – 32 years, in Lynn, Mass., so I worked just one year. I went back as an usher in 1974. The union had come in in '71 and the pay tripled. I ushered into the '74 season. Section 30, out in left field.

In the playoffs and the World Series, my job was to handle all the VIPs. I handled the Commissioner and his people and all the baseball owners and Tip O'Neill and the governors. I walked them down to the Fenmore Room, where they served food and things like that.

It's one union, but we're separate entities, the ticket takers and the ushers. '76 came and there was an opening on the ticket taker side. Ticket takers get through in the first or second inning. Ushers have to stay after the game and clear the field. It's the same money, but ushers do work on tips so you can make more money. I had to decide whether I wanted to stay late, so I talked to my wife: what should I do? I became a ticket taker in '76. I've been doing it ever since.

We open the gates an hour and a half before game time. The supervisors pull up the gates. Jerry Smith. Eddie Goode. Dave [Snyder.] They put gloves on, because that's kind of heavy, those gates going up. Sometimes the security kids help them out.

As soon as those gates go up, we're all in position. We normally put on about 18 to 20 ticket takers.

From Yawkey Way, most people go to the first three ticket takers. They're like sheep, you have to tell them, "Go down there." We have to push them down. The first gate, he'd be taking all the tickets.

We have three late gates. Gate A, one guy stays four and a half innings. The bleacher gate is four and a half innings. Gates E and B out in right field, the guys stay two innings and then

Warren Curtin
PHOTO BY BILL NOWLIN

we close them down. We go by the crowd. We usually close three about twenty minutes into the first inning. Second inning, we close the next three or four. After the second inning, we'll close another two. Then the third inning, we'll close another two, then we'll have two open and then there'll finally be one guy until the fifth inning.

Then we're all done. If it's going to be a good game, I stay. Most of us just leave. It's like a job. We work anywhere from two hours, to two hours and fifteen.

As you're taking the ticket, you glance at the date and game number. You do it fast. After taking a few tickets it comes naturally. People will come in with tickets for a game that's already gone by, or they'll mix up things. Directions are important. They say, "Where do I go?", before they even look. You know your sections, so you point them out: "Take a right, down the ramp."

I collect the stubs. The stubs go downstairs to the head usher, Larry Nowell. We have a count sheet and we write down the gate we were on, our name, and the number of tickets we took. I have a counter. We don't take it off the turnstile. Fenway has a man that comes around and reads our turnstile, to make sure we're in range. They allow us a 1% range. The turnstile number should correspond with the number on our sheet. The next day, Steve Russo, who assigns us, he'll read us how much we're off.

We used to count them ourselves. Every 25, I'd put a tab and then I'd count the tabs at the end of the night. We had a guy come in one time – he only lasted about three months – but he said, "You guys are behind the times. Why don't you buy one of these counters and have it in your hand?" We had to get it by the bosses: "Is this all right?" It's worked out good for us. In fact, we're better ticket takers because we can give directions without worrying about our count.

On our union contract, we have to make 45 out of 81 games. I average around 65. I work at the Post Office Saturdays so I can't make Saturdays or Sundays. In April and May, I'll work my Sundays and in September I'll go back to Sundays. It's pretty fair that way. If they do well, we get to work into October.

Beginning in 2004, there are no more stubs. All tickets contain bar codes and are optically scanned. The number of turnstiles, however, has increased from 18 to 30, to facilitate entry to the Park.

JOHN DEROSA
Usher

John DeRosa
PHOTO BY BILL NOWLIN

I started when I was 52. I'll be 81 in May. A friend at the Navy Yard helped me get on as an usher.

At the time, if you were there and they needed help, they'd put you on. Day by day basis. I was pretty fortunate, I think I only went home once or twice. I got two dollars a game.

They provide uniforms, yes. For years, they would give you a red suit jacket, a pair of pants; blue with a red stripe. But you'd have to provide your own white shirt. They would provide a blue tie. I left the jacket at the park, and once a year, they'd clean them.

An usher in those days had a hat, like a policeman's hat, and he stood out. Now they have these jackets. Some people come up to me and ask me if I work there!

I try to make every game that I can. I believe we're getting $46 a game this year.

You can get off if you need to, because you're hired every day, not for the season. When I first went there, they put on about a hundred ushers. Now it's down to about 35.

They don't want you there three hours before the game, so I go have a sandwich at one of the food places. After a while I mooch over and get in about 20 minutes before I'm supposed to. You go through the service gate; all the other gates are closed.

I work on the right side, if you're looking down at the dugout. When you start here, you go to the bleachers. Then you work yourself up and you're on gates. I was on a gate for a long time. If you do your job like you're supposed to, you stay in your one position all the time.

As long as people are going down to the railing to get autographs, they don't want us to kick them out from there. About ten minutes before the game you're supposed to go down and tell people to move.

Around the bottom of the ninth, I go down front. There are special seats down there, Dr. Pappas is there. I go down to keep people from jumping all over him. My partner goes out on the field. Then when the doctor leaves, I go out on the field until the music stops. That's a good fifteen minutes after the game is over. Then I go in the locker room. I've got a son-in-law working as an usher, Mark Karpowicz, and I walk down to the garage with him.

They give you printed instructions on what you have to do. "The customer is always right. They're paying your wages. You ARE the Red Sox." They want you to be cool, calm and collected at all times.

A lot of people swear and don't realize it. So you go up and you let them know it's a family ballpark. Most of them say, "OK" and calm down and that's it. You're still at a ballgame and there's going to be people rooting for their side and occasionally they're going to forget.

We're not supposed to get autographs. If a baseball comes in the stands, we're supposed to hand it back to the ball boy. You, as a fan, can keep it.

There are those numbers on the right field wall. Yaz, Cronin and so forth – people want to know what they are. I give them all the numbers, tell them who they are. They can't figure out Jackie Robinson's as yet. Cronin and Doerr, they don't know! I tell them, buy the pamphlet, [the scorebook magazine] it tells you most of the things. It has all the players in it.

They want to know who the players are. I keep one of those [rosters] in my hat. I just take my hat off and I tell them exactly who it is because I've got all the numbers. I know Garciaparra and I know O'Leary and so forth, but I don't remember every one of them, especially where they'll change them and send them down to Pawtucket. They all want to know who's pitching. I tell them to look at the scoreboard. There's a number there, but if they don't have one of the magazines, I'll take off my hat and check to see who it is.

Everybody seems to think you're making a fortune on tips. Take my word for it, you don't. I don't make even five or ten dollars, truthfully. What I've got from people is boxes of cookies. Oh yeah, cookies. One fellow brought me a pizza! How can I eat that when I'm working? Your job is to put people in their seats and that's what I do. I put them in their seats and they're happy as O'Hara!

The first four innings, I don't see much baseball. I may see a hit here and there, but I can't concentrate, because someone will ask, "Where's this seat?" or "Get these people out of my way. I can't see." So by the time I get to see the game, it's almost over. I see smidgens.

People want to know how that scoreboard works. I tell them there's two guys out there. They want to know how they can see. I tell them, well, in between some letters out there, there's a little slot they can look out.

Naturally, if they're winning it's a lot better. People are a lot happier. You don't get any of this, "Hey, you bum!"

I've met some nice people. Season ticket holders. They've been there as long as I've been there. I've seen their kids grow up.

I've met a few [VIPs] down behind home plate. I've met ex-Governor Dukakis. I've seen Seiji Ozawa. Another fellow who used to sit in my section was [Stephen] King. He amazed me. He used to be reading a book during the ballgame.

Years ago, when I worked in the bleachers, they poured beer on my head from up above, but that's standard there, you know.

RODOLFO CID
Usher

Years ago, I don't remember how many, one of the transformers went out. They had the power back within an hour and a half. Everything was under control. The only concern was the handicapped, but everything went beautiful. No problems. Since that day, they decided that everybody should carry a flashlight, that's the reason we carry the light. We haven't used it since.

I came here from Cuba, July 22, 1962. I was an accountant with the railroad company, in the payroll department.

Rodolfo Cid
PHOTO BY BILL NOWLIN

I was arrested by the G2. The G2 in Cuba is like the KGB in Russia, the secret police. I was in jail in 1960 for a couple of months. They took me out of my house about 1:30 in the morning. They brought me, with three other guys in the neighborhood that they were also suspicious about being anti-government. I distributed propaganda against Castro but they never could prove it. We never went on trial or anything like that. My brother-in-law was a lawyer. He brought them a court order. He told them. "You have to charge him, or release him, according to the law." They told him, "Take those papers and wipe your ass with it. You come back here, we're going to throw you in with him and see how you like it."

They announced, on the eve of 1961, saying it proved the generosity of the Revolution, they were going to release some of the political prisoners so they can spend the New Year with their family.

I got released but I still wanted to stay. Me and my wife worked hard. We owned a home.

Two years before Castro came in, my mortgage was all paid. My wife was a teacher. Between us, we had a decent salary.

When the government took over the school, I took my daughter who was seven years old out of the school. I said, if she's going to be in a government school at least I'm going to send her where her mother is teaching. So I sent her to the school where my wife could keep an eye on her. One day they took her to one of those revolutionary things. Young Pioneers. They started brainwashing. When I saw my daughter marching with the other kids, singing the "Internationale" – the Communist anthem – I said, "I'll see you later." That day I decided to leave.

I pay underneath the table and they give me a seat in the plane and we flew to Miami. My wife, my daughter and myself.

I went to the refugee center. I've never been a beggar. I have some pride, and I was crying when I had to search in those old clothes boxes. I'd never seen myself in that sort of situation. Three months later, they called me and said there's a church in Boston, Saint Andrew's Church in Belmont, they're going to help you.

I started at MIT almost right away. I came to Boston October 6 and on October 27 I started at MIT. They needed computer operators. I never worked in computers but I worked with other IBM type of machines.

The pay was once a month. One day the supervisor came and took my wallet out of my pocket. I said [to myself] What the hell is he doing? He looked inside and said, "You only have seven dollars here, you know." At that time I didn't know what he was saying but today I know that he was saying, "How are you going to live with seven dollars for the rest of the month?" He took me to the bursar's office and they gave me $100 in advance. I went to the A&P and bought three big steaks. I said, "For two years we haven't tasted meat. Today we're going to eat."

When I went into MIT the department I worked for was just starting. For five years, I was the computer operations manager in the accounting department.

I used to work in the Sheraton Hotel in Copley Square, in the Copenhagen Restaurant as a cashier from Tuesday to Saturday. The host in the restaurant worked as an usher. I asked him, "Can you help me get in there?"

When I came in this country, in 1963, I used to go to the ballpark. I'd pay a dollar fifty general admission and I could sit anywhere I want. The first game was between New York and Boston and the pitchers were Ralph Terry and Monbouquette. The Red Sox lost 3-2 in 11 innings, with a home run for Elston Howard.

At that time, I was glad, because I was a New York fan. I was! I used to love Joe DiMaggio and Yogi Berra – oh, yeah. My team was New York since I was five years old. I changed when I started working for the Red Sox.

In Cuba, I knew by memory the rosters of every major league team. My team in the National League was the St. Louis Cardinals, because the Cardinals had a contract with a Cuban team in Havana. Almendares. The World Series, we could hear on the radio.

I saw the Red Sox in Cuba. They went to Havana, to play an exhibition game with the Pirates. I traveled from Camaguey to Havana just to see that game. I was working for the railroad company, so I had a pass. I traveled all night long, just to watch the game the next day. I saw Ted Williams. Boy, he hit a home run to center field. It was unbelievable how far that ball went!

I used to play baseball in school, but I never was that great. I started as a catcher, but later on I moved to third base. In third base, I got a bad bounce and it hit me in the eye. I got afraid of that position and I changed to the outfield, and that's where I stayed.

I was a good hitter but not a power hitter. I was like Wade Boggs, a lot of singles. I don't have a very strong arm, but I love baseball. I used to play softball at MIT every Wednesday.

On the usher list, I am number 6. Larry Nowell is my supervisor. Gilmartin is the oldest. He's number one.

I worked at the Boston Garden for 24 years, too. The Fleet Center. I work every game at Fenway Park, because I love baseball.

I go to Spring training once a year. I spend a week and a half watching Spring training games. If I wanted to work there, I could, but I don't want to. I buy a ticket.

For the last five years, I've been saying that I'm going to quit, but I still haven't done it.

LARRY NOWELL
Head Usher

I'm the oldest usher in this place. I was born 3/28 of 1913. I started working at Fenway Park in 1947. I played in the Park League for the Squantum team. As a matter of fact, I played with Harry "The Hat" Walker in the service. And Spud Chandler, too, years ago in Camp Shelby, Mississippi.

I grew up with Eddie Pellagrini. He always admired me. Now I admire him, because he got in the big leagues.

I was working on Tremont Street in Boston for Bausch and Lomb. I was grinding, edging lenses, lining up lenses. This fellow was the chief usher, at Loew's Orpheum. I said something about getting a part-time job at Fenway Park. So he says, "Why don't you go down and see Joe Lunney? He hires all the ushers from the theaters." So I went on my lunch hour, and I said, "Any chance of working at Fenway Park as an usher?" He said, "Yeah, drop over and I'll see what I can do for you."

We used to have three men on an aisle then, top, middle and the bottom. Two dollars a game. I started at Braves Field at about '48. I worked for them, too.

I check in all the ticket takers. They come in starting about the second inning. I check them off and then sign their card, the cards that they get paid from. The late man comes in about the end of the fifth inning. From then on, I'm on my own.

All those tickets go into this large plastic bag. Then I take the sheet upstairs and they post the attendance for the night, from the tickets that I give them.

The next day when I come in, they give me this sheet of all the people who worked, if they were over or under. If they were too over or under, there's something wrong, either with their stile or with the clicker that they use. If that clicker breaks, my God, you're twenty or thirty people off.

I stay until the end of the game to sign the ushers work cards. About half an hour after the game I can leave.

There's only two women ushers. Cynthia, [Russell, who works the third base side] and Kathy Gould out in section 3 or 4. It's hard to get girls to work as ushers. There's lots more on security. That's not as tough a job.

No usher is supposed to look for problems with the fans. Even if they're getting yelled at and everything, you still have to be careful what you say. In this park, if people don't like the way you talk to them, they make out a report.

I was ushering one time and this fellow's walking along with his girl. It was game time and I was in a hurry to get the people to their seats. I put my arm towards the girl to get by her, and her boyfriend says, "Hey, take your hands off of her!" "Hey, I didn't touch her. I didn't push her. I was just squeezing through." They always give the fan the benefit of the doubt.

Larry Nowell
PHOTO BY ANDREA RAYNOR

People can get their wallets stolen pretty easy here. The "Star Spangled Banner" was playing when I was working in the first base tunnel. Everybody was backed up. They couldn't get in, so they all stood there. When the thing ended, this fellow reached in his pocket. "My wallet! My wallet's gone! I had five hundred bucks in there."

Even in the ushers room, you can't trust anybody. I was sitting here one night and there were a couple of the red jackets hung up there. A fellow walked over and took a jacket. I said, "Hey! What are you doing?" One of the ushers chased him. He wanted a jacket as a souvenir!

I don't get to see much of the game. I watch on the TV here, but I can't go up to watch the game. I've got to check the ticket takers in. If I let them do it themselves, then they wouldn't need me!

I don't know if my wife will let me keep doing this. She knows I like baseball, though. I always did.

Sox slugger Ted Williams made a surprise phone call to Larry on his 85th birthday. His sister set it up.

I said to my sister, "What did you do that for?" She said, "Well I didn't know what to get you for your birthday." I said, "Well, thank you, it was very nice."

Ted Williams, he was always a good guy, very obliging. A very likeable guy. I'd say, "Ted, I just got his ball off the umpire, would you sign this for that little kid over there?" If we went near the railing, oh Jesus, they'd be all over him. So he'd say, "Walk down to the dugout here." Then he'd say, "Do you know what his name is?" I'd say, "Yeah, I got his name. He'd be tickled to get a ball. If it's signed by you, he'd be thrilled in the years ahead of him." He was always very sociable. Never refused.

Tom Gilmartin
PHOTO BY BILL NOWLIN

TOM GILMARTIN
Usher

Larry Nowell's management now. He's not on the union list. I am number one on the seniority list. Building Employees' Union, local 254.

I started in 1961. The year Yaz came out of the minor leagues. We both started together at Fenway but I lasted longer than he did! The only difference is he made a fortune and I put bread on the table.

I was in my early 20s. I'd always been a Red Sox fanatic, grew up loving baseball and pitching for Stoneham High School. I was pretty good. The scouts were looking at me, but I was one of those unfortunate athletes that was good enough to letter in three sports and my senior year I hurt my pitching arm playing football.

I was a young family man and I used to go to about fifteen or twenty games a year, and it got to be too expensive for me. I worked with a trucking company for eighteen years in the office. A rate clerk.

I'd get through work over in Somerville and go over to Fenway Park and work the night games. My youngest daughter Erin worked on the hot dog stands. My two boys worked as vendors when they were going through high school.

I started as an usher. We were getting about $5.50 a game then. We're getting $46 a game now. When Mr. Yawkey was alive, he treated everybody like family. Since the union came in, though, management takes a hard-ass stand and it's not been as comfortable.

I started out in the right field corner, keeping the kids off the wall. They get crazy. Too many beers. I saw one guy run out in the middle of a ballgame, drop his drawers and moon the press box. I remember when all those people climbed up the screen after the last game in '67. I thought it was going to collapse. I was in front of the Red Sox dugout keeping people from going in the dugout.

I've seen kids come out from section 33 and walk along the top of the Wall.

There used to be some gamblers out there in right field. Sections 7,8, 9 – around Pesky's Pole area there. They were from down the North End there. They'd sit out there and bet on every pitch. I don't see that anymore.

You talk about gambling. I was very friendly with Ed Nottle when he was down at Pawtucket. We used to go to all his fundraisers, and one night when we were coming home I said, to Helen, "I've got a good idea how I can help Ed with this fundraiser, a high runs pool at the ballpark." Every year we give at least five hundred to the Jimmy Fund. We've given a couple of hundred to Steve Palermo's spinal cord injury fund. I even have a three hundred dollar scholarship to a Woburn High cheerleader every year in my wife's memory. Twenty dollars a week goes to the party we have at the end of the year.

We go to the Howard Johnson's and they put out a buffet, two free drinks to everybody who's been in the pool all summer. We have a good time.

In those days, when we had 80 or more ushers, they didn't even have security. They just had about 27 Boston police on detail. There'd be a Boston police officer in the tunnels and if there was any trouble we'd just send a cop down to take care of it. They squelch trouble in a hurry now. They don't hit anybody, not anymore. There were too many lawsuits and they kinda cut back on that stuff.

I worked behind home plate for years. We've got a hard-nosed supervisor that likes to impose his power on people. It's a very unfortunate situation. I'm out in right field now, even though I have the most seniority. I'm not too happy with the Mickey Mouse union we have. They don't do anything to protect us. As senior man, I should have my choice of any spot in the ball park. I'd go right back to my tunnel to the right of the screen there, where I was for fifteen years. My old section.

I can get in whenever I want. I can get my son in whenever I want, too, I used to bring my wife in. They're a little stricter about that now, but we still have ways of doing it.

You used to know the players better, too. My wife and I went to a party at Luis Tiant's house after he won that opening game of the '75 World Series against Cincinnati. I was honored to be a guest at Dave Stapleton's wedding, my wife and I. I was very friendly with Rick and Janet Miller over the years. I've been out to Cincinnati, at Timmy Naehring's parents. Bob and Joanie Stanley, too. My wife and I were pretty friendly with them. Bob is a great guy, a real down-to-earth guy. A lot of good people down through the years.

I don't usher at spring training. That's my vacation.

Thirty nine years at the ballpark has been good to me. I've got more good memories than complaints. I worked the upper boxes right behind the dugout and when Bernie Carbo hit the three run homer to tie that sixth game in '75, Denny Doyle's wife threw her arms around me and give me a big kiss! We went bananas when Carbo's home run tied that game. Then Fisk's home run won it. That was probably the highlight of my 39 years, other than the Impossible Dream year. That was pretty good, too.

My wife even got hit by a foul ball. It didn't hurt her too bad but she had to go get some ice on it. I met my second wife there. We got married two years ago. I just lost her June 9 to breast cancer.

I think there are more women baseball fans today. For the first time in years, you see more Afro-Americans and Latinos, too. It's good.

Baseball people don't change too much. The younger crowd drink more and get a little more rowdy than they used to, but the average fan is pretty much the same. New Englanders are diehard baseball fans. They love their Red Sox. When they walk into Fenway Park, it's like walking into a temple. It's a religion with New Englanders – Fenway Park and Red Sox baseball.

CYNTHIA RUSSELL
Usher

Compared to some of the others, I'm a rookie. I started April of '92. I met Kathy Gould; we both worked at the Fleet Center. She worked as an usher at Fenway, too. So I filled out an application and I got hired. We're the only female ushers.

I'm a probation officer at the courthouse [in Malden.] It's my job to monitor how well they're doing – or NOT doing! I'd like to say I don't have a lot of recidivism, but sometimes you do. I handle House of Corrections sentences.

I'm really not a sports fan per se, but I think that when you work there, you have to keep up with what's going on, especially when people want to talk about the trade that's just gone on, or about how they're pitching, how they're hitting.

It's not fun when it rains, or cold and you're standing there. In the summer, it's nice. For me, it's more the social aspect of being there. There's all these people to talk to – the fans, the people I

Jerry Smith
PHOTO BY BILL NOWLIN

work with – they make it enjoyable no matter how hot or cold it is.

When I was in left field, a lot more season ticket holders would come to the game as opposed to where I am now, which is more corporate, so you don't really get the chance to see the same people all the time.

Sometimes there are incidents, with people arguing, people not getting along, that you have to respond to. When you work things out, it's a good feeling.

When Gene [Brundage] and I were over at left field, people would get hit by foul balls. Helping them out, people come back and actually say "thank you." Nine times out of ten, those words are obsolete in the English language now. People telling you "you're doing a good job" or "you're helping us out."

When people come in, they're impressed. "You work here? How did you get the job?" I guess it's an honor to work there.

They think you're on a personal basis with the players, or in the locker room with them.

Security is done differently at the Fleet Center. We don't have the large groups of security come in like they do at Fenway. It's more intimidating. To me, if there's one person acting up, there's no reason that you need three supervisors, six blue coats and four Boston Police to ask you to leave. At the Fleet, we have only two or three people respond instead of twelve people. It's a different style. At the ballpark, I think Boston [the Boston Police] basically does all the evictions. At the Fleet Center, the security company does all the evictions; it's more professional. Of course, the ballpark's much larger and everything is pretty much on one level.

You're always going to have your problems. You're always going to have the jerk. At the ballpark, you'll have 30,000 people or whatever, and to have the minor incidents they have with the volume of people that they're dealing with, it's very minimal when it boils down to it. Things are handled better than people maybe want to portray.

JERRY SMITH
Usher Supervisor

I retired from my own business three years ago, Jerry's Canteen, my own truck. At one time I had two trucks, in Needham and Newton. That's what I did for 45 years.

A friend worked at Fenway Park and he told me to put an application in. I'm a supervisor in there. My sons Patrick and Brian both work for Twins outside, and my son Tommy works inside the big store for Twins. My grandson works for security. Joe O'Brian.

I put in for a ticket taker or an usher, but they appointed me as supervisor. A lot of people have tried to get this job for twenty, twenty-five years. I was very lucky. It was timing, and I think I knew the right person, too, to be honest with you.

They all respect me. My nickname there, they call me "The Hammer." I used to be a boxer years ago. I originally came from Bangor, Maine and went in the Marine Corps.

I love the Red Sox. I met Ted Williams when I was 13 years old. People I was brought up with, their uncle used to be the treasurer of the Red Sox, Tom Dowd.

I usually help security pulling up the gates before the game. Those gates are heavy. They're very old, with the chains and everything.

I supervise the ticket takers. If there's any problems, they come to me. My job is to be available. Once in a while we run into a few problems. People drinking, fighting, using bad words.

We usually stay twenty minutes to a half an hour after the game. I don't close the gates. That's security. When we leave the ballpark, we usually go out Gate D. After the game, we have our own locker room.

MIKE PUCILLO
Former Usher

When I was a kid, I was one of the "knot hole gang" at Braves Field. I was a fan when I started and then it became a job. The first ballgame I worked was in 1938. I was a clerk for Railway Express, midnight to eight AM. This friend of mine, Tommy, called me and said, "Mike, why don't you come to work here as an usher?" His uncle at that time – Phil Troy – was the general manager. Sure. Why not?

I stayed there until 1981. Right behind the Red Sox dugout, I had this tunnel that was my tunnel. I was right there and any bigshots that come into the game used to come down to me. They didn't have the boxes built upstairs yet. Governors and celebrities all came through me. I sat the three Kennedys one day. Box 29, I think it was. I used to seat all the governors that came to the ballpark. 32A. From Vermont, New York, Massachusetts, the state of Maine…

I used to have a lot of ways to cut corners. I lived with Frank Malzone in Arizona. He didn't charge me a dime. He was a good friend. I started driving Frank's car to Arizona, or back. I drove Carl Yastrzemski's car. I drove a lot of cars back and forth.

I haven't been there since 1982, '83. I go to spring training but not to Fenway. I enjoy spring training. It's a way to relax. I'm 83 years old, you know. To go, I've got to find a place to park, spend money. It isn't worth it, where television is so great now. I still have my season tickets, but my family uses them. When my kids go, they sit in those seats and it's seventh heaven.

I picked Joe Cronin's housekeeper right out of the box and carried her into the dugout that time she got hit. I used to seat every celebrity. If I had been stupid enough to get all their autographs, I'd have the best collection around. Every movie actor, any actress that came there, they all came through me. Those were the choice boxes. They didn't have these luxury boxes.

I had a brother-in-law who used to pitch to Ted Williams. Even down in Florida. We'd go down and he'd be working with Ted all the time. He was a left-hander and he had pinpoint control and that was what Ted wanted. He'd tell him where he wanted it and Pete would throw it. Pete Cerrone. Everybody knew him. He was connected with the Sox. A bird dog or something like that.

Mr. Yawkey used to play with my brother-in-law Pete. Pete was the equipment manager for a while and he'd take Yawkey out every day. You should see him spread the money.

In those days, I was a bartender at the Loyal Order of Moose, and I used to invite the players over to the event I put on. We had a lobster feed, the whole deal. On the way to the hall, they'd stop at the house for an hour or two until things got going. I'd start them off with a cold beer and then they'd go the Moose and have anything they wanted for free.

You could never do it today, get that many players together. You'd have to speak to their agents. I used to speak to their wives. That's how I used to get them.

GENE BRUNDAGE
Usher

I started in April of '94. I'm a retired engineer, and I was recovering from a shattered ankle and needed physical therapy. I needed to lose weight. I loved baseball so I thought I'd put an application in to Fenway to try and get a job as an usher. I got a call to come in for an interview with Mr. Corcoran, and I was hired.

I have done every game, every year for the last four years, from the strike on except for the time I was out for the heart attack.

On occasion I take the T in, because I live in Framingham. That day I didn't feel too on top of my game and when I got off the train, I thought I'd stop in at first aid and get something for my stomach, like a Tums or something. They hadn't opened the first aid room yet. I had to wait outside. Then I had the heart attack and I really don't know anything that happened between that moment and a day or so later in the hospital. I was in the hospital seven or eight days.

I did my first game after the heart attack on May 31. It felt good to go in and visit the EMTs. They remarked that it was good to see me vertical instead of horizontal!

The prognosis is good. The letter that the cardiologist wrote to give to the ballclub said no restrictions, go back to doing what you were doing.

I grew up in New York City. I'm not a Yankee fan, though. I grew up as a Giants fan. I came here in 1956. Sure, I'm a Red Sox fan. Oh, sure. I didn't really have an American League team before I came here.

Asked about the New York fans, and particularly the New York police and firemen, Gene replied:

They're so arrogant. They announce the fact that they're New York City police and they're untouchable. Typically, what they do, they come up in busloads. They drink for the four hours that they're on the bus and so they're a little tipsy by the time they arrive. A couple of years ago, they were in the bleachers and causing a commotion to the point they had to be tossed. The Boston police went up there to help security round these clowns up and evict them from the park. One guy said, "You can't do this. We're New York policemen." The Boston police lieutenant said, "Well, you oughta be ashamed of yourself. You're coming along with us anyway."

It can get rough sometimes language-wise. We're looking for two things, people who are smoking and people using offensive language. People called me vulgar names because they thought I was setting the rules. Security heard that and they just took over from there. I didn't even have to say a word, and I wouldn't have. You're not supposed to respond to that. If I hear anything offensive, I will tell them, "Cool off, please watch your language."

We had a fan hit during batting practice. A little girl, maybe ten or twelve years old, and she had been hit pretty hard. I went down to see what help I could offer, in terms of getting her ice or an EMT. Orel Hershiser, who was with Cleveland at the time, came over to the stands. He offered to run into the dugout and get some ice for her. Forget about baseball. What could

he do for this child? I thought that was a great act of being human. That makes me happy, to see that there are some individuals that aren't so egotistical that you can't talk to them.

We do see fans diving for foul balls, sure. Wherever feasible, we check them out to make sure everything's OK. I don't dive for them. We can't keep them.

TOM CASTIGLIONE
Emergency Medical Technician

Fenway Park is like a city of 20,000 to 30,000 people which convenes for 3 or 4 hours a day, 81 dates out of the year. With over-all attendance normally exceeding 2½ million fans, at an average of three hours each, that comes to seven million person hours – people living in Fenway Park. The ballclub needs to be ready to meet the inevitable medical emergencies attendant on so many people gathering in one place.

The back of the ticket warns of some of the dangers one can anticipate at a baseball game. "The holder assumes all risk and danger incidental to the game of baseball including specifically (but not exclusively) the danger of being injured by thrown bats and thrown or batted balls and agrees that the participating clubs, their agents and players are not liable for injuries resulting from such causes."

Red Sox radio broadcaster Joe Castiglione's son Tom worked as an EMT at Fenway Park. He later graduated medical school at the University of Massachusetts.

I work in the first aid department at Fenway Park. I'm an emergency medical technician. The Red Sox have a contract with Fallon Ambulance. They do all the transport work.

Each team will travel with a trainer. Most states require trainers to be EMT certified. Some teams travel with their physical therapist as well.

Each home team is responsible for providing a doctor for the players.

We've lived in Marshfield since my father came to the Red Sox in '83. When I was 14, I started as a vendor. I did that for four years and then I injured both of my knees and I couldn't climb the stairs anymore. I played baseball in high school but that knee injury ended any hopes of playing college ball. I started off selling popcorn and then I moved up to Coke. I got as far as ice cream. Hot dogs was next up.

I work about half their home games, about forty or fifty games a year. The staff is seven people and we have three EMTs on a game. They're mostly firefighter EMTs. Two of us aren't firefighters. One gentleman is an EMT for the City of Boston. I'm the only non-professional emergency medical technician. All told, there are 7 or 8 EMTs, maybe 6 nurses, and 4 doctors.

There is a station underneath the grandstand, under section 13, that is staffed by three registered nurses and two emergency medical technicians and there's a doctor on call inside the park, also an orthopedic surgeon on call inside the park.

There will be one Fallon ambulance parked right next to first aid. There's a gate so it can get out quickly. It's staffed by two emergency medical technicians and they're there to transport people to Beth Israel, the closest hospital.

We probably end up transporting in a regular homestand – which is around seven games – one or two people; with intense heat, especially on a Saturday or Sunday game, sometimes two or three. It's not all that often that we transport somebody that's highly critical. Most of it's precautionary, but we have a contract with Fallon so they're not charging the fans for the transport and they're not charging the Red Sox. So it's a ride over to the hospital for some people, to get an X-ray.

We have our cardiac arrests, our diabetic patients that are having difficulty. Some severe head trauma from balls and bats flying into the stands. Occasionally, somebody might have a bit of chest pain and they're concerned. We just send them to get checked out.

The most common problem would be heat related difficulty. Inebriation – we don't transport too often for that. There was a guy a few weeks ago that was a little drunk and he slipped and fell. He was more embarrassed than anything. I remember a woman passed out in a bathroom stall. Actually, alcohol isn't really that much of a problem. Security and the ushers are very good about identifying problems.

We have a TV inside the first aid station. You hear the crowd cheer when you see someone hitting a home run on the TV so it's still pretty exciting.

A lot goes on at Fenway that people don't realize. We're on the same radio frequency as security. They catch a lot before they become big problems. They've had everything from people walking in drunk, people using foul language, bachelor parties getting out of hand. Fenway's a very old park. There was a game where none of the toilets worked. It was very hot so people were drinking a lot of fluids. Finally they had to shut down the beer stands because men were just urinating anywhere.

No one's given birth in the last five years. I believe that women were sent over – they were going into labor – but I don't believe there's been a delivery at Fenway.

There's on average two or three fatalities a year at Fenway, usually cardiac events. You jam 35,000 people in every night with heat, people in close proximity, balls and bats flying around – a lot of stuff happens. There are maybe four cardiac arrests a year. It was probably their time and it happened to be at Fenway Park. I've heard people say that Fenway Park is the place they want to go. We've seen people sprinkle ashes on the field.

We get a lot of unusual requests in first aid. People come looking for sunscreen. Sunglasses. A lot of different things that they didn't think about before they came to the game. We've had somebody come in with a diabetic reaction. They do have an insulin injector. The nurses are able to monitor blood glucose levels. They have that type of equipment, too. It's really a first rate, very professionally run first aid station.

We open up two hours before a game. People are coming in generally throughout the day. First aid comes on two hours before the game. Back in April – a Sunday game – we were due in about 11:05 for a 1:05 game. There was an usher waiting to get in first aid, about quarter of eleven. The usher [Gene Brundage] was a little agitated, a little overheated, and he felt sort of nauseous. It turned out he had some chest pain. One of the EMTs is a firefighter from Quincy by the name of Gary Stein. Gary immediately opens up the first aid station and takes his vital signs. The ambulance isn't due until an hour and a half before the game, so Gary gets the ambulance to come in early. Once we got the guy into the ambulance, he went into cardiac arrest. Gary and the Fallon Ambulance crew were able to revive the guy, got him over to Beth Israel and into their cath lab. He came back to Fenway a few weeks ago, ready to go back to work.

He wrote a nice letter commending the first aid station, and he came in and shook Gary's hand. He shook all of our hands. His wife came in, too, and gave us big hugs. He was able to come back to Fenway, and he was excited to come back, too.

Once, a man went into cardiac arrest in the 600 Club. The response time's obviously longer in that part of the park, and they decided that they needed a first aid station based on the roof. So for every regular season game, there is a station located in the press box on the fifth level, the top level. It's stationed by one EMT and one registered nurse. They service that area. There are a lot of people up there and the response time is better.

We stay for about one hour after the game.

It's really a great place to be. People get in and they don't leave and they'd like their family to work there, too.

Richard Giglio
PHOTO BY ANDREA RAYNOR

RICHARD GIGLIO
Organist

As everyone's getting set, the organ is playing, the public address announcer reads the starting lineups and – a few minutes before game time – the National Anthem is sung. The Red Sox have two organists. One of them is the son of the oldest Red Sox season ticket holder. It would seem an impossible coincidence, but such is the case.

I am Director of Church Organ and Institutional Sales at Boston Organ and Piano. The owner, Ray Totaro, recommended me to the Red Sox five years ago.

The first game that I played for the Red Sox was the first game after the baseball strike. 1994.

I play most of the games. There's 81 home games and I play between 50 and 60, and Ray plays the rest. He's also the person who was instrumental in getting the Yamaha company to donate the use of the latest state of the art digital instrument. It's there compliments of Yamaha and Boston Organ and Piano.

An old friend of mine, John Kiley, was affiliated with this company also. I got to know John in the late 70s after I had lived in San Diego and played the organ for the Padres. John was quite a character. There was a point in time when John was the organist for the Celtics, the Bruins and the Red Sox. [A Boston trivia question – what man played for all three teams?] One time I was talking with him, and I said, "God, John. How did you get all three of those jobs?" "Oh," he said, "I just started playing here and I started playing there and then I had the jobs." And then he said, "Half the organists in town are waiting for me to die." I said, "No, John, all of us!"

He was a real sweet guy and a wonderful musician.

We have to be in our positions a half-hour before game time. They have a staff dining room so most of us will get there an hour beforehand so you have time to get settled in the booth, grab something to eat and then get back at your station.

I'm in the control booth up there with Mike Gaffney, who's running the scoreboard, and Ed Brickley, the announcer. There are eight or nine of us. The people running the instant reply and the players' pictures and all that. We can't physically see each other, the way the control booth is set up, so we talk to each other through headphones.

I'm ready to go at 6:35 but usually I end up about ten minutes of seven playing some music just to fill in before the lineups. After the lineups, usually I'll play again until the team takes the field. After the National Anthem, we have a "pump-up" CD that we play. Then I alternate with the CDs. It's about 50/50 – half live organ music and half CD, which tends to be rock music.

The only overall rule is to keep the fans jived so everything is fast, move music. We don't want anything slow.

They definitely have improved the sound system. At the beginning of the season, we did sound checks. Ray and I went over to Fenway and I played the organ, while Ray and James [Shannahan] walked around the stadium, to listen to what it sounded like in different places.

We try to pick music depending on what is going on in the game. The greatest moment of all – this was like two years ago....the Red Sox were winning 9-5 and I jumped on the organ. I played "9 to 5" – the Dolly Parton song. We're always looking for opportunities like that. Night before last, Ray told me he played "Everything's Coming Up Roses" because Brian Rose was pitching so well against the Yankees.

The "da da-da-duh-da-daaaaa!" – we don't do that at Fenway Park. They have a CD that Amy plays that gets the crowd yelling. *[The CD they rely on most heavily is one entitled* Jock Jams, *which comes in several volumes.]*

My father has been a season ticket holder at the Red Sox for fifty-nine years. His tickets are down along the first base line, right in back of the Red Sox dugout.

I love it at Fenway Park, so as long as they'll have me, I'll keep doing it. You gotta love the Red Sox – otherwise, don't stay in Boston – and I really like the guys I work with. It's a really great bunch in the control booth. It's an exciting place to be. I've actually got the second best view, I think Ed Brickley has the best, although his window is open. Every once in a while a ball will pop in and almost bean him. At least I've got good protection. I actually do have the highest seat in Fenway Park. [The organ is on the highest level platform inside the booth.]

RAY TOTARO
Organist

Boston Organ and Piano is a family business, about 42, 43 years old.

I've always been a baseball fan. As a matter of fact, in the organ booth at Fenway Park, there is a picture of me on the field as part of a check presentation. I was in the sixth grade. It was a Jimmy Fund presentation, an elementary school band did a fundraiser and I was in the band.

The Red Sox more give you direction when to play than what to play. That's a decision that's made by them. In my mind, we were just trying to copy what Kiley had done. We play a fanfare when they hit a home run. We play marchy-type stuff when the people leave at the end. We play between some of the innings. We play on some of the pitching changes. It's kind of fun.

There was one time when the game was delayed. There was snow on the outfield and they were shoveling it, so I played an hour and forty-five minutes straight. I don't know if anybody else thought it was funny, but the second thing I played was "White Christmas" and this was in April. I thought it was amusing.

The only time that I know for sure that it will be my turn is the seventh inning stretch. That's like the gospel. I know I'm going to play.

I don't think the average person in the stands is closing their eyes and totally absorbed in the music. It's background.

I get treated like a king. It's absolutely unbelievable. It's like dying and going to heaven. The biggest thing I've taken from it, in terms of the interpersonal relations, is to hope that the people who work for me at Boston Organ and

Piano feel like I feel, as an employee working for the Red Sox. It's my first experience where I was the employee and the person who took directions. They welcome my opinion. They treat me magnificently. It just couldn't be better. As far as the control room is concerned, the people that I work with, they're a joy. They're an absolute joy.

Ed Brickley
PHOTO BY BILL NOWLIN

ED BRICKLEY
Public Address Announcer

"I've never met a man who likes his job more than Ed Brickley" – Bob Kurtz, Red Sox broadcaster NESN, August 31, 1999

I started in 1997. All I can say is that I was in the right place at the right time. It was an incredibly good stroke of fortune.

I had worked with the New England Patriots for twenty years as chief statistician. That was something I truly enjoyed and loved. So I had experience with the Patriots and that got my foot in the door.

Leslie [Stirling, my immediate predecessor] decided to go back to Harvard Divinity School and could not devote the time to the p.a. duties that she had before.

Jim Healey asked me had I thought about public address work. I was kind of overwhelmed. I said that I had thought about it, in a Walter Mitty-ish kind of way, but had never really considered it. Then he asked me if I would be interested in giving it a shot, and I was thrilled.

They had me sit down at the microphone in the empty ballpark. They gave me some scripts to read and apparently it sounded good enough that I was invited to come back and try it again. I went back three times after the initial time.

The Red Sox do not want a showmanship type of public address announcer. Jim Healey emphasized to me that I was background information. I should not take away from the game,

I should provide information for people in the stadium that would help them enjoy the game.

People have been going to the park for years and year and years and have been accustomed to a certain kind of atmosphere. Because I had been going to Fenway Park for fifty years, I fully understood what it was like. I believe that I have tried to continue the same kind of public address announcements that I heard when I was a kid.

Opening Day of 1997, it was the Seattle Mariners. My previous times at the microphone had been with an empty ballpark. My maximum audience was maybe a dozen people, in the audition process.

Then to be there on Opening Day when there's 34,000 or 35,000 people, it was awesome. In all honesty, when I started to speak, I felt that the only thing which would come over the speakers would be the sound of my heart beating. I think the nerves showed, but there were no mistakes and at least I was accurate. As I said to somebody, I wish my voice were like James Earl Jones or Sherm Feller, but it's not. The Good Lord gave it to me and I'll do the best I can with it, but I wished at that time that I could have been much more powerful.

People say to me, "You have Sherm Feller's job." I say to them, "My name and Sherm's name should not be used in the same sentence. Sherm was a legend. I really feel that I'm sitting in Sherm's chair until the next Sherm comes along."

One of the names that's a delight to announce and to introduce is Nomar because of all of the syllables and the Latin sound in the name. I've loved him right from the start. He's a special kind of ballplayer but the name, too, lends itself to a little bit of emphasis. His first Opening Day with the Red Sox was my first Opening Day with the Red Sox.

In the first year, I would rehearse at home. In the bathroom, in the shower, places like that. I did it constantly. I would read the rosters. I would look at the BASEBALL REGISTER, and say the names out loud. I don't think my wife was that thrilled. Rafael Bournegal was one of the names I remember saying. What happens is that the American League publishes a book called the AMERICAN LEAGUE RED BOOK and it has phonetic pronunciations of the players that they feel need to have that kind of information provided. At the start of every series I will go and talk with a radio, TV or media representative for the visiting team. For instance, the Toronto team that was in here this weekend, Jose Cruz, Jr. I asked the TV broadcaster for the Blue Jays, "Do the folks at the Skydome introduce him as Jose Cruz or as Jose Cruz, Jr." They said, "Junior" and that's why I used the "junior."

Absolutely, positively, I have the best seat in the house. I don't mean to sound corny, but every night when I go in there, when they're playing the National Anthem, I truly thank the Good Lord because it's just spectacular. It is truly the best seat in the house. When Fenway Park is filled and it's a nice night, it's just beautiful. There's no other word to describe it. The whole setting is just magnificent.

We'll get a foul ball in once in a while. We have to be alert because they come back very, very hard. I was lucky enough to catch one on the fly last year.

One of the things that I do in addition to making the announcements is run the lights on the leftfield scoreboard – the balls and the strikes and outs, the green lights and the red lights and so forth. I do that.

Substitutes are not announced until the umpire indicates that they are in the game. I always look for the umpire's signal. They're very, very precise about the pinch hitters. I have to watch, to make sure that they point to the pinch hitter and then usually up to me.

The tough thing is when the visiting team puts a pinch runner in at second base, and they come out of that third base dugout and you can't see the jersey number. I'll say, "Can anybody see that number?" and as soon as they tell me, then I make the announcement. I've asked the fellow or the young lady down in the camera sling to help me in that kind of situation.

There is oftentimes pre-game activity. There could be a ceremonial first pitch, a special promotion, an honoring of whatever it might be. An awful lot of things relative to the Jimmy Fund. The first time I've seen the script is often that afternoon, or that evening as I show up. A lot of times, there are late changes to the script. I'll read it over and sometimes I add or change a word here or there.

Sometimes I sound better than I do at other times. I don't know enough about the technology to explain, but I know that the sound engineer can make me sound better than I am and on occasion they can make me sound a little bit worse, too. It's just a matter of their particular taste or their particular interpretation.

The sound engineer also controls the volume of the music. When Richard or Ray Totaro play the organ, they make it go out either louder or softer, or with more bass or less bass. The sound engineer controls a lot of what people hear in the ballpark.

The Red Sox provide the workers in the control room with wonderful pre-game meals. Our favorite day is Sundays because they have omelettes to order. They're the nicest and the most accommodating people you'd ever want to be with. I know when I come home at night, my wife will ask me, "What did you have to eat?" and then she'll say, "Gee, that's good. That's a great balanced meal."

After the game, I like to hang around for a while. I like to talk about what went on during the game, especially if it's a Red Sox win. We just talk baseball and perhaps catch up some on what different peoples' families are doing. It's just a very congenial and enjoyable atmosphere. Quite frankly, I love getting there and I hate leaving there every day.

Beginning in 2003, Carl Beane became P. A. announcer, and Ed hosts the Legends Suite at Fenway.

KEVIN FRIEND
Sound Engineer

We play the music. I don't know what we're called. We just play the music.

I own a company that does this for a living. BCN Productions. It comes from Boston Convention Network. We do a lot more at the other stadiums but at Fenway, all's we do is run the music.

They're proud of their heritage – and well they should be.

The experience with the other places like the Fleet Center is definitely very corporate. It's what's wrong with sports today. At Fenway, it's kind of like stepping back in time.

What I like personally and what I like at the ballpark are two different things. You don't really go there to play what you've listened to. I like to play traditional rock and roll. Some of the classic rock would be appropriate for the ballpark. We do like to mix it up. For example, I will play one song every game that's more modern, like hip-hop or something. I don't personally like hip-hop but when those songs are playing – you look out in the bleachers and people are dancing. That's what it's about. I'll always play a classic, like "Spirit in the Sky" something like that.

Amy Sill and Joe Dolan work for me. To be honest with you, Amy and Joe do it more than me. It's my company. I set it up and I probably know more about presentation than they do but they actually are the ones who do the work.

Playing the music's cool because everybody's listening. They might not be looking at the board or whatever, but it's certainly a kind of a neat thing, because you do have a little influence. It's a fun gig.

Katryna Nields
PHOTO BY BILL NOWLIN

KATRYNA NIELDS
National Anthem Singer

On the evening of August 3, 1999 Katryna and Nerissa Nields sang the National Anthem at Fenway Park.

Our manager Patty Griffin has come up with a lot of cockamamie ideas to help us promote our career. She came up with this one, because we're on Rounder Records and Rounder's in Boston.

I think this is the largest crowd we ever played. At the Edmonton Folk Festival, on the main stage, they claim there were 30,000 people there.

There are a couple of members of the band who are big Yankee fans. By sort of infusion, I've also become a Yankee fan. I'd have to say, though, that I've been brought up by parents who have told me that the Boston Red Sox were a great team and that I should always root for them. I was brought up to like the underdog.

I remember watching the Boston Red Sox in the 1970s when Carl Yastrzemski was playing with them, and I remember my mother saying, "That is a great team. You should like them." And so I've always known that the Red Sox have great moral character.

I guess it was Bill Nowlin at Rounder that helped it happen, but Rick Subrizio at the Red Sox was also a Nields fan. He's a big enough Nields fan that I recognized him. He's come to a lot of shows.

We got there around 4:30. We met Rick and he gave us our tickets. We weren't allowed to go in until 5:30 but we walked around on Lansdowne Street. I bought a Red Sox hat.

We went in as soon as they opened the gates. We found our seats and ooh-ed and ahh-ed over the whole park. Our parents came up from Washington for the occasion.

At about 6:30 we went and met Rick. Wally the mascot came over wearing a Nields shirt! Which was pretty exciting. We got pictures of that and we had Wally sign a baseball for us. Apparently, Wally is a pretty big Nields fan, too.

Rick took us out onto the field. I had asked if we could take some dirt from the Park and he said, "You can take it from the warning track, but not from near home plate." So the first thing I did when I got there was I picked up some dirt and stuck it in a container I had brought with me.

They told us that we should sing, although what most people were hearing would be the recording. If anything happened to the recording, then they would just flip the switch and they would hear us actually singing. We tested the mike and then we came back and stood around until it was time.

Because you're lip-synching and you don't know quite when the song's going to start, you're supposed to bow your head, and sort of come up singing. So you sort of start on the word "say" instead of "O"!

I read a biography of Willie Mays when I was a kid, and the thing that really stuck with me was the fact that when he was a boy, he found out that people actually got paid to play baseball. It blew his mind. My mind was similarly blown by figuring out that one could get paid to sing. I think about that all the time.

I looked out at those players and just thought, if you're a baseball player and you screw up, all the fans that had previously been cheering for you, they boo you. You don't get booed if you sing a note off-key. But if you miss a ball by a couple of inches, you can be. It's a lot of pressure.

I've never really liked that song that much. But singing it in front of that crowd, I was proud. I was proud of our country. And I was proud that our Founding Fathers felt that the pursuit of happiness was so important. Things like baseball and music and art, they're not things that are going to make us live or die, but they are going to make our life worth while. The fact that we view them as important in this country makes me happy and proud.

After it was over, we walked up through the stands and lots of people said nice things. Slapped our hands and like that. As I walked around, people would recognize me and say, "Hey, it's the singing lady!"

It was an amazing experience. It was disappointing that the Red Sox lost the game – they won the next day, though! We'll keep our fingers crossed.

JIM MCSHERRY
National Anthem Singer

Jim McSherry sang the National Anthem June 15, 1999 at Fenway Park

Jim McSherry
PHOTO BY BILL NOWLIN

I work part time at Fenway Park anyway, and the Red Sox invited me to sing on the 15th. I work for the concessionaire. I've had a 62 year on-off relationship with the Boston Red Sox. I worked for the concessionaire in 1937, when my brother and I sold peanuts.

After getting discharged from the service, I took the Boston Police examination and, oddly enough, was assigned to Station 16 which was the jurisdiction of Fenway Park. I did paid police details at Fenway Park for twenty years.

Then I retired and became a supervisor of attendance in the Boston School Department, during the busing crisis. I retired from there in 1981 and did nothing – some special investigations for some people for a few years – then I went back to work at Fenway Park again in 1986. I still work part time over there even now. I like to say I was on one side of the counter as a kid selling the peanuts and now I'm on the other side of the counter, which supplies the vendors with their wares and collects the money when they get finished.

The commissary supplies all of the vendors with the things they're going to sell. We check them out and at the end of the night, we settle up with them.

I'm the oldest one over there now. I'll be 76 in August. Aramark has been very, very good to me in the sense of saying to me, "You come in when you want to come in. We can always use an extra hand."

Here I am singing the National Anthem at a field where I knew every blade of grass, because I've been in that park so often. It was quite an honor. It's one of the high points of my life. It really was.

After I sang, I went up with my children and grandchildren. I went to the box seats that Aramark graciously donated to me, and I had eight of my family down there.

Cynthia Russell and
Gene Brundage
PHOTO BY EMMET NOWLIN

The Braves had a knothole gang but the Red Sox never did. You could sneak into Fenway, though. There was a great trick years ago. The turnstiles determine how many people are in the park. It was supposed to be a preventitive from people sneaking in. You'd stand by certain turnstile guys. You would say, "Can I turn the stile for you?" He didn't need any help! But if you hit the right guy, he would have you come in with another person so that only one registered.

Then you would stand there and turn the stile for him. They were a different type of stiles, the kind of heavy ones, you know. You'd turn the stiles for the guy and then after a while, he'd say, "All right, go ahead. You're all set."

Some of these young men that are there now, some of them started when they were fourteen or fifteen years of age. They're 26, 27, 28 now. This is a second job to them now. Some of them are married. An awful lot of them have good jobs. You'll see one of them in particular, works in the stock market, he comes in in his three piece suit, takes off the suit, changes into his uniform and sells hot dogs. He'd sell hot dogs and work like hell and end up making 95 or 100 dollars from the beginning of the game 'til the 6th inning and then go home. This was how these guys make some extra money.

6
CLUBHOUSE

Joe Cochran, Equipment Manager and
    Clubhouse Operations
Neil DeTeso, Salesman, Riddell All-American
Nick Oliva, Caterer
Joe Silva, Players' Parking Lot Attendant
Rich Zawacki, Physical Therapist
Jim Rowe, Trainer
Carlos Cowart, Red Sox Batboy
Maurice Baxter, Clubhouse Assistant
Wally McDougal, former batboy

Fred Waugh, former batboy
Joe Flanagan, Red Sox Clubhouse Security
Thomas J. Dunn, Visiting Clubhouse Security
Mike Fraser, Driver, Yankee Bus
Jack Rogers, former traveling secretary
Kevin Carson, Salesman, New England
    Household Moving
Al Hartz, Equipment Truck Driver
Mark Tremblay, Equipment Truck Driver

Joe Cochran
PHOTO BY BILL NOWLIN

JOE COCHRAN
Equipment Manager and Clubhouse Operations

I'm Joe. I went to the University of Maine, and my summer job was on the grounds crew with Joe Mooney, I've been here ever since. This is my sixteenth year.

I run the day to day operation of the clubhouse and, on the road, handle the transportation of the equipment. If they do well, we work an extra few weeks – which just makes it all that much better.

Don Fitzpatrick was the equipment manager before me. I worked the visiting clubhouse in 1990. I came over and worked this side in September of 1991. Tom McLaughlin is my right-hand man.

When you hear about the equipment truck leaving for Florida, it's a semi, filled with 25 to 30,000 pounds of personal belongings and baseball equipment. No one's ever stolen the truck. That would make for a pretty difficult spring if that happened!

Baseball equipment takes up maybe three-quarters of the truck. We dress 70 or 80 guys. A big inventory goes with us.

They keep orders going on the bats and uniforms throughout the year. A lot of stuff coming in and out to keep organized. You have a 25 man active roster. You might see forty or fifty players in the course of a season. Then you have the expanded rosters. To keep them outfitted takes a little leg work.

I'd say the players go through more bats these days. You've got some big guys. Nomar hardly ever breaks a bat, but other guys, they can break a lot.

We're out of here 45 minutes after the game. We pre-load the equipment truck with the luggage in the afternoon, and then as soon as the crowd clears out – get the truck in here. The clubhouse assistants get that thing loaded up pretty quickly. It's amazing how much equip-

ment can get packed and moved over a short period of time. We get out of here and as soon as we get that plane loaded, we're in the air.

I work closely with traveling secretary Jack McCormick. He has a truck lined up in each city. We unload the baseball equipment first, put the luggage in the back, go to the hotel and then on to the stadium.

In each city, there's a crew of batboys and clubhouse assistants and a head guy that runs the visiting clubhouse. Maybe once a year as a treat, they'll take a batboy on a trip to see what it's like outside of Fenway. Sometimes we don't see much daylight. We're in the bowels.

We have a crew of six people, including myself on this side, and a crew of five on the other side. It's pretty much like that in every park.

I come in about 11 o'clock. We usually get out about three hours after the game – we have to clean afterwards. We like to have all the laundry done before we go home. We shine all the shoes, clean up the food, clean up everything. It's a monotonous routine, but you want to get as much done that night as you can. The next morning when we come in, we'll hang up the clean uniforms from the night before. It's nicer to come in the next day without as much left to do.

During the game, I'm in the clubhouse most of the time. There's two or three innings of down time, and then it picks up quick, with the press coming in. We don't have the luxury of an equipment room or anything, so we have to get the uniforms, all right side out, check the pockets for gum. We've got a ten minute window before it gets really crowded.

You can have five pairs of new pants in a locker, but you have a lot of superstition in this game and a lot of them – the majority of them – they'd sew them up until they actually fall off their body. We have a tailor over in Somerville that we send out to. Neil DeTeso. They pick up, then bring it back the next morning.

With interleague play, we get bats for the pitchers in Spring training, because we play some National League teams. We have a pitchers' helmet bag, which we never had before. Pitchers' bat bag.

We do the food. We have a place out in Milford, Oliva's Market. We have a caterer that comes in. Nick, he does a great job. He was doing it before I came. I inherited him, really.

There's a different atmosphere here. When this place is sold out and the team's playing well, there's something electrifying that you don't see in other ballparks. Maybe Yankee Stadium with 60,000 screaming. Then you go to Anaheim where they arrive late and exit early. The fans here in Boston know the game and enjoy the baseball. It makes this place something special.

I remember seeing Tiant win his twentieth. I sat down there [points]. I was a little guy. Yeah, I remember that.

I haven't missed a home game in well over ten years, never been sick. I take a trip once a year, which gives me a break.

During the course of the game, you'll have some of the players in the clubhouse, loosening up, getting ready. We have a tee in there and a hitting net. The designated hitter will hit off the tee, or a guy that thinks he's going to get in the game. Pinch runner will do some stretching out. There's always activity.

There's a lot of history here. It's fun to be a part of it.

NEIL DE TESO
Salesman, Riddell All-American

I've been there since 1978 – we clean the uniforms and do most of the repair work, alterations, put the numbers on – and the names and numbers on the road jerseys. The company's being doing it since '58, I believe.

We were just a small local company. Now, it's Riddell All-American, a national firm. They bought us in '95. We continue to do the Red Sox the same way we always done them.

I'm a sales representative. I do Greater Boston and all up into southern New Hampshire, out to Milford, Amherst. I take care of the New England Patriots, the Boston Bruins, the Red Sox, the Carolina Panthers – which may

seem unusual but the equipment manager used to be at Boston College and still sends his stuff up here to me. He likes the way I handle his stuff.

Seven or eight years ago, they gave me a key to the visiting clubhouse. Say, the Red Sox are playing the Yankees on Monday night, I'll go in on Tuesday morning and pick up both sets of uniforms.

I'm there by 6 A.M. I back down the ramp to the visiting clubhouse, and take both sets of uniforms. As the season goes along, it gets hot and they change more. There's usually more pants than there are jerseys. Some days the Red Sox may send out as many as 60 or 65 pants. The visiting team usually it's between 45 and 55, depending on how many they have on the disabled list, and the time of year. I take them to the plant over in Somerville and then we shoot them back about 11:30 or 12.

Fridays you have to go in first thing in the morning and then back in at night, because Saturday's a day game.

When the Red Sox go on a road trip, I'll go get the home uniforms the next day. When they come in off the road, I go get the grays. I've been doing it a long time.

I only missed two games this year. I went to a wedding one day and I took my daughter back to college the other day.

The uniforms are made by Russell. I think the only team that's not Russell is Toronto. Toronto's still with Wilson. Their equipment manager is just partial towards Wilson.

We do tailoring. A lot of guys these days like their pants tight. The new thing now is that a lot of guys are sewing their stirrups into their pants as opposed to having a separate sock and pant, Joe Cochran will give me their stirrup socks and we'll cut the bottoms off and sew them right into the pant. That way they can just step right into them. Just the stirrups. Not the sanitaries.

When they make a trade or a deal, we'll put their number on the uniform. I'll go in in the morning and Joe [Cochran] has everything in a paper bag with the guy's name and number on it. We put The All-Star patch on all the uniforms. I saw an old tape of Roger Clemens on TV this week and they had the JRY with the black underneath. We did that. We did the braid when Mr. Yawkey passed away. We did the braid for Tony C. There was the Jackie Robinson patch a couple of years ago.

If a player rips their pants, or a jersey, we'll fix that. Some of the bigger guys have more pants, because when they slide, they rip them up. Canseco used to have a ton of pants in his locker. He could be pretty tough on pants when he slid. Maybe he wore them a little tight, too.

The blue workout shirts are Majestics. I don't handle any of those other than putting numbers and All-Star patches on. Joe washes those after batting practice.

I haven't lost a uniform in twenty-two years. Not a one. I hear they're worth a lot of money. I've had a pretty good record. That's probably why they gave me the key.

I have an Econoline. When I first got it, I smashed into one of the poles. I've pretty much hit every one of those poles over the years. It's gotten harder, with all the new concessions and everything. I back right down to the visiting clubhouse, then I turn around and back up to the home clubhouse. Shoot the stuff right in.

If I ever drove into the Charles River on my way over there, they probably couldn't play. We've had it happen! The last time was with Kansas City, I'm counting the shirts that morning and I thought, "There's something wrong here. There's like 19 shirts. Usually, there's 30, 35." So I called the equipment manager, "Wally, there's something wrong here. We have 19 shirts." He said, "Don't worry about it. They were probably stolen coming out of the airport. I have a whole set in the back room." I think they all have a backup. If they don't, we'd make one for them, very quickly.

NICK OLIVA
Caterer

Since '88, I do the post-game spread. After the game each clubhouse has a buffet, six or seven different items of food. I have to make sure it's hot for the end of the game. We do a couple different pasta dishes, a chicken dish, a seafood dish. I make a salad.

Usually on travel day, getaway day it's called, they get a full turkey dinner. Turkey, gravy, mashed potatoes, cranberry sauce, vegetable, along with pasta dishes. In the summertime, I'll do a lobster feed now and then, just to break it up a bit. Sometimes I do a carved prime rib.

When the players are out on the field, I'm pushing racks of food in and out of the clubhouse.

One person can do it. Say they're home for three nights, Friday and Saturday, Dana will deliver and set it up. Sunday, I'll go in and get all my pans back. The clubhouse attendants clean up.

Al or Joe park my vehicle on the corner of Van Ness and Yawkey Way. I wheel between the cars and do the home side, then I go through the crowd and do the visitors' side.

I've done a couple of private parties, for instance when Dwight Evans' son graduated from high school. One year, there was a Fourth of July celebration on the Charles, a bunch of the guys rented a yacht and we did catering on the boat for the Red Sox and their families.

We feed about 35 people on each team. When they expand the rosters, it goes up to about fifty on each side. We also feed the umpires. Their room is above the home team clubhouse, so I just make five individual dishes and run them upstairs after the game. They like the buffalo wings.

There's a steam table in each clubhouse. They put it out of the way when we're not there, but we have it out in the middle of the room. The only day we stay is the getaway day, when they have the turkey dinner or if we're carving something. Otherwise, we drop it off, watch a bit of the game, beat the traffic home.

They eat right there in the locker room. There's a couple of tables in each clubhouse. Some of them sit right at their lockers, or go in the trainer's room, or they just wander around.

The food's off-limits to the media.

Joe always teases me, "It's a tired spread." The guys, though, enjoy the chicken. Boneless buffalo wings are a big hit. Naturally, the lobsters are a big hit. Especially with the Latin guys, they like the seafood. The hard part is, you have to prepare that both teams are going to win, even though there is a loser. The team that loses, sometimes there's a lot of food left over, but the grounds crew and the clubhouse kids eat late so it doesn't really go to waste.

Saturday spreads aren't that big, they tend to go out for dinner later at night. Sunday's mostly a travel day, so that's the big spread.

In the beginning, it was like, "Wow! I don't believe I'm doing this!" Wade Boggs is asking me for this recipe. These guys, you wouldn't be able to talk to them and then it's, "Hey, Nick. Could you make me some pesto?" Wade liked the chicken pesto.

JOE SILVA
Players' Parking Lot Attendant

I work in glass distribution. We supply insulated tempered glass all over New England, New York, Philly. We have a large facility, plate glass and stuff for buildings.

I filled out an application and a week later I got called to an interview. I just asked to work anywhere. Any position with the Red Sox would have been fine.

A couple of months later, he called and said one of the kids had to go back to school. I met him here in the corner parking lot, not knowing what I was going to do. He says, "You're parking cars." I had no idea it was the players' cars! I was just in total shock. I was all excited. It's been ten years out here.

At first, you're a little timid looking at Clemens and Boggs and everybody pulling in. But after a time, you feel comfortable with them and they get very friendly. You take care of their vehicle. There's been no damage [to their cars] – it's worked out very well in that respect. You take care of their families and you take care of them and you get to be very close, you know, personal with them. They're all down to earth. They treat me with respect, as I treat them. You get a good rapport.

Joe Silva
PHOTO BY BILL NOWLIN

Myself and Al Fiorilli, we drive everything. Al's been here fifteen years. Al was a bricklayer prior to coming here, this whole ramp structure was built by Al. He did all the brickwork and all the glass block in the suites upstairs.

I show up at 1 o'clock, if it's a 7 o'clock game. It's mostly management and department heads that have to be here at 8 o'clock in the morning. They leave their keys and we take out vehicles that are inside the park. We park them out on the street. We put all the barricades out, shut the street down. Just when we finish with that, the trainers and the players start showing up.

Most of the players' vehicles are inside here. We can fit about 36 vehicles in the lot. We block a lot of them in. A player will let me know that they're going to get home right after the game, so I'll usually leave their car up front. Actually a lot of them prefer to be parked out on the street so they can leave immediately. A starting pitcher, they like to get out quick, I'll tell you.

We've had a lot of famous people come in. Billy Crystal was here last night. He was very nice to deal with, a down to earth fellow. We've had Kevin Costner, Tom Hanks, Matt Damon, Paul Newman.

Visiting players are bused in or they come by cabs. A lot of them actually walk in and nobody will even recognize them.

It's usually a good hour and a half after the game ends before we're finally able to go. We'll have the cars lined up, if there's only a few left. We'll have the security guy come and stay, then we'll leave.

I don't get to see any of the game, not really. Most times you have people bouncing in and out. You have families or somebody showing up, plus you need to make sure everything is all right on the streets and inside the parking lot. We have a radio we listen to, plus the sausage carts have them. We catch a yell – what's going on? When they go on the road trips, I watch the games. I like to get most of the highlights if I can. My wife loves baseball and when I come home, she'll start telling me all of the details, so I know basically what goes on.

Do I like night games best, or day games? A win! I like a win. We've been out here through all kinds of weather – snow, sleet even sometimes. But it's always a great feeling when they win.

RICK ZAWACKI
Physical Therapist

In 1981, I was working for someone who knew Dr. Pappas. At that time, he was looking for a physical therapist to complement the trainer, Charlie Moss. Dr. Pappas knew the woman I was working for very well. She recommended me. This will be my 20th year coming up.

We don't necessarily meet to collaborate on treatment. We're in the same area, though, on a day-to-day basis. Jim Rowe, B. J. and I are all on the same line. There isn't one of us who's the boss of the training room. Duquette talks to Jim, and we all have our own little niches, but Dr. Pappas views us all as equals.

Jim takes care of what goes on, on the field and the basic training stuff – the first aid and whatever. He'll also get involved in getting people ready to play. I'm responsible for the rehab. People who end up getting injured enough that they can't play are my responsibility, although there's a great deal of overlap between what Jim and I do. B.J. [Baker] is more general conditioning, keeping people in shape, stuff like that.

Jim goes out on the field during a game. I rarely even sit on the bench any more. I'm usually upstairs, in the training room, in the clubhouse, taking care of the pitchers. It's an art to take care of professional pitchers on a day-to-day basis. There are things that you can do – especially with the starters – to help get rid of soreness from their previous start and prepare for their next start. I spend a lot of time with pitchers while the game is going on because they

– if they're not starting – have nothing to do until five days down the road.

When it was just Charlie and I, if he had to come upstairs for something, or go to the bathroom or whatever, and something happened on the field, I would go out, but now, if Jim Rowe has to leave the bench, B.J. goes down and covers.

I talk with the pitchers a lot about preventive measures. When I first started, pitchers never really did anything until they got hurt. Now we're trying to teach people that the more you take care of yourself, and the better shape you're in, the less likely you are to get hurt.

The manager and the pitching coach do a pretty good job of protecting their people. Unless you get down to where there's a week to go in the season and there's a pennant race going on, where you might just go ahead and use somebody a lot if you had to.

A lot of these players, especially the younger ones, don't want to say anything. I can read their body language pretty good. I might say, "This guy needs a day or two off." Joe and Jimy are good about listening to that kind of information. Players try to minimize their problems, but I guess I've had enough experience after twenty years that it's kind of hard to put something by me. You can usually tell, if a guy's struggling physically, it's going to show in the way he throws. Even if they deny it, you know what's going on. Eventually, you can get them to admit that there is a problem.

I don't think it's that prevalent, but you'll find people who unless they're 100%, won't play. There's a lot of money in the game now. I'm not going to mention any names, but I know that players have been told by agents, "If you're shoulder's bothering you, just shut it down. Just go on the disabled list because you don't want to jeopardize next year or the year after." You handle those cases on an individual basis.

Diet and nutrition is B. J.'s area. I don't get involved in that.

A lot of the Hispanic players don't start doing preventative things until they've been hurt. All they've done all their life, is just play the game. As far as the Koreans or Japanese, you've got the language problem. Cho sort of understands. Okha didn't understand anything. As far as day-to-day communication in helping them out, it's tough.

B.J.'s got a conditioning manual which every player in the organization gets at the end of the year, all the way down to Single A and rookie ball.

Jim and I submit a written report every day. I type in what's been done to a player that day from a treatment point of view and then Jim will make a comment. It gets sent to the main computer and anybody can access it. We do that on a daily basis now [to protect the club.] We never used to, but now we do.

I don't usually get any late night or early morning calls. If somebody has a problem, they call Jim Rowe. Usually it's more of a sickness kind of thing, a guy's throwing up, or he's got diarrhea and wants some medication. Jim takes care of that.

It's better if I have nothing to do, if you think about, because it means everybody's healthy. If we have a lot of injuries, then the percentage would be more rehab than prevention but there are times when we're fortunate and we don't have anybody down so then all I do is just get people ready to play.

One of the two doctors, Dr. Pappas or Dr. Morgan, is there every game.

After the game, it's just putting ice towels on people. There are no treatments or anything else. Before the game, it all depends on what needs to be done, who's hurt or whatever. Nomar comes in every day to get his hamstrings worked on, because he's had hamstring problems in the past. He gets a deep massage on both hamstrings, it's something I started doing with him when he first came up and so…he's very superstitious..it's just that I'm the one who does it. He'll wait until I'm available.

We don't schedule times or anything, people just come in. What I do each day varies. There's three of us here, so we've got it pretty much covered. It's not like we have an entourage of people coming in the training room every day. There are players who don't come in — other than walking through — all year.

What I enjoy is taking care of a guy through the course of the year, and he gets through the year healthy and successful. Then the guy gives you a "thank you" at the end of the year. That's what I get out of this job. Obviously, if we get into post-season play, there's monetary stuff, but I think just helping some of these guys is a reward. You spend so much time and then you see the success. That's what I enjoy, keeping people healthy.

JIM ROWE
Trainer

"I like going to the ballpark. I like going to work. It's a lot of work but every day it's also a lot of fun." – Jim Rowe, BOSTON HERALD.

My first memory of Fenway Park is when I was five years old. We had a minor league. It was just above T-ball. They would bus us down to Fenway and we'd sit in the bleachers.

Jim Rowe, in Red Sox clubhouse
PHOTO BY BILL NOWLIN

I played baseball, football and track, but I got hurt when I was fifteen, so the docs wouldn't let me play anymore, but I had brothers behind me in school and I wanted to be with them so I started being a manager the end of my sophomore year. I went to Springfield College for sports medicine for two and a half years and then a minor league job opened with the Milwaukee Brewers in 1985.

I went to Beloit, Wisconsin for three years and then to El Paso, Texas for two years. Dan Duquette was a minor league assistant at the time I was with the Brewers. He was looking for a Triple A trainer and I had enough experience with my years in Milwaukee. He wanted someone that worked hard and thank God he said, "Yes" and gave me the Triple A job. Pawtucket. A great place. Great people. They treated me very well. I spent 1994 there and then he gave me the head trainer's job in Boston. That was '95.

When you're a trainer at the minor league level, you do just about anything. You're a traveling secretary. You're about the only guy with a college education that's on the road, so you get the accounting jobs and everything else. You'd have to do the rooming list and make sure that everybody pays their incidentals and all that wonderful stuff, plus take care of the organization's prospects at the same time. Talk about getting an education. I started spring training as a 19 year old. I was the youngest head trainer in the major leagues, starting in '95 at 30.

Charlie Moss was before me. Charlie and I were friends my entire minor league time, even when I was with the Brewers. He was the president of PBATS, the Professional Baseball Athletic Trainers, and very well known in that regard.

There is a "damaged goods" clause. We'll do our own testing. We bring him into U. Mass. Medical and do a full physical. Then we put him through an orthopedic exam. We do a lot of history at that time. If the guy needs an MRI, we'll give him an MRI. If he needs X-rays to take a look at an elbow... Since I've been here, we've turned down maybe two guys.

It's basically a full day of testing. You take the medical records they give you, and then you turn around and do your own. It's just due diligence. To cover you and the organization, you have to make sure that this is an insurable situation. You've got to pick the players you want to cover. That's a General Manager call.

Everybody has personal insurance of their own. If they're hurt while playing, they have workmen's comp. There's an extra life insurance policy that some of these guys take out. We're mired in insurance.

Right now, pitching is at such a premium, you will take an older guy that knows how to pitch, who can make an adjustment. Look at Sabes. You say, "He can make an adjustment. He knows how to pitch. So let's rehab him the best we can and see what we do."

To become a trainer, you have to graduate from an accredited college. They have a program set up by the NATA [the National Athletic Trainers Association] and they accredit and license you.

Joe [Kerrigan] is so much help to us. He knows about mechanics, and what's loading what. Rehab-wise, he is excellent. When we go into a throwing program he comes to us with a schedule for the program and all we do is sign off on it.

They're teachers first. People don't really get a feel for how good a teacher Jimy is and how good Joe is.

I'm in there bugging Jimy at the beginning of the day. I'll see him with any updates during b.p. and prior to the game. I'll update him on anything that happened during the game. And then after the game, we'll just shut the door and talk for a half hour. Every night. No matter what.

I'm the head trainer, so I'll do all the talking with Doc. Rich [Zawacki] does all the physical therapy in regards to the pitchers, whether they need a rub or a stretch. But when you're trying to take care of notifying everybody and making sure everybody's on the same page, and making sure your position players are taken care of every day, we all work together. There is a hierarchy, but there isn't.

Dr. Pappas is the medical director and the orthopedic. Dr. [Bill] Morgan is basically his assistant. Arthur can't possibly cover every night, and Billy's in there three or four nights a week. [As the 2000 season began, Dr. Morgan become the Team Physician.]

You won't see a doctor go out on the field very often. He sits so close to the dugout, though, I can say, "I need you inside."

When I go out on the field, they think you're just talking to them but you're actually doing an evaluation. The first fifteen or twenty seconds is just getting the guy to talk to you. If they got hit in the arm with a pitch, they're maybe angry and in pain. You give them time to let that pain go away and then hopefully you can talk to them and get your hands on them. If they can move their hand, if they can move their wrist, how much pain that's eliciting. Grip strength. How their nerve function is, and everything else.

You let them get to the point where they can take a deep breath. Some guys will play through anything. I just look at Jimy, and Jimy makes the call.

They say that sport mimics society. You get a lot of the same things in sports that you get in society. I wouldn't use the word "hypochondria" but yeah, you get guys that are a little tougher than other guys. There are guys that might not play unless they're a hundred percent, but there are a lot more guys who play no matter what. You're almost trying to protect them from themselves at certain points.

There are guys that you have to say, "Nope. It's out of your hands. We're done." Medically, we're not going to take a chance. You have enough time to make the call. I'll know within the first 45 seconds what I have, and then you make an informed decision. If you have a doubt in your mind, you're not going to let the guy stay there.

You're really protecting a player and thereby protecting the team. There's a difference between playing injured and paying hurt. Usually you'll weigh on the side of caution. It's hard to explain but you're watching them every minute, how they take off their jacket, or whatever. You become very astute at watching people from the corner of your eye.

We're trying to better these guys. We're not trying to make them into enormous human beings. Baseball is a game of long muscles, thinner people usually. Flexibility is a huge part of the game. That's why I'm out there. That's why B. J.'s out there on the line before the game. That's why forty minutes before the game, we'll go around and make sure everybody's been stretched. You do everything you can to prevent injury, and you try to do everything you can after games. If a guy's really tight, you get him in the tub. If a catcher's had a really long day and it's hot and you know his fluids are down, you really push the fluids. You get him in a cold tub. You do little things like that so they're more comfortable at night. A lot of these guys are so wired that they don't go to bed until three or four o'clock in the morning. Then they sleep until noon. You try to get them to the ballpark a little bit early, so they can do a maintenance program and then have time to recover by 7:05.

If you can get them on a routine that they like and it works, you leave them alone.

Jimy's amazing. He will see someone taking ground balls, say this guy who's been down for a couple of days and before I even get a word out of my mouth, he'll say, "He's not ready yet." Jimy's a very good judge. He knows what the base is for that guy.

Just about everybody's got a strength and conditioning coordinator now. There are certain guys that you just shake your head and think, "What the hell are they doing?" but they are becoming few and far between.

That kid doing his weekly program at Double A, that program's going to be the same when he comes up to the big leagues. We're not there to change anything. That program is set back in February, when they come in. They've already gone through their weekly program during the off-season.

Chris Correnti, who's my minor league coordinator, is outstanding. He rides herd on everybody.

Usually, the personal trainers are in the off-season. There are a few in other organizations that have them during the season. All of our guys work out with us.

Ethyl chloride is a cold spray that takes the bite off a little bit. You've got something cold on you, that's about it. Plus it's something to do to waste a little more time. When someone fouls a ball off your foot, there's nothing that's going to take that pain away. It's just a matter of personal taste, what protection people wear. You're trying to put a shin pad on somebody…oh no, no, no, they just don't feel right. You can tell people what to do, but they're grown men and they're going to play the game the way they play the game.

During most of the game, I will be on the bench. I'll take certain guys aside, if something's going on. It may be that the only time I'll have privacy with a player, believe it or not, is in the corner of the dugout. They'll have private or confidential questions they want answered.

They do come to us with confidential questions. It can be a family question. It can be anything. When you're with guys from February until – hopefully – October, there are times when things happen and maybe it's just a situation where, hey, my wife's pregnant. Congratulations. Sometimes they don't want to say in front of everybody. They'd rather have a quiet moment – or mess with you! That's mainly what they're doing, messing around. Trying to keep loose.

If I see something happening, I won't wait for them to come to me. I'll definitely go to them. I've got to let Jimy know if we're going to pull them. That's my job. We don't ever get into things like their swing; we don't ever do that stuff. They may come and ask a question, but you get yourself in trouble if you start coaching. We just answer physical questions.

Do you have a lot of contact with players in the off-season?

As much as possible. Everybody's got a program. Rich calls all the pitchers, and I call all the position players. Everybody in our minor league system and our major league system is called. Even if they're as healthy as rocks, we're calling them. What you do is you find out what they're doing, and there's certain things that they're going to answer and I know if they're bullshitting me or not.

Carlos Cowart
PHOTO BY BILL NOWLIN

CARLOS COWART
Red Sox Batboy

"As a kid, this is something I always hoped for. I don't know how much better it can get."

My official title is clubhouse staff, but I'm the bat boy. I put on the uniform thirty minutes before the game. I'd be running errands before that or bringing coolers out to the bullpen. I have to do pine tar, the bullpens, dugout with coolers, the helmets. It's hard. When I come in after school, most of the guys are already there.

The work before the game is easier, though, than the game itself. There's a lot of running. I try to stay down so the fans can watch. Most of the time I'm down on my knees or you can catch me on one leg.

I work at the Tobin Community Center in Mission Hill as a peer leader for pre-school kids. Somehow my community center got ahold of the applications and we checked them out and sent them in. In a week or so, we got a call telling us when to come. Me and another kid, Torey Mercer, were hired. I was 16. He works in the other clubhouse. I've worked there for three years now. I started in April, 1997, sometime after Opening Day.

Carlos told Mike Silverman from the BOSTON HERALD *that he carries photos in his school backpack to convince doubters who don't believe he works for the Red Sox.* "My friends and family, when they heard I got this job, it was like I was a baseball player, someone famous….The job is great. I love it. I never was a baseball fan, but since I got here, I get more into it. I love seeing the game. I love the excitement and the fans."

For a 7 o'clock game, we leave right after school, so I'd get in around 2:30. During the summer, 12 o'clock or a little earlier. For a 1 o'clock game on the weekends we'll come in at 7 o'clock in the morning.

The players carry their own bat out. After they've hit, I put the bat back in the rack for them. Nomar breaks maybe three bats a year. Jason Varitek breaks the most, maybe two bats a week, since I've been there.

We don't use the weight bat. We have two doughnuts. Then there's the pine tar. The wrapping thing, it's like a little cloth. The pine tar comes out of a silver can and you pour it onto a cloth. Then there's a small rosin bag. We use three a day. There's one on the mound, one in the dugout and one in the batter's box. It's this crystal material that we have to crush. We put it inside the end of a sock. A sannie. A sanitary sock. Then there's a stick of pine tar [the red stick].

Maurice brings the balls for the umpires, we usually rub them, me and a couple of clubhouse guys. If the balls are in the umpires' room, we'll do them up there. If not, we'll be in the clubhouse rubbing them.

MAURICE BAXTER
Clubhouse Assistant

I'm a clubhouse assistant. Carlos is more the bat boy. They'll call both of us bat boys, but he does the bats and I do the balls.

I started in 1998. One of the guys at the Mo Vaughn program here, Bryan Wilson, set it up for me. He knew Joe Cochran, the clubhouse man.

I've enjoyed it. I'm 17, a student at the Mo Vaughn Development Program. It's an after school program, to help us with homework, give us workshops, try to help me go to college.

I don't play a lot of baseball, but I know Mo Vaughn because this is his program. I'm a Red Sox fan. I always used to cheer for Mo.

I show up a few hours before the game, about 4 o'clock. I help set up the field for batting practice. I'd bring out the pine tar, the bag, the donuts, the net with the batting tee. The trainers mix up the Powerade and we bring that and the water out to the bullpen and to the dugout. Set up the helmets for the game.

The ground crew brings out the cage. I bring out the hitting net. It's about 5 or 6 feet high. We bring out the bag of balls for the batting practice pitcher. Set them next to the net.

The players bring their own bats out. At the end of the game you put them in the game bag.

I put on the uniform about a half hour before the game. After b. p., we clean the field off. We can get something to eat if we want, in the clubhouse. We make sure everything's looking decent. Pick up the clothes, wash them, clean off their shoes. We all take turns doing laundry.

Carlos puts the rosin bag on the mound for the pitcher, brings out the equipment for the on-deck circle. Two donuts, the rosin bag, a rosin stick and the pine tar rag. That's part of doing the bats.

I'm on the field the whole night, but Carlos comes out only when the Red Sox are up. I'm on the field when the visitors are up, ready to get balls as they come off the screen, off the net, anywhere on the field.

I bring out a bagfull of balls before the game. When I need more, I get some from the storage room, right next to the umpires' room. They're pre-rubbed.

After the game's over, you bring in the water coolers, from the bullpen and the dugout. Bring in the batting helmets, the sunflower seeds – all that stuff. I help out with the clubhouse duties, cleaning up, vacuuming. Wash the dishes, push in the chairs, pass out their clothes when they're done in the wash. That's about it. About two hours later we can leave.

Maurice Baxter
PHOTO BY BILL NOWLIN

WALLY MCDOUGAL
Former Batboy

Wally McDougal is son of Butch McDougal (mechanic for Aramark) and Patricia Orlando McDougal (checker for Aramark), and grandson of Vince Orlando.

I was around the park my whole life. I'm an insurance agent now. I started in the clubhouse, working for my grandfather. Johnny Orlando passed away when I was just a little kid. That story about his ashes scattered out there, no one ever proved that story. We don't know for sure.

There's actually a picture of me in the GLOBE when I was 7 – packing Ray Culp's bag, I think it was. When I got of legal working age, I started working there. When you were 14, you could work during the day. 1980 is when I first got on the payroll. I was 15. When I was younger, I just was hanging around, helping out.

The visiting clubhouse manager now, Tommy McLaughlin, he came in with me. His brother-in-law used to work for my grandfather; that's how he got in. It's your friends get you in. That's how it used to be. Still is. "Hey, my friend's looking for a job." "Bring him in."

In that kind of position, it's good. You know the person. You don't want someone coming in and robbing you blind. That stuff's easy to disappear. Memorabilia. Having a friend of a friend come makes things a little more comfortable.

For the most part, they're a great bunch of guys. I remember when I was a kid going out to dinner with Dwight Evans. It was more of a family atmosphere back then, the guys were a lot more fun. Now it's business. Even towards the end of the 80s, it just wasn't the same.

People say, "Oh, they're snobs now" – but society's changed. You can't be friendly to people. People said Roger Clemens is a jerk – well, Roger was one of the nicest guys if you know him personally. They'd say, "He doesn't sign autographs". Well, when you're a superstar, you have to send off that kind of aura. It keeps people away. Some of these guys give off that image that "I'm a jerk" – that gives them a bit of peace and quiet when they're with their family.

FRED WAUGH
Former Red Sox Batboy

I had a friend in high school who was a clubhouse kid for the Red Sox. Dean Lewis. I was bothering Dean for a year, telling him, "Hey, if a spot ever comes open, I'll come in."

It's all connections and everything there. It's like the Irish mafia. I think working there, there's a lot of trust involved. There's stories of kids that stole uniforms and baseball bats and stuff. That's why they like to get people they know.

There was no interview. They really work you to death when you first get there, the first thing you do is unload the truck from spring training. That's the hardest work all year, unloading those giant steamer trunks full of equipment. They've got wooden baskets in there with leather handles that you lift out, and there's a number on each wooden basket. Those are actually the trunks from when they used to make road trips on trains. They used to load those things on horse-drawn wagons, I guess, and

bring them down to the train station. Pretty cool, because their old numbers are still stenciled on them. There's a number "9" which was Ted Williams' box, I guess, that got handed down over the generations. They're only used for spring training now. They just unpack them the first time and they go up above the players' lockers, and sit there as extra storage. I wouldn't be surprised if they still use them. As you know, it's kind of a cheap organization. They save money however they can. If it works, why stop using it?

You'd get there at 2. You've got to get the uniforms from the night before from the laundry room, and put them on hangers in the lockers for the players. There's two sets of uniforms – one for batting practice and one for the game.

There's also baseballs to be signed every day. They stick dozens of balls out there in the middle of the room and the players sign them. Vinnie would send us around to each player with a box of balls and a pen and have them sign. You'd have to chase them down.

The players start coming in between 3 and 4. You'd spend a lot of time running errands. A lot of them would send us out to McDonald's, and they'd give us a couple of bucks tip.

A lot of guys were superstitious and they'd have to have their bats in the same spot. Wade Boggs used to want his helmet upside down, in with the bats. Little weird things like that. They all had their quirks I guess.

After the players took b.p. and infield, we'd launder all their wet stuff, as we called it. All the stuff they sweated in. They'd change their uniforms and everything underneath, too, usually. Some of the guys would take a shower. The older generation guys like Yastrzemski didn't even take off his uniform usually. Bill Buckner, guys like that, kind of dirty all the time and didn't care. That generation were more used to the old days of the game when you didn't have all these little extra perks, when the guys weren't making as much money and all that.

We'd be doing miscellaneous things, like putting out food for after batting practice, and making sure there was gum and chewing tobacco out. We take the shoes in the back room and use a wire brush to brush all the dirt off the cleats and then we use that liquid shoe black stuff and dress the shoes so they would look good out there.

Once a guy trusted you, he'd ask you to open his mail. If it's fan mail, put it in one place. If it looks personal, you'd stick it in his locker. A lot of them were getting fifty fan letters a day, with cards to sign and stuff. They generally set them all aside and do them all at once. Some of them didn't do them at all. That's the rumor.

You didn't hear it from me, but sometimes the kids in the clubhouse do the mail and everything. I used to do Wade Boggs' signature, and he couldn't tell it from his. If you want to do mail for a guy, you would practice his signature long and hard until it looks good enough and then he'd let you sign some of the stuff. You might get an extra tip at the end of the year.

Those guys [in the visitors' clubhouse] actually make a little more money, because they get tipped every road trip. On the home side, they tip you the last homestand of the year. You have to make a little bit more from the tips because you're making less than minimum wage from the club.

If someone got traded, you might not get anything from them. The classy guys would take care of you. There are a lot of cheap guys, though.

You try to develop relationships with the player so that you can become the "go-to" guy and make some extra money when the guy wants something. Which is what I tried to do with Wade Boggs.

I always had balls in my pocket, even in the dugout. I would watch the umpire and if he would hold up his fingers or tell me how many were needed, I'd run out and hand the baseballs to him.

When the Red Sox take the field at the top of the first, I'm just kind of sitting on the bench. If a trainer needs me to get something, or a player asks me to go get a glove or something I'll go do it. I'll make sure the Gatorade jug stays full. If it's a cold night, you have to bring down hot soup, or hot water bottles for guys to warm

their hands on. Your only duty there is if a relief pitcher comes in, I have to run out and take his coat when he's coming in from the bullpen.

Back then it was a pretty clique-y ballclub, too. There wasn't a lot of intensity. Those were not glory years.

Generally, the umpires were pretty cool. You'd do stuff for them, too, like bring them lunch and everything. Durwood Merrill was a really nice guy. He liked to talk. You'd go up and talk to him, in the umpires' room when they're getting ready, and he would tell you about pitchers. I remember he told me once he thought Bruce Hurst had the best curve in baseball, him and Bert Blyleven. Just little insider stuff like that.

When they had a clubhouse meeting, we'd either have to leave the room or go in the back where we couldn't hear anything. Whenever there was a team meeting, the trainers and all that couldn't be there, only coaches and players.

They're used to having people pick up after them, so they'd just throw their helmet on the ground even if you were standing right next to them. Some guys would make a point of handing you their stuff. Jim Rice – even after he struck out with the bases loaded – he would toss you his bat and helmet. It was usually the rookies who would do that, tossing their stuff on the ground. It bugged us, but hey, that's the price you pay for a job like this, you have to take a lot of crap from these guys. There's about thirty kids that would take your job in a second.

It's not a high-class, glamorous kind of job, really. I mean, you're washing a lot of dirty laundry and sometimes the guys are throwing shit at you. They're big babies. I had Steve Crawford stuff me in the clothes dryer once. It wasn't running, but he jammed me in there. It was kind of humiliating, but it was a two-way thing because we used to tease the players and see what we could get away with. Northeastern was doing some classes for the players and I saw him sign up, so I asked him if he was taking tractor driving or something. He didn't appreciate that, so he stuffed me in the dryer. He was a big Okie. Some guys you could joke around with, other guys just play a little rough, I guess.

My dad taught at MIT. He was a huge Red Sox fan and he was excited about my working there. Every time we'd go to a party, he'd tell people about it. My dad was always bugging me to keep a journal, but I never did

I traveled on the team charter plane, you walk in and there's a big keg of beer there for the players, and they're all kind of goofing it up on the flight. I heard it wasn't good to be a flight attendant.

At the end of the year, we got tips, anywhere from fifty to two hundred bucks. The most I ever heard anyone getting was four hundred dollars. In '82 the minimum salary [for players], I think, was $35,000. The guys with the big contracts usually gave the good tips. Jim Rice was the best tipper the whole time I was there. I think he was the only guy on the club making a million a year. Maybe Carl Yastrzemski, but I think Jim Rice was the highest paid.

Some of those guys, it's a point of pride to flash the dough around more than the other guys.

I think the media in Boston is a little...over-enthusiastic. There's a little over-zealousness there. You have very good reporters, but they all think it's Watergate. Peter Gammons was the guy we got to know the best, he would always be there early and we would just chat with him. He was a real nice guy. I think it has to do with him developing good sources, but he was there hours before anybody else.

I was on the front page of the GLOBE sports section once, picking up a bird. It flew down and sat on the first base line. They stopped play and the umpire asked me to go catch it. I was trying to throw my hat on it. It was pretty comical. It was actually on THIS WEEK IN BASEBALL, too. The bird was just disoriented. The rumor was that they put poisoned corn in the stands to kill the birds. I don't know whether that was true or not. Every time I went to catch it, it sort of squirted out of my hands. Eventually, it flew off into the stands after making me look like an idiot.

Oh yeah, you'd see rats. There was a security guard named Bill who was a little off-kilter. He would talk about how the younger generation had no respect for authority. He would work by himself all night. Sometimes you'd come in in the morning and you'd lift the garage gate and there'd be four dead rats lined up there, that he left.

JOE FLANAGAN
Red Sox Clubhouse Security

My father Lawrence worked at Fenway for Harry M. Stevens. He worked the concessions for quite a few years after he retired from the Post Office. Originally, he ran one of the stands and then he was in charge of all the cups and whatnot in the park. My kids Joe, Paul and Jimmy worked there too, hawking and peddling on the concessions.

I worked out there for the Red Sox in 1944. Hughie Duffy gave me a tryout. I went in the service right after that. I came out after the war and played around, the Park League and whatnot. In fact, I was inducted in the Boston Park League Hall of Fame and the Boston English High Hall of Fame.

I was a Boston policeman for seventeen years. I left the Police Department and worked as a court officer in Suffolk Superior Court for twenty-one years.

When I retired in 1991, I was looking for a job to keep myself occupied. My father had worked at Fenway, so I contacted somebody there.

I ran an elevator for about six years over there, just game days, when they were in town. A lot of people don't like running elevators, but I was used to working with the public, so it didn't bother me.

I'd arrive two hours before the game. People were transporting stuff up and down, for the 600 Club, the chefs and whatnot. The elevators are self-service the rest of the time. I think

Joe Flanagan
PHOTO BY BILL NOWLIN

the Red Sox wanted to have an attendant before and during the game for safety reasons and also for information. It gets jammed game days. A lot of people don't know where they're going.

There was always somebody going up and down during the game. It was constantly busy. I'd peek out once in a while from the second floor just to get the score. I was always a Red Sox fan.

I'd leave approximately an hour after the game, once they got all the people down from the second floor. Especially the wheelchairs, we had to make sure we got them down before anything.

I started working security at the clubhouse in 1997. Joe McDermott is my boss. I show up four hours before the game now. I have responsibilities not only to the players, but to the families and the umpires. They all come through the clubhouse door. Anybody that comes there, you question them what they're looking for.

Usually, the new players will introduce themselves and their families. Once the game starts, I'll lock the door to the parking lot. The fellows in the parking lot will call and ask me to open the door to certain people. Some of the older kids will go back and forth from the family room to the stands. They rap on the door and I let them in. Some of the younger kids know the park better than I do!

The media is in there until three quarters of an hour before the game starts, and then they're not allowed back in until Kevin Shea comes down. He and I will stand there and he'll make the decision. I don't let anybody in unless he gives the OK.

I'm there at least an hour after. I won't stay until all the players are gone, though. Some of the players just linger around. I wait until it really quiets down. I'll make sure everything is all right and then I'll lock the door to the parking area so nobody can get in. They can let themselves out but then they can't get back in again. It can take nine to ten hours. Some nights it goes quicker; other nights, it drags.

THOMAS J. DUNN
Visiting Clubhouse Security

This is a childhood dream, being this close to the ballplayers and to the game itself. I grew up in Manhattan. I was an ardent New York Giants fan during the 50s and the 60s. There was this intense rivalry with the Brooklyn Dodgers, so I got to love the game at a very tender age.

My wife comes from the Boston area and we felt that it would be easier for me to relocate to Boston than for her to come to New York. The quality of life is better than in metropolitan New York.

Thomas J. Dunn
PHOTO BY BILL NOWLIN

I was an insurance adjuster. When I retired a couple of years ago, one of the people who worked here indicated to me that the Red Sox were looking for someone to handle this particular spot.

It's the one job in my life that I have sincerely loved, there are so many nice people. The athletic fraternity is absolutely fantastic, and I find that in all of the executives that I meet. People like Mr. Steinbrenner. A very fine man. Just nice, nice people. I know some of the Red Sox management. Mr. Harrington resides in the same town that I reside in, and he's a very nice man. I know Mr. Buckley also, and Mr. McDermott. They're all in that same category. There aren't too many jobs in life where you can say that there are that many nice people, percentage-wise. I'd say 99.99 percent are great people.

Occasionally, we get some unruly fans or people try and crash the clubhouse, give you a story why they want to get in there, but they don't have the proper credentials. We're always on the alert for things like that.

It's a revelation and a fantastic life experience to be part of an organization such as this.

MIKE FRASER
Driver for Yankee Bus

Mike Fraser
PHOTO BY BILL NOWLIN

I have been at Yankee 18 years now. When I was a kid, I used to watch THE HONEYMOON-ERS and I was intrigued by the guy driving that double-decker bus. Most kids when they're young think "I'm going to be a doctor" or "I'm going to be this." I always told my parents I was going to be a bus driver. Ralph Kramden drove a city bus, but there was a commercial on THE HONEYMOONERS every night – it was a guy in a brand-new Greyhound double-decker bus and he'd always open that side window and he'd yell out, "Go Greyhound, and leave the driving to us!" Major league baseball player was my second choice.

Actually, I was going to be a major league coach. I went from a coach to a coach. I worked for the city of Newton for about 15 years. I was doing heavy equipment for them but I was going absolutely nowhere. Before this, I was coaching. I was a baseball coach at the high school level. I coached at Harvard University back in the 70s; I was a baseball coach there and I coached football. I was the head baseball coach at Weston High School.

I got burnt out and after I got out of coaching, I drove a school bus here in Newton. I met my wife there and married her. She was a school bus driver, too. She still drives.

This guy Eli had bought some coaches and of course when I saw those, I said Oh boy that was something I always wanted to do. He brought me over there and they were humongous; I couldn't believe how big they were. I was a little intimidated when I first saw them but then I got inside the bus and I sat down and I looked out the left mirror and I looked out the right mirror and I said, "You know, I think I could drive this." I remember he said, "Pull it out." It was parked between two columns and I pulled it out with absolutely no problem and I've just absolutely been in love ever since then.

So I took a leave of absence from the city of Newton for six months, just to go out and try this, to see if I liked being away from home some. It started out local and then long distance. And the more I got into the business, the more it was feeding another fantasy of mine and that was history. I thoroughly enjoy American history and so having on board much of the time professors and tour guides and people that are very knowledgeable about all of these places I go to, I've always had an open ear. So it's enabled me to become a licensed tour guide in Boston and Washington DC. I can do a city tour just about anywhere on the East coast, including Canada. I almost have a classroom on wheels, a captive audience. Yankee does a lot of charter work, whether it to be Washington DC or Florida. I've been to every state in the United States, with the exception of Louisiana. I enjoy Lexington and Concord. I just had a group of Harvard Business School people out there. I try to make them re-live like what it felt to be there that day. I always say, "If there were 77 of us and 700 of them, what would you do?" They were British subjects. This was treason for them. It's almost the same thing as for us as Americans sitting right here and watching the finest of the United States Army marching up Mass. Ave. and we are going to defy them! Think about how brave these 77 farmers were. Their only training was shooting squirrels out of trees or something. For Harvard people to give you a standing ovation...

I do most of the visiting teams at Fenway; I've been doing them a lot this year since Jimmy [O'Reilly] has gone to work for Coach USA. You have more runs handling visiting teams – you get to pick them up at the hotels and go to the games with them, then bring them back and then to the airport and back.

We go right on the tarmac, right to plane-side. We go to South Gate to pick them up. We usually call the airlines first and tell them we're coming over for the team and they'll meet us at South Gate with an escort – one of the trucks or one of the baggage pulleys – and then we've got an escort onto the tarmac over to planeside. You see all of the airline people lined up at the plane watching the players get off. It's kind of neat to watch that as well.

I think they're afraid that we're going to ask them for something. The Orioles came in Sunday night about 2 o'clock in the morning. I'll pick them up today [Tuesday] and bring them over in the bus about 4:30 and leave it there. Usually, I'll go watch batting practice. During the game, as the people are filing in, I go out for a walk and then I usually get something to eat outside the park, and then I come back in and go up to the roof boxes and sit up there and watch the game. Sometimes I'll come downstairs and talk to this guy Warren who's been there about 50 years, or the TV production guys. I just about have the run of the park. I move around.

They've hired us, they're in that bus and you try not to bother them. Some people like to talk and some people don't like to. This last trip, Paul O'Neill and Bernie Williams and Chuck Knoblauch are ones who struck up a conversation. Some of the players will just see the ball on the dashboard and they'll have the team sign it.

Of course, you know, they call us "Bussy." All teams call bus drivers "Bussy." I don't know where that originated from. The hockey players, the basketball players, the football players and the baseball players – they all call you "Bussy." No, the professors don't call you that.

A lot of people in my neighborhood in Newton know I pick up [visiting] teams and they say, "Ah, drive them in the Charles River! Run 'em off the road!" Typical Boston fans, you know.

On May 19, 2002, Fraser was involved in an unfortunate inci-dent, as the Yankee bus he was driving caught fire in the Ted Williams Tunnel while transporting the Seattle Mariners team to Logan Airport following a Sunday afternoon game where they were beaten by the Red Sox 3-2. Fraser was the only one treated for smoke inhalation, though manager Lou Piniella and several players were given oxygen for about half an hour at the airport. The Boston newspapers showed a charred us bearing the word "YANKEE" on the side, which was in the tunnel named after Sox great Ted Williams – a bus bearing Seattle Mariners.

JACK ROGERS
Former Traveling Secretary

Jack Rogers died in 2002. For many years in later life, he sat in the press box next to the official scorer, simply recording balls and strikes. No strenuous effort was involved. The position was clearly an emeritus slot for an old Fenway veteran. Baseball is often like that, good to people who have been around the game for a long time.

I just count how many are balls and how many are strikes. Charlie [Scoggins] calls his own shots.

I was always involved with baseball. I worked for the Boston Braves in '48 in public relations. Billy Sullivan was the boss. I was there through June of '52. My first and only position with the Red Sox was as traveling secre-tary. '69. I was interviewed by Dick O'Connell. I heard that [Tom] Dowd was going to retire. Before that, I was with Pan American World Airways.

There was very little train, it was all air by then. If we went down to Pawtucket for an exhi-bition, we'd take a bus. We'd take a train out of New York to Baltimore or Washington, but we never trained Boston to New York. You more or less have to charter. You're not going to get a scheduled airline at midnight.

I'd set up all the charters, all the hotels, all the buses. I think the Red Sox were the first baseball team to fly, actually. We'd hire a truck and a couple of buses to meet the plane. The truck would take the gear to the ballpark and the personal bags to the hotel. You'd have the same set-up when you leave. The truck would pick up the personal bags and then pick the gear up and take it to the airport.

The traveling secretaries would have what baseball calls the winter meetings. The hotel people would come in and tell us what was available, the prices and so on. We pay for the room. Movies or the mini bars – those are personal. That's up to the player. We pay for the room, period. Everything else, he pays on his own.

I was on the road with the team all year, and in spring training you'd run the whole show. You arranged for the equipment truck to take all your gear down to spring training. You're the big boss down there. The traveling secretary is in charge, but they do a lot of it out of the home office now, which they didn't do in my day. I used to do the whole thing. Every cent spent in spring training went through me.

In those days, the press traveled with us. Our usual party was roughly 45 people. We made the arrangements for the press but we didn't pay for them. In the old days, they were afraid not to travel with us, because something would happen and they wouldn't be in on it. Then frequent flyer came along and they sort of deserted us so they could get their miles. The broadcasters travel with the team now.

The scouts usually travel on their own. We don't see too much of them as a rule. They report to the manager about what's going on, and then they disappear. On to the next job.

We've had problems – trucks not there, buses not there. That happens. We got on a plane one night in New York about 8 o'clock in the evening and sat there until about 1 o'clock in the morning. But we survived.

We had a bus break down in Seattle. We were all right going down the hills, but going up, it would heat up and finally it just conked out. We all piled out and within five minutes, we had all been picked up and driven to our hotel by people driving by. They were very nice. I would guess that was in the 80's.

We had a bus to the hotel before the ball game and one back to the hotel after the game. A lot of them would go out to the park early, on their own. When it was time for the bus to go, we'd go. If they missed the bus, they'd hop a cab. As long as they show up when they're supposed to, that's all we were interested in.

If a player got sent down to the minors, we'd pay their fare to get there. Even with an outright release, they get first class fare home. First class; it's the only way they go. That's in the agreement.

I'd be in charge of tickets to the game for families and friends of the players. Four for family and two for friends. If they had six in their family, they could go to one of the other players and get a couple from him. They use them all up, one way or another.

We'd come into the hotel at 2, 3, 4 o'clock in the morning and there'd be maybe twenty people waiting. A guy that's well known, they never let him alone.

Steve August took over from me for a couple of years, then Jack McCormick took over from him. I work with Jack all the time. He does a good job. The players all like him. In the old days, the traveling secretary went on forever, but now they seem to change every few years. It's a tough job, especially for a young fellow that's got family, because you're in Florida for six weeks, then you're on the road for maybe 100 days during the season. You play 81 games but you've got days off and travel days and all that stuff.

You travel with the team. In case anything happens, you're the one that everybody turns to. I think it might be harder today. They make so much money today that they want to run everything themselves.

It was always something different. You never knew what was going to happen. It was interesting that way.

KEVIN CARSON
Salesman, New England Household Moving

I called on the Red Sox as a salesperson. I was one of the workers back then, loading the truck. Then I went into sales for the company.

Our driver is Mr. Hartz. He's solely dedicated to them. He's the guy who does it each year. Basically, it's about 90% team equipment and then there's computer equipment from the front office and whatever other things they feel they need. The trailer is full by the time we have it loaded.

They're a pretty organized group. They do all the packing themselves. They'll separate game shirts, home and away. They'll separate by size. Same thing with pants. Other boxes will contain baseballs and helmets. Everything is marked, so they can un-box in Fort Myers. We are an Atlas Van Lines agent and we have an office right in Naples, which will arrange to have some men assist in the off-loading. The unloading is really easy.

Loading here is not bad, because of the proximity of the truck to the clubhouse door. Fort Myers, on the other hand, you have to walk a couple of miles! We come in the parking lot and park over near the batting cages. That's as close as we can get. Then we have to walk about 120 feet to the door. Once you enter the clubhouse, you still have to walk another 200 feet.

We usually get there around 6:30 and start loading around 7:30. We'll probably be done 1-ish. It moves pretty quickly. I use the same crew every year and these guys know exactly what to do.

I just tell the guys, look, let's not do anything stupid. "Good things come to them who wait," I tell them, and I have to say Joe's a very decent soul and at the end of the day, he takes care of the guys. Everybody goes away with a big smile on their face and a good feeling.

It's a fun day. It really is. It's something we look forward to.

The clubhouse, it's the inner sanctum. It's the place that most people never get the chance to see. To be able to go in there and see the inside, I get a kick out of because I grew up in Boston. To be able to say, "I'm sitting in front of the locker that Roger Clemens had, and before Roger it belonged to Carl Yastrzemski. And before Carl Yastrzemski, it was Ted Williams'." That's history. Sitting right in this corner. Bret Saberhagen, I believe, has it today. As far as I know, only four people have had that locker in fifty years.

It's been a great account for us. We just moved a treadmill down to the Dominican Republic for Pedro Martinez. We've moved Roger Clemens, Nomar Garciaparra. It's afforded us the chance to do business with these guys as well.

There will be a lot of media people there Tuesday. Dan Rea is always there with a crew. He's an institution. You will see Channel 5, Channel 7. 25, 38. You'll see NESN. You'll see photographers from the GLOBE taking shots. It's the truck that gets the attention. It's a rite of spring. As far as I'm concerned, at New England Household, spring begins on February 15 this year.

Kevin Carson
PHOTO BY BILL NOWLIN

I grew up in Newton. Joe Cronin was a neighbor and a friend of my dad's. He'd call us over, "Hey, kid, come over here." He'd give me tickets to his skybox seats. I'd gather up all my buddies – it was like Our Gang, Alfalfa and all them – and we'd get on the streetcars and go to the game. One time one of the ushers grabbed me and said, "Where'd you get these tickets?" He took me into the Red Sox office and called over to the American League office and got Mr. Cronin on the phone. "We've got some kids here who have your tickets." "Who is it?" he asked. "Kevin Carson." "Oh, that's all right. He's a friend of mine. Make sure you take care of them with hot dogs and everything." For the rest of the game, my friends were calling the ushers and telling them to keep the hot dogs coming. We had a great time.

I used to go almost every weekend. One night game, around midnight my mother realized I wasn't home yet, so she called the park and had me paged. I went down to the information booth and called her and told her the game was still going on. My mother told the guy to take me and my friends and stand out on Brookline Avenue until my father came to pick me up. That wouldn't happen today, imagine telling someone from the Red Sox to stand out there with your kids. Of course, I wouldn't let my kids go in there by themselves these days. Things were different back then.

Eckersley dropped off some stuff. Jim Rice brought by a suitcase to have shipped down.

AL HARTZ
Equipment Truck Driver

Al Hartz
PHOTO BY BILL NOWLIN

This will be my third year driving the truck. I'm from Milford, always been a Red Sox fan. I don't get to too many games, though, the summer's our busy season. This really is one of the more enjoyable jobs, though.

I'll sleep in the truck, I'm with the truck all the time. The first night I'll just make it into Maryland. The second night I'll probably stay down by Florence, South Carolina. I don't push it that hard. 8 on Friday morning, I'll be there. [Fort Myers.]

If someone hijacked the truck, there'd be nothing they could really do with it. A lot of T-shirts, bubble gum, sunflower seeds...I don't know why they ship some of the stuff.

I've been with this company for over 20 years. I started as a co-op student with Northeastern – a part-time college student – and I turned around one day and I was a full-time mover. I never saw it sneaking up on me.

Al drives an 18 wheeler, a Freightliner. 4 or 5 people help load the truck, working with clubhouse staff. Al himself positioned each box, as they were brought in on two-wheelers. Material for the minor league complex is loaded first, so that will be last off. The Red Sox even ship down cartons upon cartons of soap and shaving cream – items which could easily be purchased in Florida. Gillette, though, provides it all out of their Boston headquarters and since the truck's going anyhow, they take advantage. Al says that he never really sees any players to speak of, though in 1998 Jim Corsi dropped by with a few boxes. Dennis

MARK TREMBLAY
Equipment Truck Driver

Whereas Al Hartz drives the truck to Spring training, Mark owns Pat Daley & Sons, the company which has transported Red Sox equipment within Boston since the franchise was founded.

I call it the equipment truck. All the traveling secretaries refer to it as the equipment truck.

My son Matthew has grown up with since he was five years old coming in and actually meeting the players. Coming into the clubhouse, which is very, very rare. Even the players' kids don't get to come into the clubhouse like my son has over the years. He's been overwhelmed a couple of times.

The logistics of moving baseball equipment is very, very difficult and you have to be a very organized person to do it. And you have to be extremely security conscious. They will try to steal from you any way they can, and it happens over at the airport often, where attempts are made to steal things. I'm pretty good at catching people who want to help themselves to bats and things. I've never lost a piece of equipment.

Neil [DeTeso] and I are regarded as the best in the business. We've been told this by equipment managers from all over the leagues. Both leagues. You could go out to Seattle, Texas, anywhere and ask "Who's doing the best transportation service in baseball?" and they'll say, "That guy in Boston."

Same thing for Neil. He's the best at what he does, too. Teams come in and they need uniforms in a pinch, and he's just an All-Star when it comes to doing that type of stuff.

First of all, you have to be on time. Being on time is very, very important. What I do is I get advance itineraries from all these teams coming in, from the traveling secretaries. I deal with all of them directly. Baseball is difficult in that it's a non-timed event. They can get into extra inning games, but more often the problem is with the rain delays that occur in these open stadiums. It's not too bad when it happens at home, but usually I have to bring in other teams after I bring the team out. There are teams when a team will get washed out completely and end up showing up four hours early. I have to get trucks to the airport and be prepared for all kinds of changes in scheduled times. Then there are mechanical problems and weather problems in flying. There are problems with flights being backed up. You name it and it's happened over the years.

4 o'clock in the morning, that happens all the time to me. My hours are very, very difficult. My job may look very prestigious and a lot of people say, "Boy, would I like to be doing that." But if you hang with me, it's real long hours. It's waiting at the airport sometimes for a tremendous amount of hours – actually, sleeping in the truck waiting for these flights to come in.

[On his business card, Mark has a toll free number, a regular number, his home phone number, a cellphone and a pager number.] If you can't find me with all those numbers, I'm dead. I get calls at 4 in the morning. A lot of odd things happen. Flight delays. It's very, very difficult to do. If you notice where I park the truck, you have to be an expert driver in backing out of there. They didn't design Fenway Park for trucks. You have to be an expert. I had to have those trucks specially made for Fenway Park. Trust me, I had to do a lot of homework to get it right. That door coming in, there's about 11 and ½ feet. Now normally a truck that long, which is 22 feet, calls for a 12-foot box. So I had to have that specially made – cut down. I had to have special doors put on it. Side doors. It's got a transparent roof so you can see inside it from the light up top. It's really the best truck in the league, too. It's expensive, but I like to do it right.

The Red Sox are an extremely loyal employer. They are extremely good to me, and I reciprocate and I do a great job for them. It's a lot of fun to do a good job.

Mark Tremblay
PHOTO BY BILL NOWLIN

Another thing about the Red Sox, when my mom passed away, they sent a beautiful flower arrangement. They're committed like that, and I don't forget things like that.

Let me just give you an historical perspective. Pat Daley lived in the 1800s. He started with a horse and wagon. I never knew him and I never met his son Milton, either. He did it for years. He started with the Boston Braves. The Braves were here first. He transported the Braves, with a horse and wagon. He started from day one. Whenever they started, he was the first. He lived in Charlestown and he used to take them to the train station. No airports back then. No airplanes!

Pat Daley started with the horse and wagon, like I said, and when the Red Sox came on board and they used to play by Northeastern over there [at the old Huntington Avenue Grounds, where the Red Sox played prior to the 1912 opening of Fenway Park], Pat Daley did the Red Sox, too. Again, horse and wagons and then they became mechanized. His son did it for many, many years, too.

Not only do we provide a service in transporting the equipment. We do a lot of extra favors for the ballplayers. There are players that get stuck and they need to move fast. Jeff Reardon, when he got traded to the Braves for the World Series, he had to move out of his house real quick, and I personally drove all his personal stuff and all his memorabilia stuff down to Florida for him. Roger Clemens, when he was really the superstar, I sent a half a truck just full of fan mail, all the way down to Houston. Roger Clemens got a tremendous amount of fan mail, and to my knowledge he and his wife answer all that fan mail. He wouldn't have had it trucked to Texas if he didn't care about it. I really enjoyed his friendship.

I've been doing this since 1990. I certainly believe that having a law enforcement background is extremely important for doing what we do because there's always the threat not only of people stealing equipment but there's a threat of sabotage and things like that. I make it a point to memorize everybody's equipment. I can tell you everything the Seattle Mariners carry. I can tell you the New York Yankees. I can tell you if they're missing a piece of equipment and I've done that. I take it very, very seriously. There's been times when they come in and I say, "Hey, you forgot your helmets." The equipment manager will be amazed at that, and he'll say, "Oh. We made a change this year. We put them inside trunks." If you show up here without your helmets, you're going to look awfully foolish the next day. Let's face it. There are people who hate the Yankees.

Major League Baseball's concerned about that, too. I had the privilege of doing the All-Star Game. That was my first All-Star Game and I thoroughly enjoyed doling it, but it had some real high security measures with transport. All the players coming in from all over the country and collecting their equipment at the Westin Hotel. Making sure it got from point A to point B and it was not tampered with or anything like that. There was a lot of security there. What I carry goes right into where the players are.

It's been a lot of fun. I have taken on other sports, too. I do Boston College football. Boston College hockey, and I do all the NBA teams now, too. I just do professional sports. I do have another business that I do here, a police supply business. We do some police equipment automotive stuff. I have got some calls for some very interesting high security cargo. I've done some work for the White House travel office. Presidential candidates and stuff like that. I have Secret Service clearance. When they 're looking for somebody for high security, they call. I do a couple of symphony orchestras. I don't go looking for work, but when they do call, I always like a challenge. Moving symphony orchestras, when they come in with like a $200,000 cello.

Jack Barretto took over the business from the Daleys. He had worked for them and then as the Daleys got older, he acquired it somehow. I acquired it from Jack. I'm going to tell you

this: there were a lot of people who wanted this business. I know that he liked me personally and he liked me for my commitment. He was more concerned about who was going to do a good job for the Red Sox than he was for his profit in selling the business.

I chose Gary Rich to work with because he's extremely honest and reliable. He's Mr. On Time. He's like me, what I call a "no screwup."

Nothing has ever been stolen from me. I've had several attempts. I have caught airline personnel many times, trying to help themselves to bats and balls and things like that. We did have an attempt on the Orioles, on Cal Ripken's glove. I retrieved it. I believe that individual no longer works for the airlines after I got through with him. He took the glove right out of a bag.

I've had the privilege of meeting a lot of these old-timers that have been around a long time. There's a whole new crew of equipment managers, but there are some old ones. The guy from Chicago – Chicken Willie – some of the stories I have heard are just unbelievable. They call him Chicken Willie. He used to play in the Pittsburgh organization. The guy brought a tear to my eye once. He was one of the first blacks to break into baseball and he used to have to stay at a separate hotel than the white players when they played down in Florida. He was eating peanut butter sandwiches when the other players were having steak. There was some real prejudice back then. It's amazing that I have met and known somebody in my lifetime who actually experienced that. This isn't just something that you read about like the Civil War; this was actually everyday things. We think about that as something that happened a long, long time ago, but it wasn't that long ago. Willie Thompson. He just passed away. He was a legend in Chicago with the White Sox. That guy was just a pleasure to have in my truck.

I have some celebrity players ride with me occasionally, too. They come out of the hotel and I'm just about ready to leave. They're looking for a cab and I say, "Hey, just hop in." I've had Nolan Ryan ride with me. Of course, Clemens would jump in with me. One of my favorites is Bob Uecker. Not only does Bob

Uecker know my name and recognize me and shake my hand, but he knows my kid's name and my wife's name. We've become friends. I was disappointed to see the team move to the National League, because he'd become such a good friend.

Usually my truck goes in before the game. If I don't get the vehicle into the park over an hour and a half before the game starts – because that's when they let the people in – I can't drive in.

On a normal night, what I do is I go to the hotel before the game, drive over to Fenway, go right inside and park it over by the visiting clubhouse. I'll get there if it's a 7 o'clock game, I'll get to the hotel about 3:30 and usually it's a 4:30 bus and then I go right from whatever hotel right in there.

It takes careful scheduling when a team gets in the playoffs. Let's say it's not the last game of the playoff series, but its one of those things where if the Red Sox win, they'll play another game the next day [say, the Sox are down 3 games to 2 in a best of 7 series] or if they lose, the visiting team leaves because they're at the end of their rope, or both teams are going back to another place for a series, whoever wins the game. That's when I have to have two trucks on standby in case they win or lose. That creates a logistic problem, in that all their personal gear – all their suitcases – have to be packed and put on the trucks. But if they need to stay another day, depending on how the game turns out, they have to be brought back to the hotel. There's been cases where the players have had to pack

Laundry room
PHOTO BY BILL NOWLIN

their bags and leave them in their rooms, right at the door, and if they lost the game I have to send a truck right over to pick up everything at the hotel. All those things involve me. I have to be there on standby. There are times I've had to have a third truck over at the hotel, because I need to have one truck for the equipment and one for the hotel.

There's many times when I have three teams in town. Teams will come in early on a day off. It isn't easy. But it's fun and it's a challenge. You just have to be able to make adjustments and plan for everything that could happen. I've never been late. I've never missed a trip. The company has a history of that – never being late and never missing a trip. It probably goes back to day one with Pat Daley.

Weight room
PHOTO BY BILL NOWLIN

7

CONCESSIONS

Brian Aitchison, Food Service Director,
    Gourmet Caterers
George Kirkpatrick, Jr., Cook
Jack Lyons, General Manager, Aramark
Richie Armstrong, Concessions Manager,
    Aramark
"Bones" Mason, Popcorn & Cotton Candy
    Manager
Sue Costello, Personnel Coordinator, Aramark
John Redding, Warehouse Manager
Robert White, Desk Supervisor
Patricia Orlando McDougal, Checker
Rob "Nuts" Barry, Peanut Vendor
Diana Barry, Beer Seller
Yolande Thomas-Easterling, Beer Seller

Leo LaFarge, Beer Seller
Chris Daley, Beer Seller
Tim Savage, former vendor
Dennis Keohane, former vendor
William Nowlin, Sr., former vendor
Rob Moynihan, Hot Dog vendor
Adam Birnbaum, Vendor
Jeremy Ogungbadero, Vendor
Jen Meagher, Store Manager, Lansdowne Shop
Gert Morin, Commissary Worker
Bill Horrigan, Money Room Manager
Neal Elliott, Vendor
Hank Elliott, former P.A. announcer
Nick Filler, former concession supervisor
Keith Randall, All-Star vendor

BRIAN AITCHISON
Gourmet Caterers

I'm food service director at Fenway Park for Gourmet Caterers. I also manage the corporate food service at Foxboro Stadium as well as twelve corporate cafeterias. It's a crazy business. Hopefully, my kids won't get into it, but it's too late for me.

I was a chef for seven years, I just filled in a few days ago here, it was kind of fun. You do what you gotta do in this business.

We're between 250 and 300 employees, depending on how busy the game is. I run the press and staff dining room up on the fifth floor, the 600 Club which includes the Parkview Lounge and the Fenmore Room restaurant, the corporate suites, and The Diamond at Fenway function hall. We serve anywhere from 2200 to 2500 a night.

Probably 25 employees are year-round. The rest is seasonal or for specific events. We've got twenty Christmas parties booked already. The Fidelitys and the Putnams of the world – the investment companies – they fly people in from all over. Every city has an aquarium and this and that, but every city doesn't have Fenway Park.

The executive chef, Joseph Gagliard, writes all the menus. The 600 Club menu is different eighty-one nights a year. You don't want members bringing in guests two or three nights and having the same food.

My family worked at Fenway Park when I was a kid. I had an uncle that worked here for 54 years. Jim Gately. He bled Red Sox. When we lived in Jamaica Plain, Tom Yawkey would drive him home after the game. They'd sit out front and have a few Black Labels.

My grandmother, my mother and my uncle all worked here for H. M. Stevens in the 40s and 50s. My uncle was here before World War II.

When I came on in '86, I was like a kid in a candy store. Then they went to the World Series and brought me with them. To top that off, I got a paycheck every week!

I have three sons – 11, 10 and 8. I've worked here since they were born, so it's not overly special to them – which is good, because they don't go to school and brag about it. On the other hand, my kids have played catch with Mo Vaughn, been pitched to by Roger Clemens and had their pictures on the scoreboard. Things me and you would only dream of thirty years ago.

Brian Aitchison
PHOTO BY ANDREA RAYNOR

GEORGE KIRKPATRICK, JR.
Cook

I cook for the luxury suites. I've been with Gourmet Caterers for about five years now.

During the summertime, I'll put in sixty hours a week. I make lobster croissant sandwiches, shrimp cocktail and the antipastos. I take care of putting stock away, helping out if anything is behind.

For a 7 o'clock game, I start at 9 in the morning. They order in advance how many of each thing. That has to get done by 4 o'clock in the afternoon.

A 1 o'clock game on a Saturday, I'll get there at 6. An hour and a half after the game starts we stop serving. Maybe half an hour to clean up and we're out of there.

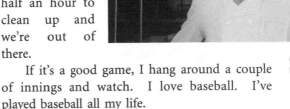

George Kirkpatrick, Jr.
PHOTO BY BILL NOWLIN

If it's a good game, I hang around a couple of innings and watch. I love baseball. I've played baseball all my life.

I had job offers from chains like Wendy's, but you have to start from scratch and the money's not as good, and the hours are even screwier than at Fenway. Now it's nice, for the first time I'm getting overtime. I work as much as I can this time of year and then relax during the winter.

I really enjoy the atmosphere. It's fun, because you're around celebrities. They had a dinner for the old-time All-Stars up on the fourth floor. I went in and pretended to help out, just so I could be around that many big wheels. I'm going, "This is amazing."

I was eighteen years managing cafeterias. I had to worry about inventory, my crew payroll and all that paperwork. Now all I have to do is the prep. I'm still making the same hourly rate, plus overtime so I love it. No worrying about sales and now if somebody doesn't show up, it's no big deal. Before, it was like the end of the world.

JACK LYONS
General Manager, Aramark

I started when I was 16, in April of 1969, making Cokes and putting them in trays and sending them up for the vendors.

I never sold in the stands but I did sell behind the concession counters. It's a different category. If you're hired as a vendor, you're a vendor. If you're hired as a concession employee, you're a concession employee.

Richie Armstrong
PHOTO BY BILL NOWLIN

I started full-time in 1975, '76. I ran the souvenir department. I was manager prior to the Aramark acquisition.

There are a lot of family ties. Just because you're related to someone doesn't automatically get you the job, but if someone's working there and they've proven responsible and they have a friend or a brother or sister that's looking for work, we'll give them a shot.

You don't see too many female vendors in the stands, we have a couple. We've had them through the years, but they don't apply for vendors jobs.

They apply as concession employees. The majority of the concession employees are female.

I never watch the game. That's when I'm on the floor, supervising, dealing with issues. When the Red Sox are out of town, that's when I watch the games, on TV.

On a game day, I'm in between 9 and 10 in the morning. If you're coming off a night game prior, you'll review the night before, look at the paperwork, look at your sales. Then you go over the night's events with your staff. We review history criteria almost on a daily basis. We're expecting 27,000 people in house. What have we done historically with a similar team and similar weather conditions?

Aramark seemed much more fan friendly than Stevens. In the first year, we did 104 different menu changes in cooperation with the Red Sox.

We do a lot of local branding, using recognized New England names. Kowloon, Papa Gino's, d'Angelo's, Legal Sea Foods, Richie's Slush.

We take vendors down to spring training each year. We call it "spring training for vendors." My concession manager Richie Armstrong runs it from January through March. I usually spend a week or ten days down there.

I have two kids but they're not old enough yet. Maybe.

Jack has gone on to national work with Aramark, and has been replaced by Julie Jordan.

RICHIE ARMSTRONG
Concessions Manager, Aramark

Originally I was with Harry M. Stevens. Combined, I've been here about 28 years. The general manager at the time, Rico Picardi, lived down the street from me in Revere, so virtually everybody in the neighborhood worked here at one time or another.

I was a popcorn man, I started out working in a little room where we made the popcorn for the vendors. I worked my way up to controlling the inventory that went in and out of the room.

I worked other jobs over the years and in the fall of '87, I went on a golf trip with one of Mr. Picardi's sons. Paul was general manager and he offered me a full-time position. In December of '94, Aramark bought out Harry M. Stevens.

I oversee all the concession stands, the staffing, the warehouse, make sure that product is ordered so that we don't run out. I staff the ballpark according to attendance.

It takes a good month, once the season's over, to break the park down, to get it winterized. We clear all the inventory out, send back the stuff that we can. We have cleaning crews doing a washout of the park. All the water is drained, because it's an open stadium and it's going to freeze if you leave water in the pipes. November and December, most of us start taking our vacation time. We don't get too much during the summer! I wouldn't mind a nice week in August, but that's the nature of the business and I understand that.

This morning – tonight there's a 7:05 game – I got in at 10:30. I'll get out of here probably midnight to 12:30. A day like today, I go over last night's event. Some stands might have had shortages or whatever. Sue [Costello] works with me, I'll go over the sheets with her. I'll get an update on attendance.

Early in an event, you might be selling more hot dogs, hamburgers and chicken. They're not snacking on the ice creams and lemonades and slush. Once the main meal is done by the fourth or fifth inning, then you pull some people off and move them over to an ice cream or lemonade stand. You've got to be out there walking the concourse and see the shift from one item to another and then you just start moving bodies around.

The vendors, the hawkers, there's four locations we run product out of around the ballpark and their cash is counted out there and they're settled up there. The managers of those four rooms come in and all the information is put in the computer.

Our employees wash down everything on the stands. They get all the inventory put away, all the perishables in the refrigerators, and then when they come in the next day, there's still cleaning to be done because it gets dusty again overnight when the cleaners are going around with those blowers.

It's an ongoing process, ordering inventory throughout the year, especially with the constraints of the ballpark. There's not a lot of storage area. Stuff that's coming from a distance like cups and peanuts and Cracker Jack, we usually stock up pretty heavily on them, for the whole home stand. But items like Coca-Cola and water, if you have a ten game home stand, you might get two, maybe three deliveries.

Hot dogs are the main staple of the ballpark. Bottled water's doing very well, it's become such a beverage now. We don't sell cigarettes or cigars in the ballpark at all any more.

We still pop the popcorn ourselves. We have a supervisor that oversees the preparation of the popcorn, the cotton candy and the pretzels. He does a great job. I know him as "Bones."

I work every game. Even when they're on the road, I'm still here Monday through Friday. The weekend's when I wouldn't come in.

BONES MASON
Popcorn & Cotton Candy Manager

I'm a physical education instructor. K through 12, at Silver Lake Junior High in Pembroke, Mass. This is a great summer job.

I started in '96. After the first year, Jack

"Bones" Mason and daughters Brandi Peters (L) and Kelly Mason (R)
PHOTO BY ANDREA RAYNOR

Lyons and Rich Roper asked me if I'd like to take over the cotton candy part of the park. I said, "Sure." I went from cotton candy the first year – and popcorn, then from popcorn to pretzels. Each year they've given me more and more.

Last year they wanted to get more popcorn added to the stands but they didn't have the space to put the machines in, so we started bagging it in the cotton candy room. That took off so then they wanted to vend it.

My two kids started working here the year after me. '97. I just said, "Do you want a job at Fenway?" You should see the number of families here. Years ago, when Stevens had the concession, they wanted families working there. They figured that if they had families, everybody would be content.

They brought in two girlfriends, and all four of them are in charge of different areas. My oldest daughter's in charge of cotton candy. The youngest one does the popcorn. The other two girls oversee the pretzels. All of them are really conscientious.

I put out anywhere from 2700 to 3000 pretzels a game. Cotton candy, I'm averaging about 1060 a game. Popcorn, 900, 910. Now, with the playoffs, the cotton candy won't sell because it's mostly adults. The popcorn and pretzels will really take off.

The pretzels come in frozen, and then I bake them. I have three pretzel machines, up in left field, up in right field, and out in the bleachers. They had two big machines – one in the commissary and one in right field – and they just couldn't get them out to the stands. It's a distance to walk out to the bleacher area from where they were made, so I have three groups of kids working it, I get the product right into the pretzel machines hot. I'm supervising four areas, really. Three pretzel areas and the cotton candy room. The cotton candy and the popcorn is all done in that room, [with competing odors] it's like working in a kitchen. After a while, you just don't want to look at the stuff. They never bring it home. They don't eat it, either. We throw out anything that is left over after every game.

Each stand gets thirty bags, we'll have another ninety ready if they need it. One vending room gets 300, the other gets 450, I'll have another 300 ready. If we have to have 900, once they make their 900 they can go home. They can get it done in five hours; sometimes they have to stay nine hours. It depends on how much is needed for that particular day. They usually are out of there before the game begins.

I wait until the seventh inning and then I pick up all the paperwork and go and punch into the computer what stands got what, and what vending room, how much they each received. This year I probably saw about three innings of baseball. I actually see more baseball when they're out of town. I'm always flipping between Atlanta and the Red Sox.

As I'm doing my pace around the park, I'll check out the monitors and see how things are going. If the stands are full of product in the fourth inning, and the game is running real fast, I don't want the kids making a lot more [pretzels], so I'm watching the pace of the game to determine how much product has to be made.

When the team is away, my daughters come in and one of them cleans up her popcorn area and the other one does the cotton candy area. With popcorn, we strip the kettles right out of the machines and boil them to get the grease and oil off. We clean the cotton candy machines and the floors and walls. Then I strip the pretzel machines on another day. One day I do paperwork. It's a three day project.

When people say "renovate Fenway Park" [instead of replacing it], they don't understand. They just see the park from a seat. They don't see the background of the park and the people that work there. People complain about how it's so crowded. The park's not built for the number of people. If you come into Gate A and go down the ramp, you've got to funnel between the commissary and stand 7. You're talking 15 to 20,000 people and they only have about a nine foot dimension to get through.

The Aramark people, especially Jack Lyons and Jack Burns, have just been super. If you have an idea you want to try, they're open. They sent the top two vendors this year down to spring training. They paid for a whole week. Then they brought in the All-Star vendors. Every game, whoever sells the most or does something different, they give them a $25 cash bonus. They do the best they can with what they have. The problem is turnover, you've got some kids that really take charge and do it, and other kids that are just there for a time and then they go.

Sue [Costello] gets the brunt of it.

SUE COSTELLO
Personnel Coordinator for Aramark

I started in February of '95. Basically, I try to keep all the stands assigned – all the workers and all the food stands – and keep track of their schedules and seniority lists. The hiring, firing, disciplinary. It's a year-round job. I started out just answering the phone. It was the year that Aramark had taken over and they had some openings and I was here and that was it.

You work ten or more days in a row sometimes. You get your vacation, usually in the winter, but they're very good about down days. Yesterday I took off. We had a nice long stretch [with the team out of town.] I had stuff to do – laundry and housework. See the kids and the husband. Stuff like that.

On a non-game day, I'm doing the sheets for the next homestand – what we call the layout sheets. All the different stands and all the different positions. You have to go through, knowing who's in, who's out, and fill out the stands. In September, it will be hard because they all go back to school. This is where it starts getting weird. We have to bring in new people and work around people's schedules.

We have time off requests, I ask for seven days notice but I'm lucky if I get that. I need to know whether or not you're coming. For the most part, they're pretty good about it. As long as it's some notice.

When I come in, the desk is littered with requests from everybody that needs the day off, so you have to start rearranging the schedule. When you end up short of bodies, I call people and try to get them to change their minds. You don't want to start closing down registers unless you absolutely have to, but sometimes it does come down to that.

We've had little bits of theft, not really a whole heck of a lot. The biggest thing is not showing up and not calling. That's the most usual offense. The first time, you're suspended. The next time, you're fired. If they're just fooling around, I'll just stick them in the crummiest job I can find for a few days. [Laughs]

Rob Barry, oh yeah, he's been suspended a few times. It's policy here at Fenway Park that vendors don't throw things because it's too small here. It's just too darn congested, so we don't promote it. Of course, in other parks, they have other policies. They did do a video on Rob in Fort Myers, which is a lot smaller stadium, and a lot more spread out. It is a mixed message. We see them on *Chronicle* and everything else. There have been injuries because people started throwing other stuff.

Sue Costello
PHOTO BY ANDREA RAYNOR

I was never a baseball fan, and I'm still not. I just show up and do my job. I don't even know who they're playing half the time. Which is good, I guess, because I'm here to work. The biggest problem we have with a lot of our employees – the big sports fans – is that they watch the game instead of being where they're supposed to be.

The warehouse guys that work during the day, they're the forgotten ones. They unload the truck, bringing product out to the stands, making sure everything's rotated. They do all the heavy work. The lumping. After the home stand ends, they're the ones who take all the product back out. Transferring and boxing up product to go back to different vendors. Cleaning the stands. Cleaning the commissary, and then they're receiving and putting away. There isn't a lot of room to put stuff away here, so once they receive it, they have to split it up and break it out and send it to the appropriate stands. Everything comes in Gate D.

JOHN REDDING
Warehouse Supervisor, Aramark

This is my fifth year at the Park. Me and Tommy Colon supervise the warehouse. If one's not here, the other one will take over.

John Redding
PHOTO BY ANDREA RAYNOR

I work until the end of November and then get laid off for a couple of months, or transfer to another area.

The help has to be here three hours before game time. We have to get all our work done before the other help comes in. We need at least three hours. At least.

The first game of a homestand is the easiest because you have time to get everything all set. Saturday morning after a Friday night game, you've got to get it all set up again.

At the end of the game, the stand porters will bring all their spoilage down, all the hot dogs that have been cooked [but unsold.] They'll have someone [in the main commissary] write them off so everything adds up. The stand porter sits there, and if the manager needs something, they go get it. There should be one for every stand. We have twenty stationary, and twelve to fifteen portable stands.

I love the job. I love it.

Joan and Robert White
PHOTO BY BILL NOWLIN

ROBERT WHITE
Desk Supervisor, Aramark

I worked for the Federal Reserve Bank of Boston as assistant vice president, in charge of statistics. Considerably larger sums of moneys there.

I came to work here when I was 14. 1953. I started in the commissary, supplying the vendors when they came in to pick up product. Inside this same office here. I worked numerous jobs throughout, 50 years now.

I'm in charge of the vendor set-up. The vendors all work on commission. You keep track of what they sell and what they return and how much money they owe, and then at the end of the night, you calculate their commission.

There's somebody at this front counter and as the vendors go out they "pay" with these checks [small tokens.] It's proved a very efficient system over the years. If a kid loses one, we're not going to charge him. We have other methods to determine whether he's playing games or not.

I usually get here about 3 o'clock for a 7 o'clock game.

In addition to keeping track of the vendors, people are constantly coming in from various concession stands – including the vendors themselves – looking for change. They might want two hundred dollars in ones, or forty dollars in quarters.

It takes time to cash out all the vendors. Most of the vendors who have been here awhile are aware that the faster they organize their bills, the faster they can get out of here.

We usually finish up in the eighth inning. The people in the money room are here for some time after the game. We've got a TV right here, [facing the work station counter], I wouldn't be here if there was no TV. Back in the 50s and early 60s, you could sit down and watch a game. Plenty of empty seats. That hasn't been the case for some time.

My dad started here in 1940. That's how I ended up here. I used to come here when I was nine or ten and sit out in the right field grandstand during batting practice.

Now my son is here. My two daughters are here.

They sell beer, all three of them. And my wife Joan started this year! A tough job interview? They were all friends, they've known her for years. She was an office manager in a dental practice. Speak of the devil, there she is right there! [standing immediately next to him, in the space she works side by side.]

The oldest grandchild is six. A little too young right now.

PATRICIA ORLANDO MCDOUGAL
Checker

I work in the commissary up until the 7th inning, then I go into the money room. I work with Bobby White up at the front desk. We check the vendors in and out. They give me the little checks. I have to know my inventory at the beginning of the ballgame, and then what they sell by the end of the game. All the money has to balance, so we know that no one walked out with a tray of product.

I started in '78. When my father [Vince Orlando] was the equipment manager, this was not a girl's place to be. I used to say, "Dad, how come I can't get a job there?" He'd say, "Oh, no, no, no, no!" Then when I finally said, "Dad, how come Rico's daughters are working here?" [Rico Picardi, manager of Harry M. Stevens.] He said, "Well, go ask Rico for a job." My father was the type "you do it yourself" – he wouldn't get you anything. So I asked, "Rico, do you need any help?" and that's when I started.

My father started in the visitors' clubhouse when he was 17, back in the 30s. My father loved the visitors' clubhouse but Mr. Yawkey needed him in the Red Sox clubhouse. My uncle Johnny was there when Ted was there. After that was Fitzie, Fitzpatrick. Then there was Pete Cerrone. He got sick, around '75, and Mr. Yawkey said to my father, "Please, would you go on the Red Sox side?" He stayed there until he retired in 1991. My father always said he loved the visitors' side. He got better tips because every three days he'd get another team of new guys [coming in with the teams that passed through. With the Red Sox guys, they'd often wait until the end of the year]…and sometimes they didn't pay up.

For my family, Fenway was just a place where your father worked, so it really didn't mean that much. Now I'm saying, "Oh my God, what if they really do tear this down? I've known this place all my life."

I started in the souvenir stand right next to the commissary, working with Rico's daughter-in-law. They kept saying, "Do you want to go in the money room?" I was very shy. I said, "Sure, because I'll never want to sell beer. Drunken men make me nervous." So I went in the money room and now I could kick myself. Those beer people make good tips. But they do take some abuse, and I'm not the type that could.

Patricia Orlando McDougal
PHOTO BY BILL NOWLIN

Then I was in the money room, counting. When it got hot, it was awful trying to count that money. Later, I started working at the vending station. Now it's both. I'm at the vending station at home plate – the commissary – and then I go in the money room late in the game.

For many years, Butch and I would go home together, but since we got [our daughter] Samantha, I take my own car and get out before him. Bill [Horrigan] knows that if it's a weekday I do not go into the money room because I want Samantha to get to bed. We bring her to work most of the time. Butch has his own office and she'll go in there and do her homework. Now I have a different job in the money room, taking care of the coin. I'm out of there by 9 or 9:30. She's sort of a night owl, anyhow, and does very well in school. Very well.

ROB "NUTS" BARRY
Peanut Vendor

The most "visible" vendor is one who's been in the news, repeatedly. From an old Fenway family, Rob "Nuts" Barry is quite a character.

My father worked here for forty years. He was a vendor himself, then a vending supervisor. He also worked in the money room. He was a

Rob "Nuts" Barry
PHOTO BY ANDREA RAYNOR

schoolteacher and a stockbroker and he got myself and my two sisters work here. My sisters both sell beer. Diana works near first base, on the stand just before Canvas Alley. Betsy's more towards right field and the foul pole there.

I started in 1981.

My father quit in '86 because there was a big hullabaloo about something I had done. In the '86 World Series a friend and I worked here, but we weren't exactly vending very hard. We were up on the roof watching the game. It was early in the game, I had sold two loads of hot dogs. I'd usually sell anywhere from 20 to 25 loads, so I wasn't exactly working my hardest. But I didn't care, I was 18 years old and I wanted to watch the World Series.

This guy – he wasn't a very nice guy, put it that way – kept coming up to me and asking for a hot dog. I told him, "I'm all out, all out." But he kept coming back. Finally I told him, "There's a hot dog stand right down there. Why don't you go and get yourself one?" If you can't understand why an 18 year-old kid would be watching a World Series game, I don't think you understand baseball in Boston.

He ended up being a reporter for *USA Today*, and he reported me and my friend Dave Buckley to my boss, and the next day he put in the paper that Fenway ran out of hot dogs in the first game of the World Series. *Good Morning America* picked it up. My boss – Rico Picardi – wasn't too happy and he turned our suspension into a firing over the off-season.

My father wasn't even informed that I was fired. He was not pleased and he quit in solidarity. He didn't need the job. He'd be getting up at 5 AM and not home until 2 AM. He didn't need that, but he did it for nearly twenty-five years. He just liked being at the ballpark. My father was a big Sox fan but when they blew the World Series in '86, not only was he bull at my boss but he was also very disappointed that we couldn't close that one out.

I fought it through the union, Local 501 or something, the Hotel Workers. [The actual union is Local 26 of the Hotel Restaurant Institutional Employees and Bartenders Union, ALF-CIO.] They don't do much except take union dues. The other vendor, Dave Buckley, they [HMS] said, "This guy hasn't been suspended before, so we'll take him back." The union guy closed his briefcase – figured he was batting .500 – and started to head out. "Hold on a second here!" I said, "I'm just a kid, eighteen years old, trying to make a buck, pay for my school". After I said my spiel, they took a vote and took me back 2-1, saying any more screw-ups and you'll be fired.

My first game, they had me selling popcorn. I made fourteen dollars and twenty cents. Hot dogs are the big moneymaker but that's really grunt work. When it's full, the hot dog bin can be 30 to 45 pounds. Not that the peanut sack's any better, but it's easier to manage. There are 36 bags in a sack, 7 ounces each. Sometimes you might carry more, like 40 or 45 bags if you go back [before you've completely emptied your sack.] A real good day would be eight to ten sacks.

I've been doing peanuts regularly about eight or nine years. The last two or three years, strictly peanuts. When it would be cool weather, I would sell hot dogs. Peanuts don't sell when people are wearing gloves. But I was getting grief from the fans: "Why don't you sell peanuts? Come on!" Now I take the hit on the money and just sell peanuts all the time.

You're known for throwing peanuts. When you first started selling peanuts, did you throw them?

Oh yeah. I used to throw ice creams before that and got to be pretty well known. When I started selling nuts, it was perfect. When it was HMS, the nuts were four ounces, almost the same as a baseball. When Aramark came in, they switched to seven ounces. Those were heavier and the bags had too much air in them so they were tougher to throw. What I came up with, I tape a tack to my finger and pop the air out of the bag and then I throw them.

So throwing pays off?

Oh yeah. I've got people that only buy peanuts off me. I have people that tip me a buck. Last year they were $2.75 a bag. You'd get a quarter every time and an occasional buck. Now they're three bucks and you get more ones. Sometimes five dollars. I threw two up to the roof boxes the other night and this guy sent me down a ten dollar bill.

If the crowd sees it, they get into it and want to catch one, too. A lot of the other vendors try to emulate it. They try to throw hot dogs. They throw Coke bottles! I've had to talk to a few of the younger vendors.

I get to the park about 6:15. Put the uniform on if I need to – I usually already have it on. Then you pick up your checks. It's a piece of plastic, an inch each way, square and flat. It says PEANUTS on it. If you were selling something else, it'd say ICE CREAM or COKE. You get four chips. Each one is worth one box of peanuts so if you sell four, you give them, I think, $324. Then they give you three more checks and so on and so forth. However many you sell, you just keep purchasing checks.

I usually vend from 6:30 to about the sixth inning and then that's pretty much it.

Aramark supplies all the clothing – cap, shirt, pants. We wash our own stuff.

Do you have to give it back at the end of the year... Do you have just one set?

Supposedly. [laughs]

We make 15 percent, so I make 45 cents on every bag. We're not as high as other parks, percentage-wise, but it's not too bad. [There is no base salary – just commission.]

The most I ever made? Peanuts-wise, I made a hundred and ninety bucks. That was maybe 13 loads. I was fired up. There was a day, I think it was 1994, where I was selling Powerade and I made four hundred bucks.

This Crunch and Munch idiot who works at the Boston Garden gets a lot of publicity. So I thought, "Well, if this guy's going to be in the paper all the time, I might as well. I ran it by my boss and he gave the OK. They did a story

on me entitled, "One of the Best Arms at Fenway." There was another story just last year, a "Service at Your Seat" type of story.

Sometimes rain delays are good, because people have nothing to watch, so they might as well watch me throw peanuts. I've actually had pretty good nights when the game's rained out. It's not a great night – you make maybe eighty or ninety bucks, but you're out of there in an hour, hour and a half.

After I finish, I walk out of there. Sometimes, I don't know who's winning or anything.

I'm friends with a lot of the players' families. I was sitting with Mo Vaughn's mother, I call her Mrs. Mo. Bret Saberhagen's wife is a good friend of mine. Lynn. She's a singer. She was at the Harp. She invited me down; put me on the Red Sox guest list. Ended up having a few beers with Saberhagen, Nomar, all those guys. A good time.

You're going to run into some jerks. I've had problems with a couple of fans, but never any fistfights or anything like that. You'll get people, who'll say, "Get out of the way!" What am I supposed to be, invisible? Hey, it's part of the game, pal. If you want perfect views, watch it at home.

Rob Barry's fingertip thumbtack
PHOTO BY BILL NOWLIN

So many people know me or know my name. I'll go out for dinner and people come up to you – I just started seeing this girl and she thinks I'm a star or something!

In '94 I threw a bag of nuts across the field and a friend of mine got a picture of it. They're hanging up in a few bars around Boston. Every game my friend Dave Buckley was like, "Hey, Girly Arm!" and it would be a longer and longer throw. I told him that I was going to throw one across the field to him. He went down the third base line and I went down the first base line. I made a joke about it, "WHO NEEDS NUTS?"

He was over the other side, screaming like a madman. The crowd was saying, "No way could you do that." I said, "Watch this!" and I threw a bag across the field. The Seattle pitcher stepped off the mound because he saw this out of the corner of his eye. He was bull! The home plate umpire called time because of all the commotion. Security came running down. I kind of tipped my hat. All the security people knew me, so they were like, "I'm not going to say anything." The crowd went crazy and I just ran down the ramp – that was my last sale of the night. You can see it in the photo, too. It was the 6th inning, 2 and 1 count. You can see the Mariners pitcher, the people pointing up in the sky like it's Superman or something.

I've been suspended a couple of times because nobody's supposed to throw anything. Some kid hit a player's family member from the White Sox. There was a big thing then: "You guys can't throw anything. If you throw anything, you're fired."

I get paid to play catch, that's the way I look at it. I was a baseball player in high school and college. I pitched in the Park League. I pitched for Mass Envelope for four or five years. That was costing me money. I was missing money at Fenway. I think my pitching career might be all done, other than pitching peanuts.

They sent us to spring training this year, six of us. They sent us down to work. We did some promotional stuff. A little girl [Amanda Bynes] had her own show on Nickelodeon, so we did an episode where she tried out to be a vendor. It was a little entertaining.

DIANA BARRY
Beer Seller

When I started, you had to know someone. That was how they hired. My father worked in the money room at HMS. '79 was my first year. I was sixteen.

Diana Barry
PHOTO BY ANDREA RAYNOR

First I sold hot dogs and sodas. I got beer at three years. It takes twelve or thirteen years now to get on beer. I've been where I am for fifteen years. I work across from the First Aid station. You see people hit by a ball or dropping from the heat and stuff.

We get $62.00 a game. We don't get commissions. We do get tips, but we don't want to mention that.

We're supposed to be there at 4, 4:30. Gates open at 5:30 so you have to be ready, in your uniform with your money and everything at 5:30. I work in an advertising agency and I'm the senior art director, I design newspaper ads, brochures. It's hard sometimes to get out [of the agency]. There's always some fire that arises when I'm trying to get out the door. We just swipe in, that gives you the slip that you use to get your money bag. They give us a starting bank of $310. They come at the top of the third to collect the first bag.

We are what's called TIP certified. I forget what it stands for. It's an alcohol seller's test. Our situation's a little different from bars. The guys only need to pull themselves together for thirty seconds to be served. That's one of the reasons we card everyone, to see how they handle their wallet. You'd be surprised how many people can't pull out their license because they're a little tipsy.

I cut off two to four people a game. That may seem like a lot until you realize that I've probably waited on 500. I usually sell about 800 beers. A lot of people get two.

Sure, we get abuse. I've had people throw food at me, throw beers back at me because we wouldn't serve them. One guy threw two trays of food once, about forty dollars worth. You're not allowed to swear back.

All the beer comes from kegs. The same kegs you buy in a store, although people are always trying to tell us it's watered down – which is ridiculous.

I've waited on Huey Lewis. Stephen King used to come all the time. I was in his birthday video – we sang "Happy Birthday" to him. I like it. It's fun, you know. I like the people. We're definitely like a family there. We've spent so much time together.

YOLANDE THOMAS-EASTERLING
Beer Seller

In '81, I was at B.U. and one of my friends worked at Fenway. She broke her ankle and couldn't work the Yankees series. She called and said, "I have a friend who can take my place. Is that OK?" I sold hot dogs the Yankees series and went back to school and that was that.

The following Opening Day, they called me back. Back then, they had cigar stands. Popcorn, cigarettes, candy and cigars. I ended up working the cigar stands for five years. I've been on beer since '86. Beer is where you want to be.

Beer is seniority. No one leaves. I have seniority there, but there are 21 people ahead of me. You really don't have much to do. You're just responsible for the beer, peanuts and pretzels. That's it. On Sundays, you don't work until 12 because of the "blue laws." We have the two and a half hour rule. There could be a rain delay. We still have the two and a half hour rule, because it's two and a half hours after the scheduled start of the game.

I have a lot of weekend regulars, and they were like, "My God! There are more Yankee people here than Red Sox people! How did they get these tickets?" As soon as the schedule comes out, they buy up the tickets, especially for a weekend series. They drive down Friday and don't go back until Sunday night, so they're here for the whole weekend. They're the most obnoxious people. You try to be nice but it's hard. When you're serving you have to deal with all the idiots and you have to be really polite and nice and they're screaming, "YANKEES! YANKEES!" and you're like, "OK. How are you?"

I'm a first grade teacher in East Boston. I've been a teacher for fourteen years.

$310 is what we start with. We get two hundred ones. We get a hundred in fives and $10 in quarters. We have the pretzels and the non-alcoholic. Sundays are usually 1:05 games and it tends to be a family day. Alcohol consumption is less and a lot of people prefer non-alcoholic.

Yolande Thomas-Easterling
PHOTO BY ANDREA RAYNOR

I don't keep track of how many beers I pour. It depends on the crowd. Yesterday, I think I started at 950 cups and I returned 300. Friday night I started with 1000. I returned 173. I used to work out in the bleachers when I first started on beer. 1000 was nothing out in the bleachers. I was selling 1050 a night, on a regular basis. I asked to leave the bleachers. I said, "I cannot deal with these kids all the time." I got tired of taking away the fake IDs, and the kids kept getting younger and younger, and rowdier and rowdier.

They tend to drink more if the team is doing well. People don't drink as much as they used to. Everybody wanted to be on beer when the Yankees came to town, because it was a big thing. People drank more; they tipped more. People are more conscious today than five, ten years ago. Which is not bad. I don't have a problem with that.

A lot of times we call security because of the ID. That's our biggest problem. If you get a fake ID, you have to take it and turn them into the office. They're always amazed. "How do you know?" The people with the fake IDs will go, "Get a cop! Get a cop!" Well, a lot of these cops have no clue. We've had cops go, "But it's him!" And we go, "Sir. It's a fake ID." We take about one a game. Sometimes we'll get three or four.

Last homestand, the guy next to me took away this guy's military ID; it was real but he altered the date on it. It was like, "You're in the military. You ought to know better." And then he had the nerve to argue until we got security. Then he was like, "Oh, I'm sorry. Just give it back. I'm going to be in trouble." Unbelievable. We gave it to security and they handled it.

There's slow times, yes. You can take a break whenever you want. We bring magazines and stuff and we're always reading. The gates open at 5:30 but there's a good hour that it's really slow. You'll get one person here, one person there. I always have a book or something.

It's a job that doesn't require much thinking. If I was to take another part-time job, I would never take a job that involved thinking or stress, because for ten months of the year, that's what I do.

So far I've made most of the games. It tends to be a long day because I get off work at 3:30 and I have to be here at 4. If it's a long homestand and I'm teaching, I take off the middle of it because I get up at quarter of five every morning.

LEO LAFARGE
Beer Seller

Leo Lafarge
PHOTO BY EMMET NOWLIN

I'm #15 on the seniority list.

My sister Susan got a job through her friend Joan McPhail. She got me a job the next year, and my other sister the next year, my other sister and my brother, they both got jobs too, but they only lasted a couple of years.

We all started off selling hot dogs, doing lunch, behind the counter. You all started off doing lunch or being a porter, moving the food from the commissary to the stands. Susan still works there.

I remember burning my arm a lot. They had these old popcorn makers made out of cast metal or something – big round bowls with a metal handle on them. They made delicious popcorn, but there was just one handle made of wood. If you missed that handle....You'd make about 50 to 70 batches a night and all it takes is just one miss and you'd get a huge burn on your arm. I'd miss about once every other homestand.

You do make more money on beer, mainly because of the tips. A lot of it has to do with your personality and how attractive you are. A lot also with how well the Sox are doing. When they do well, we do well. When they don't do well, we don't usually do well.

Somebody from security will come over when it's time to close. "All right. That's it. This is your last customer." We usually thank them for that, unless they're closing us 45 minutes early and then we're pissed off. If there's a security person there, people are a lot less likely to be banging on the grate and screaming at us.

They stopped selling beer in the stands sometime in the 70s. I think Jean Yawkey witnessed some rowdy behavior one day and said, "We've got to stop this."

When I first started on beer in '85, we'd sell 1000 beers, each beer seller. The gates would open and you'd start selling like crazy. That's not true anymore. The Red Sox have consciously tried to discourage too much drinking. The two beers at a time cuts down on it. It's a lot stricter, there's a lot less beer being sold.

This bottled water thing has taken off like crazy. What is it, four dollars a bottle? There's a fountain over there! Buy a Coke and use the cup.

I don't work in the bleachers anymore. Behind third base, it's always been a lot more relaxed than in the bleachers. Even the bleachers now are more relaxed. It would be no big deal to see at least one brawl on a Friday or a Saturday. It would be a big deal if there were like thirty guys bleeding; four or five guys bleeding was like....oh, it's Friday night. They don't let it get to that point now. They do a lot more preventive work.

For the most part, if somebody's rude to you, the best tack to take is "it's us against them" – you know, "If it were up to me, pal, I'd love to serve you. I know you're old enough. They got all this stuff up there and if I get caught, I'm gonna get fired." You give them the sympathetic "if it was up to me, pal, I'd help you, but it's them" – the big Them.

That usually does it, but if people really want to keep going, then I'll just say, "Well, I'm not serving anybody until you leave." That usually does it. The rest of the line – there may be twenty people in line – they more or less get the guy out of there. If somebody REALLY wants to be an asshole, and they don't want to leave, then I jump out there and beat the crap out of them!! No. The guy working next to me or the porter or the stand manager will just walk up the ramp and grab one of the bluecoats [security people] and that'll be the end of that.

That will happen once a Yankee series. Yeah. I had a problem with a Yankees fan – big surprise. He was 23, but he was from out of state. Our rules are basically, you've got to be 28 to 30. So he comes up and he wings his ID at me. That was pretty rude. Then I read it and it says 23 from Connecticut, and you're a Yankees fan, well, sorry. I'm not going to serve you. Then he became belligerent. If somebody throws their ID at me, he's either had too much to drink or he's just an asshole. Either one. Drinking beer at the ballgame is a privilege, not a right. I don't need to take that from anybody. I may not be the greatest person in the world, but I don't need somebody throwing things at me.

For the most part, where I work, it's corporate seating, which means it's pretty relaxed. I've been there since '86. They can be arrogant or condescending, but if I got everybody thrown out for being arrogant or condescending, well, it'd be half the ballpark.

We see the players, but it's an unwritten rule that you don't talk to them. Well, it IS a rule that you don't, but, you know, I might say hello if they happen to make eye contact, but for the most part I don't talk to them. They look at that time before the game as their time not to be bothered. We all pretty much respect that. If they want to come over and talk to me, well, then, sure. Not too many of them do. None of them, in fact.

You have to join the union, and then it's all by seniority to get on beer. There are basically fifty beer positions. Truthfully, the union could give a flying fuck about us. Our union rep is Eileen Bradley. She'll give you the whole scoop. They've negotiated the past few contracts without even asking her. Without even asking the union rep from Fenway!

I'll go up and watch the game once or twice a year. I can't tell you how many top of the ninth, bases loaded, tie ball games I've walked out on. As much as I love Fenway – and I do – it's just like any work place. You just want to get the heck out of there. So I'll go across the street and watch it on TV!

I watch about 70 per cent of the games when they're out of town, though.

I could lose my job in about ten seconds if I drank a beer while I was working. It's against company policy to be drinking on the job. They give us a little pamphlet at the beginning of the year and we go through it and see which rules we didn't violate the year before. It's usually about two out of twenty five.

I worked every single game this year. I'm probably the only one that did. If I take off a day to watch the game, I lose all the money I'd be making.

I'm the head teacher at a therapeutic day care center in Brighton. Kids that have emotional and behavioral needs. Those jobs don't pay the greatest. I like my job, but I actually make more money at Fenway.

CHRIS DALEY
Beer Seller

Chris Daley
PHOTO BY BILL NOWLIN

I started opening day in 1979. I was a senior in high school and it was a great summer job. And it was a great summer job as I went to college and, now that I'm a mother of two, it's good mother's hours and it's great money and it works. I never left, and there's a bunch of us that just never left.

My first year there I sold hot dogs. I sold a little bit of everything for about a year and a half. Then before Fenway Park became smoke-free, I sold cigars and cigarettes. You'd probaby go through 30 cartons of Marlboro a night. I was the cigar and cigarette girl for a year or two and then I went on beer and I've been on beer ever since.

I met my husband there. He was one of the old bluecoats, one of the original security people in there. I went up a ramp and he was eating a hot dog and he had mustard all down his tie – like dripping down his tie. I said, "You have mustard all over your tie" so he was very embarrassed, and then we just started talking. He said that he was going to be a senior at Framingham State College. I said, "Well, I'm going to be a freshman out there in the fall." We kept bumping into each other that summer at the ballpark. Then when I was out at Framingham State College, I did see him.

He and a buddy of his worked at Fenway together, so I said, "Gee, could I have a ride back and forth to the ballpark?" because I didn't have a car.

One thing led to another, and we got married in '85.

I got engaged there, at Fenway Park. It was in June, after the Toronto series. We went upstairs and it was behind home plate. Peter Gammons was walking towards us and they had just put the lights out and the blowers were starting up to clean up the ballpark and – lo and behold – he gave me a diamond. Behind home plate up by the refreshment stands. He said, "Come on upstairs for a minute" and we snuck back in. At the time, he had no money to buy the ring.

The timeframe didn't work out for him to keep working at Fenway, but it always did for me. I always kind of worked two jobs up until I had the children and then I just sorta did Fenway Park.

A lot of us grew up in the ballpark doing it, and we've been there for 20, 25, 30 years and we're all having kids. It's a whole new generation coming in to Fenway Park. Nine or ten years from now, maybe Nicole [daughter] will be doing souvenirs or something. Ice cream.

TIM SAVAGE
Former Vendor

I grew up in Jamaica Plain – Moss Hill. We moved to Dedham when I was 17. When I was 16, one of the guys on my paper route was Jack Rogers, the traveling secretary for the Red Sox. I barely knew the guy, but my father said, "Why don't you call and see if he can get you a job at Fenway?" He told me to go down to Harry M. Stevens and sign up. So I did.

It's all done on seniority. The first year I did lots of popcorn and Coke. You eventually move up to ice cream and hot dogs. I didn't stick around long enough to make it all the way to programs.

I worked there six years. My younger brother Matthew has been there 15 years. He's a walk-around vendor.

At the beginning of my third year – it was '85 – they asked for volunteers to sell souvenirs. We would get the big wooden booth with all the souvenirs and we would be assigned to one of four places throughout the park. You would wheel out your booth before the park opened and wait for the customers. I had the place right by the ramp where there's a stairway up to the front offices.

One of our union benefits was that they would give us really crappy roast beef sandwiches. The only way they were edible was if you piled on tons of mustard. So I went to get mustard on my roast beef sandwich. I come back and there's this big black guy standing there. "You shouldn't leave your cart unattended," he said. He was fingering a few of these little decals – which nobody ever buys – and he's like, "How much are these?" I told him and he bought a few of them. When he spoke, I noticed the gold teeth and I realized, "Wow, this is George Scott! I'm in the presence of The Boomer." I had grown up in the late 70s and of course I remembered The Boomer.

I'm standing there dealing with George Scott when Haywood Sullivan walks by. As I said, I was right at the entrance to the stairway to the front offices. He says, "George!" And George Scott immediately turns to him and says, "Hey,

Haywood, when are you going to give me a job?" Haywood stands there and he looked a little embarrassed. In mock shock, he said, "A job?" and then George Scott ambles over and throws his arm around him and the two of them disappeared upstairs. I swear to God, George Scott was the only person who ever bought any of those decals from me. They just didn't sell at all.

The best sellers were hats and pennants. The bobbing head dolls, I broke more than I sold because you have to push the cart back and forth to your position and they'd fall over and break.

I work for a non-profit now doing work on security issues in Asia. Military and nuclear weapons, international relations. We work on resource and policy, a bunch of liberal peaceniks trying to save the world.

I used to sell hot dogs to Stephen King. He had weekend season tickets, the same package my brother had, in the same section, two rows behind my brother. He was the best tipper I ever had.

DENNIS KEOHANE
Former Vendor

Dennis was a Fenway food vendor. He now works in a funeral home.

I worked for Harry M. Stevens my sophomore, junior and senior years at high school – 1987, '88 and '89. I got the job through Peter Meade, who was friends with Helen Robinson, the switchboard operator.

I started with the lowest of the low. They started me on Coke. It's more cumbersome and you didn't make as much money. This was back in the days when they had cellophane tops that they shrinkwrapped on, but they never worked and it'd spill all over the place. My first night was a Friday night in the bleachers. It was like Sodom and Gomorrah, just nuts. Everybody was drunk. I came out of there completely sticky with Coke and covered with mustard. I thought this was going to be awful. I was exhausted, and this was just my first night.

It got better though. I sold ice cream all my second year, and by the end of my third year, I was finally into hot dogs. Hot dogs are the top. You didn't have to work as long, you'd finish in the fifth or sixth inning, and you'd get more money than anybody else. I loved it.

Every game we used to go up in the sky deck and watch the last couple of innings. You get frustrated by the game while you're working, though. If someone hits a home run, it distracts everybody from what you're doing, and you kind of got upset about it. I used to go home and watch the repeat of the game on TV. The whole game, win or lose. I was a fanatic. I'd watch every game.

There was a wide range of people. Most were pretty harmless, there were some fights between fans, but I never heard of vendors getting in fights. I just enjoyed the people there. We started with ten percent, and when you achieved a certain level of sales you got jumped up a certain percentage. My average my best year was about seventy bucks a game. My worst was probably in the fifties. My best day I made a hundred and fifty bucks.

WILLIAM NOWLIN, SR.
Former Vendor

William Nowlin, Sr. is – yes – my father. When I learned at a very impressionable young age that he had sold hot dogs at Fenway Park, it was as though I'd been told he was President of the United States or something. Was there ever a better job?

After I was well underway on this project, I asked my father to tell me about the work he had done at Fenway Park.

Do you know that when you were in first or second grade, they asked you what your father did and you said your father sold hot dogs at Fenway Park?

I worked there in 1937 and 1938 and I remember that clearly because in 1939 there was going to be a World's Fair in New York and I wanted very much to go, but I couldn't afford it.

The World's Fair was the event of the century in my life. One day my father and I were at the ballgame and I said I wonder how much those kids make selling hot dogs.

We went and looked up the man in charge for H.M. Stevens, Tommy McCarthy. He was a very, very nice man, on the short side, with a big smile. I walked out of there a half hour later and I was hired. Right on the spot. You couldn't do that today. I was only 15 years old. [Tommy McCarthy later worked for many years as the steward in the old press room.]

The only other vendor I remember was the veteran of the place, an old bald-headed guy. A fat little Italian fellow, Toots Mondcllo. IIe had been there so long that he got his choice of the article he wanted to sell that day.

What happened normally is that you were given a container of soft drinks to sell. In those days, they were just chilled and in wire baskets. The orangeade and the Coca Cola and that stuff, in glass bottles. After the game was over, we had to – without being paid for it, because we were privileged to sell there – pick up all the bottles.

In later years, people began to throw bottles and that's when they went to the safer system.

I was probably too skinny in those days to get the hot dogs. It was my second year before they allowed me to sell hot dogs. Hot dogs cost the most. I think the soft drinks were a dime and the hot dogs were twenty five cents. We made twenty percent. Occasionally, we'd get a tip. But America was just beginning to recover from the Depression. People weren't that generous. I remember one time, though, two Catholic priests bought a couple of hot dogs and said, "Keep the change." I remember that very well, because it was so unusual.

It's interesting that hot dogs are still the most desirable. You had to be strong to sell hot dogs then. It was a canvas sling over your shoulders and around your neck, and a metal tray. The tray contained hot water, to keep the hot dogs hot, and mustard and piccalilli and little cardboard things that you put the hot dog in. You had to give a napkin, of course, so it took a couple of minutes. This carrier was stainless steel, with a lid over the hot water and over the mustard and the piccalilli, to keep flies off.

We had a flat knife, like a table knife, and we'd dip it in a container. You didn't even ask people do you want a lot or a little. You just sort of slathered it on. You just said, "Mustard or piccalilli, or both?" Most people said both. We didn't carry ketchup.

Doubleheader days were the best. In those days it was quite common to have Sunday and holiday doubleheaders, on one admission. So the average patron was there for five or six hours and they got hungry. The doubleheaders would start around 1 o'clock and last until 6 or later. People got hungry for hot dogs more than they did for soft drinks or popcorn.

When you went to work, you got so many dollars worth of markers. Little numbered metal tags. I think they gave us twenty dollars' worth. Then when you sold the first batch, you dumped the change in containers and it was registered by the number. At the end of the day, they didn't pay us in dollar bills, they had little cloth coin bags. I remember sitting on the back porch counting the quarters, nickels and dimes. I think I made about $40.00 on a Sunday.

I made enough money that I went to the New York World's Fair with another guy who worked with me. His name was James Sinclair. We stayed at a hotel in New York City. We took the Long Island Rail Road out, so I must have made a reasonable amount of money.

Starting in '39, I went to Northeastern. That's why I stopped at the ballpark. I may have gone back at the beginning of '39. That I don't remember. We're talking sixty years ago now.

I probably went to four or five games a year before I started working there. My father was a big baseball fan and even though we didn't have the money, he'd take me. We listened to games at home, too. We were living in Somerville then, and there was a trolley car that ran into Lechmere Station, and then you got a train to Fenway Park.

The real good memories I have is of some of the players. I remember talking to Doc Cramer, who was a center fielder, and to Jimmie Foxx, who was of course very famous. Both nice guys. I talked to Lefty Grove, who was an old crab, and had the reputation of being a drunk. I talked to Joe Cronin at one point. Just "Good luck today, Joe" – that sort of stuff. Sometimes they'd say, "Let's have a hot dog" and they'd pay for it. They always had some other kid, I guess a clubhouse attendant, go and get the money for them.

The word in those days was "hustler." We were all called hustlers. Today it means a prostitute, of course. We wore white pants, a white shirt and a white jacket. I think we wore a little white cap. Even in those days, they tried to be careful of hair falling in the food. We had a dressing room with lockers. One of my friends – the guy I went to New York with – spilled mustard all over his uniform and he thought he'd catch hell, but they didn't care if you got the uniforms dirty during the course of the day. They were freshly laundered the next day.

We were free to range everywhere in the park. Of course, people vied for the box seat areas, because that's where the big spenders were. I had good luck out in left field, in the grandstand out by the fence. I don't know why, but the people seemed bigger spenders out there. They were mostly men. There were Ladies' Days once a week or so, just to get women interested. In fact, before I met her, your mother used to go to a ballgame once a month or so.

Those were impoverished days and I was just a kid. You know, they never counted the rolls, they counted the hot dogs. During a long Sunday doubleheader, we would get hungry and rather than buy a hot dog, we would just take the rolls, slather them with mustard and eat them with no hot dog in it. It was a free lunch.

ROB MOYNIHAN
Hot Dog Vendor

I started in '81. I was fifteen. My great-uncle Frank O'Rourke had a contact at the park. He got my father and three of my uncles jobs at Fenway, back in the 50s. They did food vendoring too. It's been in the family for a while.

My two older brothers also worked as food vendors. A younger sister worked there, too. She left three or four years ago. I'm the last one. I'm trying to hang on long enough for a nephew who's only two or three now, that's a lot of years until he turns sixteen.

I actually didn't like my first year too much. I was getting things stolen from me, and then other times I'd be short money. If you don't pay attention while you're learning the ropes, you might make a mistake or drop some money or give the wrong money back.

Rob Moynihan
PHOTO BY BILL NOWLIN

I remember old Rico Picardi from HMS came in on one of those Coke days. I had got Coke all over my money and I had the bills facing all different ways. I gave it to him and he didn't say a word, just gave it back to me and made a big scene in front of thirty other vendors saying, "That is the worst money I've ever seen in my forty years!", and he sent me to the back of the line so I'd have plenty of time to straighten it out. They like to have the money organized. It makes it easier to count. Rico was very meticulous like that.

'86 and prior, they only sold hot dogs out of the home plate office, so if you wanted to go in the bleachers, you made a long run. You sold out quick because there was no one else there but then you had to spend time running all the way back. It was all strategy.

The only bank you have is the money you come with. The stand workers, they're provided a bank, but we bring our own. I don't know why.

The hot dog bin is 36 hot dogs a load. We have water in there. The whole thing weighs about 30, 35 pounds. There is a Sterno in there, to keep the water bubbling. Occasionally, you run into a problem like the water putting the Sterno out. The bins get pretty bent out of shape. Us senior guys get there early and get a nice square bin.

They used to have hot dogs in a cellophane wrapper. They used to run them through a huge microwave. There's more work involved the way we do the hot dogs since 1986 but it's a much better quality hot dog.

Also, there's more tipping when you actually service people, you know, getting a hot dog out, saying "Hey, you want ketchup, mustard?" In the old days, you used to just pull them out and slap them there, you're done in two seconds. Now you've got to make them, hand them out. You've got a chance to make a little conversation.

My all time record for hot dogs had to be last Patriot's Day, usually the best day of the year. It's April. Hopefully you get a nice cold day, which is great for hot dogs. They've got to have a hot dog for the start of summer.

People ask me, knowing you're going through maybe 300 hot dogs on average, "How do you eat that after looking at it?" Sometimes after the game, they'll have extras in a bin and I'll say, "Well, the price is right!" and I'll down a few. If there's leftovers they put them to the side and we can eat them at the end. It doesn't happen often enough.

I work as a cost accountant, at Aspect Medical in Natick. I'm getting out of work later and I usually don't eat. That's why at the end of the game, when they put those hot dogs out, I'm the first one there.

You do fast and courteous service. You make a little small talk, a joke or something. Also, just being nice to people. Every once in a while, a fan will drop a hot dog and rather than getting mad you just say, "Oh, somebody pulled a Billy Buckner" and you give them another hot dog. They'll usually throw on a nice tip.

It's part of making a fan happy. Usually, you just throw it on the side and report what happened. If you came back saying they dropped too many, you'd find yourself on Coke pretty fast.

You get the New Yorkers coming in, being loud-mouthed and stuff. They'll say, "Why don't you eat those hot dogs?" This one time I said, "Well, I can't afford to eat these hot dogs. I don't make enough." There were about five or six of them and they said, "Well, every one you eat,

we'll pay for it and we'll buy one each!" They were challenging me to see how many I could eat. I was still in school, so I needed the money. I was able to put down four hot dogs. They paid for my four and then each one bought four, and they gave me a great tip on top of it! You've got to play to the crowd to get the tips, but it wasn't easy working the rest of that game with that many hot dogs in you.

Sometimes, you'll have a friend and his boss is going to the game. He'll give me some money beforehand and send me over to say, "Oh, Mr. So-and-so, here's a couple of hot dogs from my friend." It's a way for somebody to score points with the boss.

For the most part, I don't see a lot of the game, but when a big hit happens and everybody stands up, you have to turn and look. You're not going to sell anything anyway. And your curiosity gets you. You can feel it in the crowd if the bases are loaded. As I'm getting older, I can't keep up with the younger vendors and one of my tricks is that I try to watch the game. Whenever the Red Sox have a big rally, no one's downstairs buying food. Once the rally's over the aisles are going to be clogged. So what you do is, when there's two out, watch the count and when they get a couple of strikes, go down and fill up. Then you're not stuck in the aisles.

I hope to do it a few more years. If I didn't enjoy it, I wouldn't do it. It's extra money that I can put towards a vacation or something.

Told my father's story about his free "Depression lunch," Rob nonchalantly said, "Oh, yeah. I'll do that." Some traditions live on.

ADAM BIRNBAUM
Vendor

I'm in my third year now. I just walked in and filled out an application in April 1997. Most people won't stay, so they're hiring a lot.

Right now they're telling us not to throw anything, so he's [Rob Barry] getting in trouble. I don't think Barry causes any problems, but other vendors have and they can't make an exception for him. It's pretty stupid to throw Coke bottles.

You learn on the job. I did some stupid things. I was selling pretzels my first day, Opening Day in 1997, and I was pretty unsanitary, now that I think about it, because I didn't know what I was doing. I was wearing gloves but no one told me you need utensils. I was just handing them out by hand. It was pretty disgusting. They sort of just throw you in the fire.

The best days I've had were selling bottled water in the bleachers when it's 100 degrees and the sun's just pouring down. I've made a killing out there selling water and Italian ice and stuff, but on an average game it's better to sell Cracker Jack or something.

There's all kind of drunk idiots there, they give you a ten and then claim they gave you a twenty. They want to fight about it. People leave their beers in the aisles, and somebody will knock it over. Usually, it's not a big deal, you just refill it for them, but sometimes people get upset.

I like being at Fenway and being so close to the players. It's pretty cool. You get there early for the games and when you're walking through the tunnel you'll walk right past, say, Tom Gordon. I'm sure he doesn't really notice you, but it's kind of cool to be that close.

The items that are even amounts are bad for tips. This year they raised hot dogs and peanuts to three dollars. They were $2.75 last year and all the hot dog and peanut guys used to make forty dollars in tips a game, now they get like fifteen.

They've been having problems with the Board of Health. There was an expose on HARD COPY [with a hidden camera showing some unsanitary conditions behind the scenes.] They had problems with the hot dogs not being the right temperature before they're sent out. They've been pretty careful about it this year. Also, people were touching the buns when they were serving, and that was a violation obviously. Supposedly, there've been spies in the crowd – Board of Health people – ordering hot dogs and checking to see if the vendors are touching the buns.

I'm in Dan Shaughnessy's book THE CURSE OF THE BAMBINO. My name isn't mentioned. It just says Ben Birnbaum's son, because it was his story. I wanted to stay up to watch the sixth game of the 1986 World Series, and my dad told me it was too late. He told me to go to bed and he'd wake me up if they were going to win. So of course he woke me up in the 10th inning or whenever it was, he said, "Come out. You're going to see something that hasn't happened in 70 years." So I got to come out and watch that great inning. I was crying. I got sent back to bed. That was my childhood trauma.

The next night, the same thing. I said, "If they're going to win, can you wake me up?" and he said, "Yeah." Then, I woke up the next morning and I knew they had lost because he hadn't woken me up. The minute I woke up, I knew. I was a wreck. I probably would have been worse if I'd watched the games.

JEREMY OGUNGBADERO
Soda Vendor

I'm 18. I work for Aramark as a soda vendor. I started three years ago.

I used to sell BOSTON BASEBALL outside the park but I wasn't making enough money. I knew a police officer and he knew the person who hired at Aramark so I applied. They stuck me on sodas and I've been there ever since. I work behind home plate, up in the grandstand.

I want to study film and theater, so I can make movies like Steven Spielberg. I'll keep working at Fenway while I'm in college, but if I get offered a job as a security guard, then I'll take that because it will be easier with my schoolwork. If I could get a job with a film crew, then I'd quit my job, too.

Jeremy Ogungbadero
PHOTO BY BILL NOWLIN

If people ask for a cup to get some water, I give them one of the plastic cups we use for ourself. The paper cups they control, you're given a certain number. If you drop a cup, you have to turn it back in as proof that you didn't sell it. The cashier gets in trouble, and then the manager gets involved. It's a whole ugly thing.

We have to count the cones, too, for the soft serve ice cream. There was the kid who took a cup and served himself some ice cream. He got off with a warning. We get to drink however much you need but that's really it. You can't have anything else.

The chef works right at the stand. He does sausages, chickens, stir fry, hamburgers, steak. Other employees do the hot dogs and french fries. They're not chefs, just a stand worker. The items that you have to be sure you cook really thoroughly, that's what the chef does.

When the game ends, we lock everything up. If there's two outs in the bottom of the ninth, we're still open.

When they go on the road, that's usually a time I'm relaxing. I am so tired when I get home. After work, all you want to do is sleep.

Jen Meagher
PHOTO BY BILL NOWLIN

JEN MEAGHER
Store Manager, The Lansdowne Shop

Aramark also sells souvenirs, both at stands in the park and through the Lansdowne Shop, the in-stadium souvenir store set up several years ago to ensure that the team and its concessionaires received at least a portion of the lucrative income which was otherwise flowing to Twins and other smaller shops in the vicinity.

Only the Horrigans have had more family members here. My sister Katy was the first in our family. She started on food, around '88. One of her teachers at Medford High mentioned the job to the students. She was selling hot dogs, soda, pretzels for seven or eight years.

My brother John started a year after Katy. Food, too, working at the stands. My sister Julie came next, she started on souvenirs.

I was next and started with souvenirs. My brother James followed me. Food. Then my sister Kara. She's doing souvenirs. Julie, James, Kara and myself are all working here now.

The Lansdowne Shop is partly owned by Aramark and partly by the Red Sox. I'm the store manager. I think it's been 12 years at this location, maybe a little longer.

I work year round. We open 10 to 5. On Saturdays, we're open from 9:30 to 3. Sunday we're closed. When there's a game, we stay open to the street until an hour before the game, and then we open up to the inside 45 minutes before the game starts. We close the street entrance; it becomes an exit. After a game, we'll stay open twenty minutes; if it's really busy, a little more.

I work Monday through Friday. When there is a game, I try to get out of here by 6 o'clock. One of my sisters takes over at that point. If there were any problems, my sisters have the seniority. Both of them work in the shop. Of course, I'll stay if we're short on people.

Hats sell best, and certain T shirts. Some out of towners, they'll look for something that says "Fenway Park."

The foam fingers, that's always a good item with the kids. We have little souvenir bats, baseball books, little batting gloves. Things like that never really change, but the clothing and stuff always changes.

Some places, people will go, "Oh, it's favoritism" if you have several people from the same family, but no one's ever said anything here – though some people will jokingly say the souvenir shop is the Meagher Shop.

I like the fans. I see people from England, Scotland, Australia, China, Japan. When they do the tours, the last part of the tour comes through here.

Prior to the 2004 season, the Lansdowne Shop was renovated out of existence as the club used the space to expand the third base/left field concourse, and to create a new VIP lounge. The Red Sox and Twins Enterprises have become more entwined in collaborative efforts to market Sox souvenirs and apparel.

GERT MORIN
Commissary Worker

There are a few others in the background. Gert Morin is a retired military officer, a commissary worker, who prepares food prior to the game. Bill Horrigan manages the money room, the center to which the proceeds flow. And Nick Filler, a former manager for Harry M. Stevens discusses some of the strategies to keep everyone honest.

I live in a mobile park in Weymouth and one of the women that lives here, her daughter works at Fenway for Aramark. They were looking for older people to work, because we show up and do the work. I'm 68 and I qualified as an old lady to work at Fenway Park.

We had five young girls doing the D'Angelo's sandwiches and they had to get rid of the whole kaboodle of them. These kids were having a grand time in there, playing around. They'd throw roast beef at each other, and turkey. It would sort of get out of hand. They ended up hiring two older women.

I prepare all the onions and peppers for the sandwiches. We peel up to 400 pounds of onions a day and we do many, many boxes of peppers. We do them by hand and then I put them in a slicing machine and we use the big lasagne pans, we do forty or fifty of those an evening. The chopped onions are already bought in packages that way. They are finer. The ones for the sandwiches are thicker. Those are the ones I prepare by hand.

We go on about 1 o'clock for an evening game. When it's a 1 o'clock game, we show up at 9. Most of the time we're out of there before the game starts. We park across the street and we have to be out of that lot before the game starts so they can re-rent the spot.

When I was younger, I never got involved with sports that much, but now I'm watching the Sox! Since I started working there, I'm following all of the games.

We have a bunch of women that do the pizzas. We also do D'Angelo's sandwiches. It's Aramark people that do it but we use their name and products.

I was hired to work with the peppers and onions. Not too many kids want to peel onions. I can tolerate them. They're kept in the refrigerator and they're very cold. The odor isn't that bad, and we always have a fan going, so you don't shed a tear. Unless you follow the Red Sox. That can get sad. Especially lately.

Gert Morin
PHOTO BY ANDREA RAYNOR

In 2000, Aramark started buying pre-sliced onions and peppers, so Gert moved on to making pizzas and the like. Another specialized job eliminated.

BILL HORRIGAN
Money Room Manager

I started in 1943. Just 14 years old, selling peanuts up and down the aisles. I worked as a vendor for about three years and then became involved in the service operation where we assign the kids their product and then cash them in at the end of the day. I did that for several years, what Bobby White does there during the game. In the late 60s I became involved in financial operations.

I was a teacher, senior class advisor, math and science department head, assistant principal, principal and ultimately assistant superintendent of schools. I retired in 1991. As a parallel career, I worked here summers. In addition, I used to go to the other locations that Harry M. Stevens has as well, special events and that kind of thing. Back then we had a couple of dog tracks in the area, and a couple of race tracks so when the

Bill Horrigan in the
money room
PHOTO BY ANDREA RAYNOR

team was on the road, we'd go to some of those locations.

In those years also, Harry M. Stevens had the three New York ballparks – the Yankees, Dodgers and Giants. We'd go down there and supplement their staff. Those were the glory years of baseball down there.

Harry M. Stevens came here from England and settled in Ohio. He got the concession for the minor league ballpark there, selling ice cream cones and lemonade. He came up with the idea that people might like to know who the players are on the different teams, so he developed the scorecard. He developed it both in English and in German, because there was a substantial German population living in that part of Ohio.

One cold day, ice cream and lemonade weren't selling, so he got the bright idea to buy German sausages, cook them, put them in a bun and send his workers out to sell them.

Aramark bought the company five years ago and I've continued with them. I've gone to a number of locations for them. The Kentucky Derby, they have that event. Then down to Giants Stadium, the Meadowlands. Rich Roper, who's the vice president for this area, he's also responsible for that area down there. He's had us go down for Giants games and Jets games, racing in the Monmouth Racetrack which is right close by.

We have six daughters, so a parallel career was very helpful with six college educations and six weddings and all that. All six of them worked here during high school and college on refreshment and souvenir stands.

We play down the "money room" aspect. From a security point of view, you don't want to target this area. There's a lot of security around, though, and we're pretty well buried away here. It's almost exclusively a cash business.

A beer vendor will get an opening bank of $310. During the course of the game, girls will go out and pick up money, accompanied by a

police escort, and bring it back and count it. At the end of the game, all the people bring back their individual bags.

Then it's like a production line. We have machines that count the coins and roll them. We have currency counters. They can detect mixed bills and give a running count of each denomination. We don't get too many counterfeits. It's been a few years since there's been a noticeable number.

We sell a couple of million hot dogs. It's enormous. The feeling used to be that putting in other products would hurt hot dog sales. Well, no way. People who want a hot dog are going to buy a hot dog. It's synonymous with a ballgame. But people who wouldn't buy a hot dog if Hell froze over will buy the other items that are available.

We have this TV in here to keep track of the game. Everything is timed in terms of what inning we're in. You have to keep track so we can anticipate.

Fenway does extremely well, per capita, compared to the other parks. Very well for the size of the park, a 33,000 capacity and the fact that we don't have the room here. We've got a lot more points of sale now. That's Aramark's philosophy, you offer more locations and you can do more business. Offer more options and anything you can do to move it along and cut down on the lines. People don't come here to stand in line. They come to watch the ball game.

NEAL ELLIOTT
Vendor

I sell programs before the game and then I sell a food product during the game. I'm typically at the bottom of the ramp coming down from Gate A. Then I sell Papa Gino's pizza during the games. Pizza's my main product.

My uncle Paul was the sports production manager for NBC. He later became director of Game of the Week. He threw peanuts in the 50s while he was working his way through high school and college. When they were doing the

Game of the Week, he would stop in at Fenway and say "hi" to Bill Horrigan and all his friends. He kept the relationship going.

My dad worked for local radio stations and moonlighted doing the inside-the-park public address work. When I turned 14, my dad walked me in and helped me fill out an application, and they hired me. So I became second generation in here and that was fun, to know that I already had this legacy through people who knew who my dad and my uncle were when I was just a kid.

I could only work day games at the time, supposedly. My first game was a doubleheader and they gave me this big basket that had scorecards, pencils, peanuts, chewing gum. It was so heavy! And I was so ambitious that I went bolting up and down the stairs. By the time we had gotten only to the fourth or fifth inning of the first game, I was completely burnt out. Then I realized that I was selling a lot more stuff – because I was moving a lot slower. People could see me, and stop me, and buy something. So I began to learn the technique a little bit.

In those days, Cokes were 50 cents, I think. Maybe even 25. Popcorn was 50 cents, sold out of the megaphones. Hot dogs were 35 cents. I know the ice creams with the wooden stick was 25 cents. On a good night, we came home with 10 or 12 bucks. It was cash. So I did that in '64, '65, '66 and '67. They were very dull years in the beginning.

Two of my sons work here now, and I tell them they're spoiled. They have no conception of what it's like to work in a park that's 2/3 empty. You were going, looking for customers.

'67 was a whole lot of fun. I remember a Yankee game at the end of August; it was a Friday night, the thick of the pennant race. The Yankees had just come to town. They might have been tied for first place. I walked around that park for 7 innings, and I didn't sell a blessed thing! And no one else did. No one wanted to eat a thing, and everybody shooed you out of the way. I was selling Coke that night, but nobody wanted it. In the seventh inning, the Yankees scored a run or two and that sort of broke the ice. Then people bought a few

things. But the tension was unbelievable.

I grew up, became an adult – a principal in the Boston Public Schools, and it never crossed my mind that I would do this ever again.

A few years ago, in 1998, I drove my son Matt and five friends down to sign up and I'm standing in the same room where the Harry M. Stevens office had been – and some of the same people are still there. Bill Horrigan was there. And Bob White. Jim McSherry. They were in there registering guys that Saturday morning. So I told them my woes about '67, how I worked up until September 1 but then had to go away to college and so I missed the whole end of the pennant race, and I missed the World Series, and how I just felt like it was this unfinished symphony.

Neal Elliott
PHOTO BY BILL NOWLIN

I was bemoaning my sad fate there, and my envy of my kid just starting in. So Joe, the human resources person at Aramark, says to me, "You've got a choice. You can stop moaning, or you can sign up." I said, "Yeah, right," and patted my oversized belly, at the time in middle of the winter, and my gray sideburns, but he says, "Stop moaning or sign up!"

So I did. I signed up, and when I came home, my wife said, "You're out of your mind!" I said, "I'll do one game a week, or something like that, or a weekend just for the fun of it." The first year was the wild card year with Cleveland – 1998 – and I did 62 games. It just got in my blood.

When I became a principal in the Boston Public Schools, the irony is that the two buildings I was in charge of, one on St. Mary's Street,

Josh Elliott
PHOTO BY BILL NOWLIN

off of Beacon Street – where I still park my car – and the other one down the end of Van Ness Street the other side of Boylston Street. So there I was – I couldn't get out of the neighborhood! But Fenway was just a past memory for 15 years that I was in charge of those two buildings. I look back at it now and I wish that...it would have been a great stress relief for me to have spent the whole day in the school building but then gone out a couple of nights here and there and continued working the games.

I'm an educational director now at a small school in Brookline and I bump into my students all the time now. That's fun. We talk about the games.

Matt is an unbelievable vendor. I taught him everything I knew, and then he started teaching me things. Before he went away to college, he probably had the highest per game average. He's just got a great knack. He chats with all the customers, and his tips are unbelievable so he's teaching me a thing or two. He typically sells Coke. He puts it on his head and he runs around. He's a strong kid. He works home plate.

Matt's brother Josh works in the food stands underneath. He's chosen not to go above for air. He's usually in one of two places – the main stand at the bottom of the ramp where they sell just about everything or the main stand at the top behind home plate. This is his second season. He's a high school kid. He doesn't have the inclination to be running up and down the stairs. It takes a special kind of person to do that.

HANK ELLIOTT
Former P.A. Announcer

Hank Elliott is Neal's father. He did the announcing for five years at Wonderland, the dog track. He also was public address announcer for one year, a big year in Red Sox history, 1948.

I grew up in Mattapan. One of the first games I went to at Fenway Park,

they roped off the outfield. I saw Lou Gehrig. I saw Babe Ruth. I graduated high school 1939.

The ballplayers used to just walk down the street to the park. When the Yankees walked down from the Kenmore Hotel, they had the white on white shirts, suit and tie. Always gentlemen, so to speak. The St. Louis Browns, if three or four of them in a congregation walked down the street, they looked like they came from one of the brickyards in St. Louis!

I was the 1948 public address announcer. I did the public address announcing for the Boston University Terrier football. That was how Joe Cronin heard me. Come winter time, I was shaving and my wife said, "Telephone call!" I said, "Who is it?" She said, "Joe Cronin" and I said, "Yeah, and I'm Methusaleh!" But he hired me. It was always a side job. You couldn't work 12 months around it. I did the PA in '48. The next year, the radio station WMEX wasn't able to make arrangements for me and I wasn't strong enough economically to stand on my own feet for the Red Sox job. There wasn't enough to sustain me, so I had to do something else for the family. I worked in a Chevrolet dealership that was where the McDonald's is now, right on Brookline Avenue. I was a salesman.

So I just worked the one year. I was paid $20.83 a game. 1948 ended with a one-game playoff for the pennant and the Red Sox lost to the Indians. To this day, I have never been paid for that playoff game. I didn't ask the treasurer. It slipped my mind.

NICK FILLER
Former Concession Supervisor

I was a floorwalker. I'd go out and patrol. They knew that I knew enough to spot what was going on.

I was working at Wonderland Park for Harry M. Stevens, sort of low-level management, and when Fenway was in need of someone to supervise a group of concessions or to help out in their beer room or whatever, then I got brought over.

They controlled beer by counting cups. Having been a beer vendor myself, I knew many of the tricks. Some employees re-use cups, as awful as that sounds. One of my jobs was to make sure that I didn't see any Stevens employees collecting cups out of the garbage, because they'd be used to re-sell the beer and pocket the difference.

We then put ounce counters on the beer taps, so it would just dispense a certain amount of beer. Then they'd just get some cups and they'd pour the beer and let it build up a big head and slip the extra cup under for the overflow. After four or five overflows, they'd have their own cup. That was not stealing from Stevens, of course, because Stevens was getting its dollar from each designated number of ounces, but it was stealing from the customers because they would get less beer.

They had these popcorn cones that doubled as megaphones. Once you finished the popcorn, you had a megaphone. You can't count the number of kernels, so we controlled popcorn sales by counting megaphones. Sure enough, some employees would find megaphones, bring them back and sell popcorn in them and put the money in their pockets. Not quite as bad as re-using beer cups, but that was stealing right from the company.

With soda they would put extra ice in. Then the spillover – every fourth cup – they'd sell themselves. The customer, of course, was getting more ice than soda.

It was hard to come by employees then, so all you'd do would be to say, "Hey, come on. We're watching. Don't do that." They wouldn't get fired until the second or third time. You always wondered if you saw someone pulling a cup out of the garbage, but if he didn't have a Stevens badge on, you couldn't do anything but watch to see if he delivered it to a Stevens employee.

The company had shoppers. Even so-called management didn't know when Stevens shoppers would come through. They would be deliberately rude to see how people reacted. We would get the reports, that the shopper had been through on a certain day and this is what they reported.

They would sit there in plainclothes and watch the guy who was ringing up the register just to make sure they were ringing up all the time. The count never really totaled with the register. We usually would allow 2 or 3 or 4 hot dogs a night.

KEITH RANDALL
All-Star Vendor

Keith Randall
PHOTO BY BILL NOWLIN

Keith Randall lives and works in Baltimore. I met him working at Fenway Park selling Cracker Jack for Aramark during the Home Run Derby the night before the 1999 All-Star Game. Aramark had brought in two vendors from each major league park where they have the concessions, as a treat for their employees. He was really enjoying himself selling at Fenway and wearing a different shirt from the other vendors. This one said on it: "All-Star Vendor". I asked him for his story.

I started working '88, at Memorial Stadium. My brother is a vendor, and I needed a part-time job so he asked me why don't I try it out, and I've been doing it ever since. I work University of Maryland games, the Preakness. I've been to the Kentucky Derby. I work the Ravens games, the Redskins games. I find it very lucrative and emotionally rewarding.

The last few years Aramark's been sending vendors to All-Star Games. This year our supervisor wanted to send two vendors that were in the middle of the pack, an average type as far as sales were concerned. Other criteria was personality, just who would best represent the company.

The most fun, I guess, would be hot dogs. I have a little spiel for each product I sell. Like, to get somebody's attention to pass a drink, I'll tell them, "Hey, take a sip and pass it down" or if I'm selling hot dogs, "Hey, take a bite and pass it down."

I always tell them I love my job, and when they give me a tip I really let them know I love it. They'll say, "Oh, yeah. I bet!" The last few games I tell them, "My company sent 18 vendors to the All-Star Game – I was lucky enough to be one of them. You've been served by an All-Star vendor!"

There were 18 of us. Two from each city Aramark operates in. They put us up for five nights at the Sheraton. They gave us about fifty bucks a day. I really enjoyed it. It was an honor as far as vendors are concerned.

We stopped at the Dana-Farber Clinic. The Jimmy Fund had a bunch of baseball things going on for the kids and the vendors came in and we all did a little shtick from what we do. I did an Orioles bird routine, O-R-I-O-L-E-S and you shape the letters with your body. Kids loved that. The Montreal vendor vended cotton candy in French, and gave them all some. One of the vendors from Houston, he has a bag that looks like peanuts taped to a rubber band. He throws it to you and just when you're about to catch it, he snatches it back. The kids loved that. They loved the attention.

It was fantastic. It was the best trip of my life.

8
MEDIA

Jim Healey, Vice President, Broadcasting &
    Technology
James Shannahan, Broadcasting Manager
Bob Tomaselli, Red Sox Dugout TV Camera
    Operator
Pat Cavanagh, NESN Producer, Red Sox
    Baseball
Joe Stafford, TV Camera Operator
Joe Karas, TV Camera Operator
Debbi Wrobleski, Television Reporter
Jerry Remy, Television Broadcaster

Joe Castiglione, Radio Broadcaster
Bill Kulik, Producer, Red Sox Hispanic Radio
    Network
Bobby Serrano, Broadcaster, Red Sox Hispanic
    Radio Network
Alberto Vasallo, Vice President, Caribe
    Communications
Tony Massarotti, Boston Herald Reporter
Bill Belknap, Boston Herald Staff Photographer
John Mottern, Agence France Presse
    Photographer

Jerry Remy on the Boston media:

I think it's worse now than it ever has been. When I played we had a group of writers who traveled with us all the time on the same plane and the same bus. It's much different now. There's much more coverage than when I played. There's radio talk shows, plus what you have on TV and the newspapers. They're all trying to beat each other with stories and scoops. I think at time there are some negative people who seem more happy when things are not going well. I find that disgusting. But that's the nature of the place. Would you want to be in an atmosphere like that or somewhere like Minnesota or Anaheim? I'd take the heat. I'd rather be where the action is. And I think there's a lot of players who feel that way. I wouldn't say it's cruel and mean (in Boston), but you're always on edge. – SPORTS COLLECTORS DIGEST, June 30, 2000

JIM HEALEY
Vice President of Broadcasting and Technology

Jim Healey
PHOTO BY BILL NOWLIN

Jim Healey's career track with the Red Sox is as impressive as it gets, a tribute both to Jim himself for his accomplishments and to the Red Sox for continually granting him the opportunities they have.

My parents were immigrants from Ireland. I grew up in Jamaica Plain on Child Street, right in front of St. Thomas' church. A guy by the name of John O'Neill lived in Jamaica Plain and worked in the ground crew. He worked for the construction crew that rebuilt Fenway in 1933-34.

In 1971, I walked in one day and went looking for Joe Mooney, who was groundskeeper at the time. He told me he had enough help but if I wanted to work as an usher come back on opening day. I did and I worked the 1971 season. Whenever there was a threat of rain, I would be on the tarp crew; the ushers did that then. At the end of the season, I asked Joe if I could work on the ground crew. When you worked for Joe, you worked hard. He was very fair. If you did your job, he was the best advocate you could have. I worked on the ground crew for three summers.

Gene Kirby, the VP of administration, asked me if I wanted to work in the ticket office. The reason for that was Joe. Joe knew I paid my way through school. For that, I'm forever grateful.

Arthur Moscato was the ticket manager. I sold tickets for the entire '75 season.

After the World Series, the Red Sox announced that they were putting in a video board and some new computers. I went to John Harrington and applied for that job. I had some video experience in college and I had taken computer courses. The Red Sox had nobody who had any experience in that, so I was promoted. I actually worked in the accounting department

for two years, putting our accounting system on the computer. I worked with the programmer, doing the systems analysis and training the people in the accounting department. Those people had been there a long time – a calculator was new technology then. They were using adding machines where you punch the buttons and then you crank it.

Those same computers were used for the video scoreboard, so I ran that at the same time. I would work in the accounting department during the day and run the scoreboard at night and on weekends.

A job opened up in PR as second assistant to Bill Crowley with Dick Bresciani. I wanted to move into something that was more the line of work that I had majored in at school, marketing. I worked for Bill Crowley for two years, as an assistant with Dick, and traveled with the team. Did the stats. The press notes. That was a lot of fun.

At the end of 1980, Buddy LeRoux asked me if I would set up the marketing department. Bob Montgomery and Johnny Pesky sold all the advertising for the scorebook and the billboards in the outfield. They were a couple of ex-players working on goodwill, and we developed it into a professional department. I helped them sell advertising as well as setting up Promotions, Group Sales – really getting that department off the ground. I hired a sales director who had experience in putting group packages together. I hired a promotions director. We built the suites at the time, so I had to hire food and beverage people to coordinate that. We hired some people to work with us in order to work with them.

I ran the department until 1985, when Buddy LeRoux and Haywood Sullivan and John Harrington asked me to concentrate on broadcasting. They let me hire my replacement. I hired Larry Cancro, and oversaw that for about a year until he took over complete control.

From '86 to '89, I spent most of my time working on broadcast contracts. By the time '89 came along, we had new radio and television contracts in place. Then John Harrington asked me to oversee looking for a new Spring training site, and I spent the next year and a half negotiating with different communities around Florida before we struck the deal in Fort Myers. I oversaw the design and construction of that facility. That was great experience for the new ballpark project here in Boston.

[*Jim was project manager for the replacement for Fenway Park envisioned under John Harrington's leadership, spearheading the project until new ownership took over early in 2002. The new owners favored renovation over replacement, with spectacular results.*]

I did Human Resources too. During the strike of '94, our personnel person left and John Harrington asked me to take over until we got somebody to do it full time. I wound up doing it for three years before I was able to hire my replacement, Michele Julian. Just before I got rid of that function, I was assigned the duties of information technology.

My present job responsibilities are all matters involving broadcasting. I oversee the message board/video board, the sound system, the phone system, master antenna system, all the computers and computer networking.

I'm here at just about all the games. Actually, during the game is when I get a lot of my work done.

It's not totally unique that Jerry [Remy] works for both [broadcast] teams. That happens in some places. Most broadcasting places prefer to have their own identity, but Jerry does a great job. He provides continuity to both broadcasts.

Baseball's rules allow us to offer webcasts on radio. We can't do that on television. We can't put streaming video on the web, because of contracts with Fox and ESPN. I think eventually you'll see that but it will be done on a national basis in order to keep as much parity as possible.

I represent the Red Sox on scheduling in the American League. We usually get together once a year when the schedule comes out, to kick it around, look at the problems. Our one requirement is that we be home, playing at 11 o'clock on Patriot's Day.

I was on the licensing committee back in the early 80s. Back then, licensing was done by LCA, a subsidiary of Time-Warner. We were losing money by letting somebody else do the licensing

for us, so we made the recommendation to pull it in-house. They did, and it became very, very successful. Later on, when the Baseball Network started, they put together an advisory committee and I was on that for a couple of years.

I wanted to play baseball. Didn't every kid? I played in high school but I wasn't very good. Good field, no hit. I was late inning defensive help. I have a 16 year old daughter who played varsity softball last year. I have 13-year-old twin boys. They both play hockey and baseball

Early on, they thought this was like any other father's job. As they started playing Little League, they began to realize that I was a bit different. Everybody else would go to the ballpark once or twice a year and sit in the bleachers. They'd go a bunch of times and sit upstairs in the control room or in pretty good seats. They began to realize it was something special.

We used to do the father/son game with just players, up until several years ago when we made it a family game where our kids were able to participate. They had a great time. They loved that.

My boys got to meet Ted Williams once. I was down at Fort Myers and I had a satellite dish installed at Ted's house. We had a special decoder box and instead of shipping it to him, I decided I'd drive it up and I took the kids with me. The kids got to meet Ted. Ted was great with them. They were thrilled. Ted was fabulous.

Just when we might be wondering what leadership position he might next assume, Jim Healey resigned in 2002 and soon found an executive position with the Yawkey Foundation.

JAMES SHANNAHAN
Broadcasting Manager

I started working for John Caron in the maintenance department my freshman year in college. Jim Healey is a friend of the family, he forwarded my application to maintenance and I started in March 1990.

We did the luxury boxes, the 600 Club and the press box areas. Mostly cleaning, trash removal, painting, minor carpentry – pretty much everything. Some of the coolest things happened in that position. One day in 1991, we had a ceremony honoring Ted Williams for being the last batter to hit .400 and Joe DiMaggio for his 56 game hitting streak. They needed someone to bring refreshments to them and I was fortunate enough to be given that job. I brought down a tray of fruit and some water and actually got to meet both of them at the same time. Not meet them, but...I offered them the refreshments.

DiMaggio was like I expected. He was kind of quiet and said, "No, no thank you" in a nice manner. Williams was like, "OH, NO, THANKS! I APPRECIATE IT." Very loud and outgoing. They were sitting on a golf cart underneath the bleachers talking away like they were the best of friends.

About my second week here I was washing windows in the luxury boxes and I saw Roger Clemens out running on the warning track. It was before the team had come up from spring training, I guess he was sent up earlier because he was the starting pitcher that Opening Day. He was a huge idol of mine so I ran down there just to watch. I didn't know what to expect. I just sat in the seats. He finished his running and instead of going down through the dugout into the locker room, he walked up where I was sitting and said, "Hey, how're you doing?" At that time he was having a little squabble with the press and wasn't talking to them, so I didn't expect that at all. I said, "Good. Good luck on Opening Day." He was like, "Thanks, buddy, take care." That was my first experience meeting an athlete in such a manner. They're just regular people.

In February 1996, I moved into my current position. Up here, it's like a little television studio. Our main responsibility is the electronic scoreboard and we have a lot of video equipment. I could barely get the "12:00" to stop blinking on my VCR and now I was put in a position where that's basically the nature of it, but Jeff [Goldenberg, his predecessor] got me through it and the staff is absolutely fantastic.

I oversee the electronic scoreboard, the organists, Ed Brickley, the DJ – Kevin Friend. I'm the only full time Red Sox employee up here, so all that stuff falls under my area.

I stay about 45 minutes after the game. Some of the staff stay and prepare for the next day so that everything's ready. We send out videotapes to Major League Baseball Productions which keeps a library of every game played. We get the game summaries when it's printed up by the public relations department. They need it for the television shows, and the different broadcasting teams.

A sports ticker updates the scores of the game and we have a person whose job is to enter those scores into our electronic scoreboard operation, and also to call down every inning and relay the numbers along with the pitchers' numbers, to Chris and Rich in the scoreboard. It's tough in the middle of an inning because they have to watch the game and they have to be aware if there's a hit or an error. The "hit" or "error" lights and all the balls and strikes are done by our public address announcer, Ed Brickley.

The side boards and the main electronic scoreboard are linked together. It's not supposed to happen that they are ever in disagreement but it will malfunction every now and then to where we have to quickly bring them up to speed with one another.

There's an annual scoreboard convention. In addition to the baseball people, there's a group from the NHL, the NBA, the NFL. A lot of colleges are getting electronic scoreboards as well so there's a growing number of those folks. It's called IDEA, the Information Display and Entertainment Association.

I am horrified at what some of the other scoreboard managers do: they want the scoreboard to be the main show. I think we're here just to complement the baseball. Because we are at Fenway Park, I believe we have baseball fans here, not fans who just want to be entertained.

I really hate it when they have the scoreboard tell you to cheer. Our Boston fans are coming to watch the game, I don't want them looking at the scoreboard when they should have their eyes on the mound and on the grass. I remember I went to Oakland back in 1988 and it was an unbelievable game, but the biggest cheer was for the dot race. That was just pathetic.

The objective of everyone here is to win the game. Crowd involvement is a big part of it, and that's the reason for the stress on upbeat music and why we've become a little more aggressive in that way. We want the fans to get in the spirit of becoming loud and really pulling for the nine guys on the field. We just want to create an atmosphere where that team support can go on.

When we created the "CWS" sign, when it used to be "CHI" – that was because of inter-league play. We had to differentiate between the White Sox and the Cubs. We have six slots out there, for six games going on. We have the four other American League East teams always up there, and whoever they're playing in interleague play. Then we'll also have the American League Central leader and the American League West leader up on the scoreboard. We were thinking about "CUB" for the Cubs. Very big executive decisions. Very important. [In 2000, CHI was back for the White Sox.]

We actually had to have a "BOSTON" one made up last year to post the home run hitting contest results. Because Nomar was representing Boston, we had to have an out of town "BOSTON" plate made up. The regular Boston one, of course, is permanently painted there.

When the visiting TV stations come in, I'm kind of the liaison between them and the park. They have these huge trucks which are like TV studios. Sometimes there are three networks in on one night. You have to coordinate all that. If there's a foreign pitcher performing, we'll always get an additional TV unit in to cover that game.

You can climb up inside the big electronic scoreboard. The only reason to be in there is to change the lights. They're U-shaped red, blue and green tubes. It's like a submarine up there. Ladder after ladder after ladder, up to the upper levels. There are a couple of floors so you can work in one area and then go up a ladder to another area and come across. It's kind of neat.

I've been in the manual scoreboard, too. I was down there for half an inning. I guess I earned the right to write my name in there, but I haven't yet. It was a night game and I couldn't believe how bright it was back there with all the tower lights on.

I sit right up the stairs from where Ed [Brickley] sits. I can see the whole game. I watch most of the game, but it's funny, you watch it a different way. You watch the pitch get thrown and then you quickly go from the electronic sideboard overlooking left field to be sure the count's right. Then I glance to the Green Monster to make sure that one's right. Then the one out in center field, to make sure that one's right. And then I go back to watching the game.

BOB TOMASELLI
Red Sox Dugout TV Camera Operator

I started doing Red Sox games around '94. I've been on the dugout camera since '96.

I like the dugout position the most. I love doing sports in general, but I certainly am a Red Sox fan – not a baseball fan, a Red Sox fan. It's a little different.

Bob Tomaselli
PHOTO BY BILL NOWLIN

I started in '69 doing sports with a TV station and worked my way up to director. I directed Celtics games and whatever. I left to do freelance, what you call an independent contractor. Then I broke into commercials and news. NBC News. As a camera operator.

I had the opportunity to decide what did I like. I liked the craft. I really liked the camera. When you're camera, you're in the stadium, you feel the excitement. If the Red Sox are down by three and somebody gets a home run with two guys on, the crowd goes wild. If you're right there, you feel it. So I opted for what I loved the best, and that's camera.

The dugout position is camera five. There's always someone in the opposite dugout – on third, the far end of the dugout. That's camera one.

I've been hit by baseballs, several times. I do right-handed batters. When it's not a right-handed batter, I will do the pitcher and the first baseman and second baseman. I like to go to the outfield. It's a different look. Or I'll try to get the shortstop. The double play from my position is incredible when you have the second baseman get it, he tosses it to Nomar and then Nomar throws to first and that reveals itself, right on my camera – the whole play.

Sometimes it's better that I shoot the opposite dugout than that camera, or likewise, Joe Stafford from the roof, his camera would be better going into the dugout because it's unobtrusive. If I spun my camera around on a critical situation, or where some player was mad, they don't like that camera in their face. The director will say "Get out of there" and then Joe Stafford's camera will shoot them and they don't know it.

I've been going down to Spring training since Kennedy was here. I introduced myself to Jimy Williams and to the players. So now, they know who I am. They see me in Spring training. They see me every game. They talk to me. We have fun.

They'll run my camera! Pedro Martinez will come over and find out what I'm shooting and just talk to me. Jim Rice likes to run the camera all the time. He'll actually zoom in and focus. He'll do it before the game or maybe between commercials once in a while. As a matter of fact, he did it during the last Fox game, and Fox thought that that was unusual so they came back from the commercial with Jim Rice running the camera.

Everybody has their own sport. There's only three or four of us that are really into it. Some of the guys are more into Bruins hockey, but I'm into the Red Sox. I wanted that position, the best place I could be is in the dugout. I don't lose interest! I'm all fired up. If the players are all fired up, I can hear them yelling and talking, and it fires me up.

They know I'm a fan. They know I care if the Red Sox win or lose. It's not like with the press, where they can't really cheer for one team or another. I hear all the conversation. It's terrific.

In Fenway, #1 is third base at the far end. Behind home plate is #2, in that little house under the 600 Club. As you go around, above my position, that's called high first – that's camera 3. 4 is center field. 5 is me. 6 is the left field wall, where Joe Stafford is. This year we had a tight center. That's #7. A second camera right next to the center field camera. What he does is stay tight. He'll get the signals from the catcher, the batter waist up. He'll get the ball being thrown and he stays with that batter, if he gets a hit, he takes him to first, head to toe.

We all wear headsets and we're in touch with the truck. In one ear is the director and in the other ear is the talent. The broadcasters. You always have to listen to the talent because of what they talk about. There's no script here. It's a dance, and sometimes the talent leads, and sometimes the director leads.

Sometimes you react on instinct. Sometimes the director calls a shot. They'll call me, "Five. Ready, Five. Take, Five." "Selli, get me the manager." That means the manager in the visitors' dugout.

There are stock shots that you don't have to call. Like a right handed batter, I know it's my batter. And I know I have to be waist up, because he's going to put the super in, "John Valentin, 3-for-4, his average is whatever." And then when he gets off me, the cue is "Ready, Four." Four is your center field camera. That's pitcher-batter. So he goes "Ready, Four," I go head to toe on the batter so you can see the swing. Now, if it's not my batter, I'd be on the pitcher. I might be in tight on his eyes – I like to work on the eyes on a critical play, on a tense thing. Then when he says, "Ready, Four," I get off the pitcher and I go to D [defense] and this gets back to getting hit by a ball.

I'm in the dugout and my camera's now facing first or second base but my head is facing the batter – the left-handed batter. I'm not looking in my camera, I'm looking at that batter because I don't have any protection. I get a screamer foul ball and I'm in trouble. I've got four of those this year. One hit the camera. I always duck behind the camera – BANG! – off the camera. One hit the wall behind me and, on the way out to the field, hit my chin, but it was a little deflated by the wall thing so I didn't really get hurt that much, but I got a little stunned, you know? They all scatter when you get some screamer into the dugout.

When they say, "Ready, Four," I go to the pick, which is the first baseman holding him on, to get the jump or the steal perhaps. Even if he had to jump back to first, I can get the tag. So that's another thing – if there's a man on, I would stay on first knowing that a defensive play might come up at second base as well, especially in a double play situation.

Bob Whitelaw is the director, the one going, "Ready, One. Take, One. Ready, Two. Five, give me the manager." Pat Cavanagh is the producer and he would pick replays, but also he's concerned about the breaks. The producer dictates what the format's going to be, and he cues the director on when he'd like to see stuff.

Most sporting events, you're there six hours before. In baseball, you can come in a little later. If you're set up for a homestand, you can come in four hours before. You check in to find out if there's anything peculiar that's going to happen – interviews, or anything other than the standard.

Most of the time, we come in, get the word of what's going on and then we go out to our cameras and fax. Fax stands for "facilities ready." What that does, the technical director, let's say Whitey [Bob Whitelaw] is saying, "Ready, Two. Take, Two," he's talking to a technical director that has a big keyboard in front of him. He presses camera two to put it on the air. Or to put supers or any facts that might happen. That technical director is there with us long before the director is. He switches to make sure our tallys are working, make sure we're seeing the right picture in returns....

If you think about it, that is the last live TV left. Everything else is on video tape. The show must go on. Sometimes you might have to ship in other lenses, you might have to go to a rental house. If my camera's down or the technician has to fix something, it can be hectic.

The cameras belong to companies that own TV trucks. Presently, NESN and JCS use National Mobile Television. The equipment belongs to them; these trucks are fully equipped. [NESN doesn't own it. Bob doesn't have to bring any equipment that belongs to him.]

If you have to go...you try to plan it before the game, but then nature's nature, you know. There's a little urinal just inside the tunnel from the dugout back to the clubhouse. Joe [Stafford], there's a men's room not too far away. At times, and it's very, very rare, you'll hear, "Camera 7's gotta go off" – and you'll know what that is.

There will be excitement over the headsets. "OK, Two, get ready, Two. Take, Two. READY, FIVE! FIVE! FIVE! GET OVER THERE, TWO!" Oh yeah, the excitement level in his voice goes crazy – not to miss a play. That's what he gets worked up about. I'm yelling and screaming all the time. I'm slapping five. That's why I'm there. I'm a fan. When Nomar hit the grand slam, we shook hands and I said, "Oh, that was GREAT! That was awesome!"

I told Jimy, "You know the reason I'm in this dugout? I choose to be here because I'm having fun." And he looked at me and says, "Do you know why I'm here?" I says, "Why?" "Because I'm having fun." I thought that was pretty nice.

There aren't any rules about what I cover. There might be personal choices. When it gets down to it, on my camera, I dictate what you see – what the director gets, unless he says, "Get me so-and-so."

I do like the double play, coming right at you. Last year, there was a play at second and I followed the ball, which is unusual because that's not my responsibility, but the second baseman – who I think was [Mike] Benjamin – got it and he was going to go to home and I panned right over, so the ball's in my frame the whole way, and I got the play at home and he got the guy out. They used it as a promo for NESN, so I kind of liked that.

It's instinct. You have to know the game and where things are going. I was aware that the guy was going to come home. You have to keep the ball in frame. If you're just that much behind the ball, you never catch up. You have to anticipate the action.

Because I am closer, I will iso the pitcher. I get eyeballs. Sometimes it's interesting, because you can feel the angst – if you will – of the pitcher in a crucial situation. So I zoom in. You can just feel it in his eyes, that it's a big deal at that moment.

I don't like when it rains. When it rains, they don't need me. They don't need my camera. They need a wide shot from the home plate camera. He's covered. So I go in the dugout with the players for the whole delay! We talk and fool around. That's nice, but I hate the rain thing, because it's uncomfortable.

I get paid on a per game basis. I do the Celtics and the Bruins, but baseball is the biggest thing. There's a big difference.

PAT CAVANAGH
Producer, Red Sox Baseball

Pat Cavanagh
PHOTO BY ANDREA RAYNOR

I am the producer of Red Sox Baseball [for NESN, the New England Sports Network.] The 1997 season was my first. Prior to that, I worked in other capacities on Red Sox and Bruins and other productions.

I came to NESN, as a volunteer in 1990. I just offered my services as a production assistant. They called me two or three times a month to help out, doing odd things.

NESN is owned by the Red Sox and the Boston Bruins, but we operate as if we were an independent. We don't operate under a Red Sox budget, so to speak. I'm a NESN employee.

Some people who have tried to do this, it just wears them down. It drives them insane how long the games can take, all the pitching changes and the fact that it's every day. That's not for everybody. You might find fans who would find it hard to go to 81 games a year. Try 162 – more than that! I saw about thirty spring training games. It can be ten games straight, no nights off, different time zones.

If it's a 7 o'clock home game, I'm in the office at 10. I make sure that we received statistical support information from the Elias Sports Bureau. Then I take a look at the commercial format that's provided by our traffic department. That has all the commercial breaks, where things are supposed to air – where the Budweiser scoreboard goes, the Southwest Airlines thing, the Citizen's Bank thing, the Mobil Player of the Game, the New England Ford batting leaders – all of that stuff is placed in various parts of the broadcast by our traffic and sales department. I go through, detailing each commercial break through the course of the game, to make sure things air where they're supposed to.

I'll gather up some tapes. Footage from previous games that might involve the starting pitchers, or some event that we may want to look back on. For instance, when we saw Cleveland the second time I went back and got the tapes from the first time we played them, where we had those fights. I gather all that up and head down to the truck.

The crew call is generally at 1 PM. I try to get there a little earlier, so when everybody shows up we can get to work. Six hours beforehand is a long time, but the camera people have to bring all the equipment out, hook them up, power them up, connect them to the cables that run to the truck.

The video tape operators spend the first hour making sure that they're all in time with each other, making sure that they're in synch with the switcher in the front of the truck so when they're punching cameras into their tape decks, they're all in time and everything's routed properly.

The second hour, we'll start going through some production. I'll go into the tape room and work with the four tape operators. If someone hit a home run the night before, we'll build a little package we can use when he comes to the plate. We'll build a few highlights that we might use when we first go on the air. We evaluate certain pieces of video that we want available during the course of the evening.

During the game, I will tell the tape operators, "Mark that for the highlights." Or, "Save that, we're going to look back on it next time he comes up." Or, "Give me a different angle. We're going to show that when we come back from a commercial break." That sort of thing. That's my call.

We library quite a few. I have 25 90-minute reels that are all different highlights. We did 160-plus productions when you count the Spring training games. That's how many melts I have. That's what we call them. We melt down the individual reels from each machine into one tape. We won't save everything. I go through the tapes and decide what is worth saving and what isn't. We'll probably save fifteen to twenty whole games, just package them up and send them to storage. The highlights are here and accessible.

Between two and four, we start building our elements. Our graphics guys are furiously typing in all the names and statistics. We're voicing billboards with our announcer, you know, "Brought to you by So-and-so and So-and-so." We're putting together promo graphics. "Tune in October 2 when Boston Bruins hockey starts" – that sort of thing. The lineups become available from the clubhouses and we'll put that in our system. We check through our music and make sure that that's all in order. If we have any interviews to tape, that's when that would occur.

We also have full studio support. I'm responsible for the six to eight people in the studio that track other games, out-of-town scores. They do our post-game show. I oversee that whole main studio.

That brings us to dinner from 4:30 to 5:30. At dinner, I'll discuss with Jerry Remy or Sean McDonough what we're going to present when we first go on the air.

About 6:15, the guys will stand up and tape the open on camera. We'll spend from 6:15 to 6:30 putting it all together with our animation and music and stuff. We give everybody another ten minute break until about quarter of seven and we'll do some final run-throughs checking things out. Then we hit the air at 7.

The game can be anywhere from 2:15 to 4:15 [hours in length.] After last out, we're still on the air another twenty minutes for the postgame. I spend a few minutes by myself going through what happened and what we might attack the next day. I generally leave about midnight. I'll be back again at 10:00 the next day.

I travel with the team. Some people don't have any sense of how often the team loses a night's sleep, and then they're expected to go out and play. You leave the park around midnight, then you have to load the gear. Sometimes that plane won't leave until almost two. Even to Cleveland it's about an hour and a half flight, and then another half hour to the hotel.

Some nights you get back to your hotel after a game and you're like, "What just happened?" You're so busy, you're hardly even sure who won.

Some of the newer parks are a little more conducive to what we're trying to accomplish. Outside Fenway, you see all these cables outside the building. We always keep a finger crossed. Those cables are old. Pretty soon, this is going to be the worst facility in the league. There's not even a working copy machine in the Fenway press box!

It's live TV, things are unpredictable. There are occasions when we'll have a video or audio problem, it doesn't happen often and that's a credit to the people that we work with. Generally it's corrected within a few minutes. 99 percent of the time, everything goes just as planned.

After the season, I spend a couple of weeks putting it to bed, so to speak.

I'm now off every weekend. I'm off every night. I'm on a very regular scheduled 9-to-5-ish. No one's really punching the clock. I'll wrap my three weeks of vacation around Thanksgiving and Christmas. But it's not really as much of an off-season as people think. The team reports to spring training around February 14, so we've got to have our productions up and running by the middle of January. I'll spend January on the things we want to do for the next season – creating new animation or new music, tweaking certain graphics, talking about equipment upgrades – cameras, lenses, tape machines. That takes the whole month, it really does.

When you're with them that much, they treat you as part of the team more than part of the media. They don't put us in the same category as the writers, or the national network people that are always looking for a scoop. They treat us differently.

We enjoy what we do. There's a rhythm to baseball that I think people who are drawn to it understand. It creates a lot of camaraderie. A baseball team literally lives together for eight or nine months. If the team makes it into the playoffs, though, the networks come in and it's a little weird. You spend eight months traveling with them and, all of a sudden, you're watching the most important games from your couch.

JOE STAFFORD
Left Field Wall TV Camera Operator

I've been doing Red Sox games for about eight years. I do the Bruins for NESN. I do the Celtics.

I did about 78 games this year. Home games. They don't travel anybody.

Joe Stafford
PHOTO BY BILL NOWLIN

I'm camera six. The Wall is what we call it. I've done that position for two years now. When I'm up on the Wall, I have no idea how Pedro is painting the outside corner, how his ball is moving in and out. I really can't see that. So I miss out on things like that. By the same token, there's things I see that others can't, like the stuff that

happens in the dugout, the stuff that can't be seen from other places.

I watch the re-broadcast, to pick up things that I do, or things that I should be doing. If it is an extraordinary game, where he strikes out fifteen people or something, I'll go back and I'll watch it myself.

Bob Whitelaw assigns the positions. If I had my choice, I would take high home. The central one right behind the plate, under the 600 Club.

The camera I use belongs to the trucks. The trucks are separate entities from everything else. NESN leases those trucks. We bring the equipment to wherever it has to go. All together, it weighs about sixty pounds. They're in cases. We wheel it through underneath the stands – it's kind of an archaic place – by the clubhouse and up the elevator to the fourth floor and then out to the Wall.

I'm a Yankee fan and, my God, I'm hoping the Red Sox win so maybe they'll loosen up a bit. I was raised a Red Sox fan. I don't know what happened. As far as I can remember, I think it was '76, I was watching the Yankees and the Reds swept them, just beat the pants off them. There was something about that team and ever since, I've been a Yankee fan.

I did wear a Yankee hat to a game once. Opening Day, I wore a Yankee cap. It's just a way of life. Coming into the park, I hear all this booing. I go, "What's going on?" I looked over, and they were booing me! When I went into the park, there was a little problem. I don't think the Red Sox higher-ups appreciated it very much. I didn't mean anything by it. I had to go across the street to do the political thing and bought a Red Sox hat. That's what I wear to the ballpark now.

That truck is used by NESN the whole year long. The cameras stay out in the park. But if that truck has some place to go while the Sox are gone, then we'll pack the truck and it will leave. During a homestand, though, it stays. We put bags over the cameras, called elephant bags, to protect the cameras. My camera is chained down actually, right to the platform that it rests on.

Other people with the operation have a lot to do, but we camera operators don't. They still want us there. Just in case. Just to know you're at the ballpark, they don't have to worry about you being there for game time.

In a lot of aspects, it's like an athletic team. We're together all year long. We don't do just the Red Sox. The same crew does the Bruins. We're more like some kind of dysfunctional family than we are just some guys showing up to do a job. There's a lot of hanging around, a lot of camaraderie.

When the game's over, we sit in traffic like everybody else (laughs). We usually leave the minute it's over unless we have to fill to the top of the hour or the quarter of the hour, which is very rare. They try to get off the air as soon as possible. We go back to the truck and find out if we need to come in early the next day, and to be sure that the call time for the next day hasn't changed. Then we leave, usually within twenty minutes. There used to be a time where we would hang out together and go get a beer, but with family lives and people getting older, it's kind of put a damper on that stuff.

It happens [having to go to the bathroom.] It hasn't happened to me, not yet. I prepare for it. You can't drink before you go out there. You're going to be out there for three hours. They don't want you peeing off the Wall.

I've not been hit up there. Balls have come close to me. I can remember one instance where a foul ball was hit high and I lost track of it. I saw the players running towards the left field corner, looking up. I thought, "What the heck are they looking at?" I'm looking in the sky and I can't see anything, and then all of a sudden – like magic – this whirling thing appears and it's getting bigger and bigger. It landed right by my foot, an inch away. *[On May 5, 2000, Joe took a rare night off. Filling in was Chuck Murphy, who was drilled hard in the leg by a Nomar Garciaparra foul.]*

I have visual access to the dugout, so sometimes I can see things before others see them. Things with Pedro, some of the things that he does in there – the antics, the masks that he wears – things like that.

Home runs over the Wall. It's the reason you're there, to see that kind of thing. That's kind of cool. I can remember Ken Griffey's first home run. I was there, and got that.

We're at Fenway every day. There are guys on that crew who absolutely love the Red Sox. Who have always loved the Red Sox. I just think we should be treated a little better. We see these people every day all summer, year after year. They know who we are. They know what we do. We get treated better by teams that come into the park than we do by our own home team. They don't really acknowledge us. When the visiting teams come in they'll talk to us. Just, "Hey, what's going on? What's this? What's that? How's this guy doing?" They at least give you the common courtesy to say, "Hi." That doesn't happen with the Red Sox. Mo Vaughn was somewhat friendly. So was Tim Naehring. When I can only name two, there's a problem. The Red Sox organization just pushes everybody away. They don't want anybody too close to the team.

Go to another sport. The hockey player is a whole different animal. He will come in for an interview and will talk to you and say, "Hello, how're you doing"" and when you leave he'll say, "Thanks a lot." It's unheard of in baseball. I can't put my finger on it. I'm thinking that they try to put this protective shell around themselves, that they're fragile or something. I don't know.

JOE KARAS
TV Camera Operator

I grew up in sight of Fenway Park, at 829 Beacon Street. I remember being in the living room and you'd hear the crowd erupt every so often.

I've been working Red Sox games since 1975.

I do other sports. One I enjoy most is hockey. I do basketball, boxing, wrestling, tennis. I've worked for Court TV. I did some work up at President Bush's home a couple of summers ago for some international feed; I do industrial camera work as well as entertainment and sports.

High first – that's pretty much my camera now. I operate high first for almost every game. That's an interesting position. I love the game from that point. I have double plays, pickoff plays. It's usually called the "shag camera" – I'm shagging the ball in the outfield. If a ball is hit, I try to follow the trajectory – say out to left field. Then I focus in on the left fielder and make a real tight shot of that catch.

Joe Karas
PHOTO BY ANDREA RAYNOR

I wanted to get into radio. I loved radio and I wanted to be a disc jockey. At Emerson College, my first job was working weekends at WARE in Ware, Massachusetts. My first full time radio job was in Orange. WCAT. Then I got a real great job in Springfield, where I was "Tom Brown, Springfield's Unpredictable Night Owl, hooting from midnight to six." I loved that. It was a great station.

One of the most difficult times in running a television camera is fighting the wind. You're panning and resisting the wind, and then when the wind shifts the camera can take off on you and it's almost impossible to hold it steady.

I've never really been afraid up there. When we put the cameras up, you've got to be careful because they're heavy. Sometimes you might stumble a bit. You're aware then of how high you are and that you do have to be careful up there.

The Red Sox were playing the California Angels about five years ago and a ball came up and I reached out and caught it with my left hand. I remember Jerry Remy commenting: "He runs camera and he catches baseballs."

I titled this poem "Remote Crew." That's what we used to call the people who did these games.

In beer stained stadiums and picturesque parks,
Through icy wind, searing sun, freezing rain and snow
Laboring on Sundays, holidays, weekend nights,
Hauling cable, cameras, microphones and lights.

Strong bodies unload the giant broadcast truck;
Tonight they'll follow the flight of the puck.
Tomorrow football, another basketball game,
Remote telecast artists capturing emotions in frames.

Before any player or fans arrive to cheer
They're alone with the companionship of thousands of empty chairs.
Positioning equipment, executing tests;
Some seats are filled, the crew focuses in -
Each perfect play shown and preserved on tape.

With an inner glow of accomplishment,
They disassemble and box their equipment.
Dollys are loaded rolling toward the truck,
Another drama over, sweaty silence and empty cups....

—*Joe Karas*

That kind of says it all. We're there with the companionship of thousands of empty chairs, it's another drama over and what's left? Sweaty silence – sometimes you can almost feel the sweat, particularly in basketball – and empty cups.

We've been there when there are no games, putting cable in, checking camera positions, making tests and all of that stuff, and it's nice. Meeting some of the players... Al Kaline has been there. George Kell. I haven't seen that many celebrities. Danny Kaye was there one time, and Goldie Hawn. And of course Steve King. President Bush has been there. We've seen him.

I remember my mother taking me over there, it must have been '49. I walked up to this ballplayer and I remember her saying of Ellis Kinder, "He's a baseball player. Why don't you ask him for his autograph?"

I'm somewhat of an ornithologist – well, that's a strong word. I like bird watching. It would be interesting to do something about the birds of Fenway Park. The sunsets are very nice from high first looking out. I remember something: "a sunset is heaven's door left ajar." Ned Martin used that. He liked to paint with words. I thought he was great, very poetic.

DEBBI WROBLESKI
Television Reporter

I've been working for NESN since 1995. I'm a feature reporter for a show called "Front Row." I do a lot of interviewing. They have me all over the place, but it's good. I have the best job in the world, and our offices are right here in the ballpark behind section 28 of the grandstand. We can just walk down the hall and out the door and down to the field. It's wonderful.

During the season, on a typical day I get to the office and do research. Like today, I'm going to do something with Kent Mercker, so I'll look up stories on him and get some background. Then I'll go down to the field and interview him. I'll interview Joe Kerrigan and Jimy Williams about him also.

Last year I used to do the interviews after the game, so I would stay for the game. This year, I'm not doing that so now I go to the games as a fan. There is a huge difference between watching the game in the press box and watching it from the stands. Our whole family, we're all really big sports fans. I got into it by going to my brother's Little League games up in Nashua, New Hampshire. I just really got into the games and I loved it.

For the Red Sox, I probably go to ninety percent of their home games. This year, for vacation, I'm going to California and I'll catch them in Oakland. Then I'm coming back and part of my vacation I'm going to spend at the Yankees/Red Sox games and the Patriots/Jets on Sunday.

It's different when you're not working. To go and sit in the park and just enjoy the game, I love it. I love to go up to the Spinners and I love to go see the Pawsox. It's a beautiful new park, you've got to get down there.

Debbi Wrobleski, with John Valentin
PHOTO BY BILL NOWLIN

My grandmother absolutely adored Mo Vaughn. While I was working at NESN she came to a game, and my aunt and uncle and cousins, my brother and my grandmother were sitting in the box right next to the dugout. Mo hit two home runs and was the star of the game, so after the game I interviewed him on the field. When we got done with the interview, he waved hello to my grandmother. It was just the sweetest thing. That to her was just so thrilling.

I had said, "Oh, my grandmother is over there" and he made a point to say hello. This past winter she was in the hospital. Lo and behold, one day she gets a card. "Get well. Feel better. Mo Vaughn."

Every time I walk into the park, I still get a charge. There's just something really special about the ballpark when it's empty. It's so quiet and peaceful.

The last couple of seasons, the players have been wonderful to deal with. Really good guys. I'm fortunate because a lot of these players saw me in Spring training working my butt off with Peter Gammons. Saw me there before batting practice at 8:30 in the morning and staying until after the game. Knowing that I really enjoyed what I was doing, and worked hard at it. A lot of players recognize that and tell me they're proud of me. That's really nice.

I think being a woman has helped, but I also think you have to work twice as hard at first. I had a conversation with one of the visiting players one day and we started talking about the Patriots, and he said, "Oh, wow! You really know your stuff. How do you know so much about football?" Well, that's my job. I'm a sports reporter.

Any position that you're in with any business or career, you have to ask questions, and that's something I'm not afraid to do. I think that makes you better.

Debbi has since gone on to other broadcast work.

JERRY REMY
Television Broadcaster

Jerry Remy played second base for the Boston Red Sox for 7 years, following a 3 year stint with the Angels. He grew up in Massachusetts and was always a fan favorite. Remy's last year as a player was 1984. He has now logged more years as a broadcaster than the 10 years he put in as a major league ballplayer.

Jerry Remy
PHOTO BY BILL NOWLIN

When you play, you travel with the broadcasters, but it was not something I ever expected to be in. I always thought I would be a coach, or a manager or something. After I got the job, I said, "OK, now what the hell do I do?"

I didn't have any training. It was on the job training and it was more difficult than I thought. I was lucky that I got in with a guy like Ned Martin, who had been there for years. This was 1988.

I don't think I've had a problem with overtalking. My feeling has always been, make a point and get out. I remember Ned telling me, with television they see the picture so you might not say anything for a long time, but it's not as long as you think, because you've got something to watch. With Ned, there was a relaxed atmosphere, and I think that helped me.

I think people appreciate silence. People get caught up in what's going on, and they're not listening to what the guy's saying anyway. I'd rather hear the crowd respond than some guy blabbing.

I was called a color commentator at first. I don't know what they call us now. I guess I'm an analyst or whatever. They can call me whatever they want, I don't care, I'm still in a secondary role. The play-by-play guy is the lead, you've got to play off him.

As a former player, you're on the same page with the players. You don't forget what it was like. Obviously, the guys that are playing now, I didn't play with, but you always have that common knowledge of being on the field and playing the game, and how guys feel in certain situations. That's what you try to bring across.

I never paid much attention to the broadcasters when I was growing up. I can't say that I looked up to any of them.

Doing every game is easier. You don't have to prepare as much. It was tougher doing 80 games than it is doing 162. Sometimes you'd go a week without doing a game and you'd kind of lose touch. Doing them all, it's like a soap opera. You're with them every day.

I don't keep any kind of notebook on the players, don't need it. Say tomorrow we're playing Chicago – I'll write their starting lineup on a sheet of paper and I'll make some notes on each one of them. Basically, the information part of it is for the play-by-play guy. I've got to know about the baseball end of it, and describe what's happening.

You get game notes prior to the game, which are helpful. It gives you a pretty good up-to-date. If I'm playing Detroit tomorrow, I can go on my computer and know everything I need to know about them. I'll do that, especially if I haven't seen them for a while.

I used to feel like I needed to know everything about the other team. Well, you don't. Because you're doing Red Sox games, and people in most cases don't care about the other teams. Red Sox fans don't care very much about the Twins.

JOE CASTIGLIONE
Red Sox Radio Broadcaster

Radio, of course, is the broadcast medium most older fans grew up with. Curt Gowdy, Ned Martin, Ken Coleman. There is a long tradition of Red Sox broadcasters. Today the dean is Joe Castiglione. For many years now, the Red Sox have also been broadcast over the Spanish Beisbol Network.

I always wanted to do it [broadcasting] since I realized I wasn't good enough to play, which was about age seven. I used to listen to everything Mel Allen said. I used to have my own fungo games in the backyard – by myself, announcing. It's really the only thing I ever wanted to do – except play!

Joe worked his way up in broadcasting from a number of Connecticut stations to others in Ohio.

And then in '79, I got the Indians TV job, my first baseball job.

Ken Coleman was in Cleveland for '52 to '66, well before me. A couple of years later, when I left the station, Ken's son Casey replaced me.

I did the Indians on TV, but we lost the contract. I stayed and did TV sports. A couple of years later, Casey told me his father was looking for a partner, so I called Ken and he told me where to send a tape. Of course, he wasn't the one who hired me, but the fact that he recommended me was very influential.

I did seven years with Campbell Sports network and Ken, and then we went to Atlantic Ventures, which became American Radio.

I replaced Jon Miller. New Englanders are not very open to new people. Acceptance takes a while. I had a few things that really helped. First, Ken always tried to make me look good. During my innings, he would pretty much leave so that I could establish myself. And then Johnny Pesky would sit in with me. Pesky was great and talked me up and really helped me.

I've got a couple of other jobs. Since '90 I work for the Jimmy Fund in a p.r. position. I teach sports broadcasting at Franklin Pierce in Rindge, New Hampshire and I'm in my 15th year

at Northeastern, a self-designed sports broadcasting course.

Joe Castiglione
PHOTO BY BILL NOWLIN

During the season, I get there about 4. I'll go down to the clubhouse first, see what's going on. Check the lineup. Shoot the breeze with players. Do the manager's show. Trup [Jerry Trupiano] and I alternate interviews every other day. Visit with the opposing teams. Try to find out information about them. See what's going on from other broadcasters, writers, managers and players. It's a time where you do a lot of listening and learning.

After that, I go up to the booth and do the lineup card. Do any spots that we might have. Tape the rest of the pre-game things. Have dinner in the press room, which is a great opportunity again to learn things. I try to spend most of my time with the scouts from the other teams, because they're very willing to share information that you may use down the road.

Pre-game goes at 35 minutes before, 6:30. In the pre-game typically, there's the general manager and "Around the Majors" that Trup does. Then a player interview, then the Jimy show, a couple of commercials and then game time.

Nobody else from radio travels with us on the road. Just Trup and me.

Howie Sylvester is the executive producer in the studio, back at Huntington Ave. We have an intern statistician at home, usually one of my Northeastern students. Michael O'Shaughnessy was this year. He takes care of the drop-ins, hands us the announcements, keeps the pitch count, gets coffee, runs errands. He will update the batting averages, the ERA.

Our kids have done real well. Jeff Idelson became Yankee PR director and now is PR director of the Hall of Fame. Glenn Wilburn, who works for the Red Sox as baseball information director, was with us. Don Orsillo, voice of

Pawtucket. Leslie Stirling was my student. She's at Harvard Divinity School, got the calling to be a priest. She's a wonderful lady.

[On June 2, 2001, Leslie was ordained into the priesthood at St. Paul's Episcopal Church in Boston.]

We have a pattern to the broadcasts. I do the first and second. He does the third and fourth. I do the fifth. He does the sixth and seventh, and I do the eighth and ninth. If it goes into extra innings, we alternate. It's a two-man broadcast, basically.

The ads are pre-recorded, but we read live drop-ins, usually one a half inning.

Every half inning, we have to get in, say, a Jiffy Lube drop-in. Usually you'll wait for a foul ball – so you don't interfere with the action – or a dead spot. At the end of the inning, we just have a standard cue line. "After three, Red Sox 2, White Sox 1 on the WEEI Red Sox Radio Network." Then they go to the break.

It's a lot of fun, and it's always exciting – wherever they are in the standings – just to talk baseball. We're all good friends with the TV broadcasters. Jerry Remy travels with us, because he does both. Sean's a very good friend of ours. We have friendships with other broadcasters, too – people like Ernie Harwell or Herb Carneal. People that you get to know year after year.

Bill Kulik
PHOTO BY BILL NOWLIN

BILL KULIK
Producer, Spanish Beisbol Network

The ballpark is a safe haven from some of the things on the outside.

I'm the producer of the Spanish broadcast. I've been doing this since 1993. I also write a baseball column for *El Mundo*, a weekly newspaper. I write in English, because I think in English, and then I do as much translating as I can, but to be honest with you, they correct so much that it's almost like they do it.

I speak Spanish, I would say fluently. I just can't write it. I lived for ten and a half years, in Bogota, Colombia and Buenos Aires, Argentina.

I've been writing the column for four years. I write about everything. It's almost like Peter Gammons' Sunday column. It covers the gamut from politics to personalities.

My full-time job is at Mediaone. I produce a magazine type baseball show called "Forever Baseball" which airs at Fenway Park before games.

I'm not the best guy to ask about the different uses of Spanish in the broadcasts, since technically I am a "gringo". But there are differences. As the cultures mix (especially here in the USA) the baseball language is starting to melt into one universal language. In fact, I think there is a new language which I call spanglish. You hear the ESPN guys saying "home rrron" all the time. The correct word is "cuadrangular" but a spanglish version of home run is very much accepted now.

The word I have heard more versions of is bullpen. They use "torril" or "calentador" or "bool pen" just to name a few.

Hector [Martinez] would always say "cuadrangular" whereas most of the guys would say, "Home run." Hector in some ways is right. He was the broadcaster on ESPN International. I guess because they were appealing to so many different countries they stuck with a very prim and proper dictionary of words. Everybody will know "cuadrangular" where somebody might not know "home run."

All of a sudden it's cool to be Latin. You've got Ricky Martin and Pedro Martinez shaping a pop culture almost, in music and baseball and everything. It's become cool to go back to Spanish, and listen to the game in Spanish and read about it in Spanish.

My cameraman [for Mediaone] will say, "Why are we interviewing Pudge Rodriguez? He doesn't even speak English." Well, because I might need it for something else, I'll do things for *El Mundo* or Radiolandia or something. I'll interview people in whichever language is appropriate.

I do – and I don't know if I want this printed or not – I feel sometimes like a second-class citizen, like I do not get the same access or the same respect that Joe Castiglione gets. I don't know if we deserve it yet – we don't have as much pull as he does – but you definitely know you're second. It does reflect the size of our two audiences, true, and that's why I don't know how much to read into it.

We do a quick three minute post-game wrap-up and then we do a highlights of the game. I'm really hoping that the Latin broadcast picks up steam now. It definitely picked up when Pedro came into town. Jose Canseco just didn't have the same fan appeal, and before that it was Luis Alicea and Tony Pena. While they were super-nice guys, they just didn't motivate people to come in and take a peek.

Certain guys like Pudge Rodriguez or Robby Alomar, who speak English but aren't comfortable in it, will talk to our guys more than to anyone else. You try to talk to Robby Alomar and he'll tell you to take a hike. We go to Robby Alomar and he'll say, "Sure, Sit down. What do you want to talk about?" It's because he knows he's not going to say something stupid in Spanish.

The Red Sox do reach out to the community. The Red Sox use Alberto Vasallo in particular quite a bit to translate schedules and things. They absolutely love his Latino youth day, because it makes them look great. I think he may get special breaks that other organizations at Fenway don't necessarily get. It gives them good exposure in a community they want more air time into.

BOBBY SERRANO
Broadcaster, Red Sox Hispanic Radio Network

I got this job through a friend who used to listen to me at the radio station. I did music, news, sports, everything. I'm from Puerto Rico originally. Hector Martinez, too. We have another guy from the Dominican Republic.

Bobby Serrano
PHOTO BY BILL NOWLIN

In Puerto Rico, like Cuba and the Dominican Republic, everybody plays baseball since you're five or six. I grew up in Santurce and Arecibo. My favorite team was San Juan, the Senadores. The Senators. I also followed baseball in the US. I liked Cleveland. Not the Yankees, but Cleveland. Larry Doby used to play for the San Juan team.

I work at the Police Department. I'm a civilian supervisor in charge of police reports, car accidents, stolen cars, fights, everything, including the reports from the details at Fenway.

We broadcast every home game, day or night. We don't go on the road. Not yet. We are working on that. I get there three hours before the game. I like to do some interviews, read my notes, listen to what's happening in the clubhouse. I do one or two pre-game interviews. If I interview Pedro, I speak in Spanish. If I interview Nomar, he doesn't speak Spanish so we have to translate. I'll ask the question in Spanish and then in English. Then he answers and I have to translate into Spanish, so it takes a long time.

The audience is mostly Puerto Ricans or Dominicans. Some Central Americans, some from Colombia probably. We have a good reaction from the community, through letters and phone calls. It's successful, and it's growing every day.

ALBERTO VASALLO
Vice President, Caribe Communications

I work as sports editor for *El Mundo* newspaper and Radiolandia radio 1330.

I was born in Boston, in '68. I went to BC High and then BC. We spoke Spanish at home. My father started the newspaper. We own the radio station. He came from Cuba after the Revolution. I had the advantage of our business being a family-run enterprise, so at around 11 years old, I asked to interview some players at the ballpark. It was something new to actually cover the Sox at the ballpark.

Luis Tiant was a friend of my father's from Cuba, and he said to my father, "Why don't you send him to the ballpark?" Here I was 11 or 12 years old doing my first interviews. I still have pictures. They're very funny. Very embarrassing.

Rodolfo Cid was a friend of my father, he used to find us seats. He listens to the show. He's a big fan of the newspaper and the radio. Actually, there was a time when he had a small column in the paper, "Desde Fenway" – From Fenway.

Latino Recognition Day is something we came up with five years ago, in partnership with the Red Sox. We also do it with the Celtics and the New England Revolution.

Tony Massarotti
PHOTO BY ANDREA RAYNOR

I think the Red Sox have done their part. I honestly do. I've seen it and I've experienced it. I would say they make a genuine effort to outreach to this community.

TONY MASSAROTTI
Boston Herald *Reporter*

Print media, of course, predates even radio and Boston has had a long, long tradition of first-rate baseball writing (and some other, less distinguished personalities.)

I'm the Red Sox beat reporter for the BOSTON HERALD, with the team on a daily basis. Home and on the road.

They made me a full time sports reporter the summer of '92. I covered a little bit of everything. Just sports, though. I was assigned to men's basketball at the University of Massachusetts in the fall of '94. That was my first beat.

I'm also on radio, WEEI. Usually on the Big Show with Glenn Ordway. From time to time, I'll go on with Gene Lavanchy at Channel 7, on his Sunday night show.

It's become a twelve month a year job. I go to Spring training, frequently before the players. When you're going from mid-February through October, it's really an eight and a half month season. Then November and the first half of December tend to be big times for free agent signings, trades, arbitration hearings in terms of player salaries for the subsequent season, Winter Meetings. It's one thing after the next. During the winter, it's a lot more phone work, a lot more hunting and a little bit more frustrating and stressful.

I get to the park about 3. I'll go up in the press box and unpack my laptop. I check in with my office earlier in the day, 10 or 11 o'clock.

Covering the games is like a soap opera, everyday is a new episode. If you take a few days off, you lose touch with what's going on with the individual characters. Once you get back, it takes a day or two to get back up to speed, to figure out what's going on with everyone again. It's very similar.

You almost know what you're going to write. When I leave the park on Wednesday night, having written stories for Thursday's paper, I'm already thinking about what I can do for the Friday paper.

I'll use the early part of the day to check in with different people, maybe the minor leagues, scouts, GMs from other teams, agents, etc., especially if there's any breaking story.

Once the clubhouse opens, I'll go down and check the lineup, see if there are any changes that may lead to any sort of newsworthy item. You take your spin around the clubhouse to see who's hurt, who's not, who may be upset about playing time, who isn't. You'll go through the clubhouse just compiling items that you may use in your pre-game notes.

The average fan picks up the paper and the beat guy has written a story about the game and a note book, a collection of notes and tidbits from the game. I use a notebook and a pen. I used to use a mini-cassette recorder but I found that in terms of time efficiency, it doesn't really work well. You inevitably have to go back and transcribe the tape.

The manager usually meets with all of the beat reporters around 4 or 4:30, before the team goes on the field for batting practice.

Usually I'll go over and listen to the other manager. On weekends, when they do postgame in the manager's office, they do it in waves, writers in first and then radio and TV.

A lot of times I'll stand by the cage and watch batting practice. You never know what you might pick up. Honestly, there are a lot of unwritten rules of etiquette. There really isn't one about the pre-game workout – batting practice – but I try not to conduct interviews during batting practice. I figure that's their pre-game time, to get their stuff done.

Usually the best time is to get them before or after, in the clubhouse or in the dugout.

The clubhouse remains open until 45 minutes before game time, typically from 3:30 to 6:15 every day. It's a big window. There's really no need to mess with them while they're on the field.

I'll head upstairs, and do some writing. I'll go eat 6 to 6:15, come back, finish whatever pre-game notes I've had to write, file them to my office and get ready for the game.

As the game's being played, I'm writing what we call a running game story. The only time I'll go down to the stands is if I have friends down there, otherwise I watch the game from the press box.

Fenway has one of the higher press boxes. It's pretty tough to see balls and strikes from up there. In fact, you get a much better view on a TV monitor. Frequently, if there's a close pitch or whatever, I'll just look at the monitor.

To a degree, it's like a bunch of people being together watching a ballgame. There's all kinds of natural dialogue. People crack jokes. At the same time there's a line that doesn't get crossed.

You know, the old rule of "no cheering in the press box" but it's not like a morgue up there by any stretch. Most people like to have a good time while they're covering the game.

If you were to ask any writer if they were a fan, they'd probably say, "No." Only because there's that issue of objectivity. I've grown up here so there's a part of me that has the same interest in this team that a fan would, but I don't have any problem separating that when I'm on the job.

A great deal of analysis goes on. We try to break down everything. Frequently there will be a play where someone will get thrown out at the plate and someone will say, "Was that the third base coach's fault? Did he wave the guy in when he shouldn't have? Did the runner stumble?" You can only watch so many things at one time.

A lot of times the scorer's call will get discussed. If someone thinks that maybe Charlie [Scoggins] is looking at it from a different perspective than they are, it's not uncommon for someone to say, "Charlie, do you think maybe you should take another look at that?" He never makes a call until he looks at a replay. I can't remember too many calls where we've all shaken our heads, whereas in some other cities....

I'll write in chunks. The first thing I'll write is what we call "running." For the early edition, I'm actually writing the story backwards. I write the bottom part of the story before the top half. Somewhere around the fifth or sixth inning, I send in about 60-65% of my first edition story and it will include everything that happened up to that point. How the starting pitchers did, whether any runs were scored, how the runs were scored, were there any nice defensive plays, what was the crowd like, pretty standard stuff. Then as the last three innings play themselves out, I am writing the top of the story so that as the game ends, I can just plug in the final score, send it in to my office and they'll put it on top of what I've already sent.

On the West Coast the deadline issue is extreme because you're three hours behind.

Sometimes last minute things affect you. I can't tell you how many times it's happened where you have a story ready to go that the Red

Sox won the game 4-3 and then somebody hits a 2-run homer and all of a sudden you have to rewrite. What you do is rewrite the top two or three paragraphs. Anything before that home run still happened. It's just that the impact is different. If something dramatic happens late, you just put it on top.

My copy doesn't get edited dramatically. I've had pretty good relationships with the editors. If there's any gray area, they'll call me back. They'll say, "We were thinking of changing it to this…" or "according to the wire story…" which sometimes they'll check my story against. "The wire says this and you say this. Which is right?" They'll call me before I've even left the ballpark.

I'll make any updates in the early notebook that I've written. Once you've sent your story down after the game – the final 5-4 – then you go back to the clubhouse and do all your post-game interviews. Talk to the starting pitcher. Talk to the guy who hit the home run, the player who made the error. Why did it happen? Did the ball take a bad hop, was it just a bad throw? Et cetera, et cetera. Then a lot of times, I will rewrite. Completely. Depending on how happy I was with my early edition story. Sometimes somebody says something really insightful or funny, so you'll put it at the top of your story.

It takes about five minutes to get from the clubhouse up to the press box. Other parks are closer. The best one is Kansas City. It's amazing. You get off the elevator and the doors to both clubhouses are right there. It's much easier to cover both clubhouses in Kansas City than in any other ballpark. The older parks tend to be more difficult.

I think it's good that we don't fly with them anymore. If we were on those flights, we'd be around those guys way too much. I think it would make the relationship worse. Everybody needs their space.

Sources can be pretty much anyone. You leave yourself open to all possibilities. You talk to everybody, club management, players, coaches, manager, agents, scouts from other teams, executives from other teams. The key is to know what somebody's agenda is, so if somebody gives you an opinion or a piece of information, you have to ask yourself, "Why are they telling me this? What kind of spin are they putting on it?

There are so many beat reporters – and in Boston, there are so many good ones – that it's hard to monopolize the news. Somebody's going to get something, so you can't beat yourself up over missing the little ones. You just have to get your fair share. That's what I strive for. Beyond that, the stories you remember are the special events. Pedro's game in Yankee Stadium [he struck out 17 and gave up just one hit against the Yankees in a playoff drive game in September 1999] is one I'll never forget. Roger Clemens' 20 strikeout game in Detroit. Those are special nights.

There aren't too many times when sports stories run off of page one – I mean just for the sports aspect of it – I remember that Clemens' 20 strikeout game was one of the first front page stories I had. Then when Clemens signed with Toronto, that was page one. You remember those. They're kind of neat.

It's a great business. I love the business. You take the bad with the good. The travel gets to me sometimes. Baseball is the best beat and the worst beat, at the same time. You have to be relentless. It takes a different breed to do baseball. The NFL, they play one game a week. Road trips last two days, there're only eight a year. We like to think we're the hardest working group in sports media. We joke that the football guys spend three days talking about the game that just happened and three more talking about the one that's coming up. Then they actually cover that game one day a week. In that respect, baseball's a grind. It's a long season and you can get really tired and worn out, more mentally than physically, but physically tired as well. At the same, because it's like a serial, it lends itself to the page a little bit better. People can pick up the page the next day and read the next installment.

BILL BELKNAP
Boston Herald *Staff Photographer*

I'm a staff photographer for the HERALD. If there's a game Tuesday through Friday nights, I'm there. I do the Celtics, Red Sox and Bruins. It's been a long time since I've been sent to cover anything else.

For away games, they pretty much use all AP stuff. I had a real epiphany with the [1999] All-Star Game. Major League Baseball said that the HERALD and the GLOBE were not to photograph Ted Williams throwing the first pitch. Only the AP, Major League Baseball and SPORTS ILLUSTRATED were going to do it. I looked at the guy – and I've never done this before – and I said, "Fuck you. If that's the way you are, you can fucking forget about seeing Ted Williams in the paper because we're not going to fucking put an AP picture of Ted Williams." I never said anything like that to anyone before. I was fed up with all the nonsense that was going on. The guy from the GLOBE said, "I don't care either. Screw it. If you want to be that way, fine." Ten minutes later, the guy from Major League Baseball said, "Oh, no. You guys come out. We're sorry. It was a misunderstanding."

So Williams comes down the field with Al Forester driving him in the little wagon. He was supposed to come around and stop in front, but Al drove all the way around and into the middle of the players, out by the mound. Well, the only way we could do this was to go out to the mound. So the four of us – the guy from Major League Ball and I think it was Matt York from the AP and Jimmy Davis and myself, we just walked out there. And all of a sudden, all these All-Star players are surrounding us!

Williams has got this deep booming voice and he starts teasing Griffey about his father and talking to the others guys and shaking hands. It was a very magical baseball moment. Nowadays you rarely get moments like that either in sports photography or in news photography. It's a very rare thing because everything is so controlled. This was just one of those sparkling moments.

I would have died to have a strobe with me. Out there with the lights and all that, I could have probably done a little better than I did, but I have some nice images. I can't complain. I'm not like Emily Dickinson, throwing my stuff in the trash.

Sports have been very good to me. I enjoy hockey the most, but I love Fenway in the summer. A baseball park has everything that you would ever imagine about life, from the sounds of the hawkers along Yawkey Way to the enjoyment of the fans, the depression of the fans, the excitement of the players, the ups and down of everybody there. You get some annoying drunken hecklers. But that's part of it.

Fenway Park, you have two main spots for still photographers, the third base pit and the first base pit. I work out of the first base pit, on the outside of the dugout, on the right field side. It's more aligned to first base. It's a sucky place to shoot baseball. I'd rather be next to Bob Tomaselli over by his TV camera on the inside. Most ball parks have an inside pit for still photographers on the first and third base side. From those positions, you don't really have a bad angle. You can cover first base, cover the second baseman, cover the shortstop, cover third base. You've got the pitcher and you have the full range of the outfield. [Where we are] if you're trying to cover a left-handed batter hitting to the second baseman, you get blocked by the first base coach or the frigging umpire covering the bag. Some nights there's no way you're going to get a second base picture because they're going to keep moving in and out on you.

My first deadline has to be back by 8:20. Depending on what's going on, I try to get there as quickly as I can so I can have something in the camera. Baseball can be like watching paint dry, but I've got to have something. Pre-game, you just look for the routine baseball player kind of image, them hanging around, playing around with each other. Holding their bats, pulling their gloves up or adjusting their hats.

Bill Belknap
PHOTO BY BILL NOWLIN

After batting practice, you go upstairs to get a roster. I keep a shorthand score on a scorecard, so I get a scorecard and the lineup. I keep score because it's easier to identify what I've shot. You don't spend half your time writing down everything.

I try to get at least one frame of every pitcher. They always ask, "do you have a picture of X, Y and Z pitcher?" So I always try to get the pitchers.

You don't take a frame every pitch. You tend to react when they drop their shoulder a little bit. You know they're swinging and after doing it for so long, you get a feel for when it's time to shoot. With baseball, you have to anticipate a lot more.

I bring a 400mm 2.8, a monopod, a 20-35 zoom, an 8200 zoom, a flash and three Nikon bodies, one F5 and two F4s. Some games you shoot ten or twelve rolls of film and other games you come back having shot maybe a total of six.

Nowadays we're shooting all color. It's a lot better than black and white. The HERALD uses Fuji. Color neg. It'd be next to impossible to shoot transparencies at night. We have machines to do the processing. It takes about fifteen minutes a roll.

I always stay to the final out. With baseball, you never know what's going to happen. There is a second deadline. It's called "immediate."

When I get back from a game, I produce an array of between six and eight images, and I have about forty minutes to do that. At the HERALD we edit our own film, and they'll make the choice from that array. They may give me a shopping list of what they're looking for. "Do you have something on Garciaparra? Do you have something on Varitek?" Good action is good action.

I won a World Press Foundation gold medal in '96, for a John Valentin diving back into first base. A pickoff move. He was flying in. There's a player's foot almost next to his nose and the ball's right in front of his face. He's in midair. I actually shot that from somewhere where I wasn't supposed to be. I'd been invited over to a seat by the Red Sox managers' seat. I spent a couple of innings there and I happened to nail that.

It was nice. They flew me over to Amsterdam, put me up for a night, gave me a gold medal, treated me like somebody special. Of course, I was one of a bunch of photographers there. The HERALD was pleased.

It's something like 18,000 images a year of the Red Sox. It keeps you busy. People say, "You're so lucky, I wish I could be doing that." It sounds like a lot of fun. Now I'm not griping here, but it is work. You have to be on edge and you have to concentrate, and you have the additional pressure of needing to produce something all the time. With spot news, it's like being in the U-boat, you're either waiting to sink somebody or waiting for disaster to occur to you. All of your terror can be confined to 60 seconds or less, and then you're free for another three or four weeks. Sports photography is completely different from general assignment or straight news in that with sports photography you have to produce every single day that you're there.

JOHN MOTTERN
Agence France Presse Photographer

Since the late 80's I've worked at Fenway. I started with AFP in the early 90s and have been shooting baseball ever since. I'm a full service photographer, I do news as well. I just got finished doing the [Presidential primary] debates up in New Hampshire. It's a broad range of politics, news, sports. I do about half freelance and about half AFP.

I had a front page photo in the NEW YORK TIMES and a front page photo in the WASHINGTON POST. It was fun to get both in one day. Photographs of the candidates debating in New Hampshire.

Speed is important. I have a laptop and a negative scanner, so I develop the film, dry it, edit it, pick what I want, scan it and send it over the wire. A photograph can go worldwide in about fifteen minutes.

It might take me two or three minutes to roll four rolls. Three and a half minutes in the developer. Four or five minutes in the blix. Wash for two minutes. Stabilize for thirty seconds. Then dry for five minutes. I decide which ones I want, based on looking at the negative and then I scan it. That takes forty seconds. It pops right up in Photoshop – in a positive image. You put a caption on it, and then it takes three to five minutes to transmit.

We have desk editors that make sure everything's spelled right and that it fits the format. They make the final decision. If I send them five photographs from a game, nine times out of ten they will send out five photographs. They trust our editing in the field. With digital now, it's so easy.

I'm not a Red Sox fan. I honestly could care less one way or the other. I never imagined myself as a sports shooter. It's just one of the things I do as a full service photojournalist – I've

actually gotten pretty good at it, but I'm not one of these passionate sports photographers – that's all they do, they live and breathe it and follow every statistic.

I go through four rolls of film a game. You've got to know when not to shoot, too. And the thing of it is, some days you're lucky and some days you're not.

I've done a lot of combat photography. Salvador in the late 80s. I covered Nicaragua. I was in Bosnia after the war, went into some unfriendly territory there to do stories on people who were trying to move back into unfriendly areas.

John Mottern, developing film at Fenway
PHOTO BY BILL NOWLIN

I've been hit by a baseball, too. It was back when I was fairly green. It was inner third base, between the third base dugout and home plate. Kelly Gruber gets up and just SLAMS a drive. It bounced once and hit me right between the eyes. I had the outline of a ball imprinted right between my eyes, and I couldn't focus for two days.

9

DURING THE GAME

Bob Rigby, Suites Captain
Ruth Copponi, Child Care Provider
Christian Elias, Scoreboard Operator
Rich Maloney, Scoreboard Operator
Robert Tebbetts, Boston City Policeman
Sgt. Brian Flynn, Boston City Policeman
Jonathan Mandeville, fan who ran on field
Voravut Ratanakommon, Security Officer
Mark Sweeney, former crowd control supervisor
Roland Johnson, Major League Scout,
    New York Mets

Jim Evans, American League Umpire
Wendell Kim, Red Sox Third Base Coach
Chaz Scoggins, Official Scorer
Jim Peters, Spokesperson,
    Federal Aviation Authority
Martin Allen, Banner Tow Airplane Owner,
    Aviation Promotions
Mickey Whitman, Goodyear Blimp
    Spokesperson
Jared Puffer, Radar Gun Operator
Ken Kozyra, STATS Inc. Press Box Reporter

BOB RIGBY
Suites Captain

They call me "Captain Bob."

I work in a candy factory in Cambridge – Cambridge Brands. I am responsible for all caramel products. We've been at this location for eighty years. We make Sugar Babies, Sugar Daddy, Pom Poms.

Gourmet does the company cafeteria concession here. About ten years ago, I met Brian Aitchison, who runs the Red Sox for Gourmet. He was working at Cambridge Brands and we happened to get talking about baseball. He said he was looking for a captain for the suites – the supervisor of food deliveries to the private suites. I happened to be in the right spot at the right time with the right guy. I've been there ever since.

I'm the senior captain. I do all the scheduling. We've got maybe 15 people working up there. There's 23 suites on the left side and 21 on the right. You've got the greatest view in the park, and your own bathroom, too!

We get the food all set up. There's beer and soda, and liquor in a locked cabinet. That's one of my duties – to unlock the liquor cabinets. Most people don't get involved with that. They've got the beers and the sodas and the food.

I've run into Adam Oates there, of the Bruins. I shook Dom DiMaggio's hand. Bobby Doerr. They're all great guys.

We finish up usually two hours after the game. Usually, everybody's had what they wanted. We're out the door.

Right next to the clubhouse, they have a room for the children of the players. Occasionally, they'll do some media stuff there, some special events, but mostly it's for babysitters who watch the kids. We deliver food down there once a night. This time of year, summertime, there could be twenty, twenty five kids. They've got three or four ladies who watch them.

People can stay in the suites until up to an hour afterwards, but security wants to get them out of there. We're out two hours after the game starts no matter what.

RUTH COPPONI
Child Care Provider

I retired after 32 years working as an R.N at the Norwood Hospital. I just decided that I would like to do something a little different. I sent in an application to the Red Sox and this job came up. Being the mother of six children and grandmother of eleven, I felt that I was qualified.

We show up fifteen minutes prior to game time. I like to get there a little early, in to the child care room. They call it the family room.

It's not very big. The first room that you enter is the wives' room. That has a couch, some chairs and a refrigerator. There's a closet where we hold the childrens' toys and cuddles and different games. Then we enter our room, which has a television and some chairs and tables. There's a bathroom off of that. You can't hear the players in the clubhouse. That's further back.

We very seldom see the players. We usually leave twenty minutes after the game and they're still lounging around so it's hard to meet them. If one of the children wanted to see their mother or go up and see the game, we'd get in touch with Colleen. She's with security, and she would send the mother down.

The ages range from one to ten. If they're over ten, they can go up and see the game or sit with their mother in the other room. You never know if you're going to have one child or ten. I think there's more boys than girls.

Last night we had eight children. The babysitting service is available just for the players. There has never been an occasion when we didn't have at least one child. There's always somebody. Opening Day there were nineteen children.

Any child left under the care of the babysitters must be signed in and out by their mothers. The mothers must notify the

Bob Rigby

babysitters where they are seated – the row and seat number – in case of emergency. I'm trained in CPR. We have physicians available if we need them, but we can handle things. Once in a while, a Band-Aid.

Children's Room
PHOTO BY ANDREA RAYNOR

There's usually about four of us. We draw with them. We make puzzles. We play different games – checkers for the older ones. There's all kinds of games. There's blocks, Legos, they really enjoy the Legos. We have Parcheesi but they don't usually play that. They do a lot of drawings. We hang them up on the board with their names.

We read some. They watch videos. Movies like THE LION KING and BABE. Some of the other providers are teachers and they are right up on their activities. A lot of them like to cut out things. They might make little bracelets. They keep busy. We don't like them to be in front of a video all the time. I don't think it's good for them.

If they want to watch the baseball game, they go to the wives room where there is a television.

They're excellent, well-behaved children. Very well disciplined. We don't have any problems at all. They seem to be very bright for their age. The wives are very cooperative.

They usually stay for the whole game unless the mother had to leave for an appointment or so forth. They don't always get there at game time, but they usually stay.

CHRISTIAN ELIAS
Scoreboard Operator

Christian Elias is the assistant athletic director and head baseball coach at Emerson College in Boston. He is also one of two people who work inside the manually operated scoreboard inside the Green Monster at Fenway Park.

I am one of two employees that operate the historic Green Monster scoreboard. My partner Rich Maloney and I have been doing this for years now.

As far back as I can remember, I was holding a bat in my hand. I'm a huge Yankees fan, too, but you might not want to mention that.

We get to see the whole game. There are these slots, and they're wide enough that we can see every part of the ballpark except the center field bleachers and the scoreboard there. We get an unbelievable perspective.

There's a lot of stuff written in there. A lot of ballplayers come in and sign the wall. I'd have to say that in my years there, only a handful of guys haven't been very, very nice. A lot of them come in and sign the wall. Not just the left fielders. A lot of the pitchers, because they do their running in front of the Wall before the game. A lot of guys in their first or second or third year in the major leagues, they want to check it out.

One person could do the job, and one person has at times. You're back there for three or four hours, so you go a little stir crazy if there's just one person. The other person is there more for company and just in case. We can't leave. There's no bathroom. We're sort of stuck in there. As soon as we take the numbers down, we get out of there. When you're working 81 games a year, you're itching to go home afterwards. So we clean up from the night before, then we look at the paper and write down the pitching match-ups, getting the numbers not only for the Red Sox game but all the out-of-town games.

We have an in-house phone and they'll call down between every inning; they'll say, "Toronto 2, Yankees 7 in the 5th inning" and we'll put up the scores. Nobody helps us with the game in progress. We handle that. The only thing would be the correction of a hit or an error.

The P.A. announcer controls the lights, to show the balls and strikes or hit and error. We don't do any of the electronic stuff; they do all that from up above.

The Wall at Fenway is so close that, where we're standing and watching the game in any other ballpark is probably where the left fielder is standing – that distance away. We're right there. We can listen to the outfielders. We're right on the field so we hear the players talking and positioning themselves, picking up the coaches from the dugout and so forth.

When a ball bounces off the Wall, it's fairly dull. When it bounces off the scoreboard, though, it's extremely loud, that's metal. When we're setting up during batting practice and somebody hits it off the Wall, it still startles me. It can even startle you when you know it's coming. Oh yeah, you can hear a player hit the wall, too! Depending on the game and who the guy is, we'll let him know how much room he's got.

One guy who was very very friendly, was Mike Greenwell. He was quite a character, just a good guy. He used to come back there and we talked about everything except baseball. He was funny. We had some laughs with him.

You don't really get bored. When I was in school, I was writing essays or studying for final exams out there. We've got a TV and a radio nowadays. We've done our taxes back there. Mainly, we'll sit and watch the game. Richie and I get along pretty well; we've become really close friends.

I don't know exactly how much the numbers weigh, but they're pretty heavy. The plates we use for the pitchers' numbers and the other towns' scores are one size, and the ones we use for the inning by inning scores for the Red Sox game are smaller. They're organized in the wall on pegs. We have more of some numbers, especially for the run – more 1s, 2s and 3s than the other numbers. There's a lot of pitchers' numbers. We've been known to have to paint a pitcher's number before a game. I remember Alan Mills – he used to wear number 75 for Baltimore. He's now with LA. There's a couple

of numbers we didn't have in stock, so we had to have an impromptu painting session before the game.

What's it like to hear the crowd reaction when you post an out of town score in an important game? Sometimes, as a fan watching the scoreboard, it seems as though you delay in posting a score – maybe to build the suspense.

It's fun. Sometimes we make a little game out of it. In the last couple of years, this year even going for the wild card, we had a little bit of that. '95 we had some of that when they made the playoffs. When they're important games, we know that people are focusing, so we're pretty good about putting up numbers right away. The Wall boys are temperamental sometimes! Depending on our moods, we've been known to sit on a score for a couple of innings. We don't do that on purpose…well, I don't know, maybe to bust somebody's chops.

We've really fine-tuned our cleanup. We can get it down to two or three minutes. In the control room, they've been known to time us. We can take down the inside and outside of the scoreboard quickly. By that time, we've been in there three or four hours and we're ready to get out of there.

Years ago, Bert Blyleven was pitching and when we went to dinner, he switched all the plates on the outside of the board. It was all screwed up. About the third inning, we started putting up the scores. We can't see the outside. We have a notebook telling us what plates we'd put in which positions. Of course, it was all wrong. We got a call from some guy yelling, "You guys have it all wrong." We just kept hanging up. Well, it turns out it was Haywood Sullivan, who was visibly upset. My boss called and said, "Don't hang up! Don't hang up!" So in front of 30,000 we had to go out with the ladder and switch all the plates. As we're bringing the ladder in everybody's jeering and yelling at us, everybody in the California Angels dugout were doubled over in laughter. The next time the Angels were in town Bert Blyleven came out with a big smile on his face and asked if we had ever made any mistakes. We knew right away who did it. But that's good fun. Griffey did that one time, too – switched some of the plates on the outside.

RICH MALONEY
Scoreboard Operator

I'm a production manager for Standard and Poor's. I'm not at every single game, but I'm probably at 85% of them. I've been working in the scoreboard for about 10 years now. It started as a homework assignment. Sophomore year in college at BC, in public relations class, the assignment was to write a letter to someone that you wanted their job. So I wrote to Dick Bresciani at the Red Sox. I neglected to say that it was a homework assignment so I think he thought I had a lot of initiative and offered me a job in the Wall.

It doesn't make sense for the money...but I grew up around here. I'm a Red Sox fan. It's a great job.

How long I'll keep doing this, I don't know. There's a thousand people that want this job. I could probably make more money sub-letting the job out!

If it's a big game, they let the left field scoreboard post the scores first. They call down to us. They want to make it sort of old school.

I used to go to games. You always knew someone was back there, but you never noticed it. I can't remember being at a game and actually looking at the scoreboard. Two years ago, I took a game off and actually got to go to the game. It was the game Jay Buhner caught the ball and dove into the bullpen. I just looked at the scoreboard the whole game. I knew Chris was back there by himself.

The Green Monster is metal so it retains heat or cold. The beginning of the season, it is definitely cold. If it's hot for a few days in a row, it's hot back there. If you get one day where it's not that hot, then it's actually cooler back there than it is outside.

The night Nomar had three home runs, two grand slams, I'm inside the Wall on a cellular phone negotiating a deal for the first house I ever bought.

A lot of ballparks are bringing back manual scoreboards. I think they can benefit from some design ideas. The first thing I would do is improve the sight lines. You almost have to guess that you're putting them in the right slot. When you're trying to put the numbers up, you're obstructed. There's beams and poles and everything. In the 3rd and 6th innings when you're trying to put numbers up, you have to duck. You hit your head. 3, 6 and 10, have beams right over the slots. The area we work in definitely wasn't designed with comfort in mind. Some 20th century plumbing might be nice, 21st century, I guess.

ROBERT TEBBETTS
Boston City Policeman

I'm Officer Robert Tebbetts. Like Birdie Tebbetts, the old catcher for the Red Sox. I spell my name the same way. No relation.

I've been on the force 29 years, doing details at Fenway since 1970, when I first came on. Each division handles its own area details. I could probably go to three or four games a week if I wanted to.

Captain Cellucci is usually in charge. He's from District Four. It's the same spelling as the Governor and, as a matter of fact, he makes more than the Governor. How do you like that?

There's an early shift and a late shift. The early shift shows up two hours before the game. The next shift shows up an hour before the game. We have roll call by the customer service booth, you find out what your assignment is for the game. After the game, I'm going to have a traffic post at Boylston and Ipswich. After the eighth inning, I'll go out, put on my traffic belt and pull whatever traffic I can. I stay until most of it clears out and when it lightens up, I go home.

I'm a patrolman. That's where you start and sometimes that's where you end. That's alright. I could have been a detective twenty years ago if I'd wanted to be, but I worked in a tough area and I knew if I walked around in plainclothes on a regular basis, I'd be a target.

We are not linked into the security system at the park here. If security wants us, they will come up to any officer out here and direct us to the problem. We can get on the radio and ask for more assistance if we need it. Then we just converge and take out the problem.

The Fenway security people canvass the park with binoculars on a regular basis. Anyone who might be causing disruption, they'll respond to.

You have to watch the stands and you also have to keep your eye on what's happening under the stands. It depends on the type of crowd. Usually the crowd from New York is the most rowdy. Surprisingly enough, a lot of the New York crowd are police officers! For the most part, they're just loud. But we never know when they're going to go off on a tangent.

Alcohol is the biggest problem. They serve so much beer out here, a lot of times they're not sure when to shut people off. It's hard to tell just by looking at someone.

Fairly regularly, you can get through an evening without any trouble at all. It depends on how heavily some of the younger group drinks. If they get intoxicated and obnoxious, they get ejected from the park. If they go overboard and hurt someone or themselves, they go either to the hospital or to the police station. If somebody runs out on the field, it's an automatic arrest.

I remember more than one occasion where someone's died in the seats here. Yeah, keeled over, cardiac arrest. You go down and try to resuscitate them, pick them up, rush them out, bring them to the EMTs. Later on, they say, "Well, he didn't make it." It's kind of sad.

Some women have gone into labor here, but I never saw the end results of that. That's kind of a nice happening.

Sometimes I get the wives and families section. Section 21. Right behind home plate. I got to talk to Mo Vaughn's mother and father. I've met his girlfriend. I met Tim Wakefield's girlfriend. I've talked to a lot of people over there, I don't know exactly who they are because they don't say, "Oh, I'm related to this one or that one." I just make conversation with them.

It's a leg breaker. You stand up all night. Your feet bother you. Your back bothers you. They don't really say that you can't sit down for a half an inning but they like to see you on a regular basis where you're assigned. Visibility. So if you leave, you only leave for a short time and then you go back to your post. Otherwise, these guys with the binoculars – the regular security – they'll say, "Where's the officer in section 3 or 4? I haven't seen him for an hour or so."

When you first get assigned to Fenway Park, they throw you in the bleachers. A baptism of fire, something like that. Then you get into better sections. I've worked almost every gate they have, every section with a few exceptions. They have a man in the ticket office, a man in section 21, all the gates. They increase the number when New York comes.

I didn't come here as a kid. I've worked most of my life. I started pulling groceries when I was eight or ten years old. Then I sold newspapers in Scollay Square. I used to go into the old burlesque shows – they were mostly just vaudeville – but I'd take a little peek.

You can always tell when they win or when they make a run. The crowd just roars. One night I was working a detail about a half a mile from here, at Ruggles Street and Parker Street. There was a game here and I could hear the roars from Fenway Park, all that distance. I could feel the enthusiasm a half a mile away.

Robert Tebbetts
PHOTO BY BILL NOWLIN

SGT. BRIAN FLYNN
Boston City Policeman

I don't think Bobby's ever taken the sergeant's test. Some guys just want to be a patrolman all their lives. The thing is, he'd be an excellent detective. He's got a good mind. I wouldn't want Bobby on my tail if I was wanted!

I've been working for the Boston Police for 26 years. I'm originally from Boston, but now I live in Quincy. I was born in the Mission Project, then I got rich and moved to Dorchester [laughs].

We used to go to Fenway and sneak into the games. Gates B and C had fences that only went up so high. Now they have barbed wire above. We used to cause a distraction over to one side to keep the ticket takers – they didn't have security guards then – and we'd just climb the fence and run into the crowd.

Or you'd sneak in early and hide. Stand on a toilet in the men's room stall. A couple of hours before game time, you could climb a fence, no one would be on the other side. Or you could go and beg money. At that time, I think it was fifty cents to get into the bleachers. Even if you didn't make it, they'd open the gates after the sixth inning or so.

Do you remember the Italian guys in the bleachers? It was incredible. They bet on every pitch. There was a story about them in LOOK or one of those magazines at the time. You could see the money going up and down the line. There were between 20 and 30 of them. Some in the row in the back weren't participating, they were just learning. They had hand signals and all this stuff. These were all the bookies in the North End that had already done their day's work. They weren't there taking bets from the public. It was just within themselves.

I always wanted to be a cop because I got two uncles that were cops. In those days, you had to do a strength test, vault a six-foot thing, lift a dummy that weighed 150 pounds and climb up a ladder with it and stuff. One of the first things they did was measure you. We were told they were going to measure us with our sneakers on so I had wedges under my heels. But they said, "Shoes and socks off." They had had a 5'9" height requirement. I'm only 5'7" so for five years, I couldn't get on. In fact, I benefited from the outreach for minorities, because they threw out the height requirement to get women. I got on the job in '74.

For eleven years I worked for a company that built exhibits for trade shows. I took a cut in pay to take the job with the Police Department, but I knew the opportunity was there to make more money in the long run. Plus, coming from the city, you wanted a stable job where you wouldn't get laid off. You wanted the pension. You were guaranteed – or you thought you were guaranteed – job security.

I arrested a Catholic priest once. The priest was driving under. He almost drove two teenagers off the back of the cliff on Mission Hill. He called the police himself, he said, "I called you so you'd do the right thing." I said, "I will, Father. Put your hands behind your back."

We were looking for him anyway. They wanted to force him into rehab. It just happened to work out. We had been hoping to get him, because he needed help badly. He was suspended from his priestly duties. He couldn't say Mass anymore. He did go into the rehab, but then he was diagnosed with cancer. He came out of rehab and went to a hospital, but he never came out. It was ironic – the kid he hit was a nephew of Cardinal O'Connor from New York. If the Archdiocese had complained about me, I'd have another heavy hitter with me.

This year I've been doing fairly good on details. If there's a homestand, I'll get one or two games. I'll probably end up doing 20 games, maybe 24.

They know where the trouble spots are. They like to have the sergeants available at the top of one set of stairs going into the bleachers, or down underneath. There's usually two sergeants for the bleachers, and one of us will be right near the entrance to Gate C and one will be up – not too far – in the stands. If they need us we'll escort someone out, or quiet down some trouble.

In the old days, we used to have someone standing at the top of every aisle against the wall. They only do that now during the Yankee games. I like that. Just being up there, you do away with a lot of trouble. The visible presence stops a lot of garbage. If a fight breaks out, you've got the top position. You can see from above. Now with the no smoking ban, people come up to the back to smoke. Sometimes regular cigarettes, sometimes not so regular cigarettes.

I get to watch a fair amount of the game, but you have to watch the people. A lot of the problems are between innings, people coming back and forth, spilling beer on everybody. One of the biggest problems began when they made the bleachers reserved and the busloads come in. They're half in the bag when they get there, and by the sixth inning some people can't even stand up. They're obnoxious. The language is foul. You don't want to bring a family over there and have your kids listen to the F word every other word. Even some of the chants.

I saw a guy take a real bad fall. He split his head open. Just drunk. He leaned on someone in front of him and that person wasn't there. He had an aisle seat. Nothing broke his fall. It cut from just above the eye to maybe three inches back behind the hairline, fractured his skull.

It isn't unruly fans screaming and yelling. It's the violence. They'll start a fight with little kids sitting right beside them. Something's going to have to be done or they're going to start losing families at the ballpark. It's better than five or six years ago, though. I can remember one game, right after the National Anthem some clown stood up and yelled, "We're from Vermont/And we do what we want!" Before he even finished, two kids sitting behind him whacked him – both at the same time. There was a huge fight. It turned out that there were University of Vermont buses down, and sitting right beside the sections were Salem State or Fitchburg State, one of those groups. A pitch hadn't been thrown yet, and there was a fight!

One night two sixteen year old girls are flashing themselves. Lifting up their shirt. What does that have to do with cheering for a baseball game? And the girl on the dugout? Were you there the night the girl on the dugout – the pro – got up and did an absolute lewd dance? On the Red Sox dugout. She didn't have much on to begin with, and she was very suggestive, licking her fingers after touching herself. It wasn't a case that they just threw her out. They had to go and get complaints against her in court the next day. She didn't understand what the big deal was. People actually wanted to hit her, when the cops were arresting her and taking her out, because of what she was doing in front of their little kids.

The last game I worked, I was standing at Gate A and three Irish kids come up and said, "Officer, tell us something. This is just a hypothetical. What if someone went on the field and just showed the tricolor? What would happen?" I said, "You will be arrested, and you will pay a hefty fine, probably about $500.00, at Roxbury Court." They said, "No. Really." I said, "Really! I'm not kidding you. I'm telling you, you're going to pay a heavy fine, and maybe on top of that, some court costs. So give it a thought." I said, "I don't think you have to convert too many people in Boston to the Irish cause, so I don't know why you have to run out with the Irish flag."

Everyone that they throw out, those security guards fill out a card. If they get a repeater up in Roxbury Court, that will go before the judge, and the fine will go up. Since they started using the college kids, it seems to be a lot quieter. I'll tell you, there's a lot less physical stuff we have to do because of them.

The guys who work security for the park are good. Years ago, there used to be a lot of BU football players, and a lot of them were too physical. They've weeded that situation out. Most of the guys who work there are pretty decent people. Even though people are being obnoxious and stuff, they're still human beings and fellow citizens. They're not Public Enemy #1. So you gotta be a little bit compassionate. I mean, granted we shouldn't have to put up with their behavior because they're drunk, but most of them don't know what they're doing, when they're doing whatever they're doing.

If you've got the bleachers, you have to wait until everyone's out. A lot of the people want to go over to the red seat and take a picture at the end of the game. It's like closing up a bar. They put out the lights and stuff like that. They want you to walk up to the top and say, "Let's go, folks."

JONATHAN MANDEVILLE
Fan who ran on the field

Boston Police do have to deal with the occasional fan who runs onto the field during a game. David Cataneo tells a story in his book TONY C. On his first day back at Fenway Park, in 1969, Tony was in right field when a young man "darted out of the grandstand and shook Tony's hand. 'It's nice to have you back, Tony,' the young man said. 'You're the only reason I'm here today.' 'You won't be here much longer, kid,' Tony said, as stadium cops hurried across the grass toward them."

On August 3, 1999, a fan ran out on the field and "stole second base," pulling it out of the ground. He ran around a bit, handed the base to a security guard, and unsuccessfully tried to escape. Dickie Boynton commented, "They should throw him in a dumpster, for Christ's sake. Throw him in a dumpster."

It wasn't easy to find out who he was, but the fan proved to be Jonathan Mandeville, 17, of Fairhaven. His grandmother told me, "I don't know what to make of that incident. He still doesn't know that I know. I'm kind of strict. I don't want him to think that he can get away with things like that. My husband was one of the biggest fans you ever heard. He just loved them. I told my son, I says, 'If Daddy was here, he'd probably get a big kick out of it.' My husband would have loved to have been on that field. It was on a dare, as I understand it. Friends he was with dared him to get to second base. He had to do some community service. He was dying to tell me, but I think his father told him not to."

On Opening Day, 2001, Jonathan seemed to show little regret.

One of my friends was talking about how cool that would be to get out there and just look around at 30,000 people and see what it's like. I have the reputation of being the kid who does that kind of stuff. One of my friends dared me a hundred bucks to do it.

It was the biggest adrenalin rush – the most fun probably ever. Just turning and looking around, it was the best thing ever!

I think it was Alomar at second...just looking at them, they're so big, it's like, Wow. I'm only 5' 8". These superstars get millions of dollars and I'm standing right beside one of them.

The cops were very polite and nice. The cop that actually brought me down to the police station said, "Wow, if I was 17 and had balls the size of yours, I would probably try something like that, too. Congratulations." He said, "You're going to be famous for the night." And I said, "Thanks." They were all very nice.

I was detained at the police station for about an hour. Twenty dollars bail. I had that in my pocket and I covered that and got out. I had to go to court the next day and the magistrate said, "Son, you can't be doing things like this. You'll get yourself in trouble." And I said, "All right" and he let me go.

It might have been stricter if I'd been 18. I hadn't had anything to drink. I told the judge there was no disrespect, I wasn't trying to harm anybody. I wasn't trying to destroy anything, I'm 17, I pulled a prank, I'm sorry. He forgave me. I was lucky I got off.

My grandfather was a huge Red Sox fan. Huge. He was actually in the minor leagues for the Red Sox. Albert Mandeville.

VORAVUT RATANAKOMMON
Security Officer

I was born in Thailand and came to this country when I was three.

I live in an apartment with two other people who work at Fenway and another person who works at the New England Aquarium. We all are very busy, at two or three jobs. There was a stretch where I didn't see Jay [White] for a good month and a half. I saw him at the game once in a while, but not at home, with our different schedules, relationships and stuff like that. Usually I'm at a bar watching an away game. Jay's always at the stadium.

I'm a security officer. We have supervisors and officers; that's about it. There's never anything really distinguishing except for the costume we wear. Dave Brady is my supervisor. Above him is Stephen Corcoran, and above him is Mr. McDermott. I started in 1996, at the beginning of the season.

I think they do a pretty good background check. There's some people you feel they should have done more of a check on, but I think they're pretty thorough. They get a pretty good sense of you after the first couple of games that you work, if you're going to be staying on for a while or not.

The first day I was there, I got the infamous elevator. Elevator operation. Basically, you sit there and you press the button and the elevator goes up and down. The very first day I got on the field, at deep right. There's usually a security officer there, just seeing if anybody was going to jump over the fence to grab a ball or anything like that. Before the game and during the game. It was awesome, to be right there at Fenway Park on Opening Day when all the players come on the field. It was amazing. Then on the field after the game. I was on the elevator some in the middle of the game.

That first year was such a mixed bag. People were fluctuating a lot – we had a staff of sometimes just 12 people up to maybe 60 people. They saw me there every day. I worked out in the bleachers every once in a while. I did the ramps – sometimes I was the ramp supervisor that goes down and turns around like from section 17 all the way up to 24. You just walk all the way to the bump, turn around and hang out at the ramp. I've done the Pit, which is the entrance to the 600 Club. I've opened the gates, at Gate A. That was excellent. Pull the chains to raise the grates. Of course, being a rookie, you didn't know you needed gloves and you'd pull the chains with your bare hands and then you'd have to stand there the whole entire beginning of the game with greasy palms. All the gates. Checking people, checking bags, greeting people as they pass by. The no can/no bottle policy sometimes gets really stringent.

Voravut Ratanakommon
PHOTO BY BILL NOWLIN

We had our up-front [orientation] meeting last week. We had about 80 show up. Security and ushers. Then we separate and the Aramark staff comes after us. They have like the bomb speech. The safety speech. What role we have at the stadium. How we should present ourselves. What we should wear. It hasn't changed since I was there. They still have the same speech. Same slides. They did it up in the staff dining room. This year we actually got to sit in the press box, which was pretty cool. We did the TEAM program – we got a little quiz on alcohol management. That was really a nice treat for us, because we don't usually get a tour. They want us to get to know the place a little bit more. The first year I didn't know where anything was.

We do our patrol every half an inning, to try to get good coverage and see anything suspicious. I saw THE FAN. A lot of people come through there. It varies. I work at Downtown Crossing currently and sometimes I see people who come down here to panhandle as fans at Fenway.

They tell us that we are the Red Sox. We are the closest thing that most people come to the Red Sox, so we should give a good image. Clean. Well-polished. The Friendly Fenway motto.

They supply the jacket – only for game time, though. Once a year we get a pair of sneakers that Reebok usually supplies us, because they were the supplier of the Boston Red Sox. I'm not sure what we're going to do this year.

There was no after-season party last year. They said there had been some problems. We weren't really sure. Rumors fly, as with anything else – in terms of they didn't do as well as they thought they'd do. It was a big, big shock for people. It was a really nice event. A great party.

I got to talk to people I don't usually get to talk to – even the ushers. They're working. Or you're working at the same time. It was excellent. There were a couple of years I heard that a couple people maybe had too much to drink and went out on the field. I was never there long enough to witness that. I would have my drinks and my food, and exchange pleasantries – usually, it was after a game and you'd be really tired.

We're required to show up an hour and a half before the game. At least an hour and a half. We have some people that come in four hours before. Some supervisors come in two hours before, depending. We just sign in. We gather in the stands right behind the visitors' dugout; that's where we usually congregate right before a game, to get our assignments.

They give us the one orientation and this huge packet of information, just to familiarize ourselves with the layout of the stadium, the rules, evaluations and things they feel you should know. There's the bomb packet, of course. Everything that they talked about will be in the package. Sexual harassment forms – because that's a very touchy subject right now, so there's a lot of information about that. We're not allowed to eat during the game.

Last year my primary job was to tell people not to smoke. You know that top section, along the top where the grate is? People love to smoke there. I had to patrol the whole back there to tell people not to smoke. It becomes a little tedious after a while. I used to do the alcohol-free section, 33, my third year.. It's not on the ticket, so you just try to inform people.

I never had any security work beforehand. They don't look for that. Back in earlier days – the 70s and early 80s – they would look for the biggest, the baddest, the bouncer kind. Now they're looking for the college-educated or in-college crowd, with more of the smarts than the brawn. They're trying to bring more women onto the staff.

Basically, the real conflict is more situational so it's more on the job [than something they train for.] If there was some real difficulty, I would usually call the head staff supervisor. They try to further evaluate it. Let's say it was a fight situation. They'll call the units that are needed and those units will gather up all the police necessary. I have a radio. Not everybody has them. Just the supervisors or the people that they feel...the people that have the unit numbers are the people that have the radio. Each unit is comprised of three people. The head of that unit gets the radio. We usually walk as a unit. If we stop, we'll stay closely together so that people know we're together.

[What do they tell you about bad language?] It's more like a three strikes, you're out. You have to assess the situation, to see what kind of state they're in. Just try approach them calmly and say this is a family atmosphere. There are a lot of children around. Can they please turn their language a little bit? Usually they're happy to oblige, because they know the consequences. Most people don't want to be kicked out, just for that. You have to understand. You get to the game. You're really into what the players are doing right now, and you forget where you are. In this culture and society, we think we're home.

[Agrees that most of the real problems come from excessive drinking.] Drinking is condoned. We serve the beer there. It's readily available, but the long lines do deter it. The beer sellers are really good. The people in my section, I know very very well – just working there all the time. You know when they shut down. They do so well that sometimes they want to shut down early. They just want to go home. They'll call one of us if there's a fake ID or something, and we in turn will call a Boston Police officer or anybody with arresting power to come and look at it.

We have incident forms we have to fill out. We describe what happened, the time and circumstances, any eyewitnesses that you have, things like that. I saw one really serious fight, up on the right field roof. You know how precarious it is up there. The fight started on the top of the roof and started to come down closer and closer to the edge of the roof. The participants were pretty battered up there because there's also a lot of poles and protective gear. That was pretty bloody.

A lot of fans have come up and told me how much better it is now. They'll say I was here ten years ago and some incident happened and I never came back, but now that I hear it's Friendly Fenway...especially the first year that they unveiled the Friendly Fenway program, they were like, Wow, we came back we really see a commitment to it.

People do get hit by bats and balls. We had an incident my sophomore year there. I was working there down by Canvas Alley. I turned around when this ball was hit and this woman was talking and wasn't facing the field, and the ball came and she actually turned into it and hit the ball with her nose. She really broke it. It was such a bloody mess, it was awful. Of course, we never found the ball for her. We try to do that, but of course if you get hit with the ball, it's the least of your concerns. Canseco one time let off a bat and it went right into the stands. He requested it back. We'll call the EMTs and they'll come down swiftly. We have a couple of people on staff who are trained to just handle the preliminary stuff – put pressure on contact.

There are rules about physical contact with the customers. Definitely. Like our average mall security guard, we don't have authority from the Boston Police to arrest people – which is to stop people. We have the power to observe and be a member of the Red Sox organization, so we can have other units secure them. There are a lot of Boston Police there, and that's why they're there.

I remember a couple of years when I first went there as a fan, hearing the stories of how back in the older days when there were more of the aggressive, brute type of security guards who would just bring you downstairs and pummel a little justice into you before they hand you over to the police. We don't have a holding facility. It's zero tolerance. They just go out of the stadium. There's no ifs, ands or buts. Gate D is the popular place of choice [to eject people from the park.]

They have the wagon on call. Headquarters is so nearby. There are more problems at night games than at day games, except for the day games that are on a holiday, when people have had a little chance to drink something before they come in. Night games usually are a little worse. The cover of night alone calls for less families to come in.

There are some nice stories. That's the reason I go back there. It's almost on a daily basis. Where I work, I also help the handicapped to their seats. They've expanded those areas, and pulled rows out just to accommodate. Groups come back and they remember you. I help people out all the way to their car. We provide wheelchairs within the stadium, so I'll just drop them off.

If they don't fill those seats up, they do sell the standing room. We might provide a chair so they can sit down. The stadium hasn't really grown, but the population...people have gotten bigger over the years because of better diets...well, maybe not better but more and different diets. Sometimes for folks who are bigger than their seats, we'll need a bigger seat so we usually put them upstairs. They'll be more than obliged to give you a tip. There's a lot of positive feedback all the time. Friendly Fenway, they can see it; it's working. You're encouraged to smile, and be courteous and just add that little touch of customer service that I think is lost. I've been myself to 13 major league baseball stadiums, just to observe, to see what other people do. To see the game, and have a hot dog here and there. Fenway does have a different attitude within, because people come to see Fenway itself sometimes and not even the game. It has a strange aura. You see people walking by, saying Oh my god, I've come all the way from China or all the way from Europe. I've heard of this place and I just want to see it.

Every after half inning we go down to the box seats and stand by the field. That's more of the presence. It's very, very effective. Nobody knows how many security are there, because we do have a very fluctuating staff. But you see them there. There are a number of cameras there. They cover some of the areas that you can't see, especially upstairs where there are hallways where nobody is standing there. Nobody knows where the monitors are. We call it the "wizard of Oz room." It's usually Joe

[McDermott.] I've personally never seen it, but we've always heard of it. It's a possibility [there isn't one. It's possible they just tape, in case there's a problem, but don't display on monitors.]

The people that run out on the field, we ask all the police officers they usually tell you the same thing. A fine, maybe a night in jail. But nobody really knows what the truth is. I've never spoken to anyone after the fact who's been caught.

When there's a fight, you don't know what the situation's going to be. You don't know the complexity of the fight. It could be one person, two people, three people. It could be a whole group of people on one person. So the best thing to do is to come and show that you have presence. With the uniforms, we're pretty distinctive and you can tell even from behind home plate you can look at the bleachers and you can see that there's masses of white shirts or blue shirts – depending on what outfit we're wearing that day – going to one location and that kind of gives you reassurance. That is a technique that's been employed. There's a lot of psychology involved in security today and I think they've employed it a lot at Fenway. Presence is a very important thing. They're less likely to do a crime if somebody sees you there. Sees that you're watching. You're looking around. Going in front of all the crowd and just turn around and look up. You're usually not looking at anything, but people see that you're there and there's somebody looking up there.

Every once in a while, you get a little abuse. It's a service job. It's a security job. A lot of people think that this is our only job, so we get the old mall security jokes like, "Why don't you get a real job?" But we know better. Most of those kids there are very well-educated. This is like their fun job. They don't do it because of the money. They do it because they love the game and they love the place that they work at.

We do not make court appearances. Only the supervisors. They usually will vouch for us. We try not to get to that situation. In my five years, I haven't heard of a member of our staff going to any court appearance.

I think with Fenway a lot of people feel it's such a special place. I call the baseball fields of America – and expecially Fenway – I call them churches. Fenway is almost like the Vatican City for a lot of people. My girlfriend calls it Graceland for her. She's from western Mass and it's the supreme place to go. It has a strange mystique to it. You can't put your finger on it. We know it's old. We know it's crumbling. We know all these things about it but, still, people are so attracted to it.

Boston in itself is a great city. There's so much of the past here. Downtown Crossing, there's a cemetery right there. You can drink a Sam Adams and he's buried right there. Working at Fenway just adds to it. Everybody's eyes just light up when you say, "Oh yeah, I work at Fenway." A lot of people have been working there a lot longer than I have, and the same question pops up, "Why do you keep working here?" "I love this place." Where else can you work and meet all these people and have all these experiences? You're rubbing elbows with every single economic class, and everybody is into one thing, and that's to watch baseball. I wish the world was more like that.

MARK SWEENEY
Former Crowd Control Supervisor

I was never a big baseball fan. It was just a good job. I used to go back to school and my roommate was a diehard baseball fan, and he'd ask, "Who won?" I'd say, "Red Sox." He'd say, "What was the score?" I'd say, "I don't know." He'd say, "Who did they play?" "I don't know." He'd say, "How do you know they won?" I'd say, "I got home 15 minutes earlier because they didn't have to play the bottom of the ninth."

I always thought it was an advantage for me that I didn't really care about baseball. I was the only one who was at Fenway Park when Bucky Dent hit the home run that didn't see it. I was out setting up the World Series tickets.

I started the first home stand in '76. There was some police action going on, a slowdown – they weren't going to do details or take overtime.

I was from Brookline. My father worked at Fenway during World War II. He was too young to go to war, and he worked on the ground crew for a couple of years. He worked with Al Forester and some of those guys, and when my younger brother Peter wanted to work at Fenway for a summer job, my father went in and was able to get him on.

I worked five years. I worked until '80. It's been over twenty years since I left and I still put it on my resume. When people see that on there, that I worked at Fenway Park, I still get a call every resume I send out!

At the time, it was only ten bouncers...guys. I say "bouncers" because it's easy for people to understand what we were doing. We wore gray slacks and blue blazers. We were called "blue-coats." I was the fourth one hired, and the first supervisor.

I guess you could call it an infant department – yes, and infantile! (laughs)

Before us, they relied entirely on the Boston Police and private security from Ogden. They mostly just did stationary stuff, work the gate. There were 40 police a game. There were still police there; they just wouldn't go up into the stands. It was getting to the point where they had to get somebody to become proactive instead of reactive. They were having trouble with the liquor license. Too many fights. They were still serving 22-ounce beers in the stands then! They'd take a 24-rack of 22s out and it was real beer. It wasn't light beer then. They'd sell it in a paper cup with a plastic top – like a Saran Wrap top. It was right after one of the judges in Boston had a fight break out right in front of him – about a week later that the state decided they couldn't have beer in the stands any more.

Instructions to us? They mainly told us take the drunks and throw them out. And don't get hurt. And the "don't get hurt" got thrown out pretty quick, too. They were awfully good to us, though. A lot of the kids went on to do pretty well. It was an easy job to sell the guys, to want to work.

Most of the trouble we had was with people who drank too much. The people who were smoking marijuana were so worried about getting arrested, you just walked up and said you have to leave, and they'd just walk out. Nobody was frisking them or trying to take anything off them or anything. They'd just walk out. The drunks were a pain, though.

We got hurt sometimes – stitches, mostly, and bruises – from being punched. Face, arms...I've had a lot of stitches; I didn't get any at Fenway, but I had guys that worked for me that did. I saw someone pull a knife once – it was just a drunk – but only one time in five years. It was pretty rare.

Nobody that worked for me ever got reprimanded for excessive use of force. There were lawsuits. Everybody got sued at least once. In the whole time I did it, they only got sued once, in five years. That was a kid from Norwell or Norwood. He broke his arm when he got thrown out and he sued. You know the garage gates? That are made out of real steel? Once you start one of them coming down, you can't really stop it. This kid got thrown out. We used to throw them out and then pull the door down. This kid decided he was going to run back in and just ran into the gate. He claimed somebody hit him with it and he decided to sue, and he got like $9000.00 to go away. In all the time I was there, I only went to one real trial.

By the time I left, we had 21 guys a game. They all reported to me. I would go around to the colleges and interview them, hire them and bring them in. The guys in crowd control were agents of the Red Sox. They could order somebody off the property and the cop would have to enforce it. You really wouldn't do much without a cop being there. And the cops were always scrounging for souvenirs, so it was easy to make friends with them and make sure that there was one around.

Representative Blute from Worcester was a Fenway Park crowd control guy. Peter Blute. When we hired them, it was all physical strength. That was all did. It was all physical. And smarts. I was as small a guy as they could hire. I'm just under 6 feet. At the time, I was 220. I hired guys that were 6'8", 6'9". I turned down kids with criminal records. Dumb was worse than rough. Nobody really was ever that rough. There was one guy...I had to get rid of one or two guys, out of maybe 60, that were just too rough. The key was to have more of us than them.

I was always there, from 9 AM to at least midnight. After the game, you'd start out in the bleachers. You'd toss everybody out – I mean walk everybody out – and then they would lock the gates out there first. Then they would just walk in and check all the bathrooms and everything on the way in. You'd check everything. You'd find people trying to hide out standing on the toilets inside the bathrooms; they did it all the time. When I was a kid, I'd snuck in myself. I still have Dick O'Connell's keys to the park. I haven't tried them, though.

We didn't have anybody who stayed after it was closed up. The cleaners used to lock up. We used to have a tape that would play, out at all the gates – a tape that had dog noises on it. The "dog" could go from one gate to another all night. It was one of those things where you could make a tape and have it just play over and over again on a loop. It would be silent for five minutes and then the dog would bark.

When the JFK [Navy ship] came into town, we sent 500 bleacher tickets over to the boat, for the sailors. They had this kid – they got him stiff! They stripped him down and they ended up throwing him into one of the troughs, one of the urinals. He was passed out. They got a sheet for him, brought him down to the ground crew room, gave him a ground crew uniform. As he started to figure out what kind of trouble he was in, he was all upset because he couldn't get back on the JFK [by now, it was after curfew.] It turned out that the captain of the JFK was still up in the press lounge. Tommy McCarthy used to pour drinks up in the press room. So we called Joe McDermott. McDermott went to the captain, and the captain brought the kid back in his car and the captain walked right onto the ship with no problem!

The other sailors couldn't figure out how this kid got back on the ship, with no uniform – no clothes and no I.D.

There were lots of nice stories. We used to take all the lost kids and bring them down the service gate and let them get autographs. I don't know if they still do that any more. I think the kids caught on to that after a while!

Usually people want to hear the bad stories! I haven't told a good one for a long time! I think people would be surprised at just how good everybody was. The players were great. Jim Rice was unbelievable with kids. I was at the game where his bat broke and hit a little kid. It was a sellout. Everybody stood up and you couldn't get the stretcher from the nurse's station down to where the kid was, and Jim Rice just walked over to where the kid was and picked him up and carried him through the clubhouse and up to the nurse's station.

I used to be up in the press room a lot, either working something or having a drink. It was a whole different game. I got a call one time from Haywood Sullivan one time, around Thanksgiving. Once the season was over, we didn't get tickets to start selling again until Washington's Birthday. That's changed, probably around '78 or '79. So we were all standing around in the ticket office trying to figure out where to go to lunch and about 11 o'clock Haywood Sullivan called me and asked me to go up to his office. So I went up and he said, "OK, I want you to go across the street and get some sandwiches." I was like, "Oh, OK." I went back to McDermott's office and I said, "Hey! He wants me to run out for sandwiches. I'm a college graduate!" And McDermott says, "Yeah. And he's the owner of the team. And when he tells me to go for sandwiches, I go for them. So go get the damn sandwiches!"

I got the sandwiches across the street at the Batter's Box. When I came back, we ended up going into Mr. Yawkey's bar, which was in the executive offices. Haywood Sullivan was the bartender. Buddy LeRoux – who didn't drink – was there. Jim Oliver, who was the treasurer. Joe McDermott. And me. Just sat there for a couple of hours and had a few beers and some sandwiches. It was pretty cool.

A lot of times I stayed there all night. In '78 when they had bought the World Series tickets and delivered them to the ticket office. I got two games' pay to spend the night there. I would get there at 9 in the morning and work until the game. Then I'd go on game pay and work the game. After the game, I'd run across the street and get a sandwich down at the sub shop that was next to Copperfield's. I'd go back in and spend the night on the couch in the ticket office kitchen. The kids that came in on the ground crew would wake me up at 6:30 and I'd go home and take a shower and be back at work at 9. I did that for a week.

I will say one thing for the Red Sox. I went on my first business trip and they sent me on a first class ticket. I went to a baseball security meeting in Chicago. Everyone in baseball security gets together and talks about what they do and how they do it. Now I think it's all stadium security, not just baseball.

ROLAND JOHNSON
Scout

Baseball professionals are at work during the game as well. Scouts, umpires, coaches are all active during actual play. Scouts for other teams assess the teams at play, hoping to give their team an advantage in future competition, or to evaluate players for possible trades. Umpires have their own clearly defined functions. The coaches try to get the most out of their players, both offensively and defensively, during the game in progress.

I've been a scout for the New York Mets for seventeen years. Before that, I scouted for the Cardinals for ten years.

During the season, I have the Red Sox as one of the teams to cover. We're all responsible for a team that we have a chance of playing in the World Series or the playoffs. I was covering the Red Sox just in case we met them in the World Series. Other guys were covering the Yankees, Atlanta, Houston. I saw the Red Sox for 25 games [last year.] I saw a couple of series in Boston, I think in April, and then again in

July, and then I started covering them every single game on the 17th of September.

Even before interleague play, I scouted the Red Sox. We'll be scouting for trades. And of course, the World Series. We scout all the teams during the year. We have to have a report on every player in professional baseball. When they want to make a trade, they have to have reports on these players, so we have as many scouts scouting the American League as we do the National League.

I scout major league and minor league teams, mostly in the Northeast. Some scouts scout the whole American League. They travel wherever they have to go to see the American League teams play. I've traveled to the Dominican Republic, Venezuela, Puerto Rico. I was in Australia about ten years ago. Panama. Costa Rica. Mostly amateur scouting. I've seen some of the winter leagues in the Latin countries. They have their professional winter leagues so I've seen some of those as well.

We get to the park two to three hours before the game to watch batting practice. We might see something that would help us evaluate the players. I talk to the other scouts, but we don't give any secrets away. You talk a little bit. It's part of the game, another way of getting information. Oh yeah, there's a little disinformation, too. People will try to lead you on sometime. That's always a possibility, but with experience you get a feel for what's happening.

There could be four, five, six, eight scouts at a game. In September, there might be more because some of the scouts who scout high schools and colleges during the year may have some major league teams to do in September.

The last series against the Yankees, we had two people on each team. Two people on the Yankees and two on the Red Sox. The Braves were there, too, and had two on the Yankees and two on the Red Sox.

They give you seats behind the plate, so you're all generally together in the same section. I use the radar gun occasionally. I don't score the game, really. We're just taking notes on how they hit, how they pitch and their natural ability and do you think they're going to get better, that type of thing. What kind of a major league player you think they might be now and in the future, and if they can help your ballclub.

There are some organizations that have a laptop computer that when they advance the game, they put the information right on the computer at the same time. When a guy throws a pitch, they just touch certain areas of the computer. Toronto has that. But most of the time the laptop is done back at your hotel room or at home. I just have a notebook. I have cards that have four or five players on with a lot of room to write. You can grade their abilities – their hitting, running, and throwing – that type of thing. Guys do it different ways. Some just use blank paper or they have forms that they use. It varies by team or by scout.

When you're on the laptop, if you've written a report on a player previously, you can call that up and update it. If you haven't sent it in already, you can change it as you go along. There's a big data base from Major League Baseball that has information on all the players, so you don't have to put in their height and weight and bats L and throws R. That's in there already, all you have to do is grade the player and comment about his abilities, that type of thing.

All the organizations treat you pretty well, get you pretty good seats. You can go up to the press room after batting practice for a bite to eat. You can talk a bit before the game. There's information you can get, notes on the game, the lineups, stats up until that point.

After the game you write a report on the player and send it in to the office.

They might call you and tell you they want you to look at certain players. They'll say they want you to go somewhere and see a guy pitch or a guy play. Unless they call you you're just looking at the whole team. Basically, you'll watch a team for five or six games in a row if you can. You'll get to see their starting rotation, which is usually five guys, and you see a lot of the relievers as well. You might see them earlier in the year, in the middle of the year, then late in the year and then you have a better perspective on how some of the guys are improving or not improving, and some of the new players they might have acquired during the year.

You talk to media people, they have some insights on the club. You might talk to the coaches, even the manager on the club. You might ask them about a player that they played against, or something like that. Any ways of getting information you can. It all helps, you know.

We don't talk to the players, though, unless you know the guy from the past. A couple of guys on the Red Sox played with the Mets originally – Butch Huskey and Brian Daubach. You might talk to guys like that. Just to say hi. You wouldn't talk specifically about anybody on their team, or anything like that.

I park about a quarter of a mile from Fenway. A McDonald's parking lot, the money goes to the Ronald McDonald House. It's easy to get in and out. I stay out of town, but it's only about a twenty minute ride in. In New York, I'll stay downtown and take the subway to Shea or Yankee Stadium.

I don't usually file a postgame report on a particular game. You're just constantly keeping notes on the players. If they want information on a specific player, then you'd send it in immediately. Otherwise, they might not want your reports until the middle of the year. There's the trading deadline on July 31. They might want your reports before that, and then you might even update them later on in the year. You're basically assembling information, taking and updating notes.

I read a lot of papers, too. You never know what you're going to find in there. You'll hear about someone's upset with something. You'll keep mental or written notes on that. Again, any way you can acquire information. With computers now, you can look up newspapers when you're on the road. When I'm in Toronto, I can look up the BOSTON GLOBE and follow the Red Sox that way.

I do major and minor league scouting, a little bit of everything. I've got about a third major league and two-thirds minor league at this point. I used to do high schools and colleges. I just do professional scouting now, but I did the Cape Cod League for about twenty-five years.

I've been at all the levels for the Mets. I was the scouting director for seven years. I've been an area scout for the Cardinals. I've cross-checked players across the country, and I've scouted internationally. Now I've been doing professional scouting for the last three years or so. I'll probably be doing that the rest of my life.

Cross-checking is just comparing players in different areas of the country. We have area scouts that cover regions all over the country. One guy covers New England. One covers New York, New Jersey, Pennsylvania. Another guy covers California. He has players that he's interested in, but he doesn't know how his players compare to other players, so we send people out, how does the guy in New England compare with the guy in California? You want to put them all on a preferential list before the draft so you know how you want to select these players. They may have three or four different people look at the real good players throughout the year to determine who is better than who. He's not really second-guessing the area scout. He's just comparing the area scout's players against some other area scout's players. You're trying to put them in order so that you select the best players in the draft.

Scouts still sign players. Maybe the higher ones now, the money is so phenomenal that the general manager or the scouting director himself may get involved, but down the line, maybe after the first round, the scout signs the players.

I signed Andy Van Slyke. I was an area scout back then with the St. Louis Cardinals. As a scouting director or a cross-checker, you don't get as involved. The area scout, in most cases, signs the players.

I don't go to many games at Shea Stadium. I have to scout our club but I may only go to four or five games a year. They want us to scout the Mets so we can compare the other players to our players. They want us to see such and such a pitcher and be able to say how he compares with Al Leiter. Well, if I haven't seen Al Leiter, I can't compare him to Al Leiter. The guys who do the major league scouting want us to see our club as well, so we see them a little bit in spring training and we see them a little bit during the year as well.

JIM EVANS
American League Umpire

In Boston, the dressing room is antiquated. I love the ballpark, it's a very nostalgic, historical landmark but in all honesty some of the inner things have not kept pace with the times.

To get to the umpires' room, you go in the same door as if you were going into the Red Sox dressing room. We go up the stairs. It has a window air-conditioning unit. When I first came into the League in 1972, it didn't even have that. They refurbished our dressing room maybe eight to ten years ago.

I started umpiring when I was still playing at age 14, and would work the games I wasn't playing. I developed a keen love for umpiring. I have a degree in education from the University of Texas, and after I graduated, I decided to give the professional game a try and fortunately made it.

For a 7:05 game, I'll get there around 6. Usually, we travel as a crew of four. We all take the subway over together. We go to the service gate. They know us by face. A few fans, if they're loyal fans, and have been following the game, recognize some of us that have been around for a while. This is my 28th year.

We're there an hour before the game. If there are weather conditions, we talk to the groundskeeper. We're constantly in touch with the National Weather Service.

When we go out to take the field, we share the tunnel with the Red Sox. That's another unique thing in the older ballparks. The newer ballparks have a separate entrance for the umpires.

Every game is different as to when we take the field. The home team will give us the rundown on the pre-game activities. Some places they have the National Anthem before we come out, and some places after. It all depends on their pre-game programming.

We're not informed of new players called up. Almost every night, some new player will enter the game. It's not our responsibility to know who's eligible and who is not. In amateur ball, sometimes the umpires are responsible for determining who is eligible to play, but that is not our responsibility. If you put an illegal player in there, the other team has to bring it to the League office's attention.

At the beginning of the game, we exchange lineup cards and go over the ground rules and any other issue that needs to be addressed. If it's a three game series, you discuss them the first night and leave them out the next night. Usually, it's just casual conversation at the plate after the first night.

Fenway Park does have more unusual ground rules than other parks because of all the different angles and shapes of the field.

The flavor outside the ballpark at Fenway is unique, the vendors and all that. I think that's the nostalgic part of it. I'd hate to see them do away with that.

I've written a book on the rules of baseball, and many of the rules come from the old layouts. Like Fenway, the reason the fence is so tall is that there's a street right there and they had to build the ballpark to the configuration of the real estate. They had more real estate in right and center field, but it would have been such a cheap home run to left that they said, well, we'll compensate for it and build a higher wall. The cheapest home run, though, is down by the pole in right field. It's a fascinating park.

As umpires, we change our operating system when we're here. On every ball hit into the outfield, we have an umpire in the American League who goes out to watch for catch/no catch, fair or foul, or spectator interference. In this ballpark, we divide the responsibilities different because you can have a ball that might be a home run in some parks but they hold a guy to a single here. It'll hit high on the Wall and bounce right back to the left fielder and he can throw the guy out at second or hold him to first. So, rather than have the second base umpire go out on some of those balls, like we normally do, we'll have the third base umpire go out and that leaves the sec-

ond base umpire in position for any play at second.

There are certain parks where we'll modify our system but Fenway is the only one where we'll do it because of the play at second. In Seattle in the old ballpark, and in Baltimore they have a little area down in right field where the first base umpire cannot see the ball. The ball can go out of sight on a fly ball. So we have the second base umpire take responsibilities for some catch/no catch down there. Now, the first base umpire would still have fair or foul, since he's on the line, but if the ball took him over into that area out of sight of the first base umpire, then the second base umpire assumes that responsibility. You just adjust to the ballpark.

If there is a rain delay, we have an umpire in the dugout during the whole situation unless the rains are predicted for a long time and it's raining hard. Then we might go down and check on the field periodically. During a temporary delay, we'll have somebody monitoring the field at all times. That's my ultimate responsibility, whether to continue the game, suspend play, or call it. The others will go up to the room. I'll go up or I'll send a message with the bat boy and tell them, "OK, we're uncovering the field now."

There are security officers in each dugout if we need them. It's the nature of the job, you're going to have unruly fans from time to time.

You do feel the fans closer at Fenway. Some of the new parks are getting back to that, to bring the fans more into play, more into the action.

I fear that somebody's going to be killed with foul balls, the way these guys hit today. I've seen some major, major accidents and it just breaks my heart when I see a small child sitting, say, between first base and home plate, or third base and home. I've seen people hit right between the eyes. It just scares me to death. With parks like Fenway and some of your newer parks, people are seated very close.

I've been coming into Boston 28 years. The first couple of years, you usually do the touristy things. Right now I've got my school. I'm working on curriculum, plus I'm transferring my annotation to CD-ROM and doing a lot of revisions. Plus I just produced my first video training tape, on balks. The book is OFFICIAL BASEBALL RULES, ANNOTATED. The best way to find it is check out the web page. It's www.umpire.org.

We have a professional relationship with the groundskeepers, the players and everybody else. There have been a couple of ball boys or batboys that have ended up going to my umpire school. One a few years ago was from Boston, the nephew of one of the clubhouse guys. Maybe Vince Orlando, yeah. Wally McDougal. He came back and did a lot of amateur ball. They usually initiate it by asking questions like, "How do you become an umpire? It really looks like a fun job." Then you get others that say, "Man, I wouldn't want your job for ten million dollars a year!"

Jim lost his job as a major league umpire late in the 1999 season, when the umpires staged a mass resignation hoping to get the attention of Major League Baseball regarding a number of issues the umpires' union had. It backfired. The umpires were let go and others hired. Before the 2004 season, the Red Sox built a brand new umpires' room in a different area of the park.

WENDELL KIM
Third Base Coach

I arrive at least five hours before first pitch. My first job is to pull together the advance scouting reports and other information which we have on the opposing team and enter this into my computer. I then distribute reports to our players and coaches. These show the tendencies of players on the other team. For example, does the batter like a first pitch fast ball...such as Rafael Palmiero or Tino Martinez? Will he go opposite field? How deep should our outfielders play? When does Cito Gaston send the runners? We use these reports to help us with our strategy during the game.

When I'm finished with my "paperwork", I usually do some weight training, sit-ups, and exercises that will help me perform my on-the-field duties. Once the players are dressed, about

three hours before the first pitch, I lead the team in stretching exercises which takes about 20 minutes.

During the pre-game practice, I hit fly balls to the out-

Wendell Kim
PHOTO BY BILL NOWLIN

fielders and ground balls to our infielders. Then, I alternate with the other coaches in pitching batting practice. A typical batting practice requires throwing about 200 pitches.

I get there about 11 o'clock, for night games, but usually I have players coming out early and we go in the cage for two or three hours. It's a pretty small clubhouse in Boston so you get to see most everything. There's just something about Fenway, though. It does maybe bring the team together. We're like sardines in there so I'm usually standing up ready to go on the field. I'll let the players sit. I'm in pretty good shape, so I don't mind standing and Jimy Williams does a lot of standing, along with the rest of the coaches.

When I was with the San Francisco Giants for 24 years, I had a lot of jobs – minor league player, coach and manager, and since 1989 a major league coach with the big club. I have never appeared in a major league game as a player nor has my name been carried on a major league roster. I did play minor league baseball for seven years. My best year was in 1978 when I batted .313 playing for the Phoenix, the Giants' Class AAA team. I have played every position except pitcher and first base and have been selected as a Minor League All-Star.

We have a lot of National League coaches. Kerrigan came over from Montreal. Jimy Williams came over from Atlanta. Grady Little came over from San Diego and Atlanta, and I came over from the Giants. The Red Sox have their own scouting program, which I still enter into my computer, but I don't use it a whole lot unless they don't have a player in their scouting thing and I have something on them. I think we have a very good system and our advance scouts do a very good job.

I have certain things where, say, Billy Doran – he used to be with Houston. I knew when he was stealing. He would open his right foot just a tad and I knew he was going on that pitch. I would have information like that. Certain pitchers give away pitches by the way they hold the ball in the glove, or if they have it stomach high, they're coming to first base; if they hold it belt high, they're going to home plate. There's a lot of different things that they do, unconsciously. That helps me out to study what's going on.

A lot of the players don't want people seeing them work out so I take them in the cages back in center field, and we'll work on double plays, we'll work on some drills to get his set-up ready. You don't need a lot of room. You don't have to hit ground balls all the way from home plate to second base. If they're working on their backhand, you've just got to simulate it. You're just working on the basics so you get them back where they were before. Like Nomar, sometimes when he gets out of sync. He will take off his fielding glove, and in one hand he'll have a batting glove, and I'll roll him ground balls – straight to him, then to his left, then to his right. So basically he's getting his body positioned with his hands to be in the correct position to throw the ball. At the major league level, the pros, the veterans, all they need is to be reminded of what they've done correctly. That's all you have to do. The rookies take a little bit more; you have to work into it.

Jimy Williams and the other coaches and I will get together before every series, but not before every game. After the game, I'll get together with certain players that want me, maybe to look at their films. Jimmy Rowe will go and talk with Jimy about any injuries. I do it every day, too, with Jimmy, after the game and usually before a game, too.

I want to know who's hurt. Some of them won't tell you, and that screws me up because I think they're healthy and I know how fast they can run – they should be able to make it, and then they get thrown out by ten feet...I've got to

take the heat, even though it's not my fault. I'm not going to give up the player. I'm just not going to say anything.

These reporters in Boston, they're not the greatest guys. They only talk to me once I screw up and that's usually only once a year, maybe twice at the most. That's pretty good odds that I'm doing a decent job.

With signals, I'll go over them with the whole team and individually. These signs are not very difficult once you understand the indicator and sequence. For example, if tugging at the ear is the indicator and the sequence is the second sign, than the second touch after tugging the ear will be the instruction to the player as to what they should do. Everything which occurs before the indicator or after the second touch means nothing and is intended to prevent the opposing teams from stealing our signs.

I go over it with the whole team in spring training and then if we change them, I go over them again. I know which guys have problems. I will go out and check each guy and test him.

The decisions – to bunt, or hit and run, take a pitch – it's all from the manager. I relay the signs to the hitter. Sending the runner, that's my call. The score dictates whether you're going to gamble or not. Jimy is an aggressive third base coach. He'll come up to me, even though the runner did score later, and say, "You've got to be more aggressive." I've always been aggressive but I want to be under control. A lot of times in Fenway, people are afraid to go from first to third off that left field Wall. They're going to stop on their own. I'll get the heat because the guy drops the ball, but I didn't stop him. I know what I've done and people who know the game and see what's going on, they understand what happened.

The first base coach does have an easier time than the third base coach. You don't get that kind of criticism.

I always go over the other team's outfielders with our players. Guys like Jay Buhner with Seattle, he was hurting but he was still in right field. He couldn't throw very well, so we took advantage of that. Certain guys...like Justice on ground balls is very good at throwing runners out. On fly balls, he's not as good. That's up to me.

When the other team is batting and we're in the dugout, I will chat with some of the young players, like Sadler, and try to get them to read the pitchers, get them to read his moves.

Usually in the dugout these last three years, I would put where the defense is playing against certain of our pitchers to see if it coincides with the advance scouting report. I'm always double checking certain things. Things I would do early in the game, I would probably keep the same, but if it's later with the same pitcher I will adjust my outfielders, especially my centerfielder because that pitcher doesn't have his 95 mile an hour stuff anymore by the 5th or 6th inning. Some will; some won't.

I have my computer with me on the road. I'm writing my second book. I wrote a book for Little League coaches and parents back in 1996. My mom wants me to finish my book, how I got into baseball. Nobody wanted me, and I made it out of a tryout camp with 170-something guys trying out. I was the only one to make it, and I'm still going strong. It's now my 28th year. They said I would never play.

I was not Jimy's personal pick. Well; I was and I wasn't. Every manager that was interviewed with Dan Duquette in the winter of 1996; my name was brought up. Jimy Williams when he got picked, said; "Yeah. I'll take Wendell Kim." If Jimy didn't want me, I wouldn't be here. I understand that.

Some coaches have agents, I don't, I talk for myself. I think I'm one of the lowest paid third base coaches in baseball, but maybe it's my fault. I never said, "Hey, give me more money."

Would I like to manage a Big League team? Yes! Managing in the major leagues is a goal I want to achieve. I think I do a great job of communicating with today's players. I was named Manager of the Year twice in my minor league managing career.

People ask me why I run out to the coaching box, and run back in again. All my life I've battled as a player. It doesn't take ability to hustle. It shows a lot of enthusiasm and rubs off on the players. I get a lot of comments about this from the opposing team. I like to lead by example and my fellow coaches and players appreciate it.

CHAZ SCOGGINS
Official Scorer

I am a sportswriter at the LOWELL SUN. I've been doing official scoring at Fenway Park since 1978. I've scored over 1100 regular season games. As the primary, I do all the games that I want to do. If I can't make it, they have a backup.

There are very few writers who score any-

Chaz Scoggins
PHOTO BY ANDREA RAYNOR

more. I was kind of grandfathered. I convinced my newspaper that I didn't think it was a conflict of interest and they went along with it.

I actually starting scoring in college. I was a bench-warmer at what was then Lowell State College. I was on the baseball team, but I sucked. I started keeping the scorebook for something to do. Nobody taught me how, just trial and error.

A lot of people have the misconception that I work for the Red Sox. I don't, I'm an official of the American League.

The league has a form to fill out. It doesn't look anything like a scorebook you would keep. It's just a form with lines where you keep track. You just list the at bats, runs, hits, total bases, putouts, assists, stolen bases, caught stealing, that sort of thing. Keep track of batters faced by the pitchers. You just list the name – you put Daubach, he had four at bats, scored one run, had two hits, had a stolen base. Putouts, assists, hit by pitch. You have to do it in the order in which they hit, the batting order, and keep track of pinch hitters and all that.

You mail it in within 24 hours after every game. At this point, the official scoresheet is just the official record. They update the stats off the computer ahead of time. It gets done a lot quicker than waiting for the form to show up. They're faster than the speed of light when it comes to updating stats.

I usually try to get there about an hour before the game. I have a parking pass provided by the Red Sox. I usually have some dinner. Then a half an hour before the game I'll start preparing the scorebook.

The seat I have is in the front row of the press box. The first two seats in the front row are reserved for club officials. One's a PR person responsible for making announcements in the press box. I'm two seats down from there and I have my own microphone. The League doesn't want the PR person to make the announcements for you. They want you to make the scoring announcements on your own. It's piped into the radio booth and the PA booth. After it's relayed to him, the public address announcer may announce it. They'll also put it up on the scoreboard. After I've made the decision.

It's just keeping an actual and accurate account of the game. The only controversial thing is to call a hit versus an error. The official rule book is 104 pages long. Baseball is separated into ten basic rules. The first nine rules are accomplished in the first 74 pages. Rule Ten, the scoring rules, takes up 28 pages. It's complex and very complicated. It takes up more pages than any other rule in the entire book.

One of the reasons I sit where I do is that there's where the TV monitor is. Maybe once every three years, I go down to the TV booth between innings and ask them to play back a play. Other than that, I just see the same thing that anybody else would see. Of course, some replays are better than others, that's why I don't like to rely on the replay to make a decision. The League does ask that you use the replay, but I only change my mind if I see something on the replay that I didn't see before. I don't rely on the replay to make the actual call.

Where we used to sit in the old press box, before they renovated the park ten years ago, we were in a perfect location to see the entire park but now you cannot see the left field corner at all. On Saturday's game, the final hit of the game [John Valentin singled deep into the corner to drive in the winning run in the bottom of the 9th], I have no idea what happened. They didn't even get it on TV, somebody stood up in front of the camera. I had to go down to the radio booth where they had a better angle and ask them, "Did he get a glove on the ball? What happened?" I had no way of knowing.

I cannot overrule an umpire. It's never happened to me, but if you were to find out, for example, that the umpires had forgotten how many outs there were in an inning, it's the official scorer's job to let the umpires know that there were only two outs, not three. It'd be pretty tough to let them know, because there's nothing set up for it.

If you find out guys have batted out of turn, which has happened, you're not allowed to say anything. The umpires won't call that, either. It's up to the opposing manager to complain.

I get approached to change a call maybe five times a year. The vast majority from hitters. Almost never from pitchers. Once in a while I might hear from a fielder.

The five times a year that it does come up, there's two cases that I probably say, "No, I'm absolutely satisfied with the way I called it and I'm not going to change my mind." Three times a year, they might have a gripe. It is a judgment call, so I'll give them an opportunity to talk about it as long as they're civil. If I have the chance, I'll go to the fielder, or the pitcher involved. Sometimes an umpire, if he had a good look at it. I get as much data as I can, and then maybe I'll change the call or maybe I won't.

I've received calls from the dugout in the middle of games. I refuse to deal with those. "See me after the game. We'll talk about it then." It doesn't happen often. I'll tell the manager about it and he'll make sure it doesn't happen again.

If there is a change, I try to change it that night, usually within an hour after the game. There are times when the person I need to talk to has already gone home. It's extremely rare, once every few years, that I'll actually change a call the next day.

If I'm just scoring, and not reporting, I'll go over the printout of the boxscore which is done by the ball club, which gets sent to Elias, the stats bureau. They do it all by computers, somebody in the PR department that's responsible for keeping the play-by-play and the box score of the game. They whip it out of the computer at the end of the game and I'll just double-check it to make sure that the two things jive. Once that is done, then I'll usually do the scoring form right there. It gives the traffic time to clear out of the ballpark.

In some cities, the scorers very definitely have a home town bias. There are cities where the scorers don't have enough willpower. They can be browbeaten by the home team manager or the players and they cave in. A couple of cities are notorious for that, but for the most part I don't think the home town bias really exists.

Before I was scoring, you tend to get up and just wander around the press box or talk to other people and not pay attention to the game. I found that official scoring forced me to focus on the game. And I just enjoy being busy and being a part of it.

I've learned some tricks over the years. For example, as you watch the game you can kind of cock your head when runners are running around the bases and the outfielder's picking up the ball in a corner somewhere. If he fumbles it you want to know did the guy score because he fumbled it or was he being waved home all the way? You position your head so that you can see the ball out of the corner of your eye and the third base coach out of the corner of the other eye, and see if it's a continuous play or not. Tricks like that.

I also learned to follow the ball until it's back in the pitcher's hand or time has been called. That will help on hidden ball tricks.

There was a very controversial case with Clemens and Wade Boggs. The Red Sox were in last place. It was Boggs' last year in Boston, I think. Tony Phillips hit a ball down to third base, batting lefthanded, that had gotten past

Boggs. I had not seen the play clearly, and the replay was absolutely inconclusive. So I called it an error and figured, well, if I'm wrong, I'll hear about it afterwards. Sure enough, after the game, Boggs asked me to change the call to a hit.

At the time, the Red Sox weren't going anywhere. Boggs was hitting .259. He was having a miserable year. Clemens was going for the ERA title. We were maybe three weeks away from the end of the season. Boggs wants me to change the thing and he gives me a reason: I know he was lefthanded but "the ball came in such a way I could not pick it up in the shirts of the fans, so I never really saw the ball." Which was a valid explanation, enough of a reason for me to change it. Two runs scored in the inning or something like that, which were unearned to Clemens and now they're going to become earned. In my opinion, Boggs should have just eaten the error and said, well OK maybe it wasn't an error but for the team or for Clemens, I'm going to take this. He didn't. He gave me a compelling reason to change it. I had no choice.

Clemens was never really upset with me. I didn't talk to him before I made the change because Clemens was not really involved in the play. Boggs was the only one who could really decide. The runs became earned. But I knew what was going to happen when I changed it. The entire Red Sox team was upset with Boggs. Clemens wasn't upset with me. He was just upset with Boggs for being selfish, worried about his fielding average at the time.

While it's easy to say, well, Clemens was being selfish, too, I can tell you that twice in the years that Clemens was here, he came and asked me to change errors to hits even though it cost him earned runs, because he thought they were tough plays for his fielders. One of those times he was involved in a very tough ERA race – that he ended up winning – and I told Roger, "You know, this is going to cost you earned runs if I change this" and he said, "I don't care. It was a tough play. It shouldn't be an error. It should be a hit." So I know from personal experience that Clemens wasn't being selfish about it. He didn't care about the earned runs. He just cared that here was a guy that should have taken the error.

It was a storming controversy for three or four days, and I was in the middle of it. I wasn't comfortable but it was unavoidable.

A lot of official scoring is personality, not allowing yourself to be intimidated by people who want calls to go their way, to be able to stand up for what you believe in.

JIM PETERS
FAA Spokesperson

Work goes on in the skies above Fenway as well. For as long as most fans can remember, daytime games at Fenway Park have been visited by aerial advertising agents. The most frequent flyers are single engine planes towing advertising banners. Blimps visit a few times each year. The banners often advertise a bank, a local tire or replacement glass company. Occasionally the banner bears a marriage proposal. The plane will usually circle the park three times and then move on, perhaps to make a run along the beaches or other areas where crowds congregate. It's not uncommon for two or three planes at once to be circling the park. During the 1999 All-Star Game events, there were as many as three blimps and seven planes. The day of the All-Star Game itself, fans inside Fenway were startled – some thrilled, others literally scared – when the Star Spangled Banner was punctuated by a screaming U. S. Navy F-14 flyover which came straight over The Wall at Fenway and was gone a second later. Charges flew in the newspaper the next day that the planes had shot by at half the regulation altitude, and that there had been a lot of bickering and jockeying for position among the other airborne craft seeking to display their messages above the field.

For an event like this, we have surveillance. It's part of our procedures. Air shows, air races, any kind of flyover – there will be FAA inspectors on site to make sure that the sponsor's doing what it's supposed to be doing, as well as ensuring that the pilots participating in the event are complying with Federal aviation regulations and procedures.

Blimps are considered aircraft. They are registered with FAA, meaning that the pilots have to be licensed by FAA and the blimps themselves must be maintained to an airworthy standard.

In terms of the banner tow operators, not only must the pilots be licensed and their medical examinations current, and the plane itself in an airworthy state, but we actually go out and they have to demonstrate to us their proficiency in towing the banners. There's also some equipment that is necessary. Basically, it's breakaway equipment that in the case of a problem where the banner might entangle the propeller, or the landing gear or even blind the pilot being over the windshield, you can pull something in the cockpit that releases the banner.

Helicopter traffic is a whole different animal, because of their operating nature. The fixed-wing aircraft, when they're flying over congested areas such as Fenway, must be 1000 feet above Fenway Park. Helicopters are not restricted to any altitude. The basic provision is that the pilot must identify an area where he could land safely if an emergency were to occur, or at least a route that the pilot could take out of the area. They have that auto-rotate that enables them to land if they lose power.

MARTIN ALLEN
Banner Tow Airplane Promoter

I own Aviation Promotions. We started out in Ireland in 1978 and then took the company nationwide over here. Wherever the work is, we have banner operators. For instance, we work with Myrick's, in Berkeley, Massachusetts.

The Piper Aircraft Company manufacture quite a few airplanes that are suitable for us. We fly Piper Ponys, which traditionally are agricultural spray planes. They are designed for torque more than speed and have the ability to overcome the heavy drag. We fly Piper Ponys, Piper

Cubs, Cessna Birddogs, L-19 Birddogs. We have Cintabrias. Basically, any airplane that has been certified by the FAA for towing banners.

Some of our regular customers are Fleet Bank, which is one of our biggest ones. We cover all McDonald's work from Maryland right up into Maine, Vermont and New Hampshire. NYNEX Bell Atlantic, Timberland, we do a lot of movie stuff. We did GODZILLA. We do MediaOne. We do Daewoo cars. NBC. I could go on and on.

I saw one for exotic dancers the other day and I thought that was very inappropriate, I have to tell you. There are a couple other companies around. I was a little disappointed seeing that particular banner up there.

I have refused banners because I thought the verbal content was not appropriate. Maybe I am censoring, but that's my prerogative. I won't put up swear words. Somebody recently wanted to put up a message that included the "F" word. They wanted to put "F dash dash dash" Tom Menino, the mayor. I said, "Absolutely not."

We have a lot of steady clients but we also have a lot of one-time requests. We get an awful lot of "Will you marry me's" over Fenway. Sometimes they will name the seat and section. That's always fun, because it gets everyone in the stadium looking directly at the person. We get guys thanking their wives for new babies. $595 gives them about half an hour over the stadium and then a half an hour around town, down to the waterfront, just basically showing it off to the world.

We do between 50 and 60 games a year at Fenway Park.

The altitude is dictated by the FAA, but normally it's 1000 feet above ground level, that puts us about 800, 850 over Fenway Park. We can get down much lower when we're over the water, and just flying along the beaches.

The plane flies at about 55 or 60 miles an hour. The banners are usually ½ ounce Dacron, or taffeta. Ripstop nylon is quite common. The letters are five feet high, we have a stock of them in red and black and we simply assemble them. They clip together. We lay them out on the ground and assemble the message.

I will not fly for competing companies, such as Fleet and Citizens. It's just to prevent bitching and moaning, them saying you're giving more time to one or the other.

You make a pass and pick up the banners. The rope can be from 250 to 500 feet and what you do is, you lay it on the ground. One end is attached to the banner and the other end is a loop. You put that loop up on two battens sticking up about six feet...it's like a very short goalpost, if you can imagine. The pilot releases a hook from the back of his airplane that hangs down about 15 feet. Then he's got to position that hook through the loop. As soon as he catches it he pulls straight up. He lifts the banner off the ground that way.

The banners weigh in the region of forty to sixty pounds, but weight is not the problem, it's the drag. The banners have an inch and a half aluminum tube running right through the leading edge, which we refer to as the lead pole. People often ask, "How does it stay up straight?" Well, the bridle lines that you see tapering – they all come in to a point. They're connected to that aluminum tube, at the bottom there's a two and a half pound weight. So even if it's upside down, it will always correct itself and the heavy end will fall down. Keep it flying vertical. Gravity.

The jockeying between pilots, it's done in a friendly manner because everyone's just looking to get the best exposure for their client. Irrespective of what we personally want to do, we're controlled by the FAA and they tell us where we're going to be. It was like World War II up there during the All-Star Game. There was actually eleven airplanes at one time, and five airships.

MICKEY WHITMAN
Goodyear Blimp Spokesperson

We visit Fenway Park about four days a year.

This airship, called the Goodyear Stars and Stripes, is based in Pompano Beach, Florida. It took about six days to get there. We cover between 250 and 350 miles a day. Generally it's a cruising speed of about 30. You don't want to go very fast.

We brought the TV crew in from Akron, Ohio. We own our own television equipment and our own personnel. On the blimp was a pilot, Jim Maloney, from Vienna, VA. The cameraman was Bob Rosedale. We take up still photographers at times. Sometimes VIPs, too.

Essentially, what we do is if you're ESPN or another client, you're using the blimp and showing it once per hour and there's no money transferred.

Fenway Park is a very hard place to work for a number of reasons. First of all, the air traffic, Logan Airport is very close. Plus, we operate around 1000 feet over the stadium. The park is nestled in around a lot of high buildings so you have to be extremely careful about wandering off.

The blimp is affected by winds, also by the area around it. You can get what they call "spill" off buildings from wind that will affect the blimp. During the day you get thermal activity.

It takes 22 people to operate. I am the communications liaison between the networks and the blimp. You're trying to give the networks the very best picture so you're talking to the cameraman in the blimp and you're talking to the airship, and you're talking to the director. I work out of the ESPN truck on the street outside the park.

Jared Puffer
PHOTO BY BILL NOWLIN

JARED PUFFER
Radar Gun Operator

I'm an assistant producer but I also do the radar gun. Before the games, I help out with things that need to be done for the announcers, stats and stuff. I don't get paid. It's an intern-

ship. You have to have college credit or credit from your school in order to get the job. This is my last series, I have to go back to school. It'll be by committee who takes over, I don't think they have a set person. They'll just draft one.

We go down about 3:30 and max it out. You hit this little metal thing and shoot it with the gun and it maxes out to 55. That way you know it's working. It has to be relayed back to the truck and they have to make sure they get it. Three hours before the game, we do that. I go out about twenty minutes before the game and do that again, and then just chill out until the start of the game.

If there's a new guy on deck, I tell the producer in the truck because he can't see that stuff. Or if there's someone warming up in the bullpen, or if there's a beach ball out on the field, he's got my eyes and he's also got the guy up in the booth that can tell him what's going on. With a pinch hitter, he can tell the graphics department to get that guy's name on the screen.

Sometimes it doesn't register, but most of the time you get every pitch. There's always the case where you can't get a clear, direct view but you try to get as many as you can. Before I started, they had a guy right behind the plate and the umpire and catcher got in his way, so they kind of scooted us over to the right.

The producer will tell me if I'm not getting a reading or something like that, but most of the time he'll just talk to the director or the announcers and I'll be his eyes. On my headset, I can hear both the announcers and the producer. There's two volume controls. I can turn up McDonough and Remy, or whoever the announcers are and listen to them. I like to keep Pat a little bit higher than the announcers.

Most of the time they're on point. You just try to help them out with things. They might say, "Boy, that was a live fastball" and might not have seen the reading and then I'll tell Pat, and he'll give it to the announcers. There's actually two readings. One, where it leaves his hand, from the top, and then one after it's past the plate, when it goes into the catcher's mitt. It's to see when the ball left his hand and then how fast it was when it reached the plate.

People ask to see the radar, so I'll show them. Yesterday, I was having a good conversation with the guy next to me. I try not to answer people far away, like people always screaming out, "What was that last one?" I can't be telling everyone, but the people right around me, I don't mind. I like to talk, it's not as tedious and boring.

You get a nice view of the game and the fans. It's always been one of my dreams as a child, to work for the Red Sox and to be in Fenway Park. I never thought I'd be able to do it and then I'm running the radar gun. It's unbelievable.

At first, I wanted to be an announcer, but now it's more on the producing side, like maybe a production assistant. Maybe down the line a sports manager.

KEN KOZYRA
STATs Inc. Press Box Reporter

I'm a big baseball fan and I purchased a book from STATs in 1989. In the back of the book is a paragraph saying we need people to cover various teams throughout the major leagues. So I called them up, did some training, and became part of the team to cover the Red Sox. The Red Sox were the last club in the major leagues to allow us in the press box.

John Doucette joined shortly thereafter and has been doing it for seven or eight years. This past year I did 36 games, I usually do between thirty and forty. John does in the forties, and my twin brother Kurt picks up between five and ten a year.

Prior to the game, we enter the lineups and the umpires as soon as we have them, any transactions or disabled list changes, things like that. Then we enter information from the media notes on each of the teams. It's pretty much a narrative section. We choose what we think is important, and relay it on.

When the game starts, we are live online the whole time. We use a laptop computer to keep track of everything that occurs, from every pitch – whether it's a ball, a strike, a foul ball, a foul

bunt, wild pitch to the type of hit – how hard it's hit and where it falls. We have a grid system for the whole park. We estimate the distance and I would say we're usually within five or ten feet.

Ken Kozyra
PHOTO BY BILL NOWLIN

For example, a ball hit dead to left, if it were to hit on the Wall right where the foul line is, it's 310 feet. The foul territory in left has two sections, A and B, and then fair territory starts in C [on the grid]. So if it were to hit the Wall on the fly, a hard-hit line drive would be a "C" and it would be 310 feet. It would be coded as either hard, medium or soft. If it's a liner that lands in left center, we have to guesstimate exactly which portion of the grid it fell into, and then we guesstimate the distance and how hard it was hit – whether it was sharp off the bat or not. Then of course, we have to keep track of all the fielding that occurs.

We have a very detailed score sheet that is very different from any you've ever seen. We also relay it all online to the computer in Chicago. From there it's disseminated to various sources. The Red Sox web site uses our information, so you can actually go to Redsox.com and virtually watch the game as it occurs. The text-based play-by play. That originates from us.

We're paid a flat fee. $60 a game. Occasionally, I find a conflict with my work but we have three people doing it and we're all pretty flexible to help each other out.

To put on a baseball game, you figure it's just the players on the field, but there are so many people behind the scenes. Thousands of people, every single game. I've come to know a lot of the people, and made quite a number of friends over the years.

Any time you're using a computer, there are complications. Modem communications are the most temperamental thing in the world. We've had quite a few mishaps where the computer won't work and we have to get on the phone and have someone on a computer, somewhere else in the country record the events as we talk to them. Sometimes for the whole rest of a game.

The game goes to two places from our computer – we send it to AP's desk in New York and, simultaneously, to Chicago.

We're on the phone for a couple of minutes with Chicago, double-checking our scoring. We have three people who score each game. One person is called press box reporter for obvious reasons, and then we have a person at home on a computer who is called the "starter." He does it off the TV. Then we have a third person, called the "reliever," who also does it off the TV.

The relievers are allowed to do their games on paper, but can also do them online. The starter and ourselves are the whole time online – so they can compare the two reports, in case one person missed something. They get paid significantly less – $20 a game – to do the game from TV.

Sometimes I'll be out of there in fifteen minutes. We've all been doing it for so long now that we're pretty good at what we do. If there's a difference between us and the starter we have to stay and try to figure it out, but that's rare.

I occasionally will do away games on TV as a starter. John does quite a few of them, fifty or something a year. There's another gentleman who lives here in New Hampshire, who does hundreds of them. I saw where he did something like 220 games. I know John has done two games a day sometimes – an afternoon game and a night game. John also does other sports – football and hockey and basketball. I just do baseball.

Until I get too old or too tired I'll always do Opening Day though, because on Opening Day, hope springs eternal. Everything's brand new.

Kathy Gould, usher
PHOTO BY BILL NOWLIN

10
STREET PEOPLE

Bob Whetstone, Street Minister
Dickie Boynton, Vendors' Helper
Robbie, Bottle Picker
Wayne Goff, One of the Canning People
Chris Fay, Bagpiper

Charlie, Bluesman
Germaine, Street Drummer
Chris Poteet, T-Shirt Seller
Hai Ho Nguyen, Autograph Collector

Outside the Park, there is a fascinating and changing array of people who work the streets. Jim Parry and Ken Melanson both mentioned the people who, one way or another, work around Fenway Park. For many years, there used to be a man who sat on the bridge over the Mass Pike, dressed in a priest's garb and holding a tambourine for donations. His face was weatherbeaten and often scabbed from tumbles he had taken; he gave every indication of being a falling-down drunk, though he worked the Red Sox games for at least a decade before simply disappearing at some point in the mid-1990s.

If you stand outside the park for a couple of hours prior to a game, you will note some very industrious people making regular sweeps of the trash cans along Yawkey Way and Lansdowne Street, retrieving plastic bottles and aluminum cans for the 5 cents they bring at the redemption center in the Star Market on Brookline Avenue. These are hard working people who are, perhaps understandably, reluctant to be interviewed. Some appear to be recent immigrants. At least one man and one woman are Asian — they seem rivals, not partners — and in attempting to speak with them, it's not clear how much English they possess.

The streets around the park also feature other regulars: Charlie, the bluesman who plays his electric guitar through a small battery-powered speaker; Germaine, who drums on an assortment of plastic buckets and metal objects; Dickie Boynton, who runs errands for the street vendors on Yawkey Way. Bob Whetstone works the crowds in his role as a street minister, though in his case not for personal profit. For the last few years, Luke's Lids would sell baseball caps out of the trunk of his car parked in the big lot across Brookline Avenue, flashing his flashlight on the caps to get everyone's attention as they flooded out after the game.

Approached to talk about their work, some declined to speak. Others were not fully articulate, for one reason or another. By their nature, some are solitary people who perhaps prefer to keep their thoughts to themselves.

BOB WHETSTONE
Street Minister

Anyone who gets to 2 or 3 games a season has probably seen Bob Whetsone. He's the tall guy with glasses who often stands outside Gate A or over by the Cask wearing a large pictorial sign around his neck and a cap which reads "Jesus is Lord." Bob passes out tracts from the Fellowship Tract League.

Many people work at a variety of tasks around Fenway Park. Bob's is not your usual for-profit enterprise, but he's been one of the regulars the last few years.

Bob Whetstone
PHOTO BY BILL NOWLIN

I work for the Lord.

It's a street ministry. I used to do a lot of other types of evangelism, like prison ministry and door to door, and bus ministry, and Sunday school and all that. This is for events mostly around the Boston area, New England. The Lord sent me down to Miami Beach for five winters and up in Hampton Beach for five summers.

The picture is called "The Bridge to Heaven" and it's basically showing that Jesus is the way. It's showing that the people who go through Christ have a relationship with Him, and are on the road to Heaven. The other ones are still on the Way of the World, which is the road to destruction. They need to turn to God and want Jesus to be their Savior. That's how their sins are forgiven and then they're on the Road to Heaven.

My dad worked at Bethlehem Steel for 34 years. He was a tax accountant. My brother's a schoolteacher in Pennsylvania. My sister works part-time in accounting. God told me to leave everything and go to Bible college.

When I was in the prison ministry, a lot of people were looking for answers. They were ready to be reaped, so you didn't have to do much groundwork. It was more, "What am I going to do? How do I get out of this mess?" and they were ready to receive the Gospel.

This leaflet is called "Where Are You Going to Spend Eternity?" People tell me that they read them years ago and it helped them. People have told me that they got saved from ones I gave them.

I used to go up to Hampton Beach for a day or two. Now the Lord opened the doors to stay up there for as long as I want, mostly it's around six weeks. Hampton is a place where you get to talk because they're not in a hurry.

Fenway, it's a fast-paced crowd. It's like the Celtics and the Bruins, if they win they're in a good mood. You never know who's here and what's going on in their life. We don't know that. That's God's business. Most of the time, they're wanting to get in, or they want to leave. People have told me, "Keep up the good work." Other ones think that I'm against sports, or the rock concerts. I say, "No, this has nothing to do with the event. It has to do with the crowds."

I never ask for money. Sometimes people give me food, but I never ask for anything. I have people walk up to me and say, "Here." Like last night – it was really warm – a guy came up to me and said, "Would you like anything to drink?" He gave me a nice cold water. I had people offer tickets, but I tell them no.

Sometimes I need food and I pray. The Lord works it out. He gives me places to park. I never pay for parking, in Hampton or anywhere. I pray to God, give me places to park. Same thing in Miami. Very, very rarely, maybe once a summer.

God gives me places to stay, also a van that I can stay in when I travel. I didn't have any money, no bank account, no checks. I prayed and the Lord gave me a van. It's an '86 and it runs fine. It's a conversion van so it has a bed in it.

If you go down to Florida and all that, it's more in the Bible belt, so people are more used to hearing the Gospel. In New England, people are generally not as open.

I'm sure there's a number of people that ridicule you.

Sometimes, yeah. If you're there when a team loses, they're kind of upset. Especially the Bruins. The Bruins fans are kind of aggressive, especially if it's a close game and they lose. When they're drinking and they see you, they say, "What are you here for?" You can have some hassles once in a while.

I think most people are figuring, look, I go to church on Sunday, I have my religion. They believe in Heaven and Hell. They believe in Jesus but that's as far as they want to go. They don't really think about Heaven and Hell. They just go to church. Everybody has to face reality. Sooner or later we have to find out that there's something incomplete in their life. It's a relationship with God. It's not joining religions. It's just a matter of the question: Are you going to Heaven?

There's not too many people doing what I'm doing. I know that. That's why God sends me out. Down South there is more. But if you get up in this area you won't find too many people out like this. There are Jehovah's Witnesses and Mormons and stuff, but those are cults. That's a cult ministry.

How about yourself? Have you been saved yet? You know what this means? It's a personal relationship with Christ. It's not a religion.

It's a gift from God. This isn't because God is picking certain people. We're all sinners. It's not like God is saying, "Well, I like this guy." No. There's a void that's inside us. We try to fill it up with creative things because that's all we know. But only the Creator Himself can fill it up.

When I got out of high school, I worked in Bethlehem Steel for a while, then I worked in an accounting job for a couple of years, and then in the trucking industry for a couple of years. Somehow, I sensed there was something missing but I didn't know what it was.

My thing was out of doors. I love the out of doors. I went out to the Rocky Mountains and stayed there for six weeks. I really liked it. I came back and worked that winter and then the next summer I went out for three months. That's when I started realizing there was something more, but I still didn't know what it was. I tried to read the Bible but it didn't make any sense to me. I read books on other religions but there was nothing happening.

Then my sister gave me a book by a Christian evangelist. It made sense. I got saved one night reading a Christian book. He started showing me that He wanted me to go out in a ministry down in Allentown. I started getting more and more of an interest in helping people and that's when the Lord started calling me to go to Bible college.

God bless you!

DICKIE BOYNTON
Vendors' Helper

During the summer months, Dickie comes into Boston and helps out some of the vendors on Yawkey Way. Keith Durham — who sells baseball caps — told the story about how Dickie's car caught fire on his way into Boston and he just ditched it and hopped the T, to be sure he got to the game on time. Dickie runs errands for Keith and some of the other vendors, and will man their stand for them if they need to make a quick run to relieve themselves.

Dickie Boynton
PHOTO BY BILL NOWLIN

I'm from West Boylston. I've been coming down since Ted Williams was playing. I've been to a lot of games. I went to the '75 World Series, and '67 the seventh game. The '86 Series, I was here for that.

Keith's a wonderful guy. I do errands and stuff. I go and pick up extra hats. I go to Pearl's over here. Kenmore Square. She's the lady who sells down by the subway. He's got to go to the bathroom. Jesus Christ, he can't go here, you know.

I come to maybe fifty games a year. I met Keith here, got in a conversation, got to know him. He takes care of me. He takes a hat and gets a ticket for it. He gives me a ticket. I know the fellow who sells glasses, too. Jim's a nice guy.

Keith Durham adds: Dickie's very helpful. He comes over before the game and he'll help me set up or he'll run some errands for me. Dickie's a big fan. He comes all the way from outside of Worcester. People will give me a ticket, and I'll give it to Dickie. I'll buy him lunch or throw him a few bucks here or there.

Wayne Goff
PHOTO BY BILL NOWLIN

In Massachusetts, after a prolonged battle and several public referenda, the Commonwealth passed the "Bottle Bill" to promote recycling and to provide people an incentive not to simply toss their bottles and cans by the roadside. An entire new occupational category sprang up: the men and women who gather bottles and cans so they can redeem them for 5 cents each. They'll use garbage bags to carry the empties, and often wheel "borrowed" shopping carts.

These people are scavengers, but they perform a socially useful function. This is a form of self-employment for many who might otherwise have fallen through the cracks of our economy or been forced onto welfare. Instead, they help clean urban streets and earn subsistence in the process. The Fenway area has a number of such who cruise the area around the park, in some cases almost relentlessly. Stand around for an hour or so before a game and the same person may come by 3 times.

I call them "bottle pickers;" Wayne Goff calls them "canning people." They can get competitive at Fenway. I've seen two pickers rush a trash container on the corner of Yawkey Way and Brookline Avenue and come close to fighting over the spoils – 5 or 6 cans tossed in by fans on their way to the ballgame.

Some appear to be immigrants. There's a story – not verified – that one of the group is a former stockbroker who suffered a breakdown of some sort. Most of them are very shy, neither wanting to talk about their work nor be photographed.

ROBBIE
Bottle Picker

Robbie, who comes up from Fall River for a number of homestands each year, has been doing this for 5 or 6 years now.

He says he doesn't know how much he makes. A Red Sox fan, he doesn't come to attend the games but instead to collect bottles and cans outside Fenway. On August 27, 1999 as the Red Sox opened a 7-game homestand against Anaheim, Robbie was waiting outside the park three hours before game time, Walkman in place, clutching two large plastic bags and with his Red Sox cap on. He showed his roundtrip ticket on Bonanza Bus Lines, $16.95. That's 339 cans.

While in town, he stays with his sister who lives in the area.

Once he has enough cans, he takes them to the Star Market on Brookline Avenue, the largest redemption spot in the Fenway neighborhood.

Trying to ask him what he does in Fall River was not fruitful. He was not articulate, and hard to understand. This is clearly a regular occupation for him and he must receive some satisfaction from it since he has done it for so many years.

One suspects there are many interesting stories here, but the reluctance of pickers to open up is an obstacle which nonetheless must be respected.

As it happens, by the 2000 season, Robbie had a new gig. After a night game, he will stay overnight sleeping among the sausage stands across from Gate D. These stands are not on the sidewalk, but on a 5 foot wide strip of land owned by Twins Enterprises and rented to Best Sausage Co., which also owns the snack counter across from Gate A. Robbie stays until about 10 in the morning when the main stand opens up. Ron, who shares delivery gate duties with don't want that garbage around here." "That's the sort of thing I have to put up with," says Wayne.]

WAYNE GOFF
One of the Canning People

I'm 46, a veteran, US Army. This is my second year doing this [at Fenway] but you can make quite a bit out here. If you push it, you can make twenty, thirty dollars. I work Monday through Friday, every time that the Red Sox are in town – except for weekends, of course. I take the weekends off.

The Chinese are the worst competition down here. It's a free country, so you can't really say much. I hate 'em but what can I do? It's fair game if someone throws a can in the trash.

I go to Star Market [to redeem them.] I've got some here already [shows me some redemption coupons he will later exchange for cash or credit for food purchases.] I usually do my morning run down at Faneuil Hall. You can make quite a bit down there, anywhere from five to ten bucks.

I try to get here [Fenway] right when they're setting up. I stay until the game's over. After the game, people want to spend a little bit more on the kids, you know. You can collect a whole lot more after that.

I'm a Red Sox fan, but not a big sports fan. I usually spend my winters quietly at home, living off what I make. SSI and SSDI – Social Security Income and Social Security Disability Income. I just basically live off of that. I don't get money from being a veteran. They like to kick me in the ass. It's a big hassle, so I try not to deal with them. My doctor's got me on medication.

If it's raining, I wouldn't come out. There's probably not enough here, and if there is you'd have to get wet. It's a supplementary income. It basically helps you get over that other half that you really need to get over, so other than that it's not all that bad.

[*As we were speaking, the sausage vendor asked me to move, rudely saying of Wayne, "I*

CHRIS FAY
Bagpiper

On September 21, 1999, Chris Fay set up outside the Red Sox ticket office and played the bagpipes as a street musician. It was actually the first time he ever did it. "I'm a little nervous," he confessed. Chris played some Scottish tunes, and the Marine Corps hymn for no reason other than "it's a good tune to play." By the time I talked with him – a full hour and 45 minutes before the game – he already had about 11 dollars in his case, so it looked like he was going to do pretty good. He'd taken up the bagpipes about nine months earlier. He used to play rock and roll drums – but, of course, he couldn't set up a full kit in front of the ticket office.

Chris was back Opening Day 2000, to give it another shot, but rarely showed up anytime in the next few years.

CHARLIE
Bluesman

Interviewed in October, 1999, Charlie said:

I've been playing here all year. I play during Red Sox games, but other times, too. I play rhythm & blues and blues. I play a Fender guitar, a Strat. I'm from McKenzie, Alabama, in the Montgomery area. I've been in Boston three or four years.

I do well enough. Better during a Red Sox game than not, I would say. I do have a better night after the Red Sox win, yes, I do. I'm pretty much a Red Sox fan. I wasn't a baseball fan as a kid but I've been knowing the Red Sox for a while now and I expect if they manage it right, they can win.

Charlie
PHOTO BY BILL NOWLIN

They got the material to do it, but somehow or other they don't manage it.

Yes, I've got a permit. You've got to get that from the city. In the subway, you don't.

Of course, you meet some nice people doing this. Of course.

Charlie became a regular, back again the next several seasons.

GERMAINE
Street Drummer

Germaine is a street drummer, who most evenings after Red Sox games is based on the bridge over the Mass. Pike, on the side closest to the Cask. He drums on an assortment of items – a white plastic 5-gallon paint mixer, a crisper from a refrigerator, a tin pail, a rectangular cooking pan, a pot, dishes and plates from a toaster oven – everything is positioned on metal oven racks, which also add to the percussion.

Germaine
PHOTO BY BILL NOWLIN

I do this every weekend except when it's too cold or it rains. Yeah, I do better when the Red Sox win. I've been doing it about 2½ years now.

I don't really like to answer questions about how much I make.

Sometimes I play at the Fleet Center but mainly Red Sox events or any other big events, like parades or something downtown or on the Common, the Wang Center area, all that.

I'm a Red Sox fan, yeah. I was born and raised in Boston, right down the street, so I always root for the home team.

[Germaine had about $30 or $40 at the point I spoke with him, maybe 20 minutes after the game.]

CHRIS POTEET
T-Shirt Seller

Chris Poteet, proprietor of the Somerville-based Rocket Science silkscreen shop, made up some "¡Viva Martinez!" T-shirts to sell the day that Pedro Martinez faced Roger Clemens in the 1999 ALCS. He spent most of the day before visiting city and state offices all over town, to ensure that he got the proper permits but got shuttled from office to office – and sometimes back to the first office – without resolution. On the day of the game (Saturday, October 15) he went ahead and sold the shirts anyhow, but had about 2/3 of his supply confiscated.

This summer I took a friend to her first game at Fenway and I made her a ¡Viva Martinez! shirt and people loved it. People were coming up to her saying, "Oh, you should sell those! Those are great!" I live in Central Square and had made one up for myself, too. There's a pretty big Latino population in my neighborhood and people were saying, "Oh! ¡Viva Martinez!" I follow the Red Sox because I like baseball, but also as part of the community. I've never seen Latino pride so high in Boston as it is right now, and I attribute that to Pedro Martinez. To me, that was a great thing and I just wanted to do something that would acknowledge that.

I used the old traditional Red Sox style lettering. I put it on a slant because Boston is so tradition-bound that I wanted to take the old super-conservative lettering and print something in Spanish in it.

I got everything together and ran downtown to the state offices to get a vendor's permit. I filled out the application and told them what I was doing and they smiled. "Have a great time!"

I made an arrangement with the owner of the Texaco station at the corner of Boylston and Ipswich, right behind the bleachers. I said, "I'll rent the corner parking spot in your lot Saturday afternoon." Someone who overheard our conversation came up and said, "You need a permit from the city. It costs twenty dollars. Go to 1010 Mass. Ave." So I jump in the car and got there.

I began at 8 AM and at 4 the clock ran out. Nobody said no, nobody accepted responsibility, so I just said the heck with it and went out on Saturday morning. There's already a huge crowd out, probably a thousand people in line to get tickets shouting, "Pedro! Pedro!" So we cruised down Yawkey Way wearing the shirts. A television crew rushes over and films me with the shirt. People were chanting! Wow! People were coming up to us, "Where did you get those shirts?" People in line were saying "We can't get out of line. Can you bring some to us?" So we just kept going back to the car, getting shirts, and that's how the selling was going on.

We were enjoying being in the middle of it. There were a lot of shirts saying "Death to the Yankees" and "Yankees Suck." I like that what I had wasn't anti-something else. It was more like "Go Pedro! Go Boston!" I was at the car and someone came up – a plainclothes guy – "Do you have a license for this?" "Sure do." I pulled my state hawkers and peddlers license out. He goes, "You know, you're the first smart guy out here today. You're the first person who has what he's supposed to have." He got on the walkie-talkie and said, "He's fine. He has a license."

I heard someone on the other end say "Oh, no, that's no good. We're coming over and we're bringing a uniform." The next minute, there's two guys who never identified themselves in plainclothes and a Boston Police officer. I said, "What am I doing wrong?" He said, "First of all, you're selling copyrighted material." I said, "Where's the copyright? I'm selling Viva Martinez shirts. There's ten thousand Martinezes in Boston."

At the end of the day, we had a couple of hundred shirts confiscated and the cops threw me off the Texaco lot, telling me that he would put me under arrest and take my car if I didn't get out right away.

We lost hundreds of dollars because of the police. The first guy had a badge around his neck that said "Boston Code Enforcement" and the two other guys got in a car that said Boston Code Enforcement.

They were determined that they were going to sweep the streets of all the vendors and the fact that I was licensed and everything seemed OK with me just aggravated them. They were yelling at me, asking about my car and my driver's license. It was a very obvious scene and a lot of fans saw it and spoke up.

This attorney called me and said he'd love to represent me but he worked for the Red Sox. He said it's the Red Sox that drive this. The company that has the concession to sell hot dogs and souvenirs in the park is a limited partner in the Sox and so....

He said these city inspectors are under pressure from different quarters to enforce the stuff. He goes, "Those guys see free tickets down the line. Preferential parking maybe."

There's no copyright, no Red Sox name, no player's name. I just want to get them out to people who just want to say ¡Viva Martinez! If the Red Sox win the World Series some day, there needs to be some old lady pulling her top off and dancing on the hood of a car in Kenmore Square. Any other day she should be arrested, but in that instance, she shouldn't. There should be kids selling shirts saying "We did it!" The Curse is Broken!" Spontaneous expressions. That's the experience – the culture – for me out at the ballpark. It's a shame that's so stomped on in Boston. As much as they put out the image of the peoples' team and the lyric bandbox nestled into the neighborhood, that all gets stomped on when it really comes down to it. I really thought that even if the permits and all that wasn't completely square, they would say "Hey, kid. It's a great day. There's thousands of people out. Just don't get drunk and disorderly." That they'd turn a blind eye, or at least they'd say, "Call it a day and go home" – something like that. But they were just aggressive and ugly and really over the line.

POSTSCRIPT:
December 2, 1999 Chris told me had gotten the shirts back (minus 51 of them which had been signed in but were no longer there when they were returned to him.)

It's not entirely resolved. They ticketed me for illegal vending. I challenged that and they lost.

The Red Sox are counting peanuts. They're literally trying to chase away one guy selling peanuts off a cart, to increase park revenue. From what I gather, it's become this sort of culture around there with these city agencies – how the understanding comes about, who knows – but the police and the code enforcement office are in concert with the Red Sox as far as chasing people off. Nothing exists anywhere in the statutes saying that people can't conduct these sorts of businesses on Van Ness Street and Lansdowne Street.

HAI HO NGUYEN
Autograph Collector

In the chapter "Before the Game" we met Hai, who works as a runner for BOSTON BASEBALL and also sells souvenirs for Brian Smith of Twins Enterprises. As he explained earlier, he got his start around age 12 chasing down players to get autographs, mostly just for the sport of it but later for money as well.

The first person I sold cards to saw I was getting autographs and so he came up to me and asked, "Can I buy some of them?" He was one of a pair of brothers known as "the cowboys", they travel around the United States and get autographs. They'd see kids like me and they'd buy from us. That's basically how I started out.

The first item I actually sold was Brian Leach of the Rangers. I think I got ten dollars. I was blurry to the fact that I could sell it for twenty. If the players get better and bigger, you can ask any price you want.

The best thing I ever sold was Wayne Gretsky's and Mario Lemieux's stuff. We sold a couple of gloves and a couple of hockey sticks, too. We were kids and it was easier to get when you were a kid. There's times I'd get like three autographed 8 by 10s, and I could get thirty or forty dollars for a Lemieux. I got like two hockey sticks that I could get $100 each for.

Me and Lemon had this famous jump. They put barricades in front of the Four Seasons and there's cops everywhere, but there's so many people that they can't control the crowd. Lemon saw a van drive by and he told me that was Wayne Gretsky. When he walked out, I hopped over a fence. Then Lemon hopped over and ran with me and we got Wayne Gretsky. He signed and we ran away. We got autographed sticks.

I would just come here and get autographs. It was easier to get the Red Sox players back then. You could see through the gate and stick your hand through. Now it's heavy plastic.

It goes by feelings, either they won the game, or there's a camera in front of their face. Then they'll sign. That's how baseball players are.

Some players are super nice, about ten percent of them. The rest are assholes. Frank Thomas is a really good guy. Ken Griffey, Jr. is an asshole. Griffey grew up rich. Frank Thomas grew up in the 'hood. He knows how the kids are, wanting autographs. Griffey didn't see that part. Griffey sees the business side. I've got so many Frank Thomas autographs I can't believe it. This guy was so nice. I think the background makes the difference.

The biggest baseball guy I ever got was Mark McGwire. Years ago, we didn't know Mark McGwire was going to break the 70 home runs. I got six or seven autographed cards, some pictures and some balls. His autograph is basically "M G" but if you go to a real souvenir stand, he'll write out his signature a little bit more but for collectors like us, he likes to sign it real quick.

Nomar Garciaparra, sometimes he feels like to sign, sometimes he don't. He can only sign so many a day. Sometimes he wants some time for himself. Some players, though, with the money that they make, I think they should be willing to give a guy some time, to sign some autographs.

I'm coming back this year because I saw what happened. eBay's been so good for autographs. Five dollars for Nomar's and that's just the opening bid. Keep some for myself and probably make some little money off it.

11

AREA MERCHANTS

Arthur D'Angelo, Owner, Twins Enterprises
Brian Smith, Vendor, Twins Enterprises
    Pushcart Vendor
Dana Van Fleet, Cask & Flagon
P. J. McCaul, Manager,
    Ryan Family Amusements
Mort West, former owner,
    Kenmore Bowladrome

Jimmy Rooney, Owner, Baseball Tavern
David Paratore, General Manager,
    Who's On First?
Phil Castinetti, Proprietor,
    Sportsworld at Fenway

There are the street vendors – the day of game merchants – and some have been there for years and years. There are also merchants who have set up shop in the area around the ballpark. There are restaurants, bars, souvenir shops, night clubs and more. Those mentioned here are ones whose fortunes are more closely tied to the baseball team and its schedule than, say, Osco Drug, the Howard Johnson's hotel or the rock clubs on Lansdowne Street.

First and foremost among them is Twins Enterprises, which has grown from modest activity to become a large and nationally successful business. The surviving twin, Arthur D'Angelo, is one of the larger landowners in the area, with whom the Red Sox had to achieve an accommodation in order to advance plans for expanding the day of game footprint for Fenway.

ARTHUR D'ANGELO
Proprietor, Twins Enterprises

Arthur D'Angelo
PHOTO BY ANDREA RAYNOR

I came to Boston from Italy the year Ted started with the Red Sox, 1939. We started by selling newspapers in front of the ballpark. Then we started selling souvenirs. Baseball wasn't what it is today. Back in the 1940s, the only thing we really made money on was Ted Williams merchandise, pennants and buttons and so forth. In the 1950s all we could sell was Ted Williams stuff. He kept us going. We never asked his permission, we just went ahead and done it. He'd say, "You guys never asked me." We said, "What the hell? We're making you famous!"

We came from Orsogna, Italy on the *Comte de Savoia*, the last ship that left Europe before the war, in 1938.

I was 12 years of age. My father saw the war coming and he felt it would be safer to come to the United States. We all came with the exception of my older brother.

Two or three weeks after we landed we started selling newspapers around Boston. My father always lived in Boston. He used to come back and forth from the United States to Italy practically every other year. He'd get my mother pregnant, then come back here and make some money to support her. My father was a citizen and had been here many years.

We were hungry to make money. When I say "we" it was my twin brother Henry and I. *[Their given names were Enrico and Ettore, Americanized to Henry and Arthur.]* We arrived on a Thursday. On Sunday, we wanted to shine shoes. We didn't know how to shine shoes, but we paid attention on Saturday, watching the shoe shine kids on every corner. By the following weekend, we had a shoeshine box. When we left Italy, all the grandparents gave us a couple of dollars, a going away gift. We invested a couple

of bucks and bought our supplies and were shining shoes in the North End area, which was all Italians. So we didn't have to know how to speak English.

The following spring we were exploring Boston. We learned a few words. We learned to get around a little bit. We came around Fenway Park and we found out how to buy newspapers. In those days, it would be the DAILY RECORD and the BOSTON AMERICAN, which was in Winthrop Square. We used to sell it for two cents. It cost 100 papers for $1.30. So we used to buy 50 papers – invest 65 cents – and try to sell them. You didn't make much money, but people going to the ballgames would tip you. Instead of giving you two cents, they would give you five cents. It worked out.

We did that for a couple of years and then we felt there was not enough money to be made. B.C. used to play football at Fenway Park. We started selling mums with the letters "BC" to recognize the team. There used to be a flower market on Tremont Street. You couldn't buy until you were 16, so we had to get somebody to go and buy for us. We used to make the letters with flexible wiring. We made a few dollars. They were very popular.

I got out of the service in March of '46 and we heard about the Red Sox, that everybody was coming back after the war. We were selling ice cream in front of the ballpark. You didn't know if one day was going to be cold or going to be warm. We had to get into something else. We were familiar with football, and we said, "Well, why can't we make pennants for baseball?" Prior to '46, there were no pennants sold in baseball, but in football there were. So we went to a printer in Hanover Street and bought a hundred pennants – I think we paid 15 cents each – and we sold them for fifty cents. They said "Boston Red Sox." After a few days, we sold out. We felt, what a great thing this is, and one thing led to another.

We used to sell over at Braves Field, too. We'd go from one park to another. We used to sell pennants before they went in. After they entered, we used to buy one ticket. One of us would go inside and there used to be a gambling section – Section 6 or 7 at Fenway – and the sandwiches sold inside were not that great. So we used to go to this place in the West End and buy corned beef sandwiches. Most of the gamblers were Italians or Jewish people and they liked the corned beef and the hot pastrami. So we used to throw a rope down and pull up the basket with the sandwiches and sell them to the gamblers. We used to buy them for 15 cents and sell them for fifty cents. Harry M. Stevens wouldn't like it, but they couldn't control us. We were pretty swift.

We had what we called badge boards. We used to hang everything on the badge boards. The problem was, even though you had a peddler's license, you were not allowed to sell around Fenway Park. We used to go out only at the last minute. When the people started to come out, we'd go in front of the gates.

Luckily, in 1967 the Red Sox won the pennant. That changed the whole souvenir business. Then we got licenses to produce souvenir goods and we started wholesaling. We got a license for baseball caps. We probably sell more baseball caps than anybody in the country.

The Red Sox sold very little in the way of souvenirs. I think in 1948 and 1949, they started selling some pennants and little baseball bats. We probably created this souvenir business. We were practically the originals in it.

We have a good relationship with the Red Sox. Most of the stuff that's sold there, we sell to them. Aramark has got a lot of ballparks and we sell to them.

Right now, my four sons are involved in Twins. I'm still partners with my sister-in-law. With the warehouse, the retail, and the office, we've got over 100 people working here. We have close to three acres of land and 300,000 square feet here. We have a 40-foot container coming in practically every day of the week. We do very well here.

BRIAN SMITH
Twins Enterprises Pushcart Vendor

I work outside the ballpark.

I actually went to school with Stephen D'Angelo. U. Mass. Amherst. I started filling in for a couple of people that they had given carts to, and then I got my own cart in 1991. They've been doing the carts outside for a long time. Before the '67 season. '67 was the year the Twins Souvenir shop really took off.

They keep the carts on their property. They have a garage for storage and they roll them in before and after the game. Usually it takes two people to push them uphill where there's an incline.

Souvenirs at Fenway
PHOTO BY EMMET NOWLIN

This is my brother Pat's third or fourth year out there. He works full-time for Twins. I have another brother who works part-time for the store. His name is Tommy. My dad Jerry Smith is a supervisor inside the stadium. Joe O'Brian, he's my nephew. He's a security guard inside the stadium. We got a whole bunch of us sprinkled around the ballpark.

When I first get there, we pick our stock and get our cart ready. We re-stock every game pretty much. The stuff stays on the cart when we go home at night, so we just replenish the stuff that we sold the game before. We do inventory five or six times a year. We have a manager that will count all the pieces on our cart, and make sure they match up with the quantities we've been ordering and the money we've turned in. We'll come in at the beginning of the year, in April, and spend about a week stocking our cart from scratch one. At the end of the season, our cart's bare. We return all the stuff that's not sold.

People grab stuff and run. I've had 25 people around my cart after a game and somebody will grab a hat and run. There's really not much you can do. When they do the inventory, they give us a margin for error. They've been out on the streets themselves, so they know what happens out there.

You get different types of crowds. Friday night, it's tough because everyone's drinking. When New York comes into town, it's a whole different crowd. You see a lot of strange people. You're sort of in the heart of the city, so you see a little bit of everything, you know? There are people that work around the ballpark that will come and help out. [Hai Ho Nguyen, after finishing his duties for BOSTON BASEBALL, moves over and helps Brian out.]

April and September, we'll sell sweatshirts. We'll have player shirts. When a hot team comes in like the Yankees, we'll have a special hat made up. The inventory definitely changes. There are half a dozen hats that we've been selling for ten years, the basic traditional hats. There are only a couple of out of town teams that draw interest. The Yankees, the Atlanta Braves – when they come in, they're a big draw. Cleveland. That's about it.

They sell more high end merchandise across the street. We're pretty much just selling T-shirts, hats and novelty items. You can get some real nice leather coats or a pullover or something across the street.

The traditional Red Sox cap's probably the best selling item. The blue traditional with the red "B." Some people just want the cheapest price, which is the $10.00 cotton twill, but fitted caps are really "in" right now and a lot of people like them. I have a $10.00 one, a $15.00 wool cap and a $25.00 fitted cap, and they all sell pretty good.

After caps, Nomar Garciaparra T shirts. He outsells Pedro about 20 to one. That's quite a gap. It still amazes me, to be honest with you. Pedro really only sells when he pitches.

I'll go inside the park a couple of times a homestand. I sneak in for a couple of innings. We don't push in until the third inning [push the carts back inside Twins for a few innings mid-game] and we don't have to be out until the sixth inning. So I'll just go and watch a couple of innings, grab an ice cream or something. We push in for about an hour. During the week, we'll grab dinner and then go back out. There are a couple of places around the ballpark that we like. Giordano's is one of our favorites. I go to the Beer Works a lot. Thornton's is a good place.

All the other vendors stay out there. We're the only ones that can push in because we have somewhere to put our carts. There are four of us out there.

I work on pure commission. My brother works full-time for Twins, but his vending, that's pure commission. We make more than the 13% the Aramark guys make. The four of us are making different percentages, depending on how long we've been there. We make pretty good money, and it's nice to be around the ballpark. Obviously on a ten day homestand – game eight, you get a little tired. Sometimes you don't want to be there, but overall it's a job that I really like. I've met a lot of people.

The strangest thing that's ever happened to me? I was sitting on the front steps of the Twins store on a Sunday afternoon, having my lunch, and a foul ball came over, bounced on the street – one hop, right into my lap. I didn't even have to move. I was having my sandwich and literally it landed right on my lap.

DANA VAN FLEET
Cask & Flagon

The Cask & Flagon is a family business. My father has owned it since 1969. I've been here for ten years. Right out of high school, I started working here on the door. All college, I was working my way up and then after college, I started managing and I've been managing ever since.

Red Sox games are definitely our busiest season. We do best when the Yankees are in town, as we do in the playoffs. We do better during night games. Usually the beginning of the summer is better, depending on how well the Red Sox are doing. The beginning of the season's always good, because everybody's all excited. If the Red Sox start getting down, it slows down because the interest isn't there any more. The more people come to the games, the better we do.

Outside of when the Yankees are in town, it's mostly Boston people who come here, but we do get quite a number of tourists. There are a lot of people that want to visit a ballpark, and Fenway's the one to visit.

Around 5 o'clock, we get busy. Usually we're at capacity between 5 and 5:30. Everyone comes in at 4 o'clock [the night staff.] We have a full menu. It's the place to be!

Mo Vaughn's parents have been in a few times. Most of the players that we get seem to be from the away teams, though.

It usually slows down around 8 o'clock. By the third, maybe the fourth inning, everybody's over at the game. Depending on who they're playing, we could be dead. If it's a game that's sold out, and a lot of people come to the area trying to find tickets – and fail – they have to hang out somewhere, so it will be busy during the game. We've got twelve TVs, two widescreens. And we put the game over the stereo system so you can hear it really loud. It's a good atmosphere.

[If it's a blowout game, people start leaving earlier. If it's a close game, they stay a little later.] After the game, the places packs right up again. Depending on what day of the week, they'll either stay 'til close or they'll just stay an hour, hour and a half.

Sunday we open at 10:30. We can't serve alcohol until 12. We usually don't get busy until noon. The Sunday games this year have been very, very good. Usually, they're kind of slow. The day games and the weekend day games, people usually stay until around 6 or 7 o'clock.

On the better days we do 1500 to 2000 people. The staff during a game will consist of seven bartenders, seven waitresses, nine to thirteen doormen, five cooks and a manager.

Sometimes we have rowdy fans but we work hard to make sure that it's a quiet place. That's the reason for us having up to twelve guys. Preventing the problem before it starts: that's kind of our motto.

Foul balls come over the Wall and hit our building. We used to have windows on the side of the building adjacent to Lansdowne. A couple of times those windows have been broken by balls. You won't hear it on the floor, but if you're out back, you might hear one of them hit the skylight. I've seen them hit the skylight and the rooftop. We get quite a few balls off the roof.

When the Red Sox get into the playoffs, the energy is just amazing. If it's one of those games where we have to win it to get into the playoffs, the Cask is packed and the excitement is incredible. When they win, everybody is jumping up and down. It's really a lot of fun. It's a great place to watch the game. There's a lot of excitement here.

P. J. MCCAUL
Manager, Ryan Family Amusements

One of the real oddities of Fenway Park is that it has a full-scale bowling alley in the basement! Thousands of fans go by every year and don't realize it, tucked underneath the park as it is and lacking good signage. Ryan Family Amusements also offers billiards and an array of pinball and video games. Jim Ryan began in 1958, opening an eight-lane bowling alley under the Post Office in Needham, so they're used to subterranean venues. Ryan claims to have rented over 1½ million pairs of bowling shoes over the years and he's opened a dozen alleys regionally. Jim Ryan's manager P. J. McCaul is trying to build up the business.

People know me as P.J. This place got here in the mid to late Sixties. It used to be a parking garage.

Ryan Amusement took over about 10 or 11 years ago. I've been working for the company for twenty years. I've been manager here for two years.

Dan Duquette's been down here once. He walked down with John Buckley and just walked through. Tommy Queenan, the superintendent of the building, had just done a total walkaround of the whole building. I'm trying to get a few things done around here, but they're preoccupied. The marketing department's been down, though. I gave them free bowling. They come down quite a bit.

No one knows we're here. It's tough without a sign. I want to put a new sign, but the Red Sox won't let me. It used to say "Kenmore Bowladrome." We've been running a cable ad. That's helped tremendously. The Red Sox did let me use a picture of the park for that.

P. J. McCaul
PHOTO BY BILL NOWLIN

Some of the Red Sox used to come down. George Scott used to play pool all the time. He always bitched about the price. And it was very cheap.

Upstairs where Player's Club is now, used to be King's Row. It was a bar. I remember in the Sixties, the sign said "Kenmore Bowl" and "King's Row." Mort West owned that; he was the previous owner of this place. I don't know if the Red Sox went up there. I don't think they go anywhere around here. They get out of the immediate area, to tell the truth. They go to Faneuil Hall, places like that.

We have twenty lanes, eleven pool tables, and video games. Bowling is number one throughout the year. We lose all our leagues for the summer. It's not that we can't have leagues during the summer, but parking is a nightmare. We share the parking lot across the street. We have validated parking and that helps when the Red Sox aren't in town.

We do a thing called "mystic bowling", which is with music and lights – like disco bowling. We've got a monster sound system and people bowl to the music. It's like a night club without the alcohol. That's how I got involved. I knew nothing about bowling when I took this job, but I've been in the music business for thirty-something years.

The best season is from the end of September until Opening Day. Once the kids are out of school and the tourists come in, we had some pretty good business before a game. The tourists don't realize that you can't get in the park until an hour and a half before.

Thursday, Friday and Saturday nights, we do that mystic bowling. All winter, besides our leagues, we draw off the colleges. That's what I gear the mystic bowling to. We've done corporate parties and parties for BU. There are forty colleges in just this zip code – big colleges, little colleges, everything. I've sent out advertising to all of them.

I'm in a band but I haven't had time to do it. I have a set of drums over under the third base line. We share the same boiler room and when I thought I was going to get back into it, I called up the Red Sox and said, "There's a little tiny room. Can I put my drums in there?" The guy says, "Yeah, go ahead!" So now I go in there early on Saturday and Sunday morning when no one's around and pound them for a couple of hours. I just don't have the time to do it as a career any more. I love it and I miss it but I'd rather do it for fun than to feel like I had to go out and make a few bucks at it. I'm way beyond making money at that business.

After the 2003 season, the Red Sox declined to renew the Ryan's lease and the bowling alley has been demolished, in part to provide more office space for Baseball Operations.

MORT WEST
Former Owner, Kenmore Bowladrome

I sold the Kenmore Bowladrome to Ryan. They changed the name; that's all.

Before I took over, it was a garage. Then it was bought by the Yawkey people. I was a tenant in the building and I put in a bowling center downstairs. Later, Fenway Park wanted to sell and I bought it. There were other tenants in there. One of them was a tailor shop, on Ipswich Street. When that lease was up, we built a lounge in there. King's Row. Then the Red Sox bought the building back; it was bought by

Buddy LeRoux and his syndicate. They're buying up everything now.

JIMMY ROONEY
Owner, Baseball Tavern

We've been here about 40 years. My dad, Joe Rooney, and my uncle, Lenny Coppenrath, opened the place. I grew up in the Fenway area. I used to come in Saturday mornings and help my father. When we were kids, we'd run around and grab the pans and the pretzels on the wall behind the bar – just go in and play around. As you moved up, you'd grab a mop or a broom or a towel and wash down stools or mop the floor. I grew up in a baseball tavern.

Back then, it was all industrialized around here so they came not for the Red Sox at the time. There were businesses that had three shifts a day, so it was a good opportunity.

This place really took off in '75 when they had the big teams. I became involved in 1980. I bought them out six years ago. I moved up from bartender to manager, and now I'm the owner.

Dick Radatz used to come in. A couple of the old-timers used to come in. Occasionally, you'll see the Wakefields and Tim Naehring. You don't have the Mo Vaughns and the Roger Clemens come over here. The smaller guys that aren't all hyped up on publicity, that aren't as recognizable will come in. They're much more approachable and they come in and say hello and have a beer.

We get a lot of hockey players because my brother played for the Canadiens and won the Stanley Cup in '86. Steve Rooney. He was a left wing. That's a different breed. They're approachable, more than baseball players. We get a lot of the working class people from Fenway Park, anywhere from the beer tender to the usher to the security. We've got a ton of regulars, more game day than regular staff employees.

Right now, I would say that maybe 65% of our business is baseball related. Back when we opened, it was probably 30% baseball and 70% working class.

We triple our staff during the summertime. For a game day, we would have five employees working. During an off day like this, I only have one. We sell mostly beer. Budweiser. I could pour a hundred cases on a game day. On an average Friday night, I probably go through fifty cases.

Toward the end of the week, it's better than the weekends. You don't have very many weekday games anymore, but we had one yesterday and it was outstanding. It helps when it's really hot, because we'll ice everything nice and cold, and we'll have the air conditioners going

After a win, we get more customers. They're in a better mood. They're in a spending mood. Drinking mood.

Jimmy Rooney
PHOTO BY BILL NOWLIN

DAVID PARATORE
General Manager, Who's On First?

Fenway is a relatively close community. Most of the people who run businesses in the area know each other. We're just as dependent upon each other as we are on the park. We're very close with the staff and management over at Copperfields, and the Baseball Tavern down the street. These people are our friends. We're in a business where the majority of the staff are there all day, almost every day, and so your social life is your business life. The people who are bartending there, if there's 12 games in a row, they're bartending 12 days in a row, because this is their livelihood. You become close with the other people in the neighborhood who do this.

There's no hostility; there's no competition because we're friends and we all have a niche in the neighborhood. The people who listen to live bands at Copperfields aren't the people who come in to listen to DJs and dance at Who's. The people who go sit in a quiet bar like the

Baseball Tavern aren't the people who come to us. But if somebody says, "You know what? I just want to go someplace where I can grab a beer and sit down and be quiet." That's when I'll send them to the Baseball Tavern. People go into the Baseball and say they want to go dancing somewhere, they'll send them to us.

We're not going to survive if we're always at each others' throats. I think people don't realize how closely knit all the businesses are.

I'm the general manager at Who's On First? We own things in New York and a couple of places up here in Boston that are different from Who's. We have a partnership where we have a souvenir store out in Foxboro Stadium and a couple of other sports-related endeavors. It all began with my brother Robert. He worked for the D'Angelos, managing what was then called Boston's and Who's On First?

Our hours are dictated by the Red Sox schedule because that section of town doesn't really get a huge crowd for the off-season or non-game days.

We open up for parties during the week. We're open almost every day, but our main days are Thursday/Friday/Saturday. When you've got a place that's as cavernous as we are, if you put only a hundred people in there, it looks kind of empty. It's very difficult to maintain our baseball atmosphere where you walk in and it's packed and it's fun, and also have it be small and cozy during the off-season when there aren't 35,000 people across the street. Not many people want to come in and have a drink in a place which holds 325 people but has only twenty people at the bar. It just looks empty and makes you feel like the place isn't very busy.

We've had people come back two years later, who came in from out of town for their favorite team, and who are wondering where Joe is, or where Caroline is. A lot of bartenders have their own following, people that they've made friendships with over the years. It happens a lot more than most people would expect in a bar that's not really a corner bar.

Some of the bartenders are from New York. They come in and throw on a Yankees cap. Customers will razz them, but I don't think there's any serious hatred going on. Knock on wood, we've never had a problem. People start screaming "Yankees suck…Red Sox suck" back and forth at each other. The entire room's chanting back and forth at each other, but it never really escalates with people getting really mad at each other. When it's all over, everybody's buying each other a drink and they're all talking about how the game went.

The vendors come in. We're the local bathroom stop for a lot of those guys, because there's no place else to go. The Sausage King, he's in all the time. George, the peanut vendor. Nicky, he's in a lot. A lot of them are good people who work very hard out there.

There's always at least one gentleman at the door checking IDs. We have a speaker up there so he can hear the game, and there's a TV in the souvenir store that you can watch from the door.

You have to turn away some people, like any bar. You've got to be 21 to come in. While we're serving food, you can come in and we'll sit you down at a table away from the bar and you can eat with your kids. Just like any other restaurant. Once we stop serving food, we can't have children in there. I don't think it's an appropriate atmosphere for children if people are just drinking.

We've got to keep some people out, because they've had too much to drink. We're fairly friendly with the Fenway security department. When they throw people out, they'll let us know. "We just threw out a group of six guys. You might want to keep an eye." Gate D is right down the street. All the police officers are down there. If they throw somebody out, usually the doorman outside will see it.

Not a lot of people come into the neighborhood to watch the games when they're out of town. I think that's something that happened years ago. In '86 if they were out of town, people were packing in to watch the game. Nowadays everybody's got a big TV at home or at their corner bar and there's no reason to be driving thirty minutes into Boston to watch it, but we get a fairly decent local crowd coming in to watch the game or have a beer. During the breaks, we'll play music.

PHIL CASTINETTI
Proprietor, Sportsworld at Fenway

We opened our new store in July of 1999, the week before the All-Star Game. It's Sportsworld at Fenway, more or less expanding my Sportworld store on Broadway in Everett. I opened that one in February 1986. The Patriots were in the Super Bowl. The Bruins went into the playoffs. The Celtics won the title. Marvin Hagler was on top of the world and the Red Sox went to Game 7 of the World Series. It was just a crazy year to open.

I'd been looking for another location, and a good friend owns the building on Boylston Street. Frank Russo. There was a vacant store and we just talked and ended up going partners in it.

This will be a satellite store. We're going to sell T-shirts and souvenirs and hats and stuff like that, but not have quite the depth we have in Everett. I've already noticed that some of the stuff we sell there, I couldn't give away in Everett. You're getting people that are just in town for a ball game or they wander around with their kids and buy something, stuff I wouldn't sell in the main store.

It was a great summer. It tails off in the winter, but it was a wonderful run – July, August, September and into October last year. We're working Tuesday through Saturday, 10 to 4, in the offseason. When the season opens, it'll be pretty much 10 'til 5 unless there's a game and then we'll stay until about an hour after the game.

Sportsworld at Fenway is more souvenir-ish, but we do have some memorabilia. T-shirts, hats, pennants, stuff like that. We're more in competition with Twins. They're not happy, but they're making tons of money. They won't even sell to us anymore. I guess they've got a deal and they're going to be inside the park. We're using someone else right now, out of New York.

12

CLOSING UP

◇ ◇ ◇

Rodger Auguste, Manager of Venue Services, Aramark
Michael Hardy, Supervisor of Maintenance, Aramark
Mike MacDonald, Pinkerton Security Guard

RODGER AUGUSTE
Manager of Venue Services

After the game, it's also Aramark which handles the cleaning of the grandstand, bleachers and concourses.

I'm the manager of venue services, the cleaning department of Aramark.

I started at Fenway Park in 1987. My brother Gabriel worked there. We were both on the grounds crew for Joe Mooney.

We did general grounds crew work. Help keep up the ballpark. The concrete is falling apart, and you cannot put concrete on top of concrete. We'd use epoxy. It's like cement. We'd try to repair as much as we can.

My brother's still working there, upstairs in the Group Sales Department.

Closing gate
PHOTO BY ANDREA RAYNOR

We have a temp agency, to bring people in. The agency supplies 30 to 35 people when there is games. When there is no games, I'll bring in how many I need. For the day crew in the morning, we have 6 to 7 permanent employees. After the season starts, we have about 16 or 17 people for the event, during the game. Then I have another crew in the nighttime running to almost thirty people, my own regular crew. We work around the clock.

We clean the concourses, food areas, rest rooms, seating areas. We don't go in the clubhouses. We don't do the upstairs. A different group does that. After a game, we'll go around the building and blow it down so everything's in the street. Then the city workers come in with the street sweepers. We work together with them.

Fifteen or twenty minutes after the game, as soon as they get people out, the temp agency will come in with thirty people or so and pick up all the heavy stuff. Then half an hour after, my guys start blowing down the place. [The blower is a Poulan Pro 442 model.] It takes four or five hours. It depends how many blowers we have. I try to keep fifteen or sixteen workers to blow. Usually we end up short and have just eight or nine.

I'm not required to stay, but I do. I stay day and night if I have to, until it's finished. Then I go and take a couple of hours sleep and come back again.

Many times, I'm there when the sun comes up.

We have some people who have been on the crew for ten years. The regular crew is unionized. It's local 254, AFL-CIO.

When the players go out of town we wash the whole thing down. They don't allow high pressure water. It might do some damage. We use a mixture of water and Lift.

Sometimes when it rains and there's a game the next day, everybody's left already. No one wants to come back to wash it down all over again. What we do is we wipe it down as much as we can. Certain areas might not be wiped down, and the ushers will try to take care of it. If they complain, we'll send a couple of guys out.

We do find a lot of things left. Money, food, jewelry – we find phones and beepers every day. They're supposed to return them to the office but some people just put it in their pocket. If it's a wallet or something, then they'll take the money out and bring it in. Then we take it to the lost and found.

We find clothes. Everything. The bleachers is a special area. That's where people go a little crazy. They'll take their underwear off and start spinning it all over the place, waving it, throwing it to each other. Dolls, the little butt naked dolls. They have signs [prohibiting them] but they still have them there.

We find condoms. Used ones too. Up in the blue seats, these people are crazy. They have sex right there. It's nasty. Sometimes security will catch them. During the game, they're doing that!

We find people sometimes, drunks who are knocked out. Security doesn't see them and we find them later.

We put the temps up in the stands, for cleanup and stuff. That's all we really use them for. We've got our own guys doing other things.

You can't put just anybody in the food preparation area.

I was never a Red Sox fan. I didn't even like them, I still don't. I just wanted to make some money and take care of my business. I don't get into sports that much. I don't have time to waste. I'm out there busting my butt day and night.

If the Red Sox win, though, it makes me feel better. You know why? Because my paycheck gets bigger. If they do good, that means I'm going to do good at the end of the year. If they don't do good, I'm just going to get my regular stuff with a little something. That's not good enough – I like to have a larger share! Definitely, I want them to make the playoffs, so that at the end of the year, I will know that it was worth working here.

Mike Hardy has been there for about 5 years. He's the supervisor for the night crew. He's the one I'm looking to put as manager for the nights.

I like it when the Red Sox go out of town. Then I do my own thing. I have three kids. I've got to think about college and all that stuff. The lifestyle I'm living, I've got to keep on my toes.

Rodger Auguste
PHOTO BY BILL NOWLIN

MICHAEL HARDY
Supervisor of Maintenance

I'm superintendent of maintenance. It's called Venue Services. I started in 1993. A friend referred me. He was working with Harry M. Stevens, right here in maintenance.

The pickers collect the bottles for deposits. They don't make much money. That's like an extra for them. We're really not supposed to let them do that, but they need the money. Figuring they pick up about two bags, that's about twenty bucks. The people who've been picking for the longest time get to do it.

Michael Hardy
PHOTO BY BILL NOWLIN

I started in maintenance. I was a blower, just working after games. I was working here a couple of years ago, for maintenance and the grounds crew. I worked one year for Joe Mooney, taking care of the field and stuff. I really didn't work in the off-season. I'm still not working full time. A few weeks after the season, I'm finished. I'll do a little work here, a little there, like shoveling snow. Little odd jobs.

I'll come in two hours after the game has started. The event crew will already be here. They come in two and a half hours before the game. If it's not a rainy day, it'll be about 5 to 5 1/2 hours after the game [before we're finished]. If it's a rainy day, it could be anywhere from ten hours to seventeen hours.w tired you feel, you've just got to keep going.

We should be making more money in this department, it's hard to clean this park. They're making good money, man, while we clean this park. The average player's making over a million dollars a year. They couldn't do that if the place never got cleaned. Everybody would be upset, from the front office all the way down.

It's kind of a behind the scenes job. They only notice if it's not clean, the negative side as opposed to the positive side.

Some people get paid for doing nothing at all, and they make the big bucks. I don't understand it. I'm not taking anything away from them. I'm just saying we should get more credit and more money. At every other stadium, blowers make good money, man, fourteen dollars an hour. We make eight something. We have a union, but the union's not worth a dime. They just want your money. Gimme gimme gimme gimme gimme. But I love the job. That's why I'm sticking with it. If I didn't like it, I'd have been gone long ago.

I do a lot of the hiring. We've got a lot of temps, too. There's a lot of Spanish, a lot of Cape Verdeans. No Orientals. Just Spanish and blacks and Cape Verdeans. We don't discriminate, it's just the people who apply for the job. These people picking for us, they've been here for years, before I even came. They're from the agency, but they're regulars. Even if they don't speak English, I've got a communication system with them. They understand what I'm saying. They've been around me long enough, they know what I'm telling them to do. It's either "pick this" or "go here."

After the blowers blow everything down, we have two guys with two big carts. They take one whole section and sweep it in the middle, with brooms and shovels. We do the elevator ramps, the parking lot and the sidewalk outside. A city truck comes in and picks up

The biggest problem I have with employees is people showing up for work. They don't. We get stuck short, all the time. I try to hire more than we need, but you've got to work with what you've got. If you're just sitting there whining and complaining, you're never going to get anything done. Even if I have to work myself, I don't care. The bottom line is, as long as I'm getting the place clean so the Red Sox can play their games, that's all I care about.

We used to do the bleachers first, but left field is so big that you want to get it out of the way in case it might rain. If somebody comes out of the offices upstairs, they come out over there in left field.

Rainy nights are the worst. If it just rains a little bit, then we'll be all set, but if it continues to pour while we're blowing, that makes it a pain. You've got to push all the water from under the seats first, push the peanuts as far out as you could and then push the water up to the peanuts and get it to flow down like that. If you don't do it like that, you'll be there all day. At the same time, you've got to blow the peanuts off the seats, too. The peanuts and the nachos and everything splatters all over the seats. The ushers love it, though, they get to wipe down the seats for people and get better tips. They hate when we clean the seats.

You find anything from wallets to radios to cellphones to gold chains, rings, beepers, ties, shirts, sneakers, just about anything. A pack of

Pampers. Everything. If one of the pickers finds a wallet, they have to turn it in. If they just find a five dollar bill, it goes right in their pocket. You can't trace down who that belongs to.

MIKE MACDONALD
Pinkerton Security Guard

I interviewed Mike about 2:45 AM the morning of July 25, 2000 when Rob Neyer and I stayed after a game until 7 AM the following morning, observing Fenway at rest.

I used to work for First Security, but it's now Pinkerton. We're an independent contractor which provides security for the Red Sox. We work for Joe McDermott.

I'm the overnight shift, 11 to 7. Just me. I'm in charge of the whole place. The cleaning crew is usually here for 8 or 9 hours after the end of the game. If it's a late game, then can leave at 7:30 or 8 o'clock [in the morning] sometimes. It depends on how late it goes. Or if it rains. They've got a tough job.

We stay here year-round. The only difference we have is that when the season is on, we actually have fewer hours because we don't work while the game is on. The Red Sox have their own security. We come on three hours after the game starts. If it starts at 7, I come in at 10 and work until 7 in the morning.

Thursday through Sunday night, it's absolutely crazy out here. I could have the door closed and the TV on and still hear the radios as they drive by. They're screaming. Cars are just racing around the block. It's just a madhouse until about 2:30 in the morning, once the bars get out. They've had fights out here. I've had to call the police a few times. It gets crazy out here. Just crazy. It's really nutty. I always laugh because [neighbors] complain about the game, but pretty much everybody's gone within an hour after the game. The ushers clear it out, but on Thursday through Sunday nights with the bars open, right in this whole general area, they go crazy. They're loud, they're young and they're screaming.

They drive by and yell things in. You just kind of ignore them after a while. When I first got here, I used to close the gate [roll down the metal grate cover to the chainlink fence] and keep it shut because you never know. I don't bother with that now. I just watch the gate. If the crowd is really bad, I'll close it. Usually, they don't bother me. They walk by and maybe yell something, but I've never really had any trouble. I don't think I've called the police maybe 3 or 4 times.

Mike MacDonald
PHOTO BY BILL NOWLIN

Years ago, somebody did steal home plate. I heard about it. I walked out there one day to look and there's guys running around the field. There's like five guys out there tossing a ball around. On a weekend, in the morning. I called them in and I says, "How'd you get in?" And there was a contractor working – I didn't even know about him; he had a separate key – he came in one of the gates and he had left it open, and these guys just walked in. "Hey, lookit! Fenway Park! Wow!" And they were running around. They were nice about it. Usually, when you get people doing that, you just say to them, "You can't be in here." "Oh, all right. OK."

The ground crew, they're in every day – even on Christmas Day, Joe Mooney and one other guy will come in and look around. It depends on what they've got going on. It's a business, so there's constantly people in here doing repair work and things like that. It depends on what they want to check. If they have a function upstairs during the winter, they'll have people coming in. It can get busy, even in the off-season.

We get people in starting around 4 o'clock [AM], again depending on what's happening. The cleaners who work the upstairs come in starting around 4:30. The cooks will start coming in. And then you get delivery trucks starting around 5 o'clock. It gets busy.

Post-game pickers,
cleaning crew
PHOTO BY BILL NOWLIN

[At this point in the interview, a guy outside took a running jump and leapt onto the chainlink fence, gripping it with his hands. He shouted something enthusiastic but unintelligible. Presumably he thought he would just hang on the fence, but in fact it swung on and he found himself swinging in on the ramp. Mike got up from his chair and went over and asked, "Can I help ya?" The guy was surprised and had to improvise, so he asked, "Are there any players here?" — as though they would want to chat with him. Mike came back and said, "I told him they all go home."]

Cleaning concession
stands, post-season
PHOTO BY BILL NOWLIN

If there are things going on and I have to leave the door open, like if there's caterers coming in or workers coming in, you might have 50 or 60 people in the course of an eight hour shift that will stop there and ask, "Can I come in and look?" "If I give you fifty bucks, can I come in and look?" No, you can't. You're not allowed in. What Al [Forester] does and some of the others, if they want to make a donation to the Jimmy Fund or something, then he might let them in. I have a group of out-of-town cops come one day and I called and I asked Joe Mooney. He said, "Yeah, let them in, up to the top of the ramp." They were on a tour. We usually try and take care of the police. But I don't just let anybody in. You never know.

It's an interesting place to work. I'm here when the players come in at night from the road. The regular clubhouse crew'll take care of all of that. They bring them up in buses. They usually get in between 2:30 and 4:30. When they come in from the West Coast, that'll be a late night. It'll be close to 5 o'clock in the morning. They'll usually just grab their cars and leave. They want to get home and get into bed. They just come in and get their car and they're out of here. Not very exciting, huh?

I've followed the Red Sox all my life. When I came here, it's like I'm a fan, yeah, but do you really get involved? No, not really. Working here, though, you do get a little involved because you do get to meet some of the players. You do get a little more personally involved because you're part of the overall [picture]...you do take more of an interest in what's going on. It does increase your interest a little bit. They treat us nice.

I usually sleep before. I go to bed about 2 o'clock in the afternoon and get up around 8 o'clock. I eat just before I come. When I'm in here, I have my coffee. [Does not have a 3 AM snack or anything.] I have breakfast when I go home in the mornings. I actually did bring lunch once and I put it in a little freezer over there, but then it was gone. People get hungry.

To me, working nights as long as I have, it's interesting. If you didn't have people that would work at night, a lot of what goes on during the day wouldn't happen. If you're out at 3:30 in the morning, there's people all over...there's traffic...workers. Like the guy that delivers the newspapers. Around 4 or 5 o'clock in the morning, we get our newspapers. That means he started somewhere around 2 o'clock in the morning. It's just constant. It's a whole different life. There's a whole different lifestyle.

I don't think people appreciate that when they come to the park. It's almost as if when they walk out of the gate, everything stops and there's nothing going on here. It's like a lot of places, especially sports arenas. There's a whole other eight or nine or ten hours of work that go on once the fans leave. It really never stops.

You've got the delivery trucks dropping off food and so forth. They don't consider that there's maybe 50 or 60 cleaners back here and they're walking the stands. It's raining out and they're cleaning the place. They've got all the crap that they've got to pick up and everything else, getting it ready for the next day so the team can play. Then you've got the grounds crew. The guys in the clubhouse that are washing towels and uniforms and all the rest of it. That's why I like working at night, no matter where you work. It's just a whole different thing. No matter what business it is, there's all the things that have to be done, to function the next morning. If you're in an office building, you've got cleaners. You've got repair people who come in during the night time. Guys who come in and check fire alarm systems and things like that. Just all sorts of things. The electrician we have here, he's a contractor. He's usually here in the morning, before I leave. On a game day, he's here until the game is over. The guy with the uniforms, he comes in. The catering, he's got to take his stuff out. All the things that people don't think about. There's an awful lot that goes on behind the scenes. There's a lot of people involved in getting things ready for the next day, for people to come in, sit down in a fairly clean area and watch the game. When people say, "Oh, the ticket prices are high," well, they're not paying a lot of money to the cleaning company but, still, you've got all these people in every night. You've got to pay them, all the different people that are involved. It's not just simply the guys in the clubhouse, the players and the coaches. There's an awful lot behind that, to keep everything going. People don't think about that stuff. They just go to the ballpark.

Employees only
PHOTO BY BILL NOWLIN

POSTSCRIPT

The profiles in FENWAY LIVES are just part of the picture. It is a picture that is continually evolving. As mentioned above, many of the people who appear in these pages have gone on to other work or assumed different responsibilities. Life goes on, but Fenway Park remains a vital place in the fabric of the city of Boston and the New England region.

It has been a pleasure to be able to present some of these slices of life and I hope the work prompts a better appreciation of "the team behind the team." For those fortunate enough to be able to come to Fenway Park during a ballgame, look around. Many of these people will be there, though some are inevitably working behind the scenes.

I learned a lot by getting to know some of these folks, and from walking around the Park, even getting into a few places I "shouldn't have been." I climbed a ladder up inside the large electronic messageboard which looms over the centerfield bleachers. I worked a game inside the Green Monster. I visited the laundry room, looked inside the umpires' room, and even stayed overnight – all night – wandering the park with Rob Neyer while we "observed" the cleaning crew at work after a night game.

There are so many more stories that could be told, and many more people will come to work at Fenway in the future.

Fenway Park is by no means the only workplace, and not the only ballpark, where traditions abound, nor where stories like those encountered here may be found. There are other stories and other traditions in other parks around the country. Joe Castiglione, an active observer of the venues he visits while on the road broadcasting for the Boston Red Sox, remembers Charlie Crepau from the Metrodome in Minneapolis. Charlie made fresh popcorn for the press box and the radio and TV crews in the ballpark. Just as BOSTON HERALD reporter Burt Whitman had passed away in the pressbox covering the Red Sox, "Charlie died at his post during a game one night, while standing at his popcorn machine at the press level of the Metrodome." Emil Bossard had been head groundskeeper at Cleveland Stadium. His son Harold later filled his shoes, and worked with his brother Marshall. A third brother, Roger, was head groundskeeper at Comiskey Park. [Joe Castiglione with Douglas B., Lyons, BROADCAST RITES AND SITES, Taylor Trade Publishing, 2004, pp. 115, 145]

No, Fenway isn't the only place where stories like these in FENWAY LIVES can be found. Next time you're at a ballgame, look around. Talk with some of the folks who work at the facility. Their stories will sometimes reward you.

As a Red Sox fan myself, I hope that all of the people I interviewed for FENWAY LIVES – and many, many more – will one day be able to celebrate an event that not one of the people here could possibly remember: a World Series championship for the Boston Red Sox.

~

For more photographs, interview material and other information related to this book, please visit the Rounder Books website at http://www.rounderbooks.com/, and check out the FENWAY LIVES portion of the site. I think it will be worth the visit.

Bill Nowlin
April 2004

Index

About the Author

Bill Nowlin

Bill Nowlin has co-authored nine other baseball books and over 100 articles on baseball—almost every one of them tied to the Boston Red Sox. His first writing on the Red Sox was in 1957 at age 12, for a self-produced neighborhood newspaper. After a forty year hiatus, he took up where he left off with 1997's book *Ted Williams: A Tribute*, coauthored with Jim Prime. He is a co-founder of America's premier roots music label, Rounder Records, based in Cambridge, Massachusetts. In 2004, Bill was elected Vice President of the Society for American Baseball Research.

For more information on Rounder Books, please visit our website at www.rounderbooks.com

Please also visit author site, www.billnowlin.com